The Ocean Depth

INSPIRATIONAL CHRISTIAN PROSE POETRY BY

RICKY CLEMONS

PUBLISHED BY FIDELI PUBLISHING, INC.

ISBN: 978-1-962402-19-4

Published by

Fideli Publishing, Inc.
119 W. Morgan St.
Martinsville, IN 46151

www.FideliPublishing.com

Table of Contents

The Ocean Depth

The ocean depth of God's forgiveness is God forgiving us, even if we can't forgive ourselves.

The ocean depth of God's mercy is God showing mercy on us and letting us know He will not leave us helpless.

The ocean depth of God's grace is God giving us His grace when we deserve to drop dead for sinning against him.

The ocean depth of God's joy is God giving us unspeakable joy to overpower our grief and stop it from overpowering us.

The ocean depth of God's peace is God giving us a peace of mind in a troubled and uncertain world.

The ocean depth of God's goodness can submerge souls down in the deep end of repentance that is too deep for the devil to dive down into when a lost soul repents and turns to Jesus.

The ocean depth of God's longsuffering is God suffering long over you and me to be saved in His Son, Jesus Christ, before it's too late.

The ocean depth of God's goodness is God being good to us all the time and leading us to repent of our sins that we can repeat again.

The ocean depth of God's healing is God healing us spiritually for us to glorify and praise Him even if we are physically disabled.

The ocean depth of God's chastisement is God chastising you and me because God loves us enough to correct us in our errors of not being like Him.

The ocean depth of God's mysteries is God giving us a mystery to show us that there is nothing that He can't do to solve what we can't solve.

The ocean depth of God's mind is God not changing His mind on you and me so we can know God's mind is His holy word that will never change.

The ocean depth of God's heart is God giving us nothing but pure motives and intentions from His heart to open the windows of heaven and pour out blessings upon us to have no room to receive for returning faithful tithes and offerings unto Him.

The ocean depth of God's presence is God being all around us whether we are awake in the land of the living or dead in our graves where we can't get away from God who our fate will answer to on God's judgment day.

The ocean depth of God's love is God loving us so much that He gave us His only begotten Son that whosoever believeth in Him shall not perish but shall have eternal life.

The ocean depth of God's promises is God standing firm on His promises to us who can break our promises with God as if we had never made a promise to God.

The ocean depth of God's holy word is like a two-edged sword to cut us up with the truth that can be heavy sometimes to take in, especially if we are not living the truth of God's holy word.

The ocean depth of God's salvation is God giving us His saving grace through His Son, Jesus Christ, who is our only salvation in this lost, sinful world that Jesus once lived in to save us from our sins and redeem us back to God through His blood that was shed on the cross for our sins.

The ocean depth of God's time is always on time for whatever is in God's will for us who can't question God's time that we may not live to see in some of our prayers.

The Deep Oceans of Life

In this world there are five oceans that are very limited to the deep oceans of life.

The deep oceans of life are countless oceans that can go deep down into the uncertain.

The deep oceans of life can go deep down into the unknown.

The deep oceans of life can go deep down into mysteries.

The deep oceans of life can go deep down into unpredictability.

The deep oceans of life can go deep down to the bottom floor of choosing one's own destiny.

Every day, there are countless human thoughts submerging way down in the deep oceans of life.

Every day, there are countless human words submerging way down in the deep oceans of life.

Every day, there are countless human actions submerging way down in the deep oceans of life.

Every day, there are countless human motives submerging way down in the deep oceans of life.

Every day, there are countless human intentions submerging way down in the deep oceans of life.

Every day, there are countless human opinions submerging way down in the deep oceans of life.

Every day, there are countless human ideas submerging way down in the deep oceans of life.

Every day, there are countless instances of human pride and wickedness submerging way down in the deep oceans of life.

Every day, there are countless human choices submerging way down in the deep oceans of life.

Every day, there are countless instances of human jealousy submerging way down in the deep oceans of life.

Every day, there are countless instances of human envy submerging way down in the deep oceans of life.

Every day, there are countless human lies submerging way down in the deep oceans of life.

Every day, there are countless human disappointments submerging way down in the deep oceans of life.

Every day, there are countless human deceptions submerging way down in the deep oceans of life.

Every day, there are countless instances of human favoritisms submerging way down in the deep oceans of life.

Every day there are countless human sorrows submerging way down in the deep oceans of life.

Every day, there are countless human sins submerging way down in the deep oceans of life.

Every day, there are countless human misfortunes submerging way down in the deep oceans of life.

Every day, only the Lord's mercy and grace can bring us human beings up to the ocean surface of God's love.

Every day, only the rightlessness of Jesus can bring us human beings up to the ocean surface of God's approval upon us.

Every day, only the salvation of Jesus can bring us human beings up to the ocean surface of God's joy and forgiveness upon us.

Every day, only the price that Jesus paid for our sins can bring us human beings up to the ocean surface of God's heart to gladly accept us into His eternal kingdom when Jesus Christ comes back again to take us back to heaven with Him.

The deep oceans of life are very profound to the most genius human beings who can't truly know how they will end up in life that only Jesus Christ truly knows.

The deep oceans of life go way down to the bottom floor of God's judgment day that every soul who ever lived in this world will face and be fairly judged by Jesus.

The deep oceans of life will one day part like the Red Sea for the holy saints to cross over into heaven with Jesus, who is the only one who can walk on the deep oceans of life and pull us up to the ocean surface if we repent and turn to Him.

It's up to You and Me
to Obey God's Call

God calls you and me out of the spiritual Babylon that is all about religious confusion that has been going on for thousands of years on earth.

The Lord God called me out of going to church on Sunday, which many people believed to be God's holy Sabbath day of rest.

I obeyed God's call and came in to The Seventh-Day Adventist Church that preaches and teaches all the Bible truth.

The Seventh Day Adventist Church doesn't add any words to or take any words out of the Holy Bible.

It's up to you and me to obey God's call when God calls everybody out of the spiritual Babylon that the devil loves to spread around the world.

God says that He has other sheep that are not in his fold.

There are many true faithful people who go to church on Sunday, and God will call them out and they will obey His call to come to The Seventh-Day Adventist Church just like I did when God called me out of going to church on Sunday.

Saturday is the seventh day of the week, and is the holy Sabbath day of rest to worship God in spirit and truth.

There is no truth in observing Sunday to be the holy Sabbath day of rest.

It's not written in the Bible that Sunday is the seventh day of the week to be observed as the holy Sabbath day of rest.

It's up to you and me to obey God's call to come out of the spiritual Babylon that's all about religious confusion that the Seventh Day Adventist Church doesn't preach and teach to the world.

The Bible says that the truth will set you free, and the Bible is all truth about God's will for everyone to come out of religious confusion that will preach and teach false doctrines that are not written in God's holy word.

I am so glad today that I chose to obey God's call for me to come to the Seventh-day Adventist Church that keeps all the Ten Commandments of God.

The Seventh Day Adventist Church doesn't preach and teach any false doctrines, like when you die you go straight to heaven and look down on the people in this world.

That is not written in the Bible, which says that Jesus Christ is coming back again to raise the righteous dead and take them to heaven with the righteous living.

Religious confusion is of the devil, who doesn't want you and me to believe all the truth in the Bible.

The devil deceived Eve and made her believe his lie that sounded so religious, but was not true and was the beginning of religious confusion here on earth.

The devil's religious confusion truly began in heaven where Lucifer was spreading around his false doctrines to the other angels and causing a rebellion against God.

Jesus Christ reminded the angels of all of God's truth, but one-third of the angels rejected God's truth and were kicked out of heaven.

It's up to you and me to obey God's call.

We have a free will choice to obey God's call, just like two-thirds of the angels in heaven obeyed God's call for them to live by all of God's truth.

Why Did God Create Evil?

If God is a loving God, then why did God create evil?

In the book of Isaiah 45, verse 7, it says that God created evil in the King James bible.

Many people will use that scripture to make God look guilty of being evil, when God is love to do no evil, especially to anyone who loves Him.

God put the tree of knowledge, good and evil in the midst of the Garden of Eden and told Adam and Eve not to even touch the tree.

If God had created evil against Adam and Eve, then He would not have told them to not eat of the fruit from the tree of knowledge, good and evil.

Why did God create evil?

God created evil for the purpose of destroying the devil and his fallen angels in the evilness of fire and brimstone that will be hell that God created for the fallen angels, not any human being.

God created evil against Sodom and Gomorrah to destroy all who committed wickedness against Him.

God's evilness is to one day destroy all sin that is evil and causes souls to be lost.

The devil's evilness is to possess every human being and make them rebel against God, who created evil from His strange act to cast the devil and his fallen angels and his human agents into the evilness of hell.

God is nothing but love and will not let the evilness of sin exist forever so it spreads to the unfallen worlds.

Why did God create evil that is the very opposite of God's goodness that leads to repentance?

God's evil is to destroy all the evilness of the devil, not to do any evil thing against all who believe in His Son, Jesus Christ, who lived in this world without the evilness of sin in His flesh.

God is not evil, even though God created evil out of His strange act to punish the wicked who God loves but hates their evil sins.

Those evil sins have nothing good for God to allow to exist forever.

God didn't create evil for anyone to sin against Him, but the devil created his evilness up in heaven among the angels to rebel against God.

God created evil for a good reason: to destroy that evil devil one day in hell's fire and brimstone.

Why did God create evil that is written in the book of Isaiah 45, verse 7?

Who can truly believe that God's evil is evil when the devil doesn't believe that because God allowed the devil to still exist today even though God cast him down in the earth where he tempted Eve and Adam to sin against God?

Why did God create evil?

Only God's evil is for a good cause that many people will misunderstand and make God look evil as if God is not love.

God's evil is His strange act to destroy, especially Lucifer who caused a rebellion against Him up in heaven.

God is not about evilness like the devil is.

God will one day destroy the devil's evilness and all sin that the devil created.

Why did God create evil?

God's evil is fair and allows God to chastise all who rebel against Him.

There is no fairness in the devil's evilness, which is all about causing souls to be lost in his evil sins.

Only God's evil can cause a lost soul to repent and turn to Jesus.

Why God created evil is a question that only God can always answer so very correctly.

You and I don't have a clue about God's evil coming upon even people who we believe to be Christians.

God truly knows completely everyone who is deceptive, and he will be fair with His evil and chastise pretense Christians for their evil deeds done in secrecy—they are incapable of hiding away from God.

Why did God create evil?

Evil does not seem to fit the description of God, who so loved the world that He gave us His only begotten Son that whosoever believeth in Him shall not perish but shall have eternal life.

God's evil is visited upon anyone who blasphemes His Holy Spirit, who teaches us all truth about God.

If we reject the Holy Spirit, we reject God and will one day see His wrath of evilness upon us in hell's fire and brimstone.

The only evil that God created is to truly destroy that old evil and wicked devil and his fallen angels.

It will be a very sad day to see lost human beings burning up in hell that God didn't create for any human being to be thrown into.

All who are saved in Jesus Christ can truly know that God's evil is only for good because it will burn up all sin in hell one day.

God created evil to be called hell having nothing good about it to especially destroy the devil and his fallen angels whose evilness against God began in heaven and followed them to the earth to be visited upon all human beings.

We can thank Jesus that He overcame the evilness of sin to give us the goodness of His eternal life if we believe in Him.

If Jesus had Sinned

If Jesus had given into the devil's temptations, then God would be a liar when the bible says that God cannot lie.

If Jesus had sinned against God, then all the angels in heaven and all the unfallen worlds would have been so greatly affected by it.

If Jesus had sinned against God, then God Himself and God the Holy Spirit would have lied to all existence.

If Jesus had sinned against God, then everything would be a lie.

The bible would be a lie, every Christian would be a lie and the church would be a lie.

If Jesus had committed only one sin against God, then this whole world would not exist today.

If Jesus had sinned against God, then God would have been a fool for sending His only begotten Son to this sinful world to save us from our sins.

If Jesus, who is the creator of all things, had sinned against God, then all creation would be so worthless to exist.

It's so easy to say that Jesus could have sinned against God, but we can truly thank Jesus for not sinning against God, His heavenly Father, who would have been so crushed by it and would have probably vanished away all existence from His eyesight.

If Jesus had sinned against God, then God would have been a bigger liar than the devil.

If Jesus had sinned against God, then it would have been a big lie for God to have predestined to give us salvation through His Son, Jesus Christ.

If Jesus had sinned against God, even in a thought, then our salvation would have been eliminated and vanished into thin air.

If Jesus had sinned against God, then we all would not exist at all and surely would have no minds to even think about Jesus sinning against God.

If Jesus had sinned against God, then all existence would have gone back to nothing at all, because God created existence from nothing.

If Jesus had sinned against God in the wilderness where the devil tried to tempt Him to sin, then we would not exist today to speak about if Jesus had sinned against God.

The Pharisees and religious leaders believed that Jesus sinned against God for saying that He is the Messiah and the Son of God.

The Pharisees and religious leaders believed that Jesus had sinned against God for saying that He can forgive people of their sins.

If Jesus had sinned against God when Jesus lived in this sinful world without sin in his flesh, then God's love for us would have been a big lie and there would not be anyone to exist to even pretend to be like Jesus.

Jesus had no inclinations to sin against His heavenly Father God in His suffering and bloodshed on the cross.

If Jesus had sinned against God, then we all would be crazy like the devil would want us to be and we would be under his complete control.

No one would be sane or be able to reason if Jesus had sinned against God.

Many Christians can take Jesus too lightly, as if to say that they know what Jesus could have done against God.

We will never fully know how much weight of stress and depression was on Jesus, who didn't sin against God in His suffering and pain to save us from our sins.

Our minds are too limited to think about if Jesus could have sinned against God, and our words are too empty to even say whether Jesus could have sinned against God.

Jesus is eternal above and beyond the greatest bible scholars who have sins to repent of while Jesus is pleading their case before God who cannot lie about his Son, Jesus Christ, saving us from our sins if we repent and turn to Him.

No one will ever know if Jesus could have sinned against God because if Jesus had sinned against God when He lived in this world, then no one in this world would exist to ever know that Jesus had sinned.

There would be no church for Jesus to be head of and no one would make it to heaven.

If Jesus had sinned against God, then God would be a liar and the Holy Spirit would be a liar and teach us no truth because Jesus would be a lie.

But for us to even speak Jesus' name makes the demons shake with fear and trembling because they know that Jesus can save sinners like you and me.

Many Christians will get deep and say that Jesus could have sinned when all the demons came to Him with their temptations at full force, but true Christians know their mission failed.

Those demons believed they would be successful in causing Jesus to sin against God, but they failed.

This goes to show that there are no ifs or buts about Jesus to truly be explained about, even to the unfallen worlds.

You and I should be very joyful that Jesus didn't ever sin against God.

Know that beyond our frail and curious theories, Jesus will give us the answer in person when we live with Him in heaven one day.

There will be nothing greater than Jesus telling us Himself if He could have sinned against God when He lived in this sinful world among nothing but sinners.

If Jesus had sinned against God, then death would probably have spread across all the unfallen worlds and only death would be eternal, not life that would be full of hardships to all the holy angels because heaven would have become hell if Jesus had sinned against God when He lived here on earth without sin in His flesh.

That would mean the war in heaven would have only been a big scam to the unfallen worlds where the sons of God would have truly wasted their time to come to earth to meet with God while the devil showed up to represent the earth.

If Jesus had sinned against God, then you and I would not be here right now and it would be a good thing that we were never born rather than live in a sinful world.

If Jesus had sinned against God when He lived here in this sinful world, then prayer would be so out of date and would be a big waste of time to God who would delete our prayers so they didn't exist to Him at all.

If Jesus had sinned against God, even with only one sin, then the sun would have stopped shining and all the stars in billions of galaxies and universes would have blacked out because they were all created by Jesus for His glory.

If Jesus had sinned against God, even in one thought, then every creature would have been better off with no brain or mind to make choices, and all the animals would have been better off with no fixed behavior patterns being in their brains that Jesus created to be that way.

If Jesus had sinned against God is a statement that the holy angels and creatures in the unfallen worlds would gladly erase from their minds while you and I make that statement with ease as if Jesus was only a mortal man.

Jesus is the Son of God who had no ease about seeing His Son hanging on the cross to save us from our sins.

If Jesus had sinned against God is a very profound statement that we can't ever truly imagine the repercussions of and what would have been the outcome of all existence seen and unseen if this was true.

Only God truly knows what the outcome would have been if Jesus had sinned against God, even with only one thought and one spoken word, especially when Jesus was up against the devil in the wilderness for forty days and forty nights as the devil tried to tempt Him to sin against God and failed in his mission.

On a Film

If you had watched all of my past life on a film and saw all the bad things that happened to me, then you wouldn't want to go through all of those bad things that I've been through in my past life.

If you had watched all of my childhood days and teenage years on a film, then you wouldn't want to judge me for the flaws you see in me.

If you had watched all of my young adult years on a film, then you wouldn't want to see me being lost in my sins.

If you had seen all of my motives and intentions on a film, then you might feel very sorry for me if you have a good heart and want me to be saved in Jesus Christ.

If you had seen all that I've been through in my life on a film and then see me today, living for the Lord in prosperity, then you shouldn't be envious of me for being so blessed by the Lord.

You wouldn't want to go through all of the bad things I've been through in my life, so don't look down on me and believe that you are better than me when you can make some mistakes like me.

If I had watched your past life on a film and saw you going through some hardships, then I wouldn't want to have gone through those hardships that you've been through to be who you are in the Lord today.

I don't want to be envious of you for being so blessed by the Lord with prosperity and spiritual gifts from the Lord.

If I had seen your childhood days on a film showing me your pain and suffering as a child, then I would be a fool if I had no heart of compassion for you.

If I had seen your teenage years on a film showing me your difficult changes in life, then I would be so heartless if I didn't care about you not understanding the changes in your body and mind.

Before you and I were born, Jesus foreknew all the good things and bad things we would go through in our lives.

Jesus had left heaven to walk in everyone's shoes so He could relate to every human being that He loves with an everlasting love.

Jesus was born in this world in the flesh of human beings and as He grew up and went through His teenage years and young adult years, all the angels and the celestial beings in other worlds saw this like watching a good film.

Only Jesus had no sin in His flesh to give us the power to overcome our bad experiences in our childhood, teenage, young adult and old age years.

Only Jesus was willing to go through with humility all that He knew we would go through in our ups and downs in life.

Even before we were born, Jesus foresaw our lives on his film in heaven where He also watched our destiny that we would choose.

If you watch all of my past, present and future life on a film, then if you're in your right mind you wouldn't want to walk in my shoes.

If I could watch all of your past, present and future life on a film, then I wouldn't want to walk in your shoes either.

Jesus had watched all of our past, present and future lives on His film in heaven before He left all of heaven to live among sinners like you and me.

Only Jesus was willing to walk in every sinner's shoes to save us all from our sins.

Jesus' film in heaven never runs out so He can see everyone's life choices from the beginning with Adam and Eve down to the end of this world.

Jesus foreknew before He created this world what He would get Himself into for being made flesh to become like us who can watch a bad film and never want to ever watch it again.

All of the angels and other worlds are watching you and me not always have faith in Jesus as big as a mustard seed, making our lives like a bad film that Jesus didn't allow to run out to save us from being lost in our sins.

If I could watch all of your happy days on a film, then I would know that Jesus was for you and not against you.

If I could watch all of your sad days on a film, then I would know that Jesus never left you all alone in your sadness and He wants you to be joyful in Him today.

If you could watch all of my happy days on a film, then you would know that Jesus didn't turn His love away from me.

If you could watch all of my sad days on a film, then you would know that Jesus gave me His mercy and grace so I could be cheerful about serving the Lord today with gladness for all that Jesus brought me through as the angels and other worlds watched on God's universal film that you and I are also filmed on for judgment day.

For one thousand years up in heaven all the saints will watch and see on Jesus' film the reason why all of those who didn't make it to heaven as well as the reason why one third of the angels didn't repent and turn back to God who is fair in His judgement that the fallen angels and all who are lost in their sins will know that they were wrong and God is right to cast them into Hell.

Only the film of Jesus Christ is very well preserved before God because it was Jesus who gave Lucifer and his angels a chance to repent that they didn't do.

Jesus gives a chance to all human beings to repent that many human beings will not do to get their films rolling them into having no excuse to reject Jesus who overcame the world for everybody to be saved in Him no matter what hardships they've been through and are going through today.

In the Theater of Life

One day, life spoke to me and said, "Since the day that you were born, time gave you a part to play in the theater of life."

Life told me that my scripts would be long or short, according to the choices I made in my life.

Life gave me a dressing room that was full of different costumes for me to wear on the stage floor where I had to play my part in the theater of life.

Life told me that I must be real before the audience who didn't make one sound, and it was as if I didn't see anyone as I played my part.

It was as if I was only going through the motions of life with no true purpose, not knowing why I was born into this world.

In the theater of life, I was told that I wouldn't see who I would play my part with until the day came when the theater opened and it was time for me to get on the stage.

Before the curtains opened, I would not get to see my unknown stage partner.

Life told me that I must go through and experience true reality in life to help me to be real with my unknown stage partner in the theater of life.

Life also told me I could choose to write my own scripts and play my part the way I wanted to play it with my stage partner who will be real with me before the audience I will not see, hear applauding or not applauding my performance in the theater of life.

The final day came, and the theater opened with the stage curtains rolling back and the limelight shining down on me.

At that very moment, all of my life flashed before me as Jesus walked onto the stage.

Jesus and I were all alone, standing under the limelight in the theater of life.

Jesus said, "I was there with you all of your life, giving you a free will to write your own script and live by it or not live by the script that God gave to you before you were born."

Jesus also said, "Now that you know who I am in the theater of life, you can be real with me and not play-act your scripts that I foreknew you would write before you were born."

"The reason you don't see the audience and don't hear the applause is because I haven't taken you to heaven yet.

"If you are saved in Me, you will enter into heaven and see all the angels and celestial beings in other worlds applauding you for living by my scripts that are always true and never make-believe in the theater of life."

Life told me that I have a leading role to play in my script according to my free will choices in the theater of life.

When I saw only Jesus and me on the stage under the limelight, my destiny closed the curtains and said to me that only Jesus is worthy to be the director of your life to help you to be real with your scripts and never play-act in the theater of life.

Can't Make Any More Choices Ever Again

The devil and his fallen angels can't make any more choices ever again.

The devil and his fallen angles ran out of choices in heaven and they were cast out of heaven for choosing not to repent and turn to God in heaven.

God gave Lucifer and his fallen angels plenty of chances to choose to change from their selfish ways and give all of their hearts to God before it was too late.

It might have been more than a trillion years before God cast Lucifer and his fallen angels out of heaven for rebelling against Him who time and years don't exist in because God is eternal beyond our time and calculation of years.

The devil and his fallen angels' fates were sealed forever and they will one day burn up in fire and brimstone and there will be no choices they can make to change God's mind and earn them another chance to repent.

All of those great and small who are dead in the grave can't make any more choices ever again because the dead don't know anything and can't do anything ever again.

The destiny of the dead is sealed and they can never make any more choices ever again.

The fate of the righteous dead is sealed in Jesus Christ who will give them eternal life when He comes back again.

The fate of the wicked dead is sealed in eternal death and they will one day burn up in fire and brimstone with the devil and his fallen angels in hell.

Only living human beings can make choices every day that we are alive.

A living atheist can choose to repent and turn to Jesus, but a dead atheist can't make any more choices ever again.

A living wicked man and a living wicked woman and boy and girl can choose to repent and turn to Jesus, but a dead wicked man, woman, boy and girl can't make any more choices ever again.

On judgment day, no one can say that God was not fair because He gave them plenty of chances to repent and turn to Him before it was too late.

Lucifer and his fallen angels can't say that God was unfair to them because they refused to repent and turn to Him, even though they lived in heaven for a long time before they were forced out.

When God closes His probation on this world, the wicked living can't make any more choices ever again.

They can't choose to repent and turn to God because their fate will be sealed for eternal death and many of them won't even know this until it's too late.

Only the righteous will be making it to heaven where they will make nothing but good choices forever and ever because their fate was sealed in Jesus Christ who all the righteous dead chose to believe in and be saved in before returning to the dust.

Not being able to make any more choices ever again only applies to the devil, his fallen angels and the dead — every living being in their right mind can choose right from wrong and choose to believe in Jesus Christ, who will not ever again shed His blood on the cross for us.

We have no excuse to be lost in our sins because of God's salvation to us through His Son, Jesus Christ.

Greatness

Being a friend to greatness is a great thing that will last a lifetime even after that great person passes away in the grave where greatness can be so memorable to the living.

The Lord had blessed me with a great friend who was a fighter pilot in the Vietnam War.

In all of his greatness he was a humble man who didn't boast about flying jets to make himself look good before me.

He also had a picture on his wall with him and the Washington Redskins cheerleaders standing around him.

That was a great picture to me.

He was a retired Colonel in the United States Air Force.

Even though he was paralyzed from a car accident and lying down in a bed at the Veteran's Administration hospital, I could still see his greatness in his humility toward me.

The Lord also blessed me to shake hands with greatness that was a good friend to the retired Air Force Colonel who I met at the Veteran's Administration.

He was a Commanding General over an Air Force base.

As the Colonel and General talked about flying jets in a highly intellectual language that I didn't understand, I knew I was in the presence of two great men who didn't look down on me because I wasn't high up on their level of greatness.

That was a great experience for me to be in the presence of greatness and humility in the way they interacted with me.

It was a stark difference between these humble men and many ordinary people are very proud and boast about driving a new car, which is much less complicated than having the great skill to fly a fighter jet.

No matter how great the retired Colonel and General were to me, they just don't come anywhere close to my Lord and Savior Jesus Christ, who created the heavens and earth.

Jesus is the origin of all life that He created before He knitted together babies in their mothers' wombs.

Those two great men were once babies who knew nothing and couldn't do anything but sleep, cry, wet their beds and eat baby food.

There's nothing great about that, but it goes to show that greatness is from the Lord and no one can ever be greater than Jesus Christ, who can fly any highly sophisticated jet better than any human being who Jesus is the origin of.

If Jesus can walk on water, calm the storm, heal the sick, cast out demons, feed the hungry and raise the dead, then what is there that Jesus can't do?

Jesus also ascended up into the sky before His disciples and Jesus didn't need any wings to do that.

Jesus also went back to heaven where no fighter pilot or astronaut can ever fly to.

Greatness is from the Lord, who can give greatness to anyone and can also take it away like He took away King Nebuchadnezzar's greatness and made him lose his mind and eat grass like an ox for seven years while God was ruling over the heavens.

Jesus Christ is the greatest of the great, even though He once humbled himself unto the poverty of death and rose again in His greatness of eternal life.

His eternal life is the greatest life that we can ever live, beyond the greatness of sinners who Jesus loves even though He hates all sin that is small compared to the greatness of God's grace.

No one is greater than Jesus Christ, who greatness will bow down unto and worship because Jesus gives greatness His blessings that are so great and never small.

Jesus Christ is the totality of greatness because Jesus can speak the highest intellectual words and Jesus has the most miraculous skills to build the New Jerusalem holy city with streets made of pure gold.

Whenever we pray our prayers, they go up to greatness that is very humble to answer our prayers because greatness is Jesus Christ in the highest heavens where Jesus is meek and mild to put His greatness aside and come down on our limited level of man's greatness that can come to an end.

Jesus' greatness is eternal in heaven and in other unfallen worlds that can make the greatest people in this world look so unintellectual compared to the perfect technology in the unfallen worlds.

In this world, technology is greatness, but it won't do the new earth any good because Jesus will pass away all the temporary technology because it won't be great enough to enter into an eternal new earth.

All the holy saints will live forever and ever in the greatness of God's eternal presence where no fighter pilot or astronaut can ever enter into without believing in Jesus Christ, who is the origin of greatness and can give it and take it away for His purpose that is eternal greatness.

The Church Body's Limbs

If we all only had one eye to see out of, then it would be hard to see out of one eye.

It's much easier to have two eyes to see out of.

If we all only had one ear to hear out of, then it would be hard to hear out of one ear.

It's much easier to have two ears to hear out of.

If we all only had one arm to hug one another, then it would be hard for us to hug one another.

It's much easier to have two arms to wrap all around one another with a hug.

If we all only had one hand to hold, especially something that is heavy, then it would be hard to hold something heavy.

It's much easier to have two hands to hold something that is heavy.

If we all only had one leg to stand on, then it would be hard to stand on one leg.

It's much easier to have two legs to stand on.

If we all only had one foot to walk on, then it would be hard to walk on one foot.

It's much easier to have two feet to walk on.

If it's hard to have only one of our body's limbs and it would surely disable us, then it would surely take us much longer to get things done from day to day.

It's the same way in the church body that has different body limbs to build up the church.

If the eyes have very blurred vision, it will disable the church ministries to win souls to Jesus Christ.

If the ears are hard of hearing, it will disable the church ministries to win souls to Jesus Christ.

If the arms are too weak to wrap around people with hugs, it will disable the church ministries to win souls to Jesus Christ.

If the hands are too weak to hold anything, it will disable the church ministries to win souls to Jesus Christ.

If the legs are too weak to stand upon, it will disable the church to win souls to Jesus Christ.

If the feet are too painful to walk on, it will disable the church ministries to win souls to Jesus Christ.

All of the church body parts must be in good spiritual health to work together to build up the church.

If only one of the church body limbs is not in good spiritual health, then it will spiritually disable the whole church body and it will feel the bad effects in one way or another.

All of the church body parts need to be spiritually healthy, and the only way we can get that is from the head of the church.

Jesus Christ, our Lord and Savior, is the head of the church and we must believe in Him to be saved and to build up the church with the spiritual gifts that the Holy Spirit gives to us to win souls to Jesus Christ.

The Holy Spirit gives us nothing but spiritual healthy body limbs, but if we use them for our own selfish reasons we will spiritually disable the church and Jesus will disassemble anyone from His church body for not being real about Him who is the head of the church body.

The Devil Lied on God

The devil lied on God when he told Eve that she would surely not die if she ate the fruit from the tree of knowledge, good and evil.

God told Adam and Eve that they would surely die if they ate the fruit from the tree of knowledge, good and evil.

Eve believed the devil's lie to be the truth that doesn't exist at all in the devil, who is a thief, murderer and liar every day.

The devil lied on God and he will surely use his human agents to lie on you and me, especially since we're Christians.

The devil used his human agents to lie on Jesus Christ.

They called Jesus a blasphemer and they called Jesus the devil for saying peoples' sins were forgiven and that he is the Messiah and the Son of God.

The devil's human agents will lie on you and me for loving Jesus and keeping His Commandments that the devil broke when he was up in heaven due to his pride and him wanting to be exalted above God in heaven before all the angels.

If you and I are a true child of God, we will be lied on by the devil and his fallen angels and human agents who God will reveal to be liars.

A liar is most miserable every day, and the liars will lie and say they're not miserable and pretend to be happy and content even when they are not.

The devil lied on God up in heaven and he is still lying on God today by using his human agents to say that there is no God, only a big bang that evolved everything into existence.

This belief only exists in their imaginations that are so finite before an eternal, unlimited, holy and righteous God who is self-existence and cannot lie.

Between

Between good and evil is the free will to choose to say good words and do good things or say evil words and do evil things.

Between right and wrong is the free will to choose to say the right words and do the right things or say the wrong words and do the wrong things.

Between good motives and bad motives is the free will to choose to have a good reason for doing something good or a bad reason for doing something bad.

Between life and death is the free will to choose to live a good life that can prolong our days or live a bad life that can shorten our days.

Between heaven and hell is the free will to choose to believe in Jesus Christ and be saved to one day go to heaven with Jesus when He comes back again or believe in the devil and be lost in our sins for us to go to hell.

Between today and tomorrow is the free will to choose to wise up and learn from our mistakes or to choose to learn nothing at all and keep making the same mistakes.

Between God and the devil is the free will to choose to believe that there is a true, living god or choose to be delusional and believe the devil's lies that an atheist believes because he is a fool and says that there is no God to answer to on judgment day.

Everybody in their right, mature mind knows how to exercise their free will to choose, which God will hold us accountable for.

Between Jesus representing anyone's case up in heaven and fate is the free will to choose that God predestined before He created the heavens and earth.

Between hope and despair is the free will to choose to not give up hope of seeing a better day regardless of the despair and calamities that can break our spirit.

We must keep our eyes on the only living hope who is Jesus Christ, who overcame the world to redeem us back to God.

Between being lost in sin and God's grace is the free will to choose to repent and turn to Jesus who is truth and grace from God to save us from being lost in our sins.

It will be too late to choose to repent and turn to Jesus in the grave, where the dead can't make any choices — only the living can make choices and be wise for choosing to live for Jesus before returning to the dust of the earth.

Between bible knowledge and ignorance is the free will to choose to read the bible and know God's will or choose to let the bible get covered with dust that is not ignorant toward the dead that the dust knows very well.

I was an Eyewitness of Antisemitism

Over thirty years ago, I was an eyewitness of antisemitism against a Jewish friend, Eddie, who I had met at the Veteran's Administration hospital.

I wasn't a Christian at that time, and we hung out together one day at a club with mostly white men in it.

Eddie and I went into the club and sat at the bar, intending to buy some beer to drink.

At that same time, there was a white man sitting at the bar not far from Eddie and me.

He called Eddie a slur name and began to start a fight with him.

The other white men nearby surrounded Eddie and me as we walked away from the bar.

We ended up in the middle of the club and Eddie and the first man started fighting.

I tried my best to stop the fight, but all the other white men formed a circle around the fighters and I couldn't get inside to stop things.

Eddie ended up with a bloody face, and I realized as we walked out of the club that day that those men could have killed Eddie and me.

Today, now that I am a Christian, I truly know that the Lord had His protection around Eddie and me so we wouldn't be killed in that club where I was an eyewitness to antisemitism against my Jewish friend.

The Lord is full of mercy and grace, even toward unbelievers — Eddie and I were not Christians.

The Lord was so merciful to everyone in that club, even those white men.

It is possible that some of those white men and even Eddie might be Christians today, if they are still alive.

The Lord Jesus Christ gave up His life on the cross to save all sinners from being lost in their sins.

Back in the bible days, Jesus' disciples were eyewitnesses of Jesus being crucified by the spiritual antisemitism of the devil.

The devil hated Jesus so much more than the Pharisees and religious leaders and Roman soldiers.

The devil is antisemitism against the human race and tries to cause every human being to be lost in their sins.

All Around the World

All around the world many people can see, hear, feel, taste and touch.

All around the world many people have love for their neighbors and many people hate their neighbors.

All around the world many people are very talented and many people have skills.

All around the world many people are good and many people are bad.

All around the world many people are healthy and many people are unhealthy.

All around the world many people are giving and many people are stingy.

All around the world many people are well and many people are sick.

All around the world many people are happy and many people are sad.

All around the world many people have good hygiene and many people have bad hygiene.

All around the world many people are respectful and many people are disrespectful.

All around the world many people are law-abiding people and many people are breaking the laws.

All around the world many people are fair and many people are unfair.

All around the world many people are peaceful and many people are trouble.

All around the world many people are smart and many people are dumb.

All around the world many people are wise and many people are foolish.

All around the world many people are their brother's keeper and many people are selfish.

All around the world many people are proud and many people are meek.

All around the world many people judgmental and many people are not judgmental.

All around the world many people are big and many people are small.

All around the world many people are poor and many people are prosperous.

All around the world many people are dying and many babies are born.

All around the world many people have all of their body parts and many people are physically disabled.

All around the world everybody can believe in Jesus Christ and be saved.

All around the world everybody was born in sin.

All around the world everybody can choose to repent and turn to God.

All around the world everybody has a free will.

All around the world everybody sins against God.

All around the world everybody will be judged by God.

All around the world everybody makes mistakes.

All around the world everybody has flaws.

All around the world everybody has sins to fall short of the glory of God.

All around the world God loves everybody.

All around the world everybody will have a chance to believe in Jesus Christ or reject Jesus Christ before God closes His probation on this world.

All around the world everybody who ever lived in this world and everybody who is alive today and in the future will know that God is fair to accept them in heaven or cast them into hell according to everybody's deeds that God will judge very fairly.

Even every child who is mature enough to accept Jesus or reject Jesus will be judged by God very fairly to know that God is a righteous God to be right to accept them into heaven when Jesus comes back again or to cast them into hell after the second resurrection.

All around the world everybody in their right, mature mind will not be excused by God for knowing to do right and not doing right and sinning against God, who will not allow even one sin to enter into heaven because everybody will get a chance to repent and turn to Jesus before this world comes to an end.

Only the people who have very severe mental deficiencies and can't know right from wrong as well as immature children and babies will be excused by God to be destined for heaven.

All around the world everybody in their right, mature mind who knows to choose right from wrong will be held accountable by God to be judged very fairly by God and will surely know that God is right to cast anyone into hell for rejecting His Son, Jesus Christ.

All of My True Brothers and Sisters

O Lord, be with all of my true brothers and sisters who believe in You no matter what denomination they are.

O Lord, bless all of my true brothers and sisters all around the world where Your Holy Spirit is very present in the lives of every true Christian.

O Lord, only You truly know all of my true brothers and sisters in every church here on earth that You know to truly represent You before unbelievers.

O Lord, You wink Your eye at everybody's ignorance and You truly know all who are true to You by what they know to do right unto You.

O Lord, You know all who are saved in You right now and You know all who will repent and turn to You before it's too late.

O Lord, help all of my true brothers and sisters draw closer to You in these last evil days when the devil knows that his time is very short and his evilness will come to an end.

O my Lord and Savior Jesus Christ, seal all of my true brothers and sisters all around the world to go back with You to heaven when you come back again on the clouds of glory.

O Lord, all of my true brothers and sisters all round the world love You with all of their minds, hearts, souls and strength so much beyond any ignorance they may have about You.

O Lord, You truly know every true Christian to save to one day enter into heaven beyond their ignorance that You wink at because Your amazing grace is much greater than ignorance that even a true Christian can have a little bit of.

O Lord, be with me and all of my true brothers and sisters who have sins to fall short of Your glory.

We take no pleasure in practicing to live in sin that we love to confess and repent of unto You, O Lord.

O my Lord and Savior Jesus Christ, fill me and all of my true brothers and sisters with Your Holy Spirit for us all to be like You in the presence of unbelievers so they see us representing You in this fallen world where evil will get so much worse all around the world before You come back again, O Lord.

O Lord, bless me and all of my true brothers and sisters to be a blessing to especially one another because we must love one another to be Your disciples and for unbelievers to see and know that we all belong to You, O Lord and not to the devil who lost his battle against You, O Lord, thousands of years ago.

A Tin Can Faith

We know that a tin can will easily get a dent on it if we squeeze it hard enough.

We know that a tin can will easily get smashed if we stomp down hard on it with our foot.

Some people will say that the cars these days are made out of tin cans because they can easily get dented and smashed up, especially in a car accident on the road.

If we have a tin can faith in Jesus Christ, it will get dented if we let people's false accusations against us get the best of us.

If we have a tin can faith in Jesus Christ, it will get smashed up when hardships come our way.

A tin can is very lightweight, and even a little child can pick it up.

If we have a tin can faith in Jesus Christ, even the lightweight problems in our lives will put dents in our witnessing for Jesus Christ.

We know that we can easily kick a tin can around and that's what the devil will do to you and me if we have a tin can faith in Jesus Christ.

When people buy a soda in a tin can and drink it all, they throw away the tin can because they have no more use for it.

It's the same way with the Lord Jesus Christ, who would have no use for a tin can faith in Him.

If we let the storms in our lives dent us, kick us around and smash us up like Jesus doesn't exist in our lives, then we are like an empty tin can to unbelievers.

A tin can faith in Jesus Christ will fail anyone, even if the tin can is filled up to the top, because it's still a tin can of faith that will pop open with the fizz of doubt about what Jesus can do for us especially during the hard times in our lives.

A tin can faith will fold up when sickness comes upon anyone who says that they are a Christian and then they'll blame the Lord for their sickness.

A tin can faith will get blown around in the winds of troubled times for anyone who is not rooted and grounded in Jesus Christ.

A tin can faith can come upon anyone in the church from the pulpit to the church pews.

Abraham's faith got all bent up by his fear of the Egyptians killing him if he told them that Sarah was his wife.

God could have protected Abraham if he had told the truth about Sarah being his wife.

A tin can faith can easily get kicked around, bent, smashed up and blown around in the wind if we don't stay in prayer, read the bible and live by it.

A tin can faith will show those in the church and outside the church how spiritually bent and smashed up you and I are when they see hardships come into our lives.

A tin can faith is truly a choice that we make to not believe in Jesus Christ to give us the victory over our hardships.

Only Jesus can dispose of anyone's tin can faith in Him who only wants us to grow stronger in our faith to please Him so he can fill our spiritually empty tin can with the fruit juice of His Holy Spirit.

There are many people who have a steel faith in their car to get them where they want to go without breaking down on them, but they only have a tin can faith in Jesus.

There are many people who have a steel faith in their house to not cave in on them especially when they are asleep in the night, but they only have a tin can faith in Jesus.

There are many people who have a steel faith in their jobs to not put them out of work, but they only have a tin can faith in Jesus.

There are many people who have a steel faith in the government to not shut down, but they only have a tin can faith in Jesus.

There are many church folks who have a steel faith in their ministry in the church, but they only have a tin can faith in Jesus Christ who gives them spiritual gifts through His Holy Spirit for them to have some ministries in the church.

There are many people who have a steel faith in themselves and are very proud that they're self-made, but they only have a tin can faith in Jesus when their loved one dies and they blame Jesus for not keeping their loved one alive.

A tin can faith can surely put a damper on anyone great and small and let them be kicked around and blown around in the wind so they get dented and smashed up by the uncertain adversities in life.

Only Jesus can recycle anyone's tin can faith so that it becomes a strong faith in Him if we confess and repent of our sins and turn to Him.

Jesus can recycle our tin can faith into steel faith in Him if we glorify His holy name to all the world, especially when hardships come upon us.

A tin can faith in Jesus Christ will roll down the drain of the world when the strong winds of troubled times blow sin our way.

The tin can faith in Jesus Christ will be swept away in the heavy downpour of sweeping rain of not doing right by what we know of God's holy word.

A tin can faith in Jesus Christ will easily get bent out of shape in the hands of compromising one's faith with unbelievers like Judas did with the Pharisees when he betrayed Jesus for thirty pieces of silver.

A tin can faith in Jesus Christ will sooner or later get rolled over and flattened by the big wheels of peer pressure.

If we church folks don't stand up for living right unto Jesus Christ who we claim to believe in by faith, then we only have a tin can faith that is empty and will be tossed around by false doctrines that will also crush our faith under its corrupt foot.

Jesus is mercy, truth and grace to give us all a chance to throw away that tin can faith in the garbage can of unbelief in Him that we all can have.

Even Peter, who Jesus called the rock, had an unbelief in Jesus who he denied three times for the cock to crow like Jesus predicted.

Peter had a tin can faith in Jesus during his fearful moments that got the best of him and made him deny that he was one of Jesus' disciples before unbelievers.

Peter's tin can faith in Jesus Christ was kicked around and got all smashed up by his fear of being killed if he told the unbelievers that he was one of Jesus' most loyal disciples.

You are There, O Lord

If my mind is lost in space, You are there, O Lord, to bring my mind back on You.

If I am lost and don't know where I'm going, You are there, O Lord, to bring me back on Your right course.

If I am sick and can't get well, You are there, O Lord, to heal me on Your time and no doctor can get the glory.

If no one supports me, You are there, O Lord, to support me better than anyone else can ever do.

If I don't see my way out of a bad situation, You are there, O Lord, to bring me out of a bad situation on Your time that is always on time.

If I die today, You are there, O Lord, to seal me in Your eternal life if I am saved in You, and You will take me to heaven when You come back again on the clouds of glory.

If I am weak, You are there, O Lord, to give me strength if I keep my faith in You.

If I stumble or fall, You are there, O Lord, to pick me up if I keep my trust in You.

If I make a big mistake, You are there, O Lord, to help me to not make the same mistake again if I ask You to forgive me and mean it from my heart.

If I am ignorant, You are there, O Lord, to give me knowledge of Your truth if I open up the bible and read it every day.

If I am so wrong, You are there, O Lord, to help me get things right if I admit that I am wrong.

If I am straying away from You, O Lord, You are there to bring me back to You if I repent and turn to You.

If I sin against You, O Lord, You are there to forgive me and cleanse me of my sins if I repent and ask You to give me Your Holy Spirit to help me to love You with all of my mind, heart, soul and strength.

If I am not very sure about being saved in You, O Lord, You are there to convince me that I am saved in You like no one else can do if I make my calling sure in You, O Lord, who knows me forevermore better than I can ever know myself.

I had a Supernatural Experience

I had a supernatural experience several years ago when the Lord blessed me to be a security officer.

My boss had assigned me to secure different construction sites, two trucking companies, a woman's clothing store in a shopping mall, a convenience store, a warehouse, a car lot filled with new cars and I was assigned to secure some Navy ships and private ships on a dock.

I had always worked the midnight shifts on all of my assignments.

There was one night that I was assigned to secure a Navy ship on the midnight shift, and I had a supernatural experience that was proven to be true the following morning at daybreak.

All night long, I was securing the Navy ship that I was assigned to, but I felt a strong presence of the Lord from another ship that was on the dock close to the ship I had to secure.

The other ship on the dock had no lights shining on it, so I couldn't see what the ship really looked like.

All night long I felt a strong presence from the Lord coming from that ship.

I felt so much peace from that ship all night long.

The Lord God gave me a supernatural experience for seeing the holy and wonderful name of Jesus on that ship the following morning at daybreak.

The name of Jesus is supernatural and causes the demons to tremble and flee from us when we call on Jesus.

All night long, the name of Jesus was written on that abandoned ship in big black letters that looked like it was sprayed on with paint.

I just didn't know why I was so drawn so strongly to that ship, but the Lord's presence was upon it all night long.

The name is Jesus is supernatural all day long and all night long, and gives us the power to walk on the troubled waters of wickedness.

I Can't Be You
and You Can't Be Me

I don't know what it's like to be you.

You don't know what it's like to be me.

I can't be you and you can't be me.

I don't know what it's like to think your thoughts.

I can't think your thoughts and you can't think my thoughts.

I don't know what it's like to have your feelings.

You don't know what it's like to have my feelings.

I can't have your feelings and you can't have my feelings.

I don't know what it's like to have your will.

You don't know what it's like to have my will.

I can't have your will and you can't have my will.

I don't know what it's like to breathe your breath.

You don't know what it's like to breathe my breath.

I can't breathe your breath and you can't breathe my breath.

I don't know what it's like to live in your body.

You don't know what it's like to live in my body.

I can't live in your body and you can't live in my body.

I don't know what it's like to have your flaws.

You don't know what it's like to have my flaws.

I can't have your flaws and you can't have my flaws.

I don't know what it's like to have your life to live.

You don't' know what it's like to have my life to live.

I can't live your life and you can't live my life.

I don't know what it's like to have your sins.

You don't know what it's like to have my sins.

I can't have your sins and you can't have my sins.

I don't know what it's like to have your senses.

You don't know what it's like to have my senses.

I can't have your senses and you can't have my senses.

I don't know what it's like to have your hereditary tendencies.

You don't know what it's like to have my hereditary tendencies.

I can't have your hereditary tendencies and you can't have my hereditary tendencies.

I don't know what it's like to do everything that you do.

You don't know what it's like to do everything that I do.

I can't do everything that you do and you can't do everything that I do.

I don't know what it's like to say everything you say.

You don't' know what it's like to say everything I say.

I can't say everything you say and you can't say everything I say.

I don't know what it's like to have your memory.

You don't know what it's like to have my memory.

I can't have your memory and you can't have my memory.

I don't know what it's like to have your guilt.

You don't know what it's like to have my guilt.

I can't have your guilt and you can't have my guilt.

I don't know what it's like to have your shadow.

You don't know what it's like to have my shadow.

I can't have your shadow and you can't have my shadow.

I don't know what it's like to have your faith in Jesus.

You don't know what it's like to have my faith in Jesus.

I can't have your faith in Jesus and you can't have my faith in Jesus.

I don't know what it's like to have your pain.

You don't know what it's like to have my pain.

I can't have your pain and you can't have my pain.

I don't know what it's like to have your joy.

You don't' know what it's like to have my joy.

I can't have your joy and you can't have my joy.

I don't know what it's like to have your trials for Jesus' name sake.

You don't know what it's like to have my trials for Jesus' name sake.

I can't have your trials for Jesus' name sake and you can't have my trials for Jesus' name sake.

I can't be you and you can't be me.

The Lord created me to be me and the Lord created you to be you.

The Lord created only one me and the Lord created only one you.

I am no mistake to the Lord and you are no mistake to the Lord.

The only mistake that the Lord sees is the wrong choices that you and I make.

I don't know what it's like to make your wrong choices.

You don't know what it's like to make my wrong choices.

I can't make your wrong choices and you can't make my wrong choices.

I don't know what it's like to work out your soul's salvation.

You don't know what it's like to work out my soul's salvation.

I can't work out your soul's salvation and you can't work out my soul's salvation.

I don't know what it's like to have your judgement by God.

You don't know what it's like to have my judgement by God.

I can't have your judgement by God and you can't have my judgement by God.

I don't know what it's like to repent of your sins for you.

You don't' know what it's like to repent of my sins for me.

I can't repent of your sins for you and you can't repent of my sins for me.

I don't know what it's like to choose your destiny for you.

You don't know what it's like to choose my destiny for me.

I can't choose your destiny for you and you can't choose my destiny for me.

I can't be you and you can't be me.

There are people who are good at imitating you, but they can't be you who God created to be only you.

I can't be you and you can't be me who the Lord loves the same, regardless of me being different from you and you being different from me.

I can't be you who God will judge.

You can't be me who God will judge.

I can't be you who has to answer to God.

You can't be me who has to answer to God.

I don't know what it's like to be you.

You don't know what it's like to be me.

I would be a phony to myself if I wanted to be you; I have a hard time being me.

I don't always know me who can't be you and will never know you like God does, even if I lived with you under the same roof every day.

I don't know what it's like to have your dreams in my sleep.

You don't know what it's like to have my dreams in your sleep.

I can't have your dreams in my sleep and you can't have my dreams in your sleep.

I don't know what it's like to have all of your experiences in life.

You don't know what it's like to have all of my experiences in life.

I can't have all of your experiences in life and you can't have all of my experiences in life.

I don't know what it's like to have your love in my heart.

You don't know what it's like to have my love in your heart.

I can't have your love in my heart and you can't have my love in your heart.

I don't know what it's like to have your worries in my mind.

You don't know what it's like to have my worries in your mind.

I can't have your worries in my mind and you can't have my worries in your mind.

I can't be you and you can't be me, no matter what I share with you and no matter what you share with me.

I don't know what it's like to have your testimonies about what the Lord brought you through in your life.

You don't know what it's like to have my testimonies about what the Lord brought me through in my life.

I can't have your testimonies about what the Lord brought you through in your life and you can't have my testimonies about what the Lord brought me through in my life.

I don't know what it's like to have your eyes to see this world like you see it day after day.

You don't know what it's like to have my eyes to see this world like I see it day after day.

I can't have your eyes to see this world like you see it day after day and you can't have my eyes to see this world like I see it day after day.

I can't be you and you can't be me for even one second.

If I want to be you, then I am not thankful to God for creating me in His image that has no flaws for me to not be who God created me to be in His holy will.

I don't know what it's like to have what is down in your heart.

You don't know what it's like to have what is down in my heart.

I can't have what is down in your heart and you can't have what is down in my heart.

I don't know what it's like to have your relationship with Jesus.

You don't know what it's like to have my relationship with Jesus.

I can't have your relationship with Jesus and you can't have my relationship with Jesus.

I don't know what it's like to have your cross to carry and follow Jesus.

You don't know what it's like to have my cross to carry and follow Jesus.

I can't carry your cross and follow Jesus and you can't carry my cross and follow Jesus.

I don't know what it's like to love Jesus and keep His Commandments for you.

You don't know what it's like to love Jesus and keep His Commandments for me.

I can't love Jesus and keep His Commandments for you and you can't love Jesus and keep His Commandments for me.

I can't be you and you can't be me who the Lord created to be the only one who can choose to believe in Him for myself so I can be saved in Him.

Jesus can only represent my case for me in heaven.

Jesus can't represent my case for you in heaven.

Jesus can only represent your case for you in heaven.

Jesus can't represent your case for me in heaven.

This goes to show that I can't be you and you can't be me standing before a holy and righteous God who will not switch me over to be judged before Him in your place and will not switch you over to be judged before Him in my place.

I can't be you before God and you can't be me before God who didn't make any mistake when He created you to be you and me to be me.

God will judge me fairly just like God will judge you fairly.

God was fair to create only one you and only one me.

I can't be you and you can't be me and no one's theories can be more profound than Jesus giving up His life on the cross for me as if I was the only sinner in this world where there is only one me who must make my calling sure in Jesus Christ before it's too late.

Transparency

Transparency is a good thing to many people.

Transparency is a bad thing to many people.

Transparency is how we use it at the right time to encourage someone.

Transparency is how we use it at the right time to set someone free from being burdened by self-pity and guilt.

Transparency is how we use it at the right time to bless someone's life and help them let go of their past regrets.

Transparency is how we use it at the right time to heal someone emotionally and spiritually.

Transparency is very often judged by criticizing people.

Transparency is very often judged by secretive people.

Transparency is very often judged by hurting people.

There are people who will look down on you and me for being transparent.

There are people who will look at you and me and think we're bad for being transparent.

There are people who will give you and me a bad name for being transparent about the bad things we did in our past life.

Transparency is a joy to people who love to hear someone being transparent with them.

Transparency goes on in history much more than dishonesty because transparency has enriched many people and made them not want to repeat what their ancestors did that was bad.

Transparency is from the Lord Jesus Christ who no one can ever be more transparent than.

Jesus was always transparent with everyone when He lived in this world without sin.

Jesus always spoke the truth and he did it in love, even when Jesus got angry at the merchants for selling animals in His holy temple.

Jesus was transparent with the Pharisees and religious leaders when he admitted to them that He is the Messiah and the Son of God, even though Jesus knew they would call him a blasphemer and crucify Him.

Transparency can cause you and me to make some enemies.

Transparency caused Jesus to make enemies who wanted to kill Him for being so truthful about things they had rejected.

There is no deception in transparency that can have a good effect on even a liar.

Know that being truthful is always the right thing to do by God.

God was transparent to the people back in the bible days through his prophets who many people rejected because they didn't believe that God spoke to them.

Most of all, God was very transparent in His Son, Jesus Christ, who the Pharisees and religious leaders denounced because they didn't realize what they did to Jesus they also did to God.

God is transparent today in Christians, in nature and even in many animals.

God is most transparent in the Bible that is truly all about God who so loved the world that He gave us His only begotten Son that whosoever believeth in Him shall not perish but have eternal life.

The devil hates transparency because he knows that Jesus can work with an honest person to have a change of heart to repent and turn to Him.

Transparency gives hope to many people and makes them want to keep on living when the odds are against them.

All it takes is for the truth to be told to them and they will get the help they need to survive.

The truth is transparent and will set us free from even being dishonest with ourselves.

Our thoughts are so transparent to God who sees our thoughts to be true or not true.

We can choose to change our thoughts that are transparent to God and we can think evil that is also transparent to God when no one else can see our evil thoughts.

We can choose to not speak about our evil thought and choose not to do evil but that doesn't erase the transparency that God sees in our thoughts that can be deceitful to the naked eye that can only see actions that can pretend to be true.

When Judas was at the last supper with Jesus, his actions were not true to Jesus, even though his actions looked so true to Jesus' other disciples who didn't know that Judas was only going through the motions.

His actions at the last supper were so transparent to Jesus who knew that Judas would betray Him with his actions.

The disciples believed that Judas was true to Jesus and to them as they went from place to place with Jesus who healed many sick people, cast out demons, fed many, opened the blind's eyes and raised some dead people back to life.

Judas' actions were all pretense that was so transparent to Jesus who still loved Judas regardless of his untrue actions that the other disciples believed to be true.

Only the Lord God can always see transparency.

You and I can be deceived like Jesus' disciples who were deceived by Judas giving Jesus a kiss on His cheek to betray Him.

Judas' actions with the kiss on Jesus' cheek was so transparent to Jesus.

Brilliant

There are people who are brilliant with using common sense.

They can use big and fancy words and break the words down to explain them to you and me in a plain and simple way.

There are people who are brilliant at doing small things and simple things that can go a long way in life.

Brilliance doesn't always stand out above the simple things in life.

Something might be simple to one person and brilliant to another person.

Simple things can be a brilliant thing to simple people.

Brilliant things can be a simple thing to brilliant people.

A dog can be brilliant in doing everything that the dog was trained to do.

Brilliance can be a lot of things.

The sun can shine so brilliant.

The full, white moonlight can glow so brilliant.

The stars can sparkly so brilliant.

The rainbow can show its beautiful colors so brilliant.

There are people who can invent things so brilliant.

There are people who can build things so brilliant.

There are people who can design things so brilliant.

There are brilliant people in the military.

There are brilliant people working for the government.

There are brilliant people in every job.

There are brilliant people in the church.

There are brilliant people who know that they are brilliant.

There are brilliant people who don't know that they are brilliant until someone brings it to their attention.

You might be brilliant and not know it, and there are people who see your brilliance and don't care to help you see that you are brilliant.

The Lord God created us all in His image to give brilliance to whoever God wants to be brilliant.

Birds can be brilliant and fly to warm climate areas to get out of the cold winter chill.

Brilliance is for the glory of God and not for one's own pride so you can boast about yourself or anyone else; no one can be more brilliant than God.

Jesus Christ was the most brilliant man who lived in this world, as well as being the Son of God.

No one could ever outsmart Jesus, but the Pharisees and religious leaders tried outsmart Jesus with their very clever words and tried to trap Jesus into saying something wrong, but they failed.

No one today is more brilliant than Jesus, and the devil knows that very well because he couldn't outsmart Jesus in heaven with his great brilliance that was dumb to Jesus who cast Lucifer out of heaven along with a third of his angels.

No one today is more brilliant than Jesus who sent His Holy Spirit to this world to inspire us with spiritual gifts to edify the church.

The bible is the most brilliant book that anyone can ever read and live by so they can be enlightened with the simple truth in the Bible that can change lives in Jesus' brilliant transforming power.

There are people who will see that you are brilliant and they will do all they can to make you look dumb, but if the Lord is for you and not against you no one can keep you down from blessing others with your brilliance from the Lord.

Brilliance is from the Lord to be used for good and not evil.

If you use your brilliance for evil, it will sooner or later catch up with you and you will reap what you sow.

Someone may seem so plain and simple, but a simple person might very well have some brilliance to survive in this world from day to day.

The Lord is perfect in brilliance to use the simple things to help a fool to wise up and repent and turn to Him before it's too late.

I Can Only

I can only make my own mistakes.

I can't make anyone else's mistakes for them.

I can only swallow down my own food.

I can't swallow food for someone else.

I can only talk with my own voice.

I can't talk with anyone else's voice for them.

I can only hear with my own ears.

I can't hear with anyone else's ears for them.

I can only see with my own eyes.

I can't see with anyone else's eyes for them.

I can only think with my own mind.

I can't think with anyone else's mind for them.

I can only smell through my own nose.

I can't smell through anyone else's nose for them.

I can only pick up and hold something in my own hands.

I can't pick up and hold something in someone else's hands for them.

I can only breathe my own breath.

I can't breathe anyone else's breath for them.

I can only walk on my own two legs.

I can't walk on anyone else's legs for them.

I can only use my own intelligence.

I can't use anyone else's intelligence for them.

I can only use my own common sense.

I can't use anyone else's common sense for them.

I can only use my own judgement.

I can't use anyone else's judgement for them.

I can only make my own choices.

I can't make anyone else's choices for them.

I can only confess and repent of my own sins unto the Lord Jesus Christ.

I can't confess and repent of anyone else's sins for them unto the Lord Jesus Christ.

I can only deny myself and pick up my own cross and follow Jesus Christ.

I can't deny anyone else for them and pick up anyone else's cross for them and follow Jesus Christ for them.

I can only examine myself and work out my own soul's salvation.

I can't examine anyone else for them and work out their soul's salvation for them.

I can only have my own flaws.

I can't have anyone else's flaws for them.

I can only have my own sins.

I can't have anyone else's sins for them.

I can only live my own life.

I can't live anyone else's life for them.

I can only make my own achievements.

I can't make anyone else's achievements for them.

I can only want to do better for myself.

I can't do better for anyone else.

I can only wise up for myself.

I can't wise up for anyone else.

I can only put a limit on myself.

I can't put a limit on anyone else.

I can only go as far in life as I choose to go.

I can't choose for anyone else to go far in their lives because they must choose that for themselves.

I can only love Jesus and keep His Commandments for myself.

I can't choose to love Jesus and keep His Commandments for anyone else who must love Jesus and keep His Commandments for themselves.

I can only be judged by God for myself.

I can't be judged by God for anyone else; they will be judged by God themselves.

I can only be guilty before God for myself.

I can't be guilty before God for anyone else; they will be guilty before God for themselves.

I can only believe in Jesus Christ for myself.

I can't believe in Jesus Christ for anyone else; they must believe in Jesus Christ for themselves.

I can only be saved in Jesus Christ for myself.

I can't be saved in Jesus Christ for anyone else; they must be saved in Jesus Christ themselves.

I can only choose my own destiny.

I can't choose anyone else's destiny for them.

I can only choose to do good or evil for myself.

I can't choose to do good or evil for anyone else; they will choose to do good or evil for themselves.

I can only choose to not quench the Holy Spirit for myself.

I can't choose for anyone else not to quench the Holy Spirit for themselves; they must choose not to quench the Holy Spirit speaking to them and know God loves them.

I can only choose to change to be better myself.

I can't change anyone else who must choose to change to better themselves.

I can only have a relationship with Jesus Christ for myself.

I can't have a relationship with Jesus for anyone else; they must have a relationship with Jesus for themselves.

I can only have my own heart.

I can't have anyone else's heart and feel for them.

I can only have my own actions.

I can't have anyone else's actions that belong to them to do good or evil.

I can only choose to bridle my own tongue.

I can't bridle anyone else's tongue; they must choose to do that.

I can only dream my own dreams.

I can't dream anyone else's dreams; they must dream their own dreams that must be in the Lord's will to go down in generations to come to be blessed.

I can only be real for myself.

I can't be real for anyone else; they have to be real for themselves.

I can only live my life for Jesus Christ for myself.

I can't live anyone else's life for Jesus Christ; they must do that for themselves day after day.

I can only walk my own walk for myself.

I can't walk anyone else's walk; they must do that for themselves.

I can only choose to love my neighbors for myself.

I can't choose for anyone else to love their neighbors; they must choose to love them for themselves.

I can only be humble unto the Lord Jesus Christ for myself.

I can't be humble unto the Lord Jesus Christ for anyone else; they must do that for themselves.

I can only give all of my mind, heart and soul to the Lord Jesus Christ for myself.

I can't give anyone else's mind, heart and soul to the Lord Jesus Christ; they must give those to Jesus themselves.

I can only be myself in this world day after day.

I can't be anyone else; they have to be themselves day after day.

I can only believe the bible for myself.

I can't believe the bible for anyone else; they must choose to believe the bible for themselves.

I can only be convicted of my sins for myself.

I can't be convicted of anyone else's sins; they are the only ones that can be convicted for themselves.

I can only be baptized for myself.

I can't be baptized for anyone else because they must be baptized for themselves so they can be a new creature in Jesus Christ.

The Most

The most richest people in this world are like homeless people to Jesus who fills the heavens with eternal riches.

The most genius people in this world are like dumb people to Jesus who knows all things seen and unseen.

The most righteous people in this world are so wrong without the righteousness of Jesus who makes us right with God.

The most strongest people in this world are so weak to Jesus who gave two-thirds of the angels in heaven the strength to cast Lucifer and his angels out of heaven.

The most careful people in this world are so careless to Jesus who has no sins and never makes a mistake.

The most gentle people in this world are like rough people to Jesus whose gentleness soothes the heavens and unfallen worlds.

The most talkative people in this world are like silent people to Jesus who talks to everyone at the same time through His Holy Spirit who so many people quench every day.

The most quiet people in this world are like noisy people to Jesus who always hears the heart talking loud in rebellion against Him.

The most bold people in this world are like fearful people to Jesus who cast demons out of many people with just one look on His face.

The most happy people in this world are like sad people to Jesus who filled the heavens with happiness when He rose from the grave with the victory over death and the grave.

The most healthy people in this world are like sick people to Jesus who lived in this world without sin in His flesh so that He was in perfect mental, emotional, psychological, physical and spiritual health to be the Lamb of God and give up His life to save us from our sins.

The most loving people in this world are like hateful people to Jesus because they have a sinful nature from being born in sin that Jesus hates even though He loves all souls who sin hates to be saved in Jesus Christ.

The most truthful people in this world are like liars to Jesus who cannot lie to you and me even though we can easily think a lie no matter how truthful we are in what we say.

The most giving people in this world are like stingy people to Jesus who no one can beat in giving because Jesus gave up all that He had in heaven to become poor in this world of especially spiritual poverty that only Jesus could bring us out of to give us eternal life that even the most giving people cannot do.

The most trustworthy people in this world are like promise breakers to Jesus who is worthy for us to put all of our trust in every day.

The most trustworthy people will have the best intentions of keeping their promises, but they can break them unintentionally when bad situations arise in their life so unexpected.

The most humble people in this world are like proud people to Jesus who humbled Himself unto death to save us from our sins.

Jesus humbled Himself and allowed Himself to be spit upon and beaten up really bad and didn't say one word or fight back as He was being whipped and His flesh torn.

The most humble people in this world could not have done what Jesus did, not saying a word and taking in all the suffering before dying for our sins.

The most encouraging people in this world are like discouraging people to Jesus who appeared before His disciples after He rose from the grave to give them encouragement that they were not alone.

Jesus' disciples were the most encouraging people to Him, but Peter discouraged Jesus when he denied Jesus three times, saying he didn't know Jesus.

Judas discouraged Jesus when he betrayed Him with a kiss and turned Him over to His enemies.

The most wicked people in this world are like a good chance to take to Jesus who doesn't want anyone to be lost in their sins that He became on the cross in place of the most wicked people.

Jesus gave up His life to save them and give them a chance to repent and turn to Him before it's too late.

Jonah didn't want to take a chance to warn those wicked people in Nineveh to repent and turn to God, who Jonah had disobeyed when God told him to go to Nineveh and tell the people to repent.

The Very Dark Nighttime
of this World

We are living in the very dark nighttime of this world where so many people are spiritually asleep and don't know the word of God.

We are living in the very dark nighttime of this world where spiritual predators are everywhere and prey on anyone who is not rooted and grounded in Jesus Christ.

We are living in the very dark nighttime of this world where unbelievers are so unprotected from the supreme spiritual predator called the devil who is all about setting up spiritual traps for all to live in darkness.

We are living in the very dark nighttime of this world where every day is covered over in darkness that the daily news reports, like murders, thefts, abuse, violence, political strife, wars, oppression and injustice, which are all active in the very dark nighttime of this world.

Jesus is our only hope in the very dark nighttime of this world.

Jesus is our only bright, shining light in the very dark nighttime of this world.

Only Jesus can protect you and me from spiritual predators that love to come out and attack us with lies and deceptions, especially in the very dark nighttime of this world.

We must pray without ceasing, study the bible and live right unto the Lord, who will give us His Holy Spirit if we ask Him for His Holy Spirit to dwell in us day after day.

We are living in the very dark nighttime of this world where Jesus Christ is our only source of spiritual daylight.

Jesus is our only break of spiritual daylight shining through the very dark nighttime of this world.

We are living in the very dark nighttime of this world where darkness can appear in any church with its predators mixing truth with error, but their actions speak louder than words as they prey on God's true remnant children.

These predators will fail their mission due to the light of Jesus Christ, who is the head of the church.

Imagine the Fun We Will Have in Heaven

We will sing songs unto the Lord and never lose our voices.

We will do a holy and righteous dance unto the Lord and never get tired.

Imagine the fun we will have in heaven.

We will run and never get tired.

We will play with the animals and never get tired.

Imagine the fun we will have in heaven.

We will talk to one another about the goodness of the Lord and never get bored.

We will keep company with one another and never get bored.

Imagine the fun we will have in heaven.

We will have so much holy and righteous fun and never get tired.

We will talk to Jesus and never get bored.

We will keep company with Jesus and never get bored.

We will never wear out our welcome with Jesus.

Imagine the fun we will have in heaven.

We will never wear out our welcome with one another.

We will talk to the animals and never get bored.

Imagine the fun we will have in heaven.

We will worship the Lord and never get tired.

We will get to know everybody and never get bored.

Imagine the fun we will have in heaven.

We will talk to the holy angels and never get bored.

We will keep company with the holy angels and never get bored.

Imagine the fun we will have in heaven where there will only be holy and righteous fun in our Lord and Savior Jesus Christ.

We will visit creatures in other worlds and never get tired.

We will talk to creatures in other worlds and never get bored.

Imagine the fun we will have in heaven.

We will live in our immortal bodies and never get sick.

We will live in our immortal bodies and never need to take a shower.

Imagine the fun we will have in heaven.

We will live in our immortal bodies and never need to brush and floss our teeth.

Imagine the fun we will have in heaven.

We will live in our immortal bodies and never have any moles, blemishes, freckles, scars, sores, dry skin flakes, lines under our eyes or dandruff.

Imagine the fun we will have in heaven, where fun will be eternal for all the holy saints.

We won't really know what fun is until we make it to heaven with Jesus who will give us holy and righteous fun that the people of the world can't ever measure up to or out do.

The Greatest Banquet

The greatest banquet over all the earthly banquets will be in heaven where all of us who make it there will wear our eternal long white robes and eternal royal crowns that will shine brighter than a thousand suns but won't blind our eyes.

All the angels in heaven and all the celestial beings in other worlds will join in with us to celebrate our victory in our Lord and Savior Jesus Christ who will be our eternal glorious host to excite the heavens in His celebration of all of His children who will set at the banquet table with Him and feast on the fruits from the tree of life.

At the greatest banquet in heaven we will sing victorious songs unto the Lord and we will do a holy dance like King David to marvel the angels in heaven and the celestial beings in other worlds who will clap their hands with eternal joy to fill up trillions of galaxies and billions of universes with everlasting gladness that we made it to the banquet in heaven.

The banquet in heaven will greatly be above all the best banquets in this world, and Jesus will give you and me our eternal glorious reward in a one-on-one with Him, just like any one of us was the only sinner He had to save and have at His eternally mesmerizing banquet in heaven.

To God be the glory that we are all here at this wonderful banquet being like only one drop of water in a barrel compared to the Lord's ocean of living waters that will fill up our souls with eternal life to quench the thirst of our destiny at the banquet in heaven.

To God be the glory that we are all here to have a good time with one another in our Lord Jesus Christ, who will give us all an eternal holy and righteous good time at His heavenly banquet to show all the angels in heaven and all the celestial beings in other worlds that we are His redeemed prize and eternal joy.

Our joy at this banquet won't come anywhere close to Jesus' joy.

The greatest banquet will be in heaven for all great and small to have great favor with God to win the prize of eternal life that Jesus will give to us all the same.

We all will be winners in Jesus at the greatest banquet in heaven where there will be no losers not getting their prize that will last forever.

I Don't Know What It's Like to have No Sins

I don't know what it's like to have no sins.

Do you know what it's like to have no sins?

I don't know what it's like to never think wrong.

I don't know what it's like to never say something wrong.

I don't know what it's like to never do something wrong.

I don't know what it's like to have no sins.

Do you know what it's like to have no sins?

I don't know what it's like to have never judged anyone.

I don't know what it's like to never have had a bad habit.

I don't know what it's like to have never assumed anything about someone.

I don't know what it's like to have no sins.

Do you know what it's like to have no sins?

I don't know what it's like to never hold a grudge against someone.

I don't know what it's like to never have lusted.

I don't know what it's like to have no sins to confess and repent unto the Lord Jesus Christ.

I don't know what it's like to never make a mistake.

I don't know what it's like to never get angry.

I don't know what it's like to never have been proud.

I don't know what it's like to have no sins.

Do you know what it's like to have no sins?

We were born in sin to have a sinful nature to sin against God in seen and unseen ways.

We can truly thank God for giving us His Son, Jesus Christ, to save us from being lost in our sins if we confess and repent of our sins unto the Lord Jesus Christ.

All who are saved in Jesus will one day know what it's like to have no sins when Jesus comes back again on the clouds of glory.

Jesus will give us all a new immortal body that is completely free from sin, but until then and for as long as we live in this sinful world, we will have sins to confess and repent unto Jesus Christ.

We are all sinners saved through God's grace that we don't deserve, no matter what right things we say and do.

Our righteousness is like filthy rags before a holy and righteous God.

I don't know what it's like to have no sins.

Do you know what it's like to have no sins?

When Jesus lived in this sinful world, He had no sins.

Jesus became sin on the cross to save us from our sins.

Jesus never had a corrupt thought.

Jesus never said one wrong word.

Jesus never did anything wrong when He lived here on earth without sin in His flesh.

He is our Lord and Savior and the Light of the world.

Jesus knows what it's like to have no sins so He can forgive us of our sins.

Jesus knows what it's like to have no sins so he can cleanse us of our sins.

Jesus knows what it's like to have no sins so He can save us from our sins if we confess and repent of our sins unto Him.

I don't know what it's like to have no sins.

Do you know what it's like to have no sins?

I don't' know what it's like to never have doubted God.

What about you?

I don't know what it's like to have never been jealous of anyone.

I don't know what it's like to have never been rude to anyone.

I don't know what it's like to have never hated anyone.

I don't know what it's like to have no sins.

Do you know what it's like to have no sins?

I don't know what it's like to have never eaten too much food.

I don't know what it's like to have never imitated anyone.

I don't know what it's like to have never pretended with anyone.

I don't know what it's like to have no sins.

Do you know what it's like to have no sins?

I don't know what it's like to never talk bad about someone.

I don't know what it's like to never have sinned against God.

Do you know what it's like to have no sins?

I don't know what it's like to never have overworked myself.

I don't know what it's like to never have any bad intentions.

I don't know what it's like to have no sins.

Do you know what it's like to have no sins?

I don't know what it's like to never feel any guilt.

I don't know what it's like to have never been guilty.

I don't know what it's like to have never deceived someone.

I don't know what it's like to have no sins to confess and repent of unto the Lord Jesus Christ.

Do you know what it's like to have no sins to confess and repent unto the Lord Jesus Christ?

I don't know what it's like to never offend someone.

I don't know what it's like to have never broken God's ten Commandments.

I don't know what it's like to never have taken God's grace for an excuse to do my own will.

Do you know what it's like to have no sins that Jesus became on the cross to save us from our sins if we confess our sins and repent and live for Jesus?

I don't know what it's like to never have feared anything or anyone.

I don't know what it's like to never have been wrong.

I don't know what it's like to never have made a bad choice.

I don't know what it's like to have no sins.

Do you know what it's like to have no sins?

I don't know what it's like to have never interrupted someone.

I don't know what it's like to have never wanted to get revenge.

I don't know what it's like to have never brought any hardship on myself.

I don't know what it's like to have never misunderstood someone.

I don't know what it's like to never have done someone wrong.

I don't know what it's like to have no sins.

Do you know what it's like to have no sins?

I don't know what it's like to have never quenched the Holy Spirit.

I don't know what it's like to have never been ignorant.

I don't know what it's like to have never denied Jesus before someone.

I don't know what it's like to have no sins.

Do you know what it's like to have no sins?

I don't know what it's like to have never disobeyed my parents.

I don't know what it's like to have never taken something that didn't belong to me.

I don't know what it's like to have never tried to draw attention to myself.

I don't know what it's like to have no sins.

Do you know what it's like to have no sins?

I don't know what it's like to have never been selfish.

I don't know what it's like to have never fallen short of the glory of God.

I don't know what it's like to have no sins.

Do you know what it's like to have no sins?

I don't know what it's like to have never lived in this world without sin in my flesh.

I don't know what it's like to have never eaten any food that is not good to eat.

I don't know what it's like to have never failed someone.

I don't know what it's like to have never rejected the Lord in some kind of way.

I don't know what it's like to have no sins that I was born in and only Jesus Christ can save me and you from when no one in this world can prove to be without sin to not be a sinner saved through God's grace.

I don't know what it's like to have never grieved.

I don't know what it's like to have never disappointed someone.

I don't know what it's like to have never joked about someone.

I don't know what it's like to have no sins.

Do you know what it's like to have no sins?

I don't know what it's like to have never worried.

I don't know what it's like to have never been sick.

I don't know what it's like to have never felt pain.

I don't know what it's like to have no sins.

Do you know what it's like to have no sins?

I don't know what it's like to have never been anxious.

I don't know what it's like to have never been impatient.

I don't know what it's like to have never forgotten something.

I don't know what it's like to have no sins.

Do you know what it's like to have no sins?

I don't know what it's like to have never changed on someone.

I don't know what it's like to have never pretended.

I don't know what it's like to have never been in trouble.

I don't know what it's like to have never gossiped.

I don't know what it's like to have no sins.

Do you know what it's like to have no sins?

I don't know what it's like to have never been thirsty.

I don't know what it's like to have never been hungry.

I don't know what it's like to have never been in a rush.

I don't know what it's like to have no sins.

Do you know what it's like to have no sins?

I don't know what it's like to have never disliked someone.

I don't know what it's like to have never been careless.

I don't know what it's like to have never wanted what I couldn't have.

I don't know what it's like to have no sins that only Jesus Christ was without when He lived on earth to redeem us back to God.

I don't know what it's like to have never smelled bad.

I don't know what it's like to have no sins.

Do you know what it's like to have no sins, when all sin is bad to God?

I don't know what it's like to have never been unfriendly to someone.

I don't know what it's like to have never lied to God.

I don't know what it's like to have never mistrusted God.

I don't know what it's like to have never sinned against God.

I don't know what it's like to have no sins.

Do You know what it's like to have no sins?

I don't know what it's like to have no sins in this sinful world.

I don't know what it's like to have never said something wrong even on the spur of the moment.

I don't know what it's like to have never done something wrong even on the spur of the moment.

I don't know what it's like to have never questioned God.

I don't know what it's like to have never complained.

I don't know what it's like to have no sins.

Do you know what it's like to have no sins?

I don't know what it's like to have never misinterpreted a bible scripture.

I don't know what it's like to have never given in to the devil's temptations.

I don't know what it's like to have never showed favoritism.

I don't know what it's like to have never lived in darkness.

I don't know what it's like to have never rebelled against God.

I don't know what it's like to have never turned my back on Jesus.

I don't know what it's like to have no sins.

Do you know what it's like to have no sins?

The Same Way Every Day

The sky is the same way every day and every night as it hovers over us.

The sun is the same way every day as it shines down on us.

The moon is the same way every night as it glows above us.

The stars are the same way every night as they sparkle high above us.

The air is the same way every day and every night as we breathe it in and out of our nostrils.

The ground is the same way every day and every night as we walk on it.

The mountains are the same way every day as they are there for us to climb up.

The trees are the same way every day for us to get some shade.

A house is the same way every day for us to have a roof over our heads.

A car is the same way every day for us to drive.

The ocean is the same way every day for ships to float on.

Food is the same way every day for us to eat.

Water is the same way every day for us to drink.

Clothes are the same way every day for us to wear.

Shoes are the same way every day for us to put on our feet.

Life is the same way every day for us to live.

Death is the same way every day for the dead.

We are the same way every day to be visible.

The wind is the same way every day to be invisible.

Love is the same way ever day to loving people.

Hate is the same way every day to hateful people.

Peace is the same way every day to peaceful people.

Trouble is the same way every day to people who love to make trouble.

Envy is the same way every day to envious people.

Gossip is the same way every day to people who love to gossip.

Unfaithfulness is the same way every day to people who love to cheat on their spouses.

A friend is the same way every day for being honest.

The bible is the same way every day for us to know the truth about the right way to live.

A Christian is the same way every day for being like Jesus.

God's grace is the same way every day to give us undeserved favor with God.

Salvation is the same way every day for us to be saved in Jesus.

God's goodness is the same way every day to lead us to repent and turn to Jesus.

God is the same way every day to love us even if we don't love Him.

Trust is the same way every day to all who put their trust in Jesus.

Hope is the same way every day to all who put their hope in Jesus.

Faith is the same way every day to all who believe in Jesus.

The heart is the same way every day for loving Jesus.

Our sinful nature is the same way every day for us to be a sinner who only Jesus can save from being lost in our sins that are the same way every day to break God's holy ten Commandments.

There is No End in Jesus Christ

Your marriage can come to an end.

Your house can come to an end.

Your car can come to an end.

There is no end in Jesus Christ.

Your happiness can come to an end.

Your good self-esteem can come to an end.

Your physical strength can come to an end.

There is no end in Jesus Christ.

Your memory can come to an end.

Your eyesight can come to an end.

Your hearing can come to an end.

There is no end in Jesus Christ.

Your voice can come to an end.

Your feelings can come to an end.

Your motivation can come to an end.

There is no end in Jesus Christ.

Your encouragement can come to an end.

Your success can come to an end.

Your smiles can come to an end.

There is no end in Jesus Christ.

Your hope can come to an end.

Your beauty can come to an end.

Your knowledge can come to an end.

There is no end in Jesus Christ.

Your wisdom can come to an end.

Your mind can come to an end.

Your skills can come to an end.

Your talents can come to an end.

There is no end in Jesus Christ.

Your good health can come to an end.

Your life can come to an end on any day.

There is no end in Jesus Christ, who lives forever and ever to give you and me eternal life when He comes back again on the clouds of glory.

Your choices in life can come to an end if you get so sick in your mind.

There is no end in Jesus Christ who restored King Nebuchadnezzar's mind so he could choose to bow down unto God like he should have done before he lost his mind.

He would not have lost his mind if he'd acknowledged God to be the only true living God.

King Nebuchadnezzar truly found out the hard way.

Pain

There are people who are good at hiding their pain.

There are people who are not good at hiding their pain.

There are people who are a dead giveaway in showing their pain in their eyes, looking so sad.

There are people who can hide their pain with smiles on their faces.

There are people who can hide their pain in their jokes.

There are people who can hide their pain in their work.

There are people who can hide their pain in the church, which is the best place to come together in prayer and give all of our pain to Jesus, who can strengthen us to bear our pain so we can keep going on.

Pain can cause people to hurt other people.

Pain can cause broken marriages.

Pain can cause rebellious children.

Pain can cause suicides.

Pain can cause mental illness.

Pain can cause isolation.

Pain can cause bullying.

Pain can cause proudness.

Pain can cause abuse.

Pain can cause revenge.

Pain can cause unforgiveness.

Pain can cause hatred.

Pain can cause murders.

Pain can cause greed.

Pain can cause corruption.

Pain can cause selfishness.

Pain can cause blaming God.

Pain can cause rejecting Jesus.

Pain can cause cursing God.

Pain can cause rebellion against God.

Pain can cause questioning God.

Pain can cause leaving the church.

Pain can cause wars to break out.

Pain can cause lying.

Pain can cause manipulation.

Pain can cause jealousy.

Pain can cause grief.

Pain can cause self-pity.

Pain can cause anger.

Pain can cause gluttony.

Pain caused Jesus to weep.

Pain caused God to forsake His only Son, Jesus Christ, because it greatly pained God's heart to see His only begotten Son hanging on a cross to save us from our sins that Jesus became on the cross, greatly paining God's heart.

The good news is that one day God will wipe away all the tears and there will be no pain existing in heaven where Jesus will take us to for being saved in Him.

Only those who are lost in their sins will feel great pain from God's wrath upon them in the lake of fire and brimstone.

I Lived that Street Life

I lived that street life and I don't want to live it ever again.

That street life is nothing but trouble on every side, every day and every night.

That street life is only a proud life for fools who love to live the street life.

I was just a wanderer living the street life because I was following a bad crowd of people who used drugs, smoked cigarettes, drank a lot of alcohol and slept with prostitutes.

I lived that street life and had nothing but bad influences around me.

I was a wanderer and was so lost in my ignorance that I didn't know what a fool I was for following that bad crowd.

I lived that street life that was full of people who loved to use anyone they could use to get them what they wanted.

I lived that street life that was full of potheads and alcoholics and sex addicts.

That street life had me under its spell and deceived me and made me believe that my life was good.

I believed that I would find my soulmate on that street life where every man was only looking out for himself and wanted to take the woman I liked away from me.

Even I'm a Christian, the fact that I lived that street life still haunts me today.

I see some of that street life in the church where there are people who are spiritual potheads and spiritually drunk and living in spiritual adultery against God.

That spiritual street life is worse than the physical street life because there are people in the church mixing truth with lies and believing they are right with God.

I lived that street life and it was peaceful compared to the spiritual street life in the church where there are people who know the truth of God's holy word but want to add their opinions to it to suit their way of living day after day.

With the physical street life, I pretty much knew who I hung out with from day to day, but when I gave my life to the Lord, He didn't promise me that I wouldn't see anyone living the spiritual street life in the church.

The spiritual street life in the church has its bad people who are all about themselves and not about the Lord Jesus Christ who is the head of the church and will clean up the spiritual street and spiritually rehabilitate all who repent and turn to Him.

Everybody in the church will not repent and turn to Jesus because they choose to live that spiritual street life of scheming and conniving and manipulating people, even in the church, which makes the physical street life look so peaceful and uncorrupt in comparison.

I know from my own experience what is true and not true about the street life I once lived.

If I Believed that there is No God

If I believed that there is no God, then I wouldn't even want to say the word god.

For me to speak the word God means that God exists to me.

The devil wants many people to believe that there is no God.

The devil believes that there is a God who cast him out of heaven with one third of the angels in heaven.

The devil doesn't want anyone to believe that there is a God because the devil knows that we can enter into heaven one day for believing in God's Son, Jesus Christ.

The devil can't return to heaven ever again and he doesn't want you and me to be saved in Jesus Christ who is coming back again to take all who are saved in Him to heaven.

Anyone who believes that there is no God is admitting that there is a God from the tip of their tongue.

The devil doesn't want anyone to speak the name of God because he knows that there is power in God's name and that even an atheist may very speak it if their life is in great danger.

An atheist can realize that it is good to call on God at once if death is closing in on them because there is nothing good about death.

If I believed that there is No God, then I wouldn't want to waste my time trying to prove to anyone that there is no God.

The only thing that would convince me that there is no God is if good things didn't exist at all in this world where it's a good thing to me to be alive and in my right mind and in good health.

If this world was full of only evilness, then I can believe that there is no God whose goodness leads to repentance.

The devil believes that there is a God who will cast him into hell fire and brimstone one day.

It's a good thing to even say God's name because that proves the devil is right to fear and tremble when we call to God's name.

For anyone to say that there is no God is really saying there is a God for speaking God's name that can surely can cause emotions to erupt in an atheist's heart like a volcano eruption because of being challenged by those who believe that there is a God.

Why even speak the name of God if you believe that there is no God?

It comes to show that you haven't fully convinced yourself to believe that God doesn't exist.

Just by speaking God's name, God exists to you in some kind of way deep down in your heart where your doubts got the best of you because of misfortunes in your life.

Your misfortunes, heartaches and hardships corrupted you and made you believe that there is no God who predestined you to exist in this world before the devil could ever deceive you into believing that there is no God.

The devil knows that if he can get the best of you and me with his lies, telling us that evil is the way to live and believe, then he can convince us that there is no God.

An atheist dislikes the weakest of Christians who call on the name of God before them because they know that the name of God can surely stir up their emotions that are no match to God who is slow to anger, which the devil hates.

The devil knows that God sent His Son into this world to also save the atheists from being lost in sin.

God is not quick to get angry and destroy any lost soul who doesn't believe in His Son, Jesus Christ, who gave up His life on the cross for the atheists' sins too.

If I believed that there is no God, then I wouldn't want to know what is right and wouldn't care to do anything right.

Even an atheist can want to be loved, and it is not wrong for an atheist to want this because love is good to be right even for an atheist.

Love is from God, but an atheist can say that there is no God, even though he or she believes in love and won't reject love, especially from someone who they truly love.

If I believed that there is no God, then I wouldn't care about anyone else not believing what I believe to be right because what would matter to me is that I am right and don't need anyone else on my side to back me up.

I have talked to an atheist whose body language was not near to an atheist who says that there is no God.

I recognized God in the atheist's good ways beyond her words, and her body language just didn't convince me that she had shut God out of her life.

Just because someone tells you and me that they are an atheist, it doesn't always mean that God is not with them.

God could be working on them when they don't know it.

You and I can believe that there is no God, even right in the church where we can say that there is no God in our body language if we don't have love for one another when God is love.

If I believed that there is no God, then I wouldn't talk to anyone who believes that there is a God and I wouldn't want to hear and speak the name of God that many atheists will speak to try to prove their point that there is no God who greatly exists on the tip of their tongue for saying the word God.

The atheists believe that there is no God, but they want to be all-knowing and all-seeing and all-powerful like God who they can't be, so they try to eliminate God and pretend He is not the origin of all life.

By doing this, they instead eliminate themselves and make themselves nothing, like thin air.

The air that the atheists breathe is from God who the thin air will acknowledge and obey to be breathed in and out of our nostrils so we can live.

The atheists believe that there is no God, even though nothing at all became all things from God who created all things from nothing, including the atheists who choose to be atheists who God also loves even though He is against their sins.

If I believed that there is no God, then I surely wouldn't be able to be positive about writing this to share with anyone who believes that there is a God like I believe that there is a God whose goodness can lead an atheist's heart to repent and turn to His Son, Jesus Christ, who is one with God and the Holy Spirit.

May Have Been God's Deepest Mystery

The free will to choose may have been God's deepest mystery that God revealed to the angels before He revealed it to this world.

It's like a deep mystery that a perfect angel who God created wanted to be like the most-high God who gave all the angels the free will to choose to love and obey Him.

Lucifer and one third of the angels in heaven chose to rebel against God.

Knowing why Lucifer's heart got filled with flaws that ruined his perfection in heaven is like a deep mystery that no human being can ever solve.

The free will to choose may have been God's deepest mystery to solve because God gave all the angels all of Himself who is nothing but everlasting love that Lucifer and one third of the angels chose to take for granted.

If the free will to choose is the deepest mystery of God, then how can we ever truly know that super-intelligent angels can make foolish choices like Lucifer and one third of the heavenly angels made and fell down from their perfection before God to be cast out of heaven?

God gave all the angels the free will to choose in their eternal perfection but they traded that in for no good outcome to their eternal destiny in hell that God created to cast them into one day.

The free will to choose may have been the deepest, most profound mystery of God because the free will to choose caused a war to break out in heaven and still causes wars to break out in this world where God gave everybody the free will to choose.

The free will to choose has caused heartaches, murders, thefts, abuse, violence, deceit, greed, selfishness, envy, hatred, prejudices, injustice, discrimination, rapes, molestations, and many more hardships.

It may have been the deepest mystery of God to create the free will for angels and human beings to choose to love and obey Him or choose to rebel against Him who is nothing but love all the time that is like a deep mystery to haters of God.

There is no mystery that God can't solve, because God solved the deepest mystery through His Son, Jesus Christ, who had predestined the free will to exist before He created the heavens and the earth in His self-existence.

The free will to choose may have been the deepest mystery of God who foreknew the choices that all the angles would make and all the choices that every human being will make.

God will never force anyone to choose to love and obey Him.

Could it be a very deep mystery of God to have a strange act to destroy the fallen angels and rebellious human beings in the lake of fire when God is nothing but love that is a deep mystery to the unfallen worlds seeing God giving up His only begotten Son to save sinners from being lost while we have the free will to choose our destiny that God won't force anyone to choose?

You and I don't know all the choices we will make while we live with the free will to choose that may have been the deepest mystery of God.

Lucifer may not have known for billions of light years that he would choose to rebel against God along with one third of the angels in heaven.

It may have been the deepest mystery of God to give the angels the free will to choose.

God's love can be a very deep mystery, especially when God allows a very wicked man to live a very long life just so he has a chance to repent and turn to Jesus.

There's no telling how long God gave the rebellious angels in heaven to repent; it may have been trillions of years.

The angels may have chosen to rebel against God who gave them the free will to choose this path, which may have been the deepest mystery of God revealing it to all existence.

Adam and Eve just didn't know from the beginning that they would choose to disobey God.

They didn't see that coming to them in their complete perfection that God created them with.

Their free will to choose may have been the deepest mystery of God.

Even though it may have been the deepest mystery of God to create us with the free will to choose, God gives us His Holy Spirit to encourage us to make good and right choices day after day, but God won't force us to make good choices.

Making good and right choices through our free will to choose may be like a deep mystery to rebellious people who don't care about making good and right choices through their God-given free will to choose, even if there may be no mystery about the bad choices they made.

When We See the Face of Jesus

When we see the face of Jesus and look into His eyes, our hearts will be overflowing with joy that will last forever and ever.

When we see the face of Jesus and look into His eyes, we will experience eternal freedom from all that we have seen in this world.

When we see the face of Jesus and look into His eyes, all life in this world will be like a flash of light passing through the night into eternal light.

When we see the face of Jesus and look into His eyes, we will see all mysteries being solved in glory and praises unto Jesus.

When we see the face of Jesus and look into His eyes, we will see the countless teardrops drying up like they never existed.

When we see the face of Jesus and look into His eyes, we will see everlasting love looking back at you and me and filling up our eyes with His eternal victory over this sinful world.

When we see the face of Jesus and look into His eyes, we will see ourselves as being the only sinner who Jesus gave up His life on the cross to save from being lost in sin.

When we see the face of Jesus and look into His eyes, we will experience nothing but total eternal wholeness in our souls while having no earthly words to express to Jesus.

When we see the face of Jesus and look into His eyes, we will see all of our days on earth being like only a shadow passing over the landscape.

There won't be any numbers on our days that won't exist in Jesus' eternal presence before us in heaven.

When we see the face of Jesus and look into His eyes, we will see all existence traveling faster than the speed of light in our eyes to behold the Creator of all things.

When we see the face of Jesus and look into His all-seeing eyes, we will see all the things that we could never have imagined in this fallen world of sin that filled the eyes of Jesus with tears and grief and made Jesus leave heaven to be born in the flesh of men and live among sinners without sin to save us from our sins and redeem us back to God.

When we see the face of Jesus and look into His eyes, we will see complete eternal perfection looking back at us and filling us up with no trace of memories of this sinful world that we now live in and will not pass away with for being saved in Jesus.

When we see the face of Jesus and look into His eyes, we will experience eternal presence as if time never existed to us because there is no existence of time in heaven that Jesus created with an eternal great smile on His face.

When we see the face of Jesus and look into His eyes, we will see our faith and hope and obedience kissing the streets made of pure, everlasting gold that Jesus created for us to walk down wearing our white robes and crowns on our heads for not taking our eyes off of Him in this eroded world where all the gold is temporary and will pass away one day in fire and brimstone.

We Can't Get By

We can't get by one another and get to God

I can't get by you and get to God

You can't get by me and get to God

We can't get by one another and get to God.

I can see you, but I can't see God.

You can see me, but you can't see God.

We can't get by one another and get to God

If I don't love you, then how can I love God?

If you don't love me, then how can you love God?

We can't get by one another and get to God.

If I don't forgive you, then God won't forgive me.

If you don't forgive me, then God won't forgive you.

We can't get by Jesus and get to God.

If I don't trust Jesus, then I don't trust God.

If you don't trust Jesus, then you don't trust God.

If I deny Jesus, then I deny God.

If you deny Jesus, then you deny God.

If I don't love Jesus, then I don't love God.

If you don't love Jesus, then you don't love God.

We can't get by Jesus and get to God.

If I reject Jesus, then I reject God.

If you reject Jesus, then you reject God.

Jesus Christ is the Son of God and is one with God.

We can't get by one another and we can't get by Jesus to get to God, who so loved the world that He gave us His only begotten Son that whosoever believeth in Him shall not perish but have eternal life.

Will Give All
the Glory and Praise to God

All of the atoms will give all the glory and praise to God.

All of the proteins will give all the glory and praise to God.

All of the molecules will give all the glory and praise to God.

All of the neutrons will give all the glory and praise to God.

All of the electrons will give all the glory and praise to God.

All of the DNA will give all the glory and praise to God.

All of the elements in the earth will give all the glory and praise to God.

All of the stars will give all the glory and praise to God.

All of the planets will give all the glory and praise to God.

All of the galaxies will give all the glory and praise to God.

All of the universes will give all the glory and praise to God.

All of the genetics will give all the glory and praise to God.

All of the unknown will give all the glory and praise to God.

All of nature will give all the glory and praise to God.

All of the mysteries will give all the glory and praise to God.

All of the living cells will give all the glory and praise to God.

All of the species will give all the glory and praise to God.

All of the possibilities will give all the glory and praise to God.

All of the chances will give all the glory and praise to God.

All of the truth will give all the glory and praise to God.

All of the freedom will give all the glory and praise to God.

All of the unfallen worlds will give all the glory and praise to God.

All of the angels in heaven will give all the glory and praise to God.

God is the Father, the Son and the Holy Spirit being eternally complete in oneness to be the beginning and the end that all existence can't go beyond.

All existence is limited to the self-existing Trinity Godhead who created all seen and unseen things before we were born to see nothing, hear nothing and know nothing in our mother's womb.

All of the rocks will give all the glory and praise to God.

All of the deep waters will give all the glory and praise to God.

All of the mountains will give all the glory and praise to God.

All of the birds will give all the glory and praise to God.

All of the animals will give all the glory and praise to God.

We human beings were the only ones who God created in His likeness for us to be so much like God who many human beings degrade and believe that there is no God.

We human beings were the only ones who God created in His likeness for us to communicate with God who many people will not pray to because they believe that there is no God to hear them and communicate with them.

We human beings were the only ones who God the Father, the Son and the Holy Spirit created in their likeness to be so much like God in His character, but many human beings, even in the church, will live their lives like God doesn't exist and didn't give us His only begotten Son to save us from our sins and redeem us back to God.

We human beings were the only ones who God created in His image for us to reason like God, but many people, even in the church, will cherish their selfish reasons in doing things and not be in line with God's holy word that is filled with the Holy Spirit and God's promises to us for believing in his Son, Jesus Christ who is one with God and the Holy Spirit.

We will never fully understand that Trinity Godhead who created human beings in their likeness that is worthy of all of our glory and praise, even though many people don't give that to God.

God surely gave us all of Himself when He created us human beings in His image, but many people shun away from God through their animalistic lifestyle doing things like they don't have a mind to think.

All of the good things and right things will give all the glory and praise to God the Father, God the Son Jesus Christ, and God the Holy Spirit who cannot lie to us, but many people, even in the church, will lie to God the Holy Spirit who anointed them with spiritual gifts in the church when they carry on in the church like they anointed themselves and grieve the Holy Spirit.

All of the time here on earth will give all the glory and praise to God who is so long-suffering and merciful to all in the church and not in the church to not overlook our short time in the land of the living where now is the time for us all to repent and turn to Jesus not only in words but also in actions.

All of the actions in billions of universes will give all the glory and praise to God, but the actions of many people, even in the church, are so unstable to unbelievers who see nothing different from them to not be convicted to want to change from their selfish ways that deny the glory and praise that is due to God forever and ever.

We Live in a World

We live in a world where there are all kinds of addictions that people have in their lives day after day.

I was watching a program on TV one day that showed a woman who was addicted to drinking human blood and animal blood.

There was another woman who was addicted to eating baby diapers that were filled with urine, and there was a man who put leeches on his body because he believed that it would heal all the ailments in his body.

This is the kind of world we live in, where sin is like a king sitting on his throne and ruling over anyone who bows down unto him.

We live in a sinful world every day, so we need to choose to confess and repent and live our lives unto Jesus Christ who can give us the victory over our addictions.

We live in a world that Jesus once lived in without sin or addictions in His flesh so Jesus Christ, our Lord, could save us from our sins.

We live in a world of so many addictions that people have from day to day.

There are big and little addictions that we can give to Jesus in prayer of confessions and repentance and we can turn to Jesus who the devil has no power or authority over.

We live in a world that Jesus overcame to give you and me the power to overcome our addictions if we want to deny ourselves and pick up our crosses to follow Him day after day.

No addiction is too hard for Jesus to cleanse us from for believing in Him who came into this sinful world to save us sinners from being lost in our sins.

We live in a world where everybody has some kind of addiction for being born in sin that only Jesus can forgive us of and cleanse us of and save us from if we choose to confess and repent of our sins and turn to Him who the demons will fear and tremble before when we call on Jesus' name that can cause the devil to flee from us.

To Stay in its Place

God created the sun to stay in its place with no free will to choose to move out of its place in the universe.

God created the moon to stay in its place with no free will to choose to move out of its place in the universe.

God created the stars to stay in their places with no free will to choose to move out of their places in the universe.

God created this world to stay in its place with no free will to choose to move out of its place in the universe.

God created the sky to stay in its place with no free will to choose to move out of its place hovering over this world.

God created the clouds to stay in their place with no free will to choose to move out of their place up in the sky.

God created the mountains to stay in its place with no free will to choose to move out of their place on the ground.

God created the hills to stay in their place with no free will to choose to move out of their place on the ground.

God created the oceans to stay in their place with no free will to choose to move out of their place above the ground.

God created the ground to stay in its place with no free will to choose to move out of its place in the world.

God created human beings with a free will to choose to move around here and there.

God created human beings with a free will to choose, which animals can't do because they have a fixed behavior pattern that God gave to all animals.

It is not for us to question why God did what He did.

God created our sleep to stay in its place with no free will to choose to move our dreams around from place to place.

God created the air to stay in its place with no free will to choose not to enter into our nostrils.

God created only us human beings in this world with a free will to choose to move from place to place because we were created in the image of God, who sometimes moves around in mysterious ways and doesn't stay in one place, especially in the areas of our minds and hearts that God loves to travel to from day to day.

We Don't Usually Like to Talk About Death

We don't usually like to talk about death because many people fear it will come their way if they talk about it.

We don't even like to think about death because most people love to live from day to day.

Who in their right mind would want to die, even fighting in a war where every soldier hopes to live through the fight regardless of whether they get wounded?

We don't usually like to talk about making out a will because we love to live from day to day being in our right minds.

Even many very sick people don't want to die because they want to get well, which is what life is pretty much about from day to day.

From the beginning, God created all creatures to live forever, but we all fall short of that now because of Adam and Eve disobeying God and causing death to come upon all living creatures here on earth.

We don't usually like to talk about death and we don't usually like to see anyone die, even an animal.

Only hateful and evil people take pleasure in killing other people.

Even good soldiers fighting in a war take no pleasure in killing the enemy soldiers, but they have no other choice but to kill them or be killed.

Jesus Himself took no pleasure in talking about His death on the cross to His disciples.

Jesus knew that He had to die to save us from our sins that Jesus became on the cross in that moment in time.

All Christians would mourn and be heartbroken over the death of Jesus for eternity, if He hadn't risen again and shut the bad mouth of death for all sinners to receive God's grace.

We don't usually like to talk about death because many people don't want to face up to the fact that they will die because it is terrifying, especially to many people who don't live their lives loving and obeying Jesus Christ who has conquered death to give us eternal life for being saved in Him.

Favor

Many people will give you their favor as long as you are giving them no trouble.

Many people will give you their favor as long as you are helping them.

Many people will give you their favor as long as you are going along with whatever they say and do.

Many people will give you their favor as long as you are educated like them.

Many people will give you their favor as long as you are rich like them.

Many people will give you their favor as long as you are talented like them.

Many people will give you their favor as long as you are healthy like them.

Many people will give you their favor as long as you are foolish like them.

Many people will give you their favor as long as you are intelligent like them.

Many people will give you their favor as long as you are bold like them.

Many people will give you their favor as long as you are great like them.

Many people will give you their favor as long as you look like them.

Many people will give you their favor as long as you do what they do.

Many people will give you their favor as long as you kiss up to them.

Many people will give you their favor as long as you give them what they want.

Many people will give you their favor as long as you are bad like them.

God gave us all His favor when we were ignorant and didn't know His holy word.

God gave us His favor in our mother's womb for us to be born.

God gave us favor to be here in the land of the living where many people will give you and me their favor as long as we keep our mouths closed and let them get away with their wrongdoings.

Your favor and my favor can cause jealousy, division and strife, even in the church where God favors everybody to spread the gospel of Jesus Christ with the spiritual gifts that the Holy Spirit gives to us in the church.

God gave favor to all sinners to be saved in His Son, Jesus Christ.

Your favor and my favor can cause a soul to be lost, even in the church where favoritism exists that even a child can see.

God gave us favor when we had favored our selfish desires over that still, small voice speaking to our hearts to turn away from the pride of life.

Favor is very popular in this world where the rich get so much more favor than the poor, no matter what the color of their skin may be.

The educated get so much more favor than the uneducated.

God gives us all in this world favor to repent and turn to His Son, Jesus Christ, who many people will not give their favor for blessing their lives.

You and I can't hide all of our favoritism, especially from God, who knows our whole hearts when we can have favor for someone who we don't know and may not mean you and me good and well.

I Can't do Good Things Better than You Can, O Lord

I can't do good things better than You can, O Lord.

I can't change anyone's mind and make them believe in You better than You can, O Lord.

I can't change anyone's mind and make them pick up their cross and follow You better than You can, O Lord.

I can't change anyone's mind and make them serve You better than You can, O Lord.

I can't change anyone's mind and make them humble themselves unto You better than You can, O Lord.

I can't change anyone's mind and make them pray to You better than You can, O Lord.

I can't change anyone's mind and make them trust You better than You can, O Lord.

I can't change anyone's mind and make them put their hope in You better than You can, O Lord.

I can't do anything better than You can, O Lord.

I can't win a soul to You better than You can, O Lord.

I can't help anyone better than You can, O Lord.

I can't talk to anyone better than You can, O Lord.

I can't love anyone better than You can, O Lord.

I can't change anyone's mind and make them love You better than You can, O Lord.

It's Your goodness, O Lord, that leads to repentance.

There is no goodness in me that leads to repentance.

I can't do anything better than You can, my Lord and Savior Jesus Christ.

I can't change anyone's mind and make them wise up better than You can, O Lord.

I can't change anyone's mind and make them do better in life better than You can, O Lord.

I can't help myself better than You can help me, O Lord.

I can't love myself better than You can love me, O Lord.

I can't love anyone better than You love everyone, O Lord.

I can't do good things better than You can, O Lord.

I can't speak any good words better than You can, O Lord.

I can't listen better than You can, O Lord.

I can't relate to anyone better than You can, O Lord.

I can't encourage anyone better than You can, O Lord.

I can't motivate anyone better than You can, O Lord.

I can't understand anyone better than You can, my Lord and Savior Jesus Christ.

It's Your goodness that leads to repentance, O Lord.

My goodness can be taken as being weak.

It's Your goodness that leads to repentance, O Lord.

My goodness can especially spoil a child so they grow up to be a spoiled brat.

It comes to show that my goodness is like filthy rags.

I can't do good things better than You can, my Lord and Savior Jesus Christ.

You are so good to all the birds that you feed day after day so they don't have to worry about where they will get their food.

I can't do good things better than You can, O Lord, because the good things I do can be overlooked, even by many in the household of faith where there can be questions as to whether I have good motives or bad motives.

It's Your goodness that leads to repentance, O Lord, because I can't do anything better than You.

My good deeds can be judged by even many in the household of faith.

I can't do good things better than You can, O Lord, whose goodness leads to repentance when my goodness can be taken in the wrong way, even in the household of faith where everyone is not good.

I can't do good things better than You can, O Lord, because it's Your goodness that suffers long for sinners to repent, when my goodness can give up on people and lead them to be lost in their sins.

Jonah in the bible is a good example for us all because Jonah had a selective kind of goodness that was only for his people and not for the people in Nineveh.

It was surely God's goodness that led them to repent.

I know that I can't do good things better than You can, my Lord Jesus Christ.

All of the prophets of old failed to do anything good better than you, O Lord.

The Best Place to Hang Out

The best place to hang out is the church where you and I can hang around church folks who are trying to love and obey the Lord.

There are people who love to hang out in restaurants where there is plenty of food to eat, but they love to talk about themselves and say nothing about the Lord.

There are people even in our kinfolk's family that want you and me to hang out with them, but they have no interest in the spiritual things of God that you and I love to talk about because we're Christians.

They want you and me to hang out with them as if they have something better to talk about than glorifying and praising the Lord.

The best place to hang out is the church, because people there are making an effort to be real about wanting to get to know the Lord Jesus Christ who helps us to be real with one another.

The best place to hang out is the church where there are some real Christians who will not lead you and me astray.

The Lord who knows much better than you and me if people don't want to hang out with you and me if they don't have any real interest in the spiritual things of God.

There are people who love to hang out anywhere else except the church, which is the best place for them to see you and me trying to better ourselves to also tolerate them and their proud ways.

The church is the best place to hang out so the Lord can get ahold of sinners like you and me and change us from our selfish ways.

A real, true Christian will take no pleasure in hanging out with anyone who knows how to do right by the Lord and doesn't do it because they like hanging out with the devil who will cause their souls to be lost.

Don't think that you, as a Christian, can hang out with unbelievers and they won't affect your relationship with the Lord.

If you put your hand in fire, it will burn you.

The best place to hang out is the church, even though there are no perfect people in the world.

The church is the best place to let our guard down so the Lord can set us free from hanging out in the wrong places with fools.

Fate Said to Life

One day Fate and Life crossed each other's paths and they had nothing in common to share with each other.

They looked at each other in the eyes with a hard stare, and Fate said to Life, "I have been taking many of your children down to the grave."

Fate said to Life, "I show no respect to any human being to live from birth to old age to meet their fate on any day."

Fate said to Life, "I am the king sitting on the throne of this sinful world where no human being can get past me who can take away their life from them even when they may least expect it."

Fate said to Life, "No human being, rich or poor, educated or not educated, good or bad can override me and live beyond, even one second longer than I decide."

Life asked Fate, "Are you through talking to me? I agree with everything you said to me."

Then Life said to Fate, "There is an afterlife in someone who gave me life and His name is Jesus Christ and He's coming back again to give eternal life to all who are saved in Him."

Life said to Fate, "You will exist no more for all of God's children who will live forever and ever in heaven with Jesus Christ who you, Mr. Fate, could not keep in the grave. Jesus rose from the grave with eternal life, crushing you, Mr. Fate."

Life said to Fate, "You are only temporary in this fallen world, no matter how unpredictable you are or how many countless numbers of human beings you send to the grave."

Life said to Fate, "You surely don't care anything about anyone's age from birth up to old age — you take them all to the grave."

"Life said to Fate, "I will live on forever and ever in Jesus Christ just like the many of His righteous children who will be alive when He comes back again on the clouds of glory."

Life said to Fate, "You are like a withered flower compared to God's eternal abundance of life for all who are saved in His Son, Jesus Christ."

Life said to Fate, "You have no power over the giver of life who is very fair to all human beings from the time they're young until old. He will take them to heaven when you, Mr. Fate, can't judge them.

"God knows all of His children, young, middle aged, and old, as well as the unborn babies who God owns.

My Bible Said to Me

I woke up one day, early in the morning, and could not get back to sleep.

So, I picked up my phone and began to look on Amazon's website to see what was there.

Then I turned on the TV and changed the channels, looking for a good TV program to watch.

Then I turned the TV off and went downstairs to give one of my dogs some water to drink because he was whining for me to give him some water to drink.

I went back upstairs after I gave my dog some water to drink, sat down in my chair and looked at my stereo with my bible sitting on top of it.

My bible said to me, "Open me up and read me and I'll tell you about a true, living God who loves you so much that he gave You His only begotten Son to save you from your sins."

My bible also said to me, "I am always here for you, so open me up and read me every day and I will tell you the truth and nothing but the truth about a holy and righteous Lord God who created heaven and the earth."

My bible told me even more things about being here for thousands of years for people to read, even when they read from scrolls.

My bible said, I told them about the true, living God who cannot lie and lives forever and ever."

My bible kept talking to me, saying, "I am not here in your presence to keep silent about the Lord and Savior Jesus Christ who filled me up with nothing but the truth through His Holy Spirit, inspiring men who loved God to write me into existence for you to open me up and study me day after day so you get to know your true purpose in this sinful world.

My bible also said to me, "No one can talk to you more than me because you need the Holy Spirit to help you fully understand me whenever you open me up and read me."

My bible said to me again and again, "Nothing in this world can change your life for the better like me who will also tell you everything about this life on earth that you need to know as well as your own life that is defined by the truth in me."

Being Persecuted for Jesus' Name Sake

Being persecuted for Jesus' name sake is not only going through some physical hardships for Jesus' holy name sake.

Being persecuted for Jesus' name sake is also going through some mental hardships for Jesus' holy name sake.

There are people who will argue with you and me about the bible scriptures to prove that they are right and you and I are wrong about the word of God.

They will misinterpret the word of God and believe that you and I are misinterpreting the word of God.

They will add their own opinions to the word of God to suit their way of living day after day.

Being persecuted for Jesus' name sake is not only a physical hardship that you and I will go through.

Being persecuted for Jesus' holy name sake is also an emotional hardship that you and I will go through for Jesus' holy name sake.

There are people who will have ill feelings towards you and me and will stop talking to you and me because we stand up for our belief in Jesus Christ.

They can make it hard on us emotionally, especially if they are our kinfolks who have some different beliefs about God's holy word and do not see eye to eye with you and me.

Being persecuted for Jesus' name sake is not only a physical hardship that we must go through for Jesus' holy name sake.

You and I will go through a psychological hardship for Jesus' holy name sake.

There are many people who will not go to church, especially on the holy Sabbath day of rest, and they will do their own will day after day.

That will bring some hardships on our minds if we are living the right life that we know by God's holy word.

You and I know in our minds that what they are doing is not in line with God's holy word that we can think on and get a peace of mind in Jesus.

Being persecuted for Jesus' name sake is not only going through some physical hardships for Jesus' holy name sake.

You and I will go through a spiritual hardship for Jesus' holy name sake.

The spiritual hardship is the worst hardship that Jesus Himself went through on the cross because His heavenly Father God had forsaken Him to feel nothing but spiritual darkness to save you and me from the darkness of our sins.

There are people who will call you and me everything but a child of God to make it hard on us spiritually and there are people, even in the church, who will say that you and I are playing church.

You and I know that we are trying our best to love and obey our Lord Jesus Christ, but there are people who will try their best to break our spirit so we're broken by their opinions about you and me who only the Lord Jesus Christ completely knows so He can be the judge of our hearts.

There are people who don't believe in Jesus Christ and they will make it hard on us spiritually because we believe in Jesus Christ who can heal our broken spirits in His holy name that every evil spirit will fear when we call on Jesus' name.

Being persecuted for Jesus' name sake is not only a physical persecution that you and I will go through for Jesus' holy name sake.

Jesus was persecuted mentally, emotionally, psychologically and spiritually before He was persecuted physically to save us from our sins.

You and I can't ever be more persecuted than Jesus was when He lived in this sinful world without sin in His flesh.

What can be worse than God forsaking you and me?

Jesus experienced that hardship on the cross where He became sin in our place.

That spiritual hardship on Jesus was much harder on Jesus than the mental, emotional and physical hardships that He went through to redeem you and me back to God.

Many people will only believe that persecution is a physical hardship that Jesus went through for you and me, but that physical hardship didn't come close to the spiritual hardship Jesus endured on the cross.

Our Lord Jesus' heavenly Father God had forsaken Him and he lost His spiritual connection with God.

That must have felt like nothing but spiritual eternal pain to Jesus, beyond his mental, emotional and physical pain that was only for a moment to Jesus.

All Good Things Come from the Lord

All good things come from the Lord who is good all the time.

The good that is in people is from the Lord.

It's a blessing to talk to good people, no matter what the color of their skin is.

It's a blessing to talk to good people, no matter what their religion is.

It's a blessing to talk to good people, no matter what their gender is.

It's a blessing to talk to good people, whether they're educated or uneducated.

It's a blessing to talk to good people, no matter if they are rich, upper middle class, middle class, lower middle class or poor.

All good things come from the Lord.

All good people are from the Lord whose goodness leads to repentance, no matter how evil many people are from day to day.

The good that is in anyone is from the Lord.

There is nothing good in the devil who is evil all the time but can pretend to be good like the devil pretended with Eve in the Garden of Eden.

The devil pretended to be good, causing Eve to eat that unforbidden fruit because the devil talked so good to her with his smooth words that were nothing but lies he spoke to deceive her and make her eat the fruit.

There is no pretense in God's goodness and we all can get that from the Lord who gave us all a free will to choose to do good or do evil from day to day.

All good things come from the Lord who is filled with goodness all the time.

We receive good things that we don't deserve from the Lord Jesus Christ.

The good that is in you and me doesn't come from you and me because we have a sinful nature to sin against God and there is nothing good about sinning against God.

Even a wicked man can be good to his children, but that good in him comes from the Lord who gives His goodness to sinners too in the hope they will repent and turn to Him.

The good that is in people comes from the Lord, whether they go to church or don't go to church.

The good that is in people comes from the Lord, whether they believe in the Lord Jesus Christ or don't believe in the Lord Jesus Christ who is so good all the time to you and me who are not always good to the Lord.

Just Because the Lord is Forgiving

Just because the Lord is forgiving doesn't mean that we have an excuse to sin against Him.

Just because the Lord is forgiving doesn't mean that we can knowingly sin against Him.

Just because the Lord is forgiving doesn't mean that we can willfully sin against Him.

If we know what is right by the Lord and don't do right, the Lord will not keep on forgiving you and me.

If you and I make a habit of sinning against the Lord, He will not keep on forgiving us.

Just because the Lord is forgiving, it doesn't mean that we can make a practice of sinning against the Lord.

There are people who will knowingly sin against the Lord and then say that the Lord will forgive them.

They take the Lord for granted, as if He will always forgive them of their sins.

Just because the Lord is forgiving it doesn't mean that we can live in sin like the Lord will give us His approval.

If we know to do right and make it a practice of doing wrong, the Lord will not keep on forgiving us.

The Lord is not weak and He will not keep on forgiving us when we know to do right by Him and make it a habit of doing wrong anyway.

I read an article a Christian wrote that said the Lord is forgiving.

The author had entered into a profession that is against her Christian values and she knew that she was doing wrong, but she wrote in her article that it was okay because the Lord is forgiving.

The Lord is truly forgiving, but there comes a time when the Lord's patience will run out for anyone who makes it their practice of sinning against Him and knowing that what they're doing is wrong.

You and I can't make it a habit to sin against the Lord and believe that He will forgive us for the wrongs that He is against.

We can't mistake the Lord's forgiveness for weakness like many people do and then use that as an excuse to do their own will that will sooner or later be their downfall.

Just because the Lord is forgiving, it doesn't mean that we can willfully break His Commandments day after day and expect the Lord will just sit back on His holy throne and do nothing about it.

The Lord will not let anyone get away with their practice of sinning against Him.

The Lord is always forgiving to anyone who makes a practice of confessing and repenting of their sins unto Him who we must turn to every day.

Once we are saved it doesn't mean that we are always saved in the Lord.

We must take it one day at a time to be saved in the Lord.

We will sin against the Lord in some kind of way, but a true Christian won't make it a practice to sin against the Lord day after day.

A real, true Christian won't willfully sin against the Lord because a true Christian knows what is right by the Lord's holy word and lives it day after day.

If we sin against the Lord on the spur of the moment without thinking, the Lord is more willing to forgive us than if we think about doing something wrong before we do it.

If we do things by practice that we know are wrong to do and use the Lord's forgiveness as an excuse, then we are on that wide and broad road of destruction that will cause our soul to be lost because we're treating God's forgiveness like waste to be flushed down the toilet.

The Facts of Life

No one knows the facts of life better than Jesus who was tempted by the devil in so many ways that no man or woman can count.

Jesus lived in this world for thirty-three years with no sin in His flesh.

There were so many things that Jesus did that were not written about in the bible because there wasn't enough space to write down everything Jesus did in this world without ever sinning against His heavenly Father God.

The facts of life were all wrapped up in Jesus who was faithful and true to God in every word that he said and everything that He did when He lived in this world with no sin in His flesh.

Jesus experienced many things that we can't ever imagine as He grew up from a little child into an adult who overcame every obstacle the devil put before Him.

No one knows the facts of life better than Jesus who talked to the most brilliant religious leaders and teachers back in the bible days.

Jesus shared His great wisdom with them at the tender age of twelve years old.

Jesus baffled their minds because they had never heard or seen a young boy quote all the scrolls written by all the prophets of God.

No one knows the facts of life better than our Lord and Savior Jesus Christ who the devil came at full-force with all of his temptations that Jesus didn't give in to.

The devil knows this to be a true fact of life better than you and I will ever know until we live in heaven with Jesus when He comes back again.

When we live with Jesus in heaven, Jesus will show us all the facts of life that He encountered in this sinful world.

All the books that the prophets and disciples wrote cannot contain everything that Jesus experienced in His life that the facts of life rest its case in.

The Way to Know When God is Speaking to You

The way you know when God is speaking to you will be in line with God's holy word.

If the preacher is speaking to you according to God's holy word, then God is speaking to you.

If the bible school teacher is speaking to you according to God's holy Word, then God is speaking to you.

If the gospel singer is singing songs to you according to God's holy word, then God is speaking to you.

If someone is giving you advice according to God's holy word, then God is speaking to you.

The way to know when God is speaking to you will be in line with God's holy word.

If anyone is speaking to you according to God's holy word, then God is speaking to you.

The devil will speak to you and me, but his words won't be in line with God's holy word.

God will always speak to you and me according to His holy word.

God will not say anything to you and me if it's not in His holy word.

God speaks to you and me in our thoughts so that we think on His holy word.

The way you know when God is speaking to you and me will be according to His holy word that we must study in order to know that God is speaking to us.

There are people who do bad things and believe that God told them to do those bad things.

If they study the bible, they will know that God is righteous and will only tell them to do good things that are in line with His holy word.

The best way for you and me to know that the devil is speaking to us is for us to know God's holy word that we have studied and know.

The devil will never tell anyone to say something or do something or even write something that's in line with God's holy word.

That lets us know what the devil is about and how he came into existence.

The best way for you and I to know when God is speaking to us is for us to study His holy word and know that God is holy and righteous and everlasting love.

There are people who do evil things and say that they did them in the name of God.

They will pray to God to accept their evil deeds.

Anyone who knows God's holy word and lives by it will know that God hates sin and that every evil thing that comes about is not in line with God's holy word that He speaks to you and me every time we open up the bible and read it.

I Need You So Much, O Lord

The strong winds of uncertainty blow hard on me in this uncertain world.

I need You so much, O Lord.

The wildfires of the unknown burn me to a crisp.

I need You so much, O Lord.

The unpredictable chokes me day after day.

I need You so much, O Lord.

The heatwaves of the world try to give me a spiritual stroke.

I need You so much, O Lord.

The snow blizzards of deception try to freeze me day after day.

I need You so much, O Lord.

The tornadoes of lies try to rip me apart.

I need You so much, O Lord.

The earthquakes of doubt try to take me down.

I need You so much, O Lord.

The air pollution of fear tries to suffocate me.

I need You so much, O Lord.

The mudslides of the world try to bury my existence in this world day after day.

I need You so much, O Lord.

The volcanic eruptions of the world try to melt my dignity in the lava of prejudice day after day.

I need You so much, O Lord.

The sinkholes of pretense religion try to take me down in their truth mixed with errors and lies.

I need You so much, O Lord.

The bad accidents of the world try to spiritually shock me and make me waver in my faith in the Lord Jesus Christ.

I need You so much, O Lord, twenty-four hours around the clock, day after day.

The hurricanes of injustice try to oppress me day after day.

I need You so much, O Lord.

The water floods of favoritism in the world try to drown me in discouragement.

I need You so much, O Lord.

The spiritual crimes of compromising the truth of God's holy word in the church try to make me look so wrong for defending my true conversion in the truth of God that I know.

I need You so much, my Lord and Savior Jesus Christ.

The dreams in my sleep take me from place to place, departing from me who has no consciousness to help myself from being vulnerable in my dreams.

I need You so much, my Lord and Savior Jesus Christ, even in my dreams where I can't choose what to dream about in my sleep.

When Compared to the Lord Jesus Christ

We all are no good compared to the Lord Jesus Christ who is good all the time.

We all are corrupt compared to the Lord Jesus Christ who has no corruption in Him.

We all are bad compared to the Lord Jesus Christ who has nothing bad in Him.

We are all messed up compared to the Lord Jesus Christ who has no mess in Him.

We are all weak compared to the Lord Jesus Christ who has no weakness in Him.

We all are hopeless compared to the Lord Jesus Christ who is the living hope.

We all are helpless compared to the Lord Jesus Christ who is our best help in times of need.

We all are screwed up compared to the Lord Jesus Christ who can unscrew the top off of anyone's life and pour out every sin if we repent unto the Lord Jesus Christ.

We all are a phony compared to the Lord Jesus Christ who is always real with us.

We all are poor and homeless compared to the Lord Jesus Christ who filled the heavens with eternal riches and wealth and made heaven to be our real eternal home if we are saved in Him who is coming back again to take us to heaven.

We are all dead compared to the Lord Jesus Christ who got the victory over death and the grave when He rose again and went back to heaven where life is eternal above and beyond our days that have a short number and we can even die so unexpectedly.

We all are like a flower that withers away when compared to the Lord Jesus Christ who is the gardener to give us living waters on the hard soil of our lives that He also plants for us to grow up in His beautiful living garden that the Lord nurtures from day to day if we love and obey Him.

We all are like a shadow moving over the landscape and then disappearing when compared to the Lord Jesus Christ who the shadows will obey and not move even an inch over the landscape of our lives if we repent before the Lord who will save us from our sins.

We all are nothing compared to the Lord Jesus Christ who is every good thing in the heavens and in other worlds and here on earth.

We all are the dust of the earth compared to the Lord Jesus Christ who rose from the grave because He is the resurrection over the dust of the earth.

Some Things
We Have to Leave Alone

Some things we have to leave alone to keep from stirring up feelings, especially in innocent people who don't know any better.

Some things we have to leave alone to keep from causing disunity, especially among believers in our Lord and Savior Jesus Christ.

Some things we have to leave alone to keep peace that we especially need in the church.

Some things we have to leave alone to keep our sanity.

Some things we have to leave alone to keep someone from falling into sin.

Some things we have to leave alone to allow the Holy Spirit to convict people to repent and turn to Jesus Christ.

Some things we have to leave alone to allow someone to learn things the hard way so they wise up.

Some things we have to leave alone in the church, especially for new believers to grow stronger in the Lord.

Some things we have to leave alone for you and me to move beyond the past, especially the bad things that happened in the past.

Some things we have to leave alone, especially in the church where we will be wise to let Jesus pull up a tare when we may pull up a wheat for believing it to be a tare.

Some things we have to leave alone like we've never seen it, heard it or experienced it in our lives so you and I can keep a good outlook on life that is too short for everyone to leave alone their soul's salvation in Jesus Christ who didn't leave alone the cross to die on and save us from our sins.

Jesus didn't leave alone the grave that He rose from to give us an afterlife of eternity in Him.

Some things we have to leave alone, especially if they can hinder someone from giving their life to our Lord God who has to leave alone a reprobate's mind.

Everybody is Guilty Before the Lord

Everybody is guilty of thinking something wrong before the Lord.

Everybody is guilty of assuming something wrong before the Lord.

Everybody is guilty of saying something wrong before the Lord.

Everybody is guilty of doing something wrong before the Lord.

Everybody is guilty in one way or another way before the Lord.

Everybody is a sinner and is guilty of being born in sin before the Lord.

Everybody is guilty of having a sinful nature before the Lord.

You and I are guilty of some pretense before the Lord.

You and I are guilty of showing some favoritism before the Lord.

You and I are guilty of having some selfishness before the Lord.

Everybody in the church is guilty of some lack of love before the Lord who says that love is the greatest gift in the church.

Everybody is guilty before the Lord Jesus Christ who once lived in this sinful world but Jesus wasn't guilty about anything before His heavenly Father God.

The scribes and Pharisees believed that Jesus was guilty of blasphemy for claiming to be the Son of God.

Jesus took on all of our guilt and sins on the cross He hung on and died on.

Jesus rose from the grave being so guiltless before God for you and me to be set free from all of our guilt in His righteousness to make us right before God if we confess and repent of our guilty sins and turn to the guiltless Lord and Savior Jesus Christ.

There is Nothing Wrong About What We Need

There is nothing wrong about what we need when our every need is good and right for us.

There is nothing wrong about what we need that is always satisfying to even a bad person who needs to give their life to the Lord before it's too late.

There is nothing good about denying the things that we need that will surely outweigh our wants.

What we need is always much better than what we want because if we have what we need it will be so right for us above any wants that can be so sinful and so wrong to desire.

There is no sin in getting what we need because every need is from the Lord who will supply all of our needs.

There is nothing wrong about what we need when every day we need more things than we can count because we need even things that we don't think about, but the Lord knows them all.

If the Lord gives us only the things that we want, then those wants would surely drive us insane.

Our needs will surely help to keep us sane and satisfy our souls, because when we get what we need in our lives it does us right.

If we turn away from something that we need then we do ourselves wrong, but if we want something that we don't need it can be a delusion for us.

There is nothing wrong about what we need; only a fool would be too proud to accept a need and believe that a want is a need.

The Lord says that He will supply all of our needs.

The Lord didn't say that He will supply all of our wants, because the Lord knows that our wants can surely ruin us like Lucifer's wants ruined him and caused him to be cast out of heaven.

God gave Lucifer everything he needed, but it wasn't good enough for Lucifer because he wanted to sit on God's holy throne and be God.

There is nothing wrong about the things that we need from day to day, because what we need can't ruin our lives but wants have already caused many people to go to an early grave because they were greedy for worldly gain.

There is nothing wrong about what we need because there is no sin in the things that we need that the Lord will supply us with, but the Lord can surely give us something that we want to show us that our wants will never be greater than our needs.

Is a Very Beautiful Gift

The free will choice is a very beautiful gift from God and nothing in this world is more beautiful than our free will choice.

We all have a free will choice to believe whatever we want to believe day after day and night after night.

No matter what bad choices we make, it won't tarnish our very beautiful gift from God.

The free will to choose is a very beautiful gift from God and the free will choice is a true beauty that will never age or get old.

Our free will choice is a real, true beauty that is attractive to everyone's imagination to choose to bring into action what we create in our free will mind.

The free will choice is a very beautiful gift from God who gave us all a free will to choose.

God didn't give us this gift so we would destroy ourselves with selfishness.

God gave us all this very beautiful gift out of His great love for us so we could have the freedom to choose to love Him who so loved us first.

Our very beautiful free will gift from God is walking down the runway of other worlds being so captivated by us for choosing to believe in God's Son, Jesus Christ.

It's Jesus who gives us His white robe of righteousness for choosing to deny ourselves and pick up our crosses to follow Him on the runway of eternal life that we will receive one day for being saved in Jesus.

The free will choice is a very beautiful gift to us all from God, but it's up to us all to choose to do the right things that we know and the right things that are presented to us, especially from God who has His true children to encourage us to choose to go to church and worship His Son, Jesus Christ, in our words and in our actions, which are evidence of our free will choices.

A Church that Helps People

A church that helps people is a church that has faith and works unto the Lord.

A church that helps people will give out food to needy people.

A church that helps people will give out clothes to needy people.

Many people will only come to the church to get some food to eat and some clothes to wear, and then after they get what they need you and I won't see them again anytime soon.

Even if people don't come back to the church after they get what they need, they know that the church is there for them and they can hold onto that.

They know who the church stands for and that is Jesus Christ, which means they see you and me representing Jesus Christ when we give them food to eat and clothes to wear.

It would be great if those needy people would come to church to worship the Lord every holy Sabbath day of rest unto the Lord.

Even if people come to the church to get some food to eat, they will see the children of God being on one accord, showing that we have love for one another and them as we help them in their need.

Even if those needy people don't come back to the church, our work is not in vain because we gave them our Lord and Savior Jesus Christ through our actions they witnessed meaning they saw the love of Jesus in us.

A church that helps the needy is not a dead church, even if none of the poor and needy people come back to the church after they get their food and clothes.

What they got most was Jesus being in the minds and hearts of His children who are you and me having faith and works in Jesus.

A lot of those same needy people would come to the church again when we are giving out food for them to eat because they know the church is a good place where the Lord dwells.

So Many People Will

So many people will accept evil over good.

So many people would rather read evil books than Godly books.

So many people love to keep company with wicked people rather than Christian people.

So many people will marry proud people rather than humble people.

So many people will help bad people rather than good people.

So many people will judge people rather than getting to know people.

So many people will hate people rather than love people.

So many people will put people down rather than esteem people.

So many people will gossip about people rather than talk to people.

So many people will want what people have rather than give something good to people.

So many people will envy people rather than be happy for them.

So many people will kill people rather than forgiving people.

So many people will oppress people rather than help people bear their burdens.

So many people will lie to people rather than tell people the truth.

So many people will give up on people rather than pray for people.

So many people will call Christian people hypocrites rather than getting to know Jesus for themselves.

So many people will not step one foot into the church rather than seeing even a little child being active in the church for the Lord.

So many people will lie on a Christian rather than believing the change in a Christian's life.

So many people will let their bible look brand new rather than open it up and study until the pages get worn out.

So many people will want to go to heaven rather than believe in Jesus Christ who they can't slip by on judgment day and enter into heaven.

The People the Devil Will Possess

The people the devil will possess are the people who make a practice of rejecting God's Holy Spirit who always tells the truth to everyone to live the truth of God's holy word.

The people the devil will possess are the people who make a practice of rejecting the Holy Spirit who will always tell us all to do the right thing from day to day and that if we speak evil words and do evil things we are possessed by the devil.

The people the devil will possess are the people who live to please their own selfish desires that the devil will take full control over and put people's fate in his bondage so those peoples' souls are lost.

The devil can't possess everybody because everybody will not reject the Holy Spirit who teaches us all the truth about Jesus Christ, the Son of God, who people can reject and still have a chance to repent and turn to Jesus.

If anyone makes a practice of rejecting the Holy Spirit, he or she will not be forgiven by God because the Holy Spirit will never tell anyone to say something wrong or do something wrong.

The devil will possess anyone who makes a practice of rejecting the Holy Spirit who Jesus sent to this world to tell us all the truth that the devil wants everybody to reject Jesus so he can possess everybody and keep them from being saved in Jesus Christ.

Nobody in this world can be like Jesus and live for Jesus without the Holy Spirit being in them.

The devil can't possess anyone who has the Holy Spirit dwelling in them to love and obey Jesus Christ who the Holy Spirit ascended upon in the form of a dove when John the Baptist baptized Jesus.

The people the devil will possess are the people who make a practice of rejecting the Holy Spirit who is the God in this world to convict everyone of their sins and convert everyone who chooses to believe in Jesus Christ.

The Holy Spirit always speaks the truth about Jesus and not about Himself who we would be a fool to reject so the devil could possess us, which he can do even in the church where many church folks can reject the Holy Spirit and make excuses for their sins.

So many people in this world make a practice of not obeying that still, small voice giving them warnings of harm and danger and death just waiting for them to walk into its death trap.

Many people do walk into that trap and meet their fate of death.

That still, small voice is the Holy Spirit who so many people make a practice of rejecting day after day so the devil can possess them with his sins of death and eternal death.

The people the devil will possess could be you and me if we make a practice of living in sin and rejecting the Holy Spirit who can speak to us in our lives even when things get very hectic and we are in a rush.

If anyone practices listening to and obeying that small inner voice being the Holy Spirit speaking to us, then the devil can't possess us because we are being like Jesus and not rejecting the Holy Spirit speaking all the truth to us about Jesus Christ who has redeemed us all back to God.

It is our choice to deny ourselves and pick up our crosses and follow Jesus every day.

There are People Who Believe

There are people who believe that they can pray to You any kind of way, O Lord, and they also believe that You are supposed to answer their prayers.

There are people who take you, O Lord, lightly as if You will allow them to get away with anything they say and do.

There are people who believe that You, O Lord, are supposed to bow down before them and give them whatever they ask You for.

There are people who believe that You are weak, O Lord, and are supposed to listen to their nonsense words when they speak to You as they believe they are right in their own eyes.

There are people in the church who believe that You only exist, O Lord, when things are going good in their lives.

When things begin to go wrong for them, they believe there is no God to get them out of a bad situation.

There are people in the church who believe that every word they say and every thing they do is from You, O Lord, who truly knows that everybody, even in the church, will misunderstand You in some kind of way for being a sinner saved through Your grace.

There are people in the church who believe they can be a friend of the world and a friend to You, O Lord, and they do not believe this makes them an enemy to You, O Lord.

They believe they can please the people of the world and please You at the same time, but that is impossible for them to do and makes them an enemy to You, my Lord and Savior Jesus Christ.

O Lord, You are a holy and righteous God and no one can bring you down on their level, even John the Baptist, who was the greatest prophet, said that he was not worthy to untie the straps on your sandals.

You Don't Really Know

You don't really know what people are like just by looking at them, but when people talk you will pretty much know what's on their minds.

You don't really know what people are like just by looking at them, but when people do something good or bad you will pretty much know what's in their hearts.

You don't really know what people are like just by looking at them, but if someone gives you a smile you will pretty much know that you are not disliked.

You don't really know what people are like just by looking at them, but if someone gives you an evil eye look you will pretty much know that you are disliked.

You don't really know what people are like just by looking at them, but when people talk you will pretty much know if they are wise, intelligent or foolish.

You don't really know what people are like just by looking at them, but when someone does something good or evil you will pretty much know their behavior.

You don't really know what people are like just by looking at them, but when people talk you will pretty much know if people are educated or ignorant.

You don't really know what people are like just by looking at them, but when people talk to you and me we will pretty much know if they keep their mind on Jesus Christ.

You and I don't really know what people are like just by looking at people, but when people show us their actions we will pretty much know whether their heart is in Jesus or in the devil's darkness of sins.

God Gave up His Greatest Love

God gave up His greatest love to save us from our sins.

Can you imagine giving up your greatest love, that might be your child, to die for a good cause?

Can you imagine giving up your greatest love, that might be your spouse, to die for a good cause?

Can you imagine giving up your greatest love, that might be your mother, to die for a good cause?

Can you imagine giving up your greatest love, that might be your father, to die for a good cause?

We just can't ever imagine how God felt giving up His greatest love, which was His only begotten Son who gave up His life on the cross to save us from our sins.

If we can feel very deep pain from the death of our loved ones who we shed tears over, then what about God who gave up His greatest love?

Can you imagine giving up your greatest love, that might be your pet, to die for you?

God and His Son, Jesus Christ, were bonded together forever before death separated them.

We can't imagine an eternal God giving up His greatest love to show us that He gave us sinners all of His heart-felt love by giving up His Son, Jesus Christ, to save us from our sins.

Life in this World

Life in this world is short for even people who live to be over 100 years old.

Life in this world is short under the sun, moon and stars that have been around for thousands of years.

Life in this world is short while the life in heaven goes on forever and ever.

Life in this world is short while life in other worlds goes on forever and ever because of having no sins.

It's a blessing from the Lord that a baby is born in this world where life is short.

It's a blessing from the Lord for a child to grow up into the teenage years in this world where life is short.

It's a blessing from the Lord that many of us have grown up to adulthood in this world where life is short.

It's a blessing from the Lord that many of us have reached the golden years in this world where life is truly short compared to the hundreds of years that people lived before the flood that God spared Noah and his family from.

Life in this world is short, no matter how healthy people are, because the best healthy foods that we eat may not benefit us to live to be one hundred years old.

There are people who eat healthy food and exercise and they don't live a long life, but eating right and exercising will help add more years to anyone's life.

Life in this world is short but it's wise to live our life unto the Lord Jesus Christ and not live our life unto ourselves.

Life in this world is short and many people will live their lives like there is no God for them to answer to.

Life in this world is short and many people will live their lives like there is no God to judge them by every thought they think, every word they say and by everything they do from day to day.

Life in this world is short lived for everybody compared to the afterlife that only Jesus Christ can give to us if we are saved in Him who was the life eternal even before He created heaven and earth.

Life in this world is short and what better life we can live beyond living our life unto Jesus who gives us an abundant life that no one else can give us in this world where everyone has sin in their genes to not escape from death.

Life in this world is short for us sinners saved through God's grace that is all wrapped up in our Lord and Savior Jesus Christ who no one can question about how long He will let us live.

The Lord allows some wicked people to live a hundred years and He allows some good people to die at a very young age.

Life in this world is short and it's always wise to love the Lord and His Commandments and trust the Lord to number our days that won't be less or too many for Him to not save us.

Life in this world is short and no one can number our days to live without the Lord allowing it because the Lord has the last say-so about everyone's life.

Freedom Is

Freedom is encouragement from the Lord who gave us all a free will to choose.

Freedom is goodness from the Lord who gave us all a free will to choose.

Freedom is truth from the Lord who gave us all a free will to choose.

Freedom is trust from the Lord who gave us all a free will to choose.

Freedom is grace from the Lord who gave us all a free will to choose.

Freedom is peace from the Lord who gave us all a free will to choose.

Freedom is justice from the Lord who gave us all a free will to choose.

Freedom is mercy from the Lord who gave us all a free will to choose.

Freedom is a blessing from the Lord who gave us all a free will to choose.

Freedom is a second chance from the Lord who gave us all a free will to choose.

Freedom is right from the Lord who gave us all a free will to choose.

Freedom is joy from the Lord who gave us all a free will to choose.

Freedom is kindness from the Lord who gave us all a free will to choose.

Freedom is favor from the Lord who gave us all a free will to choose.

Freedom is rest from the Lord who gave us all a free will to choose.

Freedom is unity from the Lord who gave us all a free will to choose.

Freedom is power from the Lord who gave us all a free will to choose.

Freedom is a gift from the Lord who gave us all a free will to choose.

Freedom is laws from the Lord who gave us all a free will to choose.

Freedom is love from the Lord who gave us all a free will to choose.

Freedom is salvation from the Lord who gave us all a free will to choose.

Freedom is life, health and strength from the Lord who gave us all a free will to choose.

Freedom is healing from the Lord who gave us all a free will to choose.

Freedom is patience from the Lord who gave us all a free will to choose.

Freedom is humility from the Lord who gave us all a free will to choose.

Freedom is the answer from the Lord who gave us all a free will to choose.

Freedom is contentment from the Lord who gave us all a free will to choose.

Freedom is fairness from the Lord who gave us all a free will to choose.

Freedom is eternal from the Lord who gave us all a free will to choose.

Even all the animals love to be free from being locked up in a cage.

Freedom is Jesus Christ who sets us free from living in sin if we confess and repent and live for Him.

Freedom is believing in Jesus Christ who will save us from our sins when the devil loves to lock us up in his chains and shackles.

The devil's sins caused him to be doomed to eternal death that we are free from for being saved in Jesus Christ.

Freedom is protection from the Lord who gave us all a free will to choose.

Freedom is vengeance from the Lord who gave us all a free will to choose.

Freedom is restoration from the Lord who gave us all a free will to choose.

Freedom is revival from the Lord who gave us all a free will to choose.

Freedom is judgment from the Lord who gave us all a free will to choose.

God's judgment is fair to everybody great and small and good and evil.

Having a God-given free will to choose is freedom.

Freedom is all good things from the Lord who gave us all a free will to choose that is more valuable than anything in this world.

I Want to Sleep in You, O Lord

One day when I go to the grave, I want to sleep in You, O Lord.

I hope that my mother and father are sleeping in You too.

I hope that my spiritual brothers and sisters who have passed away are all sleeping in You, my Lord and Savior Jesus Christ.

I hope that all of my loved ones who have passed away are sleeping in You, my Lord and Savior Jesus Christ.

I believe You are coming back again to open the graves of all who are sleeping in You so You can raise all the righteous dead who are sleeping in You, O Lord.

All of Your children's joy and tears are sleeping in You, my Lord who will come back again on the clouds of glory and wipe away all of your children's tears.

I want to sleep in You, O Lord, if You don't allow me to be alive until You come back again.

I just want to be saved in You, my Lord Jesus Christ, whether I'm alive or dead when You come back again.

It will be my greatest joy to see You shining brighter than a thousand suns that won't blind my eyes for being saved in You.

If I die before You come back again, O Lord, I want to sleep with Your seal upon me and wake up in the first resurrection along with a number of holy saints that no one can count except You, my Lord and Savior Jesus Christ.

I so long to sleep in You, my Lord, with my faith, hope, trust, love and obedience unto You who knows all of my mind, heart, soul and strength that only You can judge fairly with no questions about my destiny.

I want to sleep in You, my Lord, and I know if I die today I can't take anything with me to the grave except my destiny to heaven or my destiny to hell.

I know I can't pass by You, O Lord, and exist without your final say-so that can put a limit on eternity.

I want to sleep in You, my Lord and Savior Jesus Christ, because sleeping in You will be better than living in riches and wealth if my soul is lost.

I want to sleep in You, my Lord Jesus Christ, because my sleep in You will only be one moment that I close my eyes.

My eyes will open out of my sleep in a split second to see You on the clouds of glory for all the years in this world to be like a twinkling of an eye that I and all of the holy saints will be changed from mortal to immortality like we never slept.

I want to sleep in You, my Lord Jesus Christ, because it doesn't matter to me if I am alive when You come back again.

It would be great if I am alive, but I know my Lord my sleep will be like the speed of light traveling through the grave to wake me up into your eternal life that has no time above the grave that's been existing for thousands of years being only like the spur of a moment to You, My Lord and Savior Jesus Christ because You live forever.

I want to sleep in You, O Lord, whenever that time comes.

Hopefully that time will not be soon because I love living my life unto You as if death doesn't exist at all.

All it takes is a Split Second

All it takes is a split second to think right.

All it takes is a split second to think wrong.

All it takes is a split second to say something right.

All it takes is a split second to say something wrong.

All it takes is a split second to get in a car accident.

All it takes is a split second to change our minds.

All it takes is a split second to blink our eyes.

All it takes is a split second to get choked from eating some food.

All it takes is a split second to get killed.

All it takes is a split second to doubt someone.

All it takes is a split second to feel good.

All it takes is a split second to feel bad.

All it takes is a split second to call on the name of Jesus and make the demons tremble and flee from you and me.

All it takes is a split second to hurt someone's feelings.

All it takes is a split second to disrespect someone.

All it takes is a split second for someone to disrespect you and me.

All it takes is a split second to deny Jesus Christ.

All it takes is a split second to get angry.

All it takes is a split second to misunderstand someone.

All it takes is a split second to show favoritism.

All it takes is a split second to make a bad choice.

All it takes is a split second to make a good choice.

All it takes is a split second to show you and me if we are strong in the Lord or if we will fall apart in our split-second difficulty that can cause us to feel so helpless as if the Lord doesn't exist and won't miraculously remove the difficulty as though it never existed in our split second of not having control over our difficulty.

Trouble

There are people who are trouble in their house.

There are people who are trouble in their neighborhood.

There are people who are trouble driving on the road.

There are people who are trouble on their job.

There are people who are trouble to their pets.

There are people who are trouble wherever they go.

There are political leaders who are trouble in the White House.

There are lawyers and judges who are trouble in the courtrooms.

There are correctional officers who are trouble in the prisons.

There are police officers who are trouble to be so quick to pull the trigger.

There are people who are trouble to talk to.

There are people who are trouble to keep company with.

There are people who are trouble to help out.

There are people who are trouble to be a friend to.

There are people who are trouble to be near.

There are people who are trouble to teach.

There are people who are trouble when you give them something good for them.

There are people who are trouble to themselves

There are people who are trouble to anybody they don't like.

We know that criminals are always trouble to society all around the world.

There are church folks who are trouble in their church.

There are church folks who are trouble to the Lord Jesus Christ.

The Pharisees and religious leaders were trouble to Jesus every day that they were trying to make it hard for Jesus to win souls to believe in Him and make it to heaven having no trace of trouble.

There are church folks who are trouble to a real, true Christian who loves everybody like Jesus loves to save every soul no matter how bad that person may be.

There are people who are trouble just looking at them.

There are people who are trouble just walking by them.

Trouble won't always last for you and me if we keep our faith in Jesus Christ who already defeated that troublesome devil at Mount Calvary.

There are People

There are people who love to encourage other people.

There are people who love to talk about people's flaws

There are people who love to help other people.

There are people who love to talk good about people.

There are people who love to look down on people.

There are people who love to be kind to people.

There are people who love to be mean to people.

There are people who love to give a kind eye look to people.

There are people who love to give evil eye looks to people.

There are people who love to treat people right.

There are people who love to treat people bad.

There are people who love to save people's lives.

There are people who love to kill people.

There are people who love to give gifts to people.

There are people who love to steal from people.

There are people who love to make peace with people.

There are people who love to fight people.

There are people who love to respect people.

There are people who love to be rude to people.

There are people who love to talk to people.

There are people who love to ignore people.

There are people who love to accept people for who they are.

There are people who love to judge people.

There are people who love to see the good in people.

There are people who love to see the bad in people.

There are people who love to heal people.

There are people who love to break people's hearts.

There are people who love to love people.

There are people who love to hate people.

There are people who love to see people set free from bondage.

There are people who love to control people.

There are people who love to show compassion for people.

There are people who love to make it hard on people.

There are people who love to be real with people.

There are people who love to be a phony to people.

There are people who love to be good to people.

There are people who love to be bad to people.

There are people who love to spread the gospel of Jesus Christ to people.

There are people who love to deny Jesus Christ to people.

There are church people who love to keep the Commandments of God.

There are church people who love to make excuses for their sins.

There are church people who love to give testimonies about the hardships that Jesus brought them through.

There are church people who love to carry themselves like they had it so good all of their lives.

There are church people who love to study the bible.

There are church people who love to study people.

There are church people who love to bury their spiritual gifts.

There are church people who love to see their spiritual brothers and sisters prospering in the Lord.

There are church people who love to see their less fortunate spiritual brothers and sisters stay down under them in every way.

There are church people who love to live their lives unto the Lord.

There are church people who love to try to serve the Lord and the world at the same time.

There are church people who love to humble themselves unto the Lord.

There are church people who love to carry themselves like they are self-made.

There are church people who love to love everybody.

There are church people who love to love only who they highly favor.

There are church people who love to live right by example before everybody.

There are church people who love to pretend to live right but only out in public and in the church, while in their homes they can't fool their families.

There are church people who love to be more and more like Jesus.

There are church people who love to put people and material things above the Lord Jesus Christ.

There are church people who are filled with the Holy Spirit.

There are church people who love to pick and choose the fruit of the Spirit that they would like to have to best suit them.

There are church people who love to worship Jesus Christ and give Him all the glory and praise.

There are church people who love to be in church, but have no heart to confess and repent of their sins unto Jesus Christ.

There are church people who love to be true about loving Jesus.

There are church people who love to go through the motions of service unto Jesus to make themselves look good, but they have no true love in their hearts for Jesus.

There are church people who love to keep Jesus first in their lives every day, no matter what they go through good or bad.

There are church people who love to put Jesus last in their lives from day to day because they look at their problems and think they're bigger than Jesus, who is always ahead of every problem that has a dead end when it comes to Jesus.

Jesus is endless in working out all of our problems for us to be fit to be rooted and grounded in Him.

Tithes and Offerings

Returning a faithful tithe and offering is mostly about receiving the fullness of God's blessings that are mostly spiritual blessings, not material and physical blessings.

There are people who return a faithful tithe and offering and will expect the Lord to bless them with more money and more material things.

The Lord will bless us with the fullness of His spiritual blessings that we need the most for returning faithful tithes and offerings unto the Lord.

There are people who believe that their car wont' break down and their house won't need repair work if they return faithful tithes and offerings unto the Lord.

There are people who believe that they won't get sick and won't get in a car accident if they return faithful tithes and offerings.

The Lord never promised anyone that no hardships will come their way if they return faithful tithes and offerings unto Him.

The purpose of returning faithful tithes and offerings unto the Lord is to help strengthen our faith in the Lord as we draw closer and closer to Him.

If the purpose of returning faithful tithes and offerings unto the Lord is to get more and more material things like money, then everyone won't waste any time returning faithful tithes and offerings unto the Lord.

There are people who don't return faithful tithes and offerings and they are blessed with riches and wealth and good health, but they are missing out on the fullness of God's blessings that are mostly spiritual blessings like having a peace of mind.

When we return faithful tithes and offerings unto the Lord God, He will open the windows of heaven and pour out His blessings upon us that we may not have enough room to receive.

It's mostly the spiritual blessings in the fullness of God blessing us with love, joy, peace, goodness, kindness, temperance, patience and so on.

The spiritual blessings are lasting for us to hold onto and are much more than the material and physical blessings that have no lasting good effects on our soul's salvation.

Prayer is Sacred

Many people believe that prayer is not sacred.

They believe that they can pray to the Lord and ask the Lord for anything they believe the Lord is supposed to give to them.

Prayer is not sacred to many people who believe that the Lord is weak and is supposed to give into all of their prayers.

Many people believe that the Lord is supposed to suck up their prayers while they do whatever they want to do.

Prayer is not sacred to many people who are living in darkness while believing that the Lord will answer their prayers as if the Lord will excuse their evil deeds.

Prayer is sacred, but many people even in the church take this too lightly because they believe that their prayers are supposed to change the Lord, when actually prayer is supposed to change you and me for the better and is a way to love and obey the Lord Jesus Christ.

Prayer is sacred but many people will overlook this and instead look at prayer like it's a little toy that they can play with until they get tired of it.

Prayer is sacred but many so-called Christians think that we must pray to the Lord with polished and captivating words to get the Lord's attention, when in reality a simple child's prayer can get the Lord's attention because it is real and from the heart.

Prayer is sacred but many people believe that they can turn it on and off like a light switch because they only turn on prayer if they are in trouble and need to get well from an illness.

These same people then turn off prayer if things are going very good in their lives.

Prayer is sacred, whether we pray to the Lord with polished words or broken words, it's the fact that the prayer comes from our hearts that pleases the Lord.

Like the Seasons that Change

Let us not change on the Lord like the seasons that change from summer to fall and from winter to spring.

When we pray to the Lord to work things out for us, we must trust Him and leave things in His hands.

Let us not change on the Lord and want to take things out of His hands and then try to work things out on our own by putting things in our hands.

That can surely mess things up.

Let us not change on the Lord like the seasons that change from summer to fall and from winter to spring on our good days when things are going our way and the way we want them to

On our good days, when things are going the way we want, it's so easy to thank the Lord for blessing us real good.

Let us not change on the Lord on our bad days and begin to doubt what He can do for us when things are not easy and aren't going our way.

Let us not change on the Lord like the seasons that change from summer to fall and from winter to spring.

The Lord will not change on us, no matter if we change on Him.

As long as we are well and not sick, then we are joyful and have no complaints with the Lord and we have no problem about keeping our eyes on Him.

Let us not change on the Lord when we are sick and feel no joy and then complain about how sick we are as if the Lord's eyes are not upon us and He can't make us well.

Let us not change on the Lord like the seasons that change from summer to fall and from winter to spring.

We can also change on one another if we change on the Lord.

No One is All Right Without the Lord

On a Sunday morning I went out to the Walmart store and it was pretty crowded with people shopping to buy whatever they wanted to buy.

I was about to push my grocery cart out of the lane I was in for a short time when one of my neighbors and his wife came into my lane.

As my neighbor was pushing his grocery cart in my direction, he looked at me and asked, "Are you all right?" as if I didn't look all right to him.

I said to him in return, "I'm all right," and we went our separate ways.

When I got back home, the Holy Spirit spoke to me and said, no one is all right without the Lord's blessings upon their life.

The Holy Spirit said to me, no matter how well someone looks, he or she is not all right without the Lord.

The Holy Spirit said to me, no matter how well someone dresses, he or she is not all right without the Lord.

The Holy Spirit said to me, no matter how rich someone may be, he or she is not all right without the Lord.

The Holy Spirit said to me, no matter how educated someone may be, he or she is not all right without the Lord.

The Holy Spirit said to me, no matter how talented someone may be, he or she is not all right without the Lord.

It's the Lord who keeps us in our right mind for us to be all right in our sane mind, no matter where we go here and there so that we can truly say we are all right when someone asks if we're all right.

Will Not Stand Still

The seconds will not stand still and will continue to move on to add up to a minute.

The minutes will not stand still and will move on to add up to an hour.

The hours will not stand still and will move on to add up to a day.

The days will not stand still and will move on to add up to a week.

The weeks will not stand still and will move on to add up to a month.

The months will not stand still and will move on to add up to a year.

The years will not stand still and will move on to add up to a decade.

The decades will not stand still and will move on to add up to a century.

We can stand still by holding grudges and not move on into forgiveness.

We can stand still in fear and not move on to boldness.

We can stand still in the past and not move on to the present.

We can stand still in the present and not move on to the future.

We can stand still in our opinions and not move on to the facts.

We can stand still in conflict and not move on to peace.

We can stand still in favoritism and not move on to loving everyone the same.

We can stand still in pride and not move on to humility.

Life will not stand still, it moves on into eternal life in Jesus Christ who did not stand still in the grave and instead moved on into heaven to sit on the right-hand side of His heavenly Father's holy throne.

The church will not stand still and will move on to be the bride of Jesus Christ, who will not stand still in heaven and will move on to coming back again on the clouds of glory to get His church bride.

Common Sense and the Bible

Common sense will let us know that it's wrong to tell a lie.

The bible will let us know that the devil is the father of lies.

Common sense will let us know that it's wrong to kill.

The bible will let us know that the devil is a murderer.

Common sense will let us know that it's wrong to steal.

The bible will let us know that the devil is a thief.

Common sense will let us know that it's wrong to treat people bad.

The bible will let us know that we must love our neighbors.

Common sense will let us know that it's wrong to have sex with another man's wife.

The bible will let us know not to commit adultery.

Common sense will let us know that it's wrong to believe you're better than others.

The bible will let us know that God hates pride.

God gave us all a free will to choose with common sense that will let us know that it's wrong to break the laws that are good for our well-being.

The bible will let us know that God gave us His ten Commandments that are always right for us to choose to keep every day.

Common sense will let us know that if some of our five senses are missing then we are mentally handicapped.

The bible will let us know that God created us in His likeness and that we can do all things through Christ, who strengthens us.

Walking Down the Christian Road

Walking down the Christian road is a struggle every day, because it's easy to get full of pride on any day.

Walking down the Christian road is a struggle every day, because it's easy to have a bad motive on any day.

Walking down the Christian road is a struggle every day, because it's easy to say something wrong on any day.

Walking down the Christian road is a struggle every day, because it's easy to be selfish on any day.

Walking down the Christian road is a struggle every day, because it's easy to do our own will on any day.

Walking down the Christian road is a struggle every day, and we need the Holy Spirit to dwell in us.

Walking down the Christian road is a struggle every day, and we need to deny ourselves and pick up our crosses to follow Jesus Christ.

Walking down the Christian road is a struggle every day, and we need to pray to the Lord Jesus Christ to give us the strength to bear whatever bad situation comes our way.

Walking down the Christian road is a struggle every day, and we need Jesus to help us to live right by example before fellow Christians and the people of the world.

To be Like Jesus

I must respect you for me to be like Jesus.

You must respect me for you to be like Jesus.

I must forgive you for me to be like Jesus.

You must forgive me for you to be like Jesus.

I must esteem you for me to be like Jesus.

You must esteem me for you to be like Jesus.

I must help you for me to be like Jesus.

You must help me for you to be like Jesus.

I must be honest to you for me to be like Jesus.

You must be honest to me for you to be like Jesus.

I must love you for me to be like Jesus.

You must love me for you to be like Jesus.

I must be good to you for me to be like Jesus.

You must be good to me for you to be like Jesus.

I must share my testimonies with you for me to be like Jesus.

You must share your testimonies with me for you to be like Jesus.

I must pray for you for me to be like Jesus.

You must pray for me for you to be like Jesus.

I must edify you with my spiritual gifts for me to be like Jesus.

You must edify me with my spiritual gifts for me to be like Jesus.

We need the Holy Spirit to help us to be like Jesus because we can't be like Jesus on our own intellect.

We can't be like Jesus on our own strength.

We can't be like Jesus in our own ways of saying things and doing things.

I must be humble before you for me to be like Jesus.

You must be humble before me for you to be like Jesus.

I must be live right by God's holy word before you for me to be like Jesus.

You must be live right by God's holy word before me for you to be like Jesus.

I must be filled with the Holy Spirit before you for me to be like Jesus before you.

You must be filled with the Holy Spirit before me for you to be like Jesus before me.

To be like Jesus is to have the fruit of the Holy Spirit in you and me.

All good things will always be good things in the Lord, who gives me good things for me to be like Him before you and he give you good things for you to be like Him before me.

There is nothing good in the devil, who can appear to be an angel of light that only looks good but has nothing good to give to you and me for us to not be like Jesus.

Pride Can Talk Right in the Church

Pride can talk right in the church, where some church leaders will say, "I am this" and "I am that" and they don't say that the Lord has blessed them to be who they are today.

Pride can talk right in the church, where some church folks will say, "I did this" and "I did that" and they don't' say that the Lord has blessed them to do this and do that.

Pride can talk right in the church, where it can be so easy to say prideful words to make yourself look good and not make the Lord look good, as if the Lord had nothing to do with your achievements in life.

Even right in the church there are some church folks who are puffed up with pride, and it's not just educated church folks but also some uneducated church folks.

Pride can get into anybody in the church, where humility is only something small to some church folks.

Let us church folks make a practice of saying that the Lord is blessing me to do this and that.

Let us church folks make a practice of saying that the Lord has blessed me to be successful.

Let us church folks make a practice of saying that the Lord has allowed me to be who I am today and has cast that proud Lucifer out of heaven.

Let us church folks make a practice of saying that it was the Lord who allowed me to get a good education.

It's so easy to get full of pride right in the church, where someone in the church has the gift of discernment from the Lord to see right through prideful people in the church.

Pride can talk right in the church, where a true child of God will pick up on it real easy like a balloon will burst if you stick a pin in it.

Even though pride can talk right in the church, it is still the best place to be because Jesus Christ, our Lord, is the head of the church and will cast pride out of the church like He cast that proud Lucifer out of heaven with his proud fallen angels.

So, let us all in the church talk humility unto the Lord by acknowledging that it's the Lord who has made us all who we are to be where we are at today.

We didn't accomplish anything on our own because it's the Lord who keeps breath in our bodies for us to move here and there day after day.

All it takes is one church leader or one church member to cause pride to spread like a wild fire in the church, but Jesus will surely put it out sooner or later with the water hose of His holy word.

Pride can talk strong right in the church, but Jesus hates pride and will cut it up into pieces with His holy word being like a two-edged sword.

O Lord, I want to See You on the Clouds of Glory

O Lord, I want to see You on the clouds of glory and I want to go back home with You to heaven when You come back again.

This world is not my home and I don't want to make this sinful world my home.

This world is all about hurting my heart and letting me down.

This world is all about oppressing me and discouraging me.

This world is all about showing favoritism against me.

This world is all about cheating me and deceiving me.

O Lord, I want to see You on the clouds of glory when You come back again to take me home with You, and I know You will dry up all of my tears.

O Lord, this world is not my home and I don't want to make this fallen world my home.

As I live in this world, I want to love You and keep Your Commandments day after day when You, O Lord, are my only hope.

This world will only give me false hopes and will try to take away whatever it is that You give to me, my Lord and Savior Jesus Christ.

This world has been letting me down since the day I was born into this selfish world that breaks its promises to me.

O Lord, this world loves to crush my dignity.

This world loves to scorn my faith in You, O Lord.

This world loves to beat me up with its criticism for being a witness of You, especially in my body language day after day.

O Lord, I want to see You coming back again on the clouds of glory to take me back to my real home in heaven where there is no sin beyond this sinful world that loves to fill my life with regrets.

I don't want to make this world my home, O Lord, because since I've been living in this sinful world it's been trying its best to keep me from denying myself and picking up my cross to follow You.

This world tricked me with its deceit and this world robbed me of my true purpose, but this world has failed to eliminate my free will choice to repent and turn to Jesus.

O my Lord and Savior Jesus Christ, I want to see You on the clouds of glory one day soon as I live for You today and this world can't shatter my free will into pieces for me not to have an excuse to believe that this sinful world can control my choices in life.

O Lord, I want to see You on the clouds of glory when this sinful world can't keep You from appearing before my eyes that will see You in the fullness of your eternal glory if I am saved in You, my Lord and Savior Jesus Christ.

When Jesus Left Heaven

When Jesus left heaven to live on earth, it must have been like leaving a big mansion to live on the mean streets.

When Jesus left heaven to live on earth, it must have been like giving away a trillion dollars to receive a penny.

When Jesus left heaven to live on earth, the angels must have been confused to see Him leaving His heavenly throne to become a man who has sins in His flesh.

When Jesus left heaven to live on earth, it must have been like leaving a beautiful, faithful wife to live with a prostitute.

When Jesus left heaven to live on earth, it must have been like leaving a seven-figure salary to receive a minimum wage salary.

When Jesus left the riches and wealth in heaven to live on earth, it must have been like leaving a lifetime of freedom and peace to volunteer to live in prison among the worst criminals.

You and I just cannot imagine the everlasting love and everlasting life that Jesus left behind in heaven to live on earth where our first parents made a deal with the devil who conned Adam and Even into giving him their dominion over the earth.

When Jesus Christ left heaven to live a sinless life on earth, it must have been like living among a tribe of barbarians who didn't know what it's like to be civilized.

When Jesus left heaven to live on earth, it must have been like trading in a new Rolls Royce car for an old rusty bicycle.

Jesus lived a sinless life in this sinful world among sinners so He could set us free from being slaves to sin.

When Jesus left heaven to live on earth, it must have been like leaving a good community to live in a graveyard.

Jesus left all of heaven to go through the agony, pain and suffering for you and me.

Jesus left all of heaven to go through the agony of suffering and death for you and me to live with Him in heaven where Jesus went back to with power and the victory over death.

When Jesus left heaven to live on earth, it must have been like leaving college with a PhD degree and being forced to do hard labor work at a trash dump.

Will we leave all the possessions we have for Jesus Christ's name sake?

Only Jesus knows all who will leave life to die for His holy and precious name.

Jesus is Coming Back Again

Jesus Christ is coming back again, regardless of wolves in sheep's clothing that might be you and I, who can howl like a wolf in our words and actions and not give Jesus our whole hearts.

Jesus is coming back again to vanish away bias opinions, cliques and monarchy attitudes that will not prevail against the church.

Jesus is coming back again to destroy ignorance, stupidity, pride, arrogance, cunning techniques, charming deceit and refined conceit and He will destroy clever expressions and putting people down.

Jesus is coming back again to crush intellectual, seductive and revengeful minds that will not prevail against the church that Jesus has given wisdom and knowledge through His holy word so that you and I can detect errors of intellectual evil that can appear to be words fitly spoken.

Jesus is coming back again to mock the mockers who make fun of you and me in direct and indirect ways and can disguise themselves and make us think they love you and me when their hearts are full of resentment toward us.

Jesus is coming back again to put self-righteousness to shame for deceiving many church folks and making them believe they're doing Jesus a favor by spreading the gospel, when Jesus' favor can turn against us if we believe we're worthy to be anointed by the Holy Ghost.

Jesus is coming back again to wipe away death that will not prevail against the church where anyone can persecute Jesus for showing partiality when Jesus loves us all the same.

Jesus is coming back again to wipe away death that will not prevail against the church that Jesus has given His Holy Spirit to raise the spiritual dead from a dead consciousness to confess their faults, but hypocrites will believe themselves to be perfect in their own minds which will not prevail against the church regardless of their exceptional qualities and having favor with people who have no heaven to put you and me in.

Jesus Christ is coming back again for souls yearning for the Creator of every soul.

Only the pure of heart will see God, who is not impressed by status, skills, achievements, degrees or riches and wealth, because all of these things belong to Jesus who can take them all away before He comes back again.

The Mind

What goes into the mind is the origin of what you and I believe.

The mind is very powerful and controls your life and my life.

If good thoughts are in the mind, good actions will be seen.

If bad thoughts are in the mind, bad actions will be seen.

The mind will control what you and I say, good words or bad words.

The mind is the master of actions, so it controls our actions and decides whether we do good things or bad things.

The mind controls what you and I believe.

The mind is master of our tongues and decides whether we say good words or bad words.

The mind is the master of actions and controls whether we do good things or bad things.

If there is anger in the mind, anger will be in our words.

If there is anger in the mind, anger will be seen in our actions.

The mind is a gift from the Lord, who has given you and me a mind to think on Him.

The mind will control the body's movements and the mind will tell the body what to do and not to do.

If the mind is disciplined, the body will be disciplined.

If the mind is ill, the whole body will do ill things.

The mind is the tunnel that choices pass through.

The mind is the house that is furnished with beliefs.

The mind is an expressway for thoughts to travel on.

The mind is an open window for knowledge to fly through.

The mind is an open door for wisdom to walk through.

The mind is a battleground for you and I to fight with ourselves, who can be trouble to ourselves

The mind is an artist that draws with imagination.

The mind is the architect that designs self-esteem.

The mind is the light switch to turn our behaviors on and off.

The mind is either a captive of the truth or a captive of lies.

The mind is pure gold motives or counterfeit motives.

The mind can be strong and overpower stress, or the mind can be weak and allow stress to overpower it.

The mind that thinks of Jesus Christ will get the victory over doubt and fear.

The mind that stays on Jesus will cause the prince of darkness to flee.

The mind that knows God's word will paralyze false doctrines.

The mind that is filled with the Holy Spirit will love Jesus and keep His Commandments.

The mind is where our change begins by free will choice, but the mind can also be where there is no change, which also comes about by the free will choice.

Having one's mind on Jesus creates unity in the home, neighborhood, on the job and in church.

We Have Nothing to Complain About

We have nothing to complain about if we think on how blessed we are to be alive and in our right minds.

Everything we go through in life should be with no complaints if we are truly thankful unto Jesus Christ for bringing us this far in life when we deserve to be six feet down in the ground.

If we live our lives like we own something, we will begin to complain about the things that belong to the Lord.

If we live our lives like people owe us something, we will begin to complain about people who belong to the Lord.

If we are not content with what God has given to us, we will begin to complain about the things that belong to God.

We have nothing to complain about if we trust Jesus Christ to work out our problems and move our stumbling blocks out of the way on His time and not on our time.

If we believe that we made ourselves and our achievements in life, we will begin to complain about those not on our educational level, when the Lord can use a donkey to get His message out and save a lost soul.

Is it wise to complain when the knowledge we have can swell our heads and cause us to complain about what we know to be so right, when contentment is of the Lord?

If we are content with one another, we wouldn't complain about one another.

We must love one another to be Jesus' disciples.

Complainers are people who are not satisfied with what the Lord has blessed them with.

We will not complain about one another if we stay focused on the goodness of God.

Complaining is an insult to God who can work out all of our problems.

We have nothing to complain about if we deny ourselves, take time to be content and take more time to be like Jesus.

We are so Blessed to be Different

We are so blessed to be different and we should be joyful about our differences in this sinful world.

You don't want my mistakes to be your mistakes and I don't want your mistakes to be my mistakes.

You and I have plenty of our own sins that we need to confess and repent of unto the Lord.

I was born in sin and I don't want anyone else to act exactly like me and have all of my same changeable and stubborn ways.

I can't imagine someone else thinking and talking and doing everything exactly like me.

Would you want me to be exactly like you?

Would you want me to think all of your thoughts, speak all of your words and do everything exactly like you?

You and I are different and we will not agree on everything.

It's a blessing to me to be around people who are different from me in good ways.

The wrong thing about being different is being different in a bad way.

I'm not better than you and you are not better than me for being different.

Many people are proud of being different and believe they're better than other people because of those differences.

Being different in a good way is a blessing from the Lord who made no mistake when giving you and me different personalities to serve His holy purpose.

Our Lord Jesus Christ created you to be different from me to give us some space that we need to identify ourselves and be different from one another.

You can be different in a good way and someone else may dislike you, even in the church.

Being different will be a problem to anyone who thinks highly of themselves or very low of themselves.

The people who you and I can dislike the most are people who have some of the same bad ways you and I have.

Many people will make being different to be a bad thing and reap what they sow, but you and I are so blessed by God to have different personalities that belong to the Lord to use for His glory.

We can always be glad about having our own good personality that Jesus always respects, even if we are opinionated by criticizing people.

No Matter What Age

We are not so broken that Jesus can't fix us, no matter what age we are.

Life is not too hard on anyone whose burdens are not too hard for Jesus to make them light as a feather to fly in the sky.

Many times, we make life hard on ourselves by being selfish, no matter what age we are.

You and I cannot always blame our failures on peer pressure and on bad things that other people have done to us.

We have a free will choice to give Jesus a try after everyone and everything has failed us.

No matter what age we are, we are usually good at giving the things in this world a try but the things in this world are temporary and will fail us.

There is nothing new under the sun where every generation of people has their victories and defeats.

Life is not as bad as many people make it out to be, because life is a gift from God who can bless anyone's life to prosper in good health and in good financial status no matter what age we are.

Age has no number to Jesus.

Age may make a difference to you and me, but Jesus shows no respect of age and doesn't care if you're young, middle aged or old.

Many people will love the middle aged and old people, but despise the young people.

Jesus is not like you and me, who can show respect of age, as if the young people are superior to the middle aged and old people.

Age is no number to Jesus, who is against us living in sin no matter what age we are.

For the wages of sin is death upon every age of people who Jesus wants to save from being lost in sin that has no power over any age group of people to not choose to repent and live for Jesus.

Everybody Wants to be Believed

Everybody wants people to believe what they say.

Everybody wants people to believe what they do.

Everybody wants to be believed.

Everybody wants people to believe their ideas.

Everybody wants people to believe their life.

Everybody wants to be believed, whether they tell the truth or lies.

Even a little child wants to be believed.

Everybody wants people to believe their opinions.

Everybody wants to believe themselves.

Everybody wants to believe their eyes.

Everybody wants to believe their feelings.

Everybody wants to believe their senses.

Everybody wants to believe their intelligence.

Everybody wants to be believed.

Everybody wants to believe their taste buds.

Everybody wants to believe their hearts.

Everybody wants to believe their minds.

Everybody wants to be believed, whether they are good or evil.

Anyone not in their right mind wants to believe that they say and do things right.

Even a fool wants to believe they are right.

Everybody wants to be believed, but only Jesus always knows the height and depth of what everyone believes from day to day.

Everybody wants to be believed, but it can't reach up any higher than God's holy word that is eternal belief about Jesus Christ.

The devil wants to be believed day after day to cause many people to tell his lies, because the devil is forever lost in his sins against God.

Most of all, Jesus wants to be believed, and we should believe Him to be the Son of God and our Lord and Savior.

Everybody wants to be believed, but nobody can rise above Jesus who the demons fear and tremble from, because Jesus and His angels cast them out of heaven.

Everybody wants to be believed, and there are people who are so much more believable than you and me.

They can get a lot of things done because they are so much more believable than you and me.

Everybody wants to be believed, but nobody can out-do all the good things that Jesus did when He lived here on earth without sin.

Everybody wants to be believed, but the cross was much more believable even to the demons who saw Jesus being nailed to it and die on it in the place of every sinner from the beginning of time on earth to the last days.

Everybody wants what they say and do to be believed, but nobody can be more believable than Jesus Christ who rose from the grave with victory over death for our lives to be believed today.

The grave is not more believable than Jesus, who is coming back again on the clouds of glory to raise the righteous from death and change the righteous living from mortal to immortal.

Everybody wants to be believed, but who knows our hearts better than Jesus, who we can believe with all of our hearts?

Our hearts can't be more believable than Jesus.

Our works can't be more believable than Jesus.

Our lives can't be more believable than Jesus.

Everybody wants to be believed, even when time is not on our side and we can die today with not enough believable faith in Jesus to be saved.

Everybody wants to be believed; people who invent things want to be believed.

Everybody wants to be believed; people who write and publish books want to be believed, whether their books are fiction or non-fiction.

Everybody wants to be believed; people who solve a mystery want to be believed.

Everybody wants to be believed; people who are sick and get well want to be believed that they are well.

Everybody wants to be believed; people who make a new discovery want to be believed.

Everybody wants to be believed; people who survive a life-threatening situation want to be believed.

Everybody wants to be believed in one way or another.

Everybody wants to be believed, whether they are a Christian or an atheist.

What is forevermore believable than everybody in this world is Jesus Christ who is the truth, the way and the life of all existence in heaven and on earth.

Everybody wants to be believed, but everybody will not have enough evidence to prove themselves to be believable, especially in the courtroom.

Everybody wants to be believed, but only Jesus Christ is always believable and the demons know that better than everybody in this world.

The demons will fear and tremble because they believed too late that Jesus is forevermore powerful than they are.

Everybody wants to be believed, but nobody can ever be more believable than Jesus Christ, who cast the devil and his angels out of heaven so long before any human being existed.

Lucifer wanted to be believed and thought that he could be God, but he deceived himself and one-third of the angels in heaven.

Everybody wants to be believed, but if anyone believes they are more believable than Jesus Christ, then all the darkness of sin will over-shadow their soul and it will be lost.

Everybody wants to be believed about something, but only Jesus will always have proof of everything that He has done and is doing today.

Everybody wants to be believed, but everybody can't prove themselves believable for saying one thing and doing another thing.

Everybody wants to be believed, but everybody will fall short of the glory of God, even if they mean good and well.

Only Jesus Christ is worthy to always be believed in His holy word.

Jesus is the foundation for anyone to stand on and know that He is always believable in a world of so much disbelief about Jesus Christ, even in many churches.

Everybody wants to be believed in the church, but everybody doesn't love everybody in the church so they are not like Jesus, who loves everybody in and out of the church.

Everybody wants to be believed, but everybody's body language will be observed saying much more than words can say.

Everybody wants to be believed; people who are full of themselves want to be believed.

Everybody wants to be believed and it will sooner or later prove to be good or bad in their lives, showing that the truth is always believable over every lie and that the truth will sooner or later prevail.

Everybody wants to be believed, whether they are telling the truth or telling lies.

Jesus Christ is the only living eternal truth to forever be believed over lies that will one day pass away and not be believable to all the holy saints going with Jesus back to heaven when Jesus comes back again.

Everybody wants to be believed regardless of their personality.

Everybody wants to be believed regardless of their gender.

Everybody wants to be believed regardless of their skin color.

Everybody wants to be believed regardless of their religion.

Everybody wants to be believed regardless of their education.

Everybody wants to be believed regardless of their mental health and physical health.

Everybody wants to be believed by what they say, whether it's the truth or a lie.

Everybody wants to be believed by what they do, whether they have good motives or bad motives.

Everybody wants to be believed, whether they are living free in society or in prison.

Everybody wants to be believed, whether they are free or a slave.

Everybody wants to be believed, whether they are rich or poor.

Everybody wants to be believed, whether they are sane or insane.

Nobody can ever be more believable than Jesus Christ, who the Holy Spirit speaks the truth about in the bible that only a fool would not believe.

Everybody wants to be believed, but not everybody will believe in Jesus Christ who is forevermore believable to all the angels in heaven and forevermore believable to all the unfallen worlds.

Everybody wants to be believed and everybody has that in common.

We all relate to one another that we want to be believed for the rest of our lives.

Everybody wants to be believed, whether they are ignorant, foolish or just down right wicked, but only the Lord Jesus Christ is always worthy to be believable.

Jesus is believable in His holy word and in the lives of devout Christians because many people have repented of their sins and turned to Jesus even way back in the bible days and up to this day.

Everybody wants to be believed, but everybody won't believe Jesus Christ, who is the highest believable supernatural being who gave up His life on the cross to save everybody from their sins.

Jesus rose from the grave to conquer death that wants to be believed by sinners.

The Beginning

The beginning was here before we were born.

Our lives began in our mothers' wombs, forevermore after the beginning.

The beginning was here before the heavens and earth that the beginning created.

The beginning was here before the universe existed.

The beginning was here before other worlds.

The beginning is the source of life.

No one knows how the beginning began.

The beginning didn't begin with a big bang.

The beginning was here before any kind of theory.

The beginning is God.

The beginning was the word of God.

The beginning was made flesh in the image of God.

The beginning spoke to prophets.

The beginning was here before the angels.

The beginning created the angels.

The beginning created a man and woman.

The beginning created all the animals.

The beginning created the sun, moon and stars.

The beginning created all things in heaven and on earth.

The beginning was here before all things.

You and I began in our mothers' wombs.

The beginning began with God.

No one knows how God began.

No one knows when God began.

We can believe that life began with God and not with a big bang in the outer space.

No one knows where God began.

The beginning is forevermore beyond our imagination.

The beginning is forevermore beyond our knowledge.

The beginning is forevermore beyond science and technology.

The beginning is forevermore beyond our wisdom.

No man or woman was there in the beginning.

No angel was there in the beginning.

Only God was there in the beginning, which was God.

The beginning is eternal.

The beginning is all-powerful.

The beginning is everlasting life.

The beginning is eternal glory.

The beginning is everlasting love.

The beginning is God the Father, God the Son and God the Holy Spirit.

They were there in the beginning and we will never understand that because our minds are fallible to the beginning.

The beginning is forevermore real beyond luck.

The beginning is forevermore real beyond any mystery.

The beginning is forevermore real beyond any phenomenon.

The beginning is God and Jesus Christ and the Holy Spirit.

No one can explain their existence in the beginning.

It's like trying to read and explain all the published books in the world.

It's like trying to explain what everyone is feeling in their hearts.

It's like trying to read and explain what is in everyone's minds.

We know that only God can do that.

No prophecy can explain the beginning that existed before any prophecy.

The beginning is God, and no one can question how God began.

We don't usually think about how water began, we just love to drink it to quench our thirst.

We don't usually think about how food began, we just love to eat food when we are hungry.

It's the same way with God.

We don't need to know how God began, but we can truly love God and be thankful that God can quench our thirsty souls and satisfy our hungry souls every day.

The beginning is God, who is also the end, and will put an end to death.

God will do that in the end to create a new earth.

In the beginning was God and not evolution or chance.

God was here for billions and billions of years.

God is the beginning of all life in heaven and on earth.

God is the beginning of all life in the universe.

God's end is eternal life.

In the beginning was God and not theories and science.

In the beginning was God and not an educated guess.

In the beginning was God and not creation.

In the beginning was God and no man knows how God began.

Who can reason that God began from evolution?

No man's reason can go back to the beginning and figure out God's existence.

No man's theories and imagination can erase God, who is the origin of life.

In the beginning was God, who is also the origin of love.

In the beginning was God, whose end is infinite when our end is short here on earth.

God's end is endless forevermore beyond all the stars that look so endless in the universe.

The beginning was God and is God forevermore beyond the beginning of a baby born into this world.

Worthy is the Lamb of God

O Lord, I deserve to have my back lashed a hundred or more times.

O Lord, I deserve to be spit on one hundred times.

O Lord, you didn't deserve to get lashes on your back.

O Lord, you didn't deserve to be spit on.

O Lord, I deserve to have 100 bruises on my head.

O Lord I deserve to bleed my blood all over my body.

O Lord, you didn't deserve to get bruises on your head.

O Lord, you didn't deserve to bleed any blood.

O Lord, you did it all for me as if I was the only sinner who You want to save from my sins.

O Lord, I deserve to have nail prints in my hands.

O Lord, I deserve to have nail prints in my feet.

O Lord, you didn't deserve to get nail prints in your hands.

O Lord, you didn't deserve to get nail prints in your feet.

O Lord, you did it all for me, who deserves to die and be lost in my sins.

Worthy is the Lamb of God is You, my Lord and Savior Jesus Christ.

I can shed a million tears for all that you've done for me, O Lord, and it doesn't come close to how you felt in the Garden of Gethsemane where you, O Lord, had sweat so very intense to look like drops of blood dripping down from your face.

You knew, O Lord, that the cup of God's wrath was so bitter for you to drink in my place.

Worthy is the Lamb of God, is You, my Lord and Savior Jesus Christ, who had left all of heaven and given up all of your riches to come to this sinful world to save a poor sinner like me and one day give me Your eternal riches and wealth of eternal life.

If our Lord and Savior Jesus Christ had not laid down His life for the sins of all the world, then Enoch would have had to leave heaven and go to the grave.

If Jesus had not laid down His life on the cross for the sins of all the world, then Moses would have had to leave heaven and go to the grave.

If Jesus had not died on the cross and risen again, then Elijah would have had to leave heaven and go to the grave because he was not more worthy than Jesus, who created the heavens and earth.

Worthy is the Lamb of God, is Jesus Christ, who humbled Himself like a lamb before the religious leaders and Pharisees and before the Roman soldiers who were like hungry wolves waiting to devour Jesus.

Jesus held back all of His power to become like a helpless little lamb to be preyed upon by the hungry wild beast called the devil, who along with his human agents, could not tempt Jesus to sin against God.

Jesus was the lamb who heard and answered His master God calling Him out in the wilderness of the sinful world.

God let Jesus know that He was not alone even when Jesus felt all alone on the cross.

The devil cut the throat of Jesus' life and let it bleed out on the cross, but God had predestined His supernatural power to heal Jesus' wounds and raise Him from the dead with victory over the hungry, devouring wolf of death.

Greatness is the Lamb of God.

Glory and honor and praise to the Lamb of God, who is worthy to exist forever beyond all existence seen and unseen.

Worthy is the Lamb of God, who is Jesus Christ, to take away our sins and cast them into the deep sea.

Worthy is the Lamb of God, who is Jesus Christ, to carry all the world's governments on his shoulders.

Worthy is the Lamb of God, who is Jesus Christ, who is coming back again on the clouds of glory with all the angels to gather you and me and all of His children to take them to heaven.

Worthy is the Lamb of God, who is Jesus Christ, who has all power and glory in heaven and in other worlds.

Worthy is the Lamb of God, who is Jesus Christ, who stooped down very low to be slaughtered like a little helpless lamb to save you and me from our sins.

Every time that we sin against Jesus, we slaughter him over and over again.

Lower Than

Jesus came down lower than any sinner when He hung on the cross that made Him become sin in our place.

Jesus came down lower than any sinner when His heavenly Father, God, turned His back on Him causing him to ask, "Why hast thou forsaken me?"

It was too hard for God to see His only begotten Son becoming sin on the cross and dying on the cross in our place.

You and I have no excuse to believe that Jesus doesn't know what we are going through in our lives.

You and I have no excuse to believe that Jesus doesn't understand our hardships.

You and I have no excuse to believe that Jesus never felt all the emotions we've felt.

You and I have no excuse to believe that Jesus can't bring us through anything because nothing is too hard for Jesus.

No one has any excuse to believe that their sins are too many for Jesus not to cleanse them of and save them from their sins.

No one has the excuse to believe that their sins are too bad for Jesus not to cleanse them of and save them from their sins.

Jesus came down lower than any sinner when He hung on the cross and become sin in our place to save us from our sins.

Jesus rose from the grave with the victory over the worst kind of sin called death, being the worst kind as a result of our sins.

No one is too much of a sinner that Jesus can't save them from their sins if they confess and repent, which anyone can choose to do.

Jesus chose to give up His life on the cross before He created this world that He came to by choosing to live among sinners like you and me.

No one can believe that they are too low down of a sinner that Jesus can't save them from being lost in their sins.

Jesus became our sins on the cross to become so much lower than any sinner.

If anyone is lost in their sins, they can't tell God on judgement day that they didn't have a choice to choose to believe in His Son, Jesus Christ, and be saved.

Jesus made it possible for even the worst sinner to be saved in Him who died on the cross and rose from the grave.

No sinner has ever come down lower than Jesus who became sin on the cross in our place.

Jesus became sin and took on every sin that no one could ever bear because there are too many and it is too hard for us.

Jesus came down lower than any sinner, when He was on the cross.

Eternity witnessed this and walked away with tears rolling down its cheeks.

God loved the world, so He gave His only begotten Son so whosoever believeth in Him shall not perish but shall have eternal life.

If People Go to Heaven After They Die

If people go to heaven after they die, then the bible would be a lie for saying that Jesus Christ is coming back again to raise the righteous dead.

If people go to heaven after they die, then there would be no one in the grave for Jesus to raise from the dead.

The purpose of Jesus Christ coming back again is to raise the righteous dead and change the righteous living from mortal to immortal and take them to live with Him in heaven forever and ever.

If people go to heaven right after they die, then there would be no need for Jesus to come back again.

If people go to heaven after they die, then what is the use of putting their body down in the ground? That would be a waste of time.

If people go to heaven after they die, then why would they want to come down from heaven and reappear before you and me in this sinful world?

Why would they want to see you and me suffer in sickness when they can't be with us to comfort us?

If people go to heaven after they die, then there would be no need to bury anyone because there would be no body to bury.

If people go to heaven after they die, then there would be no one's body rotting in the grave because there would be real bodies in heaven, not people floating around in thin air.

If people go to heaven after they die, then what is the use of having funeral homes and funeral services if the dead wake back up again within the next day, week, month or year?

If people go to heaven after they die, then why would they want to reappear before us when they can't constantly be with us or do things with us?

That would be torture for them for God to take them to heaven right after they die, where they could see you and me going through hardships while they live on easy street in heaven looking down on us.

If people go to heaven after they die, then Jesus would have had no need to die on the cross for our sins that we can't take to heaven with us.

If people go to heaven after they die, then the bible would be so worthless to read and study about Jesus Christ coming back again on the clouds of glory to raise the righteous dead.

If people go to heaven after they die, then why would we waste our time grieving over our loved ones?

That would be so unfair to you and me for them to reappear before us who would be so very limited compared to their joy in heaven as we go through our ups and downs in this sinful world.

If people go to heaven after they die, then Jesus Christ would not be the Resurrection to raise the dead because there would be no dead to be raised.

If it was true that people go to heaven after they die, the devil would not waste his time killing people.

Why would the devil want people to go to heaven after they die, when that would mean he had a lost mission to destroy people?

If people go to heaven after they die, then the devil would not be able to take anyone to hell with him because everybody would be in heaven, whether they are good or evil.

The devil knows that he is going to hell and he is trying his best to take as many people with him as he can.

Jesus will raise the wicked dead and judge them to be cast into the lake of fire.

If people go to heaven after they die, then Jesus is a liar who won't come back again and raise the righteous dead and change the righteous living from mortal to immortal.

If people go to heaven right after they die, then why would anyone waste their time living in a very troubled, sinful world when they could be in heaven enjoying the eternal peace of God?

If it was really true that people go to heaven after they die, then everyone would want to die and leave this world so they could live in heaven.

No one would want to wait for Jesus to come back again because that would be a waste of time if we go to heaven right after we die.

The devil would just be wasting his time causing souls to be lost if people go straight to heaven after they die.

If people go to heaven after they die, then it would not make any good sense for the grave to exist and tombs would be so empty.

God says that we will return to dust after we die, but if we go to heaven right after we die then how can we return to dust?

We would have no need to be buried in the grave if we go to heaven after we die.

God is not that kind of God to allow you and me to go to heaven after we die.

God won't let us enter into heaven without Jesus taking us there when He comes back again.

Jesus' death on the cross would have been so worthless if we can go to heaven right after we die.

Heaven was wrapped all up in Jesus' death and resurrection that covers over everyone who ever lived in this world from the beginning of time.

There are people who are in heaven right now, and that's because of Jesus' profound reasons.

Those people who are in heaven didn't enter into heaven without Jesus being there with them.

They couldn't pass by Jesus and enter into heaven.

No one can leave Jesus out of their lives and go to heaven.

No one can go to heaven if Jesus is not there, and no one today will go to heaven before Jesus comes back again on the clouds of glory.

No one has ever entered into heaven without Jesus being there to accept them, just like He accepted Enoch, Moses, Elijah and those who Jesus resurrected from the grave when He rose from the grave and took them back to heaven with Him.

If people go to heaven after they die, then Jesus would have no purpose to come back again.

Why would Jesus tell us in His holy word that He is coming back again if there is no one to raise from the dead?

There would be no righteous dead that Jesus would raise and take to heaven with Him.

No one will go to heaven if Jesus doesn't come back again, and no one who is dead will be raised from the dead before Jesus comes back again.

The dead have no power to raise themselves after they die; they have to stay in the grave until Jesus comes back again.

None of our dead loved ones are looking down on us from heaven because they can't enter into heaven before Jesus comes back again to raise them from the dead if they are saved in Him.

When you and I die, we won't go to heaven after we die because we will stay right in the grave where we will know nothing until Jesus raises us from the dead when He comes back again on the clouds of glory.

After we die, we won't go to heaven and float around in the thin air without our bodies that Jesus will make new when He raises us from the dead to live forever in our new immortal bodies that will be real to touch and feel.

If people go to straight to heaven right after they die, then why would hell even exist.

It would be a waste of God's time to cast wicked people into hell if this was true.

Jesus will not take everybody to heaven when He comes back again, and surely no one can go to heaven right after they die because God won't accept them in before Jesus comes back again to raise the righteous dead who will truly know that Jesus raised them right on time.

If people go to heaven after they die, then why would time even exist?

It would be of no good use to anyone because time would never be too late for anyone to die and go straight to heaven with no need to wait on Jesus to come back again.

When Jesus comes back again that will be the real, true supernatural thing for only the righteous to enter into heaven and they will truly know that they didn't die and make it to heaven without Jesus raising them from the dead.

Many people believe that after they die they will go straight to heaven without Jesus coming back again to raise them from the dead.

Death and the grave truly know that they will keep us in the dust and we will know nothing and do nothing until Jesus Christ comes back again to raise us from the dead if we die being saved in Him.

If everybody goes to heaven right after they die, then why would our free will exist?

It would be so useless to God, who created us with a free will to choose to love and obey His Son, Jesus, who is our only way to enter into heaven when He comes back again.

If we go to heaven right after we die, then it will be so useless for Jesus Christ to be the head of the church, because we won't need Jesus to come back again if the righteous die and go straight to heaven.

The church would have no need to wait for Jesus Christ to come back again if we go straight to heaven after we die.

We would have no need to wait for Jesus Christ to come back again if we go to heaven right after we die.

We would have no need to sing any songs about Jesus coming back again.

Preachers would have no need to preach sermons about Jesus coming back again if we go to heaven right after we die.

The church would be so useless to go to and hear about Jesus coming back again to take us to heaven if we go to heaven right after we die.

This would make Jesus so obsolete to the church.

If the bible is not true when it talks about Jesus Christ coming back again to raise the righteous dead and change the righteous living from mortal to immortal and take us to heaven, then it's impossible for heaven to even exist if the bible is a lie.

The only truth is in the bible, because without the bible truth the church is lying for telling people that they will go to heaven right after they die.

The bible says that Jesus Christ is coming back again on the clouds of glory to raise the righteous dead and change the righteous living from mortal to immortal and take all to heaven who are saved in Him.

No one can get ahead of Jesus and go right to heaven after they die.

That is an insult to Jesus, who resurrected from the dead and went back to heaven to make a way for you and me to enter into heaven when He comes back again on the clouds of glory.

Fallen angels from heaven can appear to be our dead loved ones talking to us from heaven, and they can also appear to be our dead friends.

They have the power to deceive us that way if we don't read and study God's holy word and know the truth about only Jesus having the power to take us to heaven when He comes back again.

No one will go to heaven right after they die.

Without Jesus being in heaven, there would be no people in heaven beginning with Enoch who was the first one Jesus translated and took to heaven before Moses and Elijah, and before those who Jesus resurrected when he resurrected and went back to heaven.

No one else will go to heaven until Jesus comes back again on the clouds of glory.

Jesus Sees No Color of the Skin

Jesus sees no color of the skin because that doesn't concern Jesus; He will take every color of skin to heaven with Him when He comes back again.

The color of the skin doesn't matter to Jesus when it comes to giving eternal life when He comes back again.

The color of the skin is a big problem to controlling people who don't know what love is.

Jesus sees no color of the skin because Jesus loves everybody, regardless of their skin color.

The color of their skin has caused people to be disliked.

The color of their skin has caused people to be discriminated against.

The color of their skin has caused people to be treated unfairly.

The color of their skin has caused people to be disrespected.

Jesus sees no color of the skin, because skin color is no problem to Jesus at all from day to day.

The color of their skin has caused people to be hated.

The color of their skin has caused people to dislike themselves.

The color of their skin has caused people to kill themselves.

The color of their skin has caused people to lose their minds.

Jesus sees no color of the skin, no matter who you are.

The color of their skin has caused people to be killed.

The color of their skin has caused people to be depressed.

The color of their skin has caused people to be proud.

Jesus sees no color of the skin, which is a difficult thing to believe for many people, but not Jesus.

The color of their skin has caused people to feel superior.

The color of their skin has caused people to behave badly.

The color of their skin has caused people to do bad things.

The color of their skin has caused people to be unreasonable.

Jesus sees no color of the skin to give an abundance of life to those who believe in Him.

The color of their skin is causing hardships for people today.

The color of their skin is causing injustice to people today.

The color of their skin is causing strife for people today.

Jesus sees no color of the skin and will open the windows of heaven and pour out blessings upon anyone who returns faithful tithes and offerings unto Him.

The color of their skin is causing people to miss out on their true love today.

The color of their skin is causing people to be judgmental today.

The color of their skin is causing people to have mistrust today.

The color of their skin is causing people to be ignorant today.

Jesus sees no color of the skin to be His church bride.

Jesus sees no color of the skin to be His wheat in the church where the wheat and tares will grow together for only Jesus to separate.

No skin color can stop that from happening.

Jesus sees no color of the skin to prosper in this world, where the color of your skin is a threat to people who are insecure.

Jesus sees no color of the skin to be for you and not against you if you love Him and keep His Commandments that are for every color of the skin to keep day after day.

The color of their skin has caused people to tell lies to oppress equality even today, but Jesus sees no color of the skin and everyone is equal in His holy eyesight.

Before I Knew God's Holy Word

When I was a little boy, I lived in my grandfather and step-grandmother's house with my mother, little sister, one of my aunts and my girl cousins.

We all lived in a small two-story house in a peaceful neighborhood where everybody on the street block was friendly.

This was before I knew God's holy word.

My living conditions weren't so easy because at night I had to use a pot to discharge my waste in, and then dump it out in the backyard outhouse the following morning.

There was no indoor bathroom in the house.

I had to wash up in a bowl to clean myself up.

This was before I knew God's holy word.

My mother, little sister and I moved out of the house in the summertime and moved in with a middle-aged married couple who smoked cigarettes.

The husband also drank alcohol to the point of getting drunk.

This was before I knew God's holy word.

When my mother, little sister and I lived in the two-story house with the middle-aged couple, my mother worked a job to pay the couple for our room and board for the summer.

My mother, little sister and I moved out of the couple's house before the summer was over and moved into our own one-story apartment that was only a few blocks away from the middle-aged couple's house and my grandparents' house.

This was before I knew God's holy word.

When my mother, little sister and I lived in our apartment, I had to attend a different junior high school that was integrated with black and white students.

This was something new and different for me.

This was before I knew God's holy word.

I had no problem fitting into this new environment in the junior high school, and was there from sixth grade to eighth grade.

Even though I didn't know God's holy word, I know today that the Lord was with me, my mother and my little sister every step of the way in our lives.

I thank the Lord for blessing me and my sister to go to high school and graduate.

This was before I knew God's holy word.

When my mother, little sister and I lived in the middle-aged couple's house I had to sleep on a folding chair that could open up so I could lay down.

I had to sleep that way in the same room with the middle-aged married couple, with my folding chair bed placed at the bottom of the couple's bed.

It was hard for me to fall asleep because of their loud snoring.

I thank the Lord today that He kept a roof over my head, regardless of some sleepless nights.

All of this was before I knew God's holy word that was active in my life, my mother's life and my little sister's life even though we were ignorant to God's holy word.

I am so blessed today to know God's holy word that is all about my Lord and Savior Jesus Christ.

I was redeemed when I didn't know it.

I remember when my mother made me go to church during the time my mother, little sister and I lived in the married couple's house that was only a few blocks from the church that we went to on a Sunday.

I went to that Methodist church, but I didn't know God's holy word that the preacher talked about up in the pulpit.

I had heard God's holy word, but I just didn't know the true meaning of it until I joined the Seventh Day Adventist church.

The Lord had my name, my mother's name and my little sister's name on the roster of the Seventh Day Adventist church before we knew God's holy word.

The Lord foreknew that I would choose to worship Him on His holy Sabbath day of rest that everybody will not choose to rest on.

In my early childhood, I didn't know God's holy word because it wasn't taught to me in my home, but I'm so glad today that God winked His eye at my mother's ignorance, my ignorance and my little sister's ignorance of not knowing His holy word.

Everyone has a story to tell about the choices they make, whether they are good or bad, but the Lord is fair to everyone and will not interrupt anyone's free will choices.

This is only a little story of my past life that the Lord put here for me to love Him and keep His Commandments day by day.

Everyone who is still alive has a story to tell, and they have no excuse to leave God out of their story.

You and I Might Be Surprised

You and I might be surprised about who we see in heaven if we make it to heaven when Jesus comes back again.

Some people who might believe they will make it to heaven might not be there in heaven where Jesus will take you and me if we are saved in Him.

Some people who we might believe to be lost in their sins might be there in heaven with you and me because only Jesus truly knows all who will confess and repent of their sins before it's too late.

Only Jesus truly knows everyone's hearts and is not surprised about who He will take to heaven when He comes back again on the clouds of glory.

Only Jesus truly knows all who are saved in Him right now.

Only Jesus truly knows all who will become saved in Him before it's too late.

You and I might be surprised if we end up in heaven with Jesus when He comes back again because we don't truly know if we will make it to heaven.

We can only pray and hope that we will be in heaven with Jesus when He comes back again.

You and I might be surprised about who we might see in heaven and we might be surprised that we are there to not wake up in the second resurrection.

For death is only a short sleep to Jesus, who won't be surprised about waking us up in the first resurrection or in the second resurrection.

You and I might be surprised to wake up in the second resurrection unto eternal fire and brimstone that we will face if we are lost in our sins.

You and I just don't know if we are truly saved in Jesus, for we can only pray and hope that we will be in heaven because our works can't enter us into heaven, only Jesus can do that.

You and I can't believe that we are so holy and righteous and on our own way to heaven.

Only Jesus knows all of His true remnant children, so Jesus will not be surprised about who will go to heaven with Him when He comes back again on the clouds of glory.

Only we sinners saved through God's grace are prone to be surprised about anything, and especially about something going wrong when we believe to have it all together.

You and I might be surprised about who we will see in heaven, but we will be happy that they made it to heaven because of believing in Jesus Christ.

You and I will be happy that we made it to heaven but there will be some people who will be surprised to see you and me in heaven.

There will be many people who will be surprised to be raised up from the dead in the second resurrection.

Many so-called church folks will be surprised to be raised up in the second resurrection, where they will be lost in their sins to die again in the eternal death of hell's fire and brimstone.

Jesus will not be surprised about who will make it to heaven and who will go to hell.

Surprises are only for we imperfect human beings who were born with a sinful nature to sin against God who was not surprised about Lucifer and one third of the angels in heaven rebelling against Him.

No one can surprise God, who sees all and knows all things in heaven, in other worlds and in this world.

All existence would vanish away before anyone could surprise God, who was not surprised about Adam and Eve disobeying Him.

Hopefully you and I will be saved in Jesus and make it to heaven, where you and I might be surprised to see who we helped to make it to heaven with us.

Even though we might not know them or might never have seen them, we truly will be happy that they made it to heaven and be happy that we made it to heaven for believing in Jesus Christ.

You and I might be surprised about who we see in heaven because a wicked person who we know may confess and repent of their sins and turn to Jesus Christ during their last hour in this life before they die.

You and I might be surprised about some church brothers and sisters who aren't in heaven, but the Lord God is the supreme Judge who will show us why they didn't make it to heaven.

God will also show you and me why we made it to heaven.

Only the Lord Jesus Christ won't be surprised about who will make it to heaven and who won't make it to heaven.

One thing for sure, the righteous will make it to heaven and the wicked will go to hell and there will be no surprises about that because the bible tells us so.

You and I don't know all the people who are righteous to be saved in Jesus.

You and I don't know all who are wicked to be lost in their sins, but Jesus knows all who are righteous and all who are wicked and will not be surprised about who will enter into heaven and who will go to hell.

Jesus knows the heart of every person and they can't surprise Him, even though you and I might be surprised even about ourselves making it to heaven when we know that our righteousness is like filthy rags for only Jesus to make us perfect before God and His righteousness.

You and I, who claim to be Christians, might be surprised about waking up in the second resurrection among the wicked for holding on to even one unconfessed and unrepented sin that we can make excuses for and hold onto.

Not even one sin will enter into heaven before a holy and righteous God.

God won't be surprised to see anyone who He knows to love Him and keep His Commandments.

All who have lived in this world and are alive today might be surprised about their destiny to enter into heaven or enter into hell because God will judge everyone, dead or alive, and knows without any surprises about who will enter into heaven when Jesus comes back again on the clouds of glory.

You and I can only pray and hope that we make our calling sure in the Lord Jesus Christ while we are alive today, because chances will be slim for the righteous to enter into heaven where Jesus is not surprised about whose case He is pleading for before God.

You and I just don't know if our case has been closed already.

It's never good and wise for anyone to live their lives rejecting Jesus until they are on their dying bed and wanting to believe in Jesus because by then it might be too late for Jesus to not be surprised.

Only Jesus is not surprised about anyone being saved in Him in their last hour of life, but you and I might be surprised about seeing someone in heaven who we believe to be lost in their sins.

But if you and I don't make it to heaven, someone might be surprised to not see us in heaven, especially if we had convinced them to believe that we were Christians.

Only Jesus truly knows and isn't surprised that we missed out on heaven.

Medicine Can't Cure the Sin-Sick Soul

Medicine can't cure the sin-sick soul.

Only Jesus Christ can cure the sin-sick soul.

Medicine can't cure bad motives.

Medicine can't cure bad intentions.

Medicine can't cure bad words.

Medicine can't cure flaws.

Medicine can't cure bad habits.

Only Jesus Christ can cure the sin-sick soul.

Medicine can't cure wrong-doings.

Medicine can't cure bad thoughts.

Medicine can't cure ill feelings.

Medicine can't cure selfishness.

Only Jesus Christ can cure the sin-sick soul.

Medicine can't cure mistakes.

Medicine can't cure the sinful nature.

Only Jesus Christ, our Lord and Savior, can cure our sin-sick souls through His precious blood that was shed on the cross for our sins.

Medicine can't cure the sin-sick soul.

Medicine will never be strong enough to cure this sin-sick soul.

Medicine can't cure anyone from sinning against the Lord.

Medicine can't cure anyone from breaking God's commandments.

The very best medicine can't stop anyone from saying anything wrong and doing anything wrong.

Only Jesus can cure the sin-sick soul.

The Greatest Test of Our Faith

The greatest test of our faith in Jesus Christ is to be willing to give up our life for Jesus' name sake.

Would we be willing to get our heads cut off of our bodies for Jesus' name sake?

Would we be willing to get burned up in hot flames of fire for Jesus' name sake?

Would we be willing to get shot up by a firing squad for Jesus' name sake?

Would we be willing to get thrown off a high mountain Cliff for Jesus name sake?

Would we be willing to get tied up with ropes and thrown in the ocean to drown for Jesus' name sake?

The greatest test of our faith in Jesus Christ is to be willing to give up our lives for Jesus' name sake.

Would we be willing to be thrown in a wood-chipper for Jesus' name sake?

Would we be willing to be thrown out of an airplane flying thousands of feet above the ground for Jesus' name sake?

Only Jesus knows if you and I have that kind of faith in Him to be willing to give up our lives for His holy name's sake.

Would we be willing to get rolled over by a speeding train for Jesus' name sake?

Would we be willing to be thrown in a lion's den for Jesus' name sake?

Would we be willing to be thrown in a pond full of crocodiles for Jesus' name sake?

Would we be willing to get thrown in a pit full of poisonous snakes for Jesus' name sake?

Only Jesus knows if you and I will pass the greatest test of our faith.

The Lord will not put on you and me more than we can bear.

Only the Lord knows if you and I can bear our greatest test of faith.

Would we be willing to get thrown in a pool of boiling oil for Jesus' name sake?

Would we be willing to get thrown in a gas chamber for Jesus' name sake?

Would we be willing to get thrown off a high bridge for Jesus' name sake?

Only the Lord knows who will be willing to give up their own life for His holy name's sake.

You and I just don't know if we will pass the greatest test of our faith in Him.

The Devil's Mind-Control Techniques

The devil causes many people to believe that what they say wrong is right.

The devil causes many people to believe that what they do wrong is right.

The devil causes many people to believe that they have a good reason to kill people.

The devil causes many people to believe that their good works can save them.

The devil causes many people to believe that they are saved through God's grace and don't have to keep God's commandments.

The devil causes many people to believe that after they die they will live again in the form of an animal.

The devil causes many people to believe that they have no sins to confess and repent of.

The devil causes many people to believe that a man can forgive them of their sins.

The devil causes many people to believe that they can talk to their dead loved ones.

The devil causes many people to believe that the Bible is not true.

The devil causes many people to believe that they can live in their sins and make it to heaven.

The devil causes many people to believe that they are better than others.

The devil causes many people to believe that everyone doesn't have human rights.

The devil causes many people to believe that they are worthless.

The devil causes many people to believe that there is no devil.

The devil causes many people to believe that Jesus Christ is not the creator of all things.

The devil causes many people to believe that a lie is the truth and the truth is a lie.

The devil caused the Pharisees to believe that Jesus Christ was the devil.

The devil caused the Pharisees to believe that Jesus Christ was not the Son of God.

The devil caused the Pharisees to believe that Jesus Christ was a blasphemer.

The devil's mind-control techniques are nothing new today.

The devil's mind-control techniques have been around for thousands of years.

The devil causes many people to believe that they are self-made.

The devil causes many people to believe that when they die they will go to heaven before Jesus comes back again.

The devil causes many people to believe that God doesn't love them.

The Devil
Has His Human Agents

The devil has his human agents who will tell you and me lies that they want you and me to believe are the truth.

The devil has his human agents who won't give you and me what we deserve.

The devil has his human agents even in the church.

There are people in the church who will deceive you and me and make us believe that they are honest, when they are not honest.

The devil has his human agents who will steal from you and me, and kill you and me with joy in their hearts.

The devil has his human agents who are very selfish and only think about themselves and getting worldly gain.

The devil has his human agents who love to use you and me to help them prosper.

The devil has his human agents who don't care if you and I lose everything that we have.

The devil had his human agents who gave Jesus Christ, our Lord, a hard time when He lived here on earth.

The devil had his human agents who tried to make Jesus look bad.

The devil had his human agents who nailed Jesus on the cross.

The devil has his human agents today that are full of pride, jealousy, and greed.

The devil has his human agents today who will come in the church and cause strife and division amongst church members.

The devil has his human agents who go to church to draw attention to themselves, because they don't want Jesus to get your attention and my attention.

The devil has his human agents who will smile in our faces and plan evil deeds against you and me.

The devil has his human agents who want you and me to believe that they are Christians, when they are living in their sins.

The devil has his human agents who will cause you and me to believe that they are fair with us, when they are cheating us.

Many People Live By

Many people live by the things that they see.

Many people live by their jobs.

Many people live by their education.

Many people live by their skills.

Many people live by their talents.

Many people live by their wealth.

Many people live by their money in the bank.

Many people live by their retirement.

Many people live by their careers.

Many people live by eyesight.

Many people live by their greed for worldly gain.

Many People live by their lust of the flesh.

Many people don't live by faith in Jesus Christ, because they don't believe that Jesus can supply all of their needs — they don't believe that Jesus will never fail them.

Many people will live by their appetite.

Many people will live by the house they live in.

Many People will live by their car.

Many people will live by their truck.

Many people will live by their airplanes.

Many people will live by the clothes on their backs.

Many people will live by the things that they see.

They believe that the things they see can secure their lives.

Many people will live by their hairstyles.

Many people will live by their pets.

Many people will live by the money that they saved up.

Many people will live by their paychecks.

Many people will not live in faith by Jesus Christ, because they don't believe that Jesus can make a way out of no way for them — they don't believe that Jesus can open doors for them.

Many people will live by their jewelry.

Many people will live by their good looks.

Many people will live by their business.

Many people will live by whatever they can get their hands on.

Many people don't believe that Jesus can work anything out for them.

Before I was Born

O Lord, You planned out my life before I was born.

O Lord, You foreknew that I would have some misfortunes in my life when You planned out my life.

O Lord, You foreknew that I would have some heartaches when You planned out my life.

O Lord, You planned out my life before I was born into this sinful world.

O Lord, You foreknew that I would have some disappointments in my life when You planned out my life.

O Lord, You foreknew that I would have some good days and some bad days when You planned out my life.

O Lord, You foreknew that I would make some mistakes in my life when You planned out my life.

O Lord, you foreknew that I would make some bad choices in my life when You planned out my life.

Before I was born, O Lord, You planned out my life for me to have no excuses to not deny myself and pick up my cross and follow You, my Lord and Savior Jesus Christ.

Before I was born, O Lord, You planned out my life for me to have no excuses to not choose to believe in You and love You and keep Your Commandments.

Like a Slap in Jesus' Face

If we don't thank Jesus for sparing our lives from death, it's like a slap in Jesus' face.

When we get well from a sickness and don't thank Jesus Christ for making us well, it's like a slap in Jesus' face.

When we achieve things in life and don't give Jesus the glory and praise, it's like a slap in Jesus' face.

When we get out of trouble and don't thank the Lord Jesus Christ, it's like a slap in Jesus' face.

When we go through some hardships and come out safely and don't give the glory and praise to Jesus Christ, it's like a slap in Jesus' face.

When someone helps us and we don't thank the Lord Jesus Christ, it's like a slap in Jesus' face.

If we don't thank Jesus Christ for all that He does for us, it's like a slap in Jesus's face.

If we don't love and obey Jesus Christ, it's like a slap in Jesus' face.

It's a Very Hard Thing

It's a very hard thing to be locked up in prison for something that you didn't do.

It's a very hard thing to lose your mind.

It's a very hard thing to lose innocent casualties in a war that is an ugly thing.

It's a very hard thing to be lied about.

It's a very hard thing to not know where you are going.

It's a very hard thing to lose your loved ones.

It's a very hard thing to be discriminated against.

It's a very hard thing to be attacked.

It's a very hard thing for a friend to turn their back on you when you need encouragement and support.

It's a very hard thing to lose everything you worked hard to get.

It's a very hard thing to get rejected.

It's a very hard thing to get sick and not be able to get well.

It's a very hard thing to be hated for being a Christian.

It was a very hard thing for Jesus Christ to live in this world among sinners.

It was very hard for Jesus Christ to be in the wilderness for 40 days and 40 nights without any food to eat.

It was very hard for Jesus Christ to suffer on the cross for our sins.

The Chickens and the Eagle

There was an eagle raised in a chicken coop.

The eagle didn't know he could fly because he'd never seen the chickens fly.

One day, he flapped his wings and lifted himself up off the ground.

It felt so good to him to flap his wings and spread them wide.

He began to realize that he was different from the chickens, so the eagle flapped his wings more and more and lifted himself up off the ground.

One day, the eagle looked at the chickens and then looked up in the sky.

He had to decide whether to stay on the ground or flap his wings and fly out of the chicken coop.

The eagle saw the chickens running around on the ground and the eagle decided he'd had enough of that, so he flew out of the chicken coop.

When we get enough of the devil's lies, we must fly to the truth of God's holy word because that is a great place for an eagle Christian to make his or her nest.

Peace of Mind

Having peace of mind is doing the Lord's holy will.

There is no peace of mind in doing our own will.

Doing our own will can sooner or later cause trouble in our minds.

Having peace of mind is from the Lord, who we need to keep our minds focused on every day.

The devil loves to trouble our minds with this world's temporary things that have no peace to give us.

We live in an uncertain world where anything bad can happen at any time of the day and night.

There is no peace in the uncertain things in this troubled world.

Only the Lord can give us peace of mind for loving Him and keeping His Commandments.

Peace of mind from the Lord is a big threat to the devil, who loves to cause chaos in our lives that would be troublesome without the Lord's peace.

Yesterday, Today and Tomorrow

We had to get through yesterday to get to today.

It was not easy for many people to get through yesterday because it was not a good day for them.

It's truly the Lord who got you and me through yesterday so that we could see today.

Many people died yesterday and won't see today.

We must get through today to see tomorrow.

We know what yesterday brought us, but we don't know what today will bring us.

Today will bring many people sickness and death.

Today will bring many people success.

Today will bring many people some good things in their lives.

Today will bring many people some doubt.

Today will bring many people some depression.

We must get through today to see tomorrow.

You and I can only pray and hope that we will be among those people who will see tomorrow come.

If we see tomorrow, we can surely thank the Lord for blessing us with another day.

The Lord got us through yesterday, that now seems like a dream that fades away for many people who had a hard day yesterday.

Many people didn't know if they would make it through yesterday and they may have believed that they would breathe their last breath.

Many people didn't make it through yesterday and they did breathe their last breath and will not see today.

Today can't promise us that we will see tomorrow, and today will be the last day for many people who will die and not see tomorrow.

You and I can only pray that we won't die today and so that we'll see tomorrow like many other people because tomorrow is meant to be for many to live for Jesus Christ, who gives people a chance to live to see today and tomorrow.

Yesterday, today and tomorrow depend on the Lord to give you and me life to live to do His holy will, which is meant for us to do yesterday, today and tomorrow here on earth where our days are numbered to be short to God.

Yesterday was a great day for many people.

Yesterday was a terrible day for many people.

Yesterday was an uncertain day for many people.

Yesterday was a good day for many people.

Yesterday was a painful day for many people.

Yesterday was a blessed day for many people.

Yesterday was a hopeful day for many people.

Yesterday was the last day to live for many people.

We had to make it through yesterday to see today, and we can only hope and pray that today won't be like yesterday.

Today will be a joyful day for many people.

Today will be a great day for many people.

Today will be a prosperous day for many people.

Today will be a sad day for many people.

Today will be a stressful day too many people.

We must live through today to see tomorrow.

If we live through today, it is because of God's mercy and grace upon us.

Many people will live tomorrow because of God's mercy and grace.

You and I can only pray and hope that we will live tomorrow, but only God can promise that to us.

Yesterday, today and tomorrow is limited to us compared to the Ancient of Days who is God who lives forever and ever beyond our yesterday, today and tomorrow.

Our days are short under the sun, but the Ancient of Days who is God is eternal and will never end beyond yesterday, today and tomorrow that covers over you and me like a rooftop that has a water leak.

The leak will get worse and worse if we don't get it fixed.

Yesterday, today and tomorrow can only be fixed by God, who will fix it when He sends His Son, Jesus Christ, back to this world again to give eternal life to all who are saved in Him.

Yesterday, today and tomorrow will not exist in the eternal life that is all present in God and we will have no days that are numbered when we make it to heaven.

When the Lord Tells Us to Do Something

When the Lord tells us to do something, we must do it.

The Lord will never tell us to do something bad.

When the Lord tells us to do something, it is always a good thing to do.

There are people who do evil things and they believe that the Lord tells them to do those evil things.

The Lord will never tell anyone to do something evil.

When the Lord tells us to do something, it's always for our good and for the good of others.

There are people who will say that the Lord told them to do something wrong, when it was surely the devil who told them to do that wrong thing.

There is no evil thing in the Lord who is good all the time.

The Lord doesn't tempt us to do evil.

It's the devil who tempts us to do evil things.

When the Lord tells us to do something, we will surely be blessed.

When the Lord tells us to do something, nothing will go wrong.

The Lord will never tell us to do something that we can't do.

The devil will tell us to do something that we can't do and make us look bad.

If you know that you can't walk on water, the devil will tell you that you can walk on water.

If you know that you can't walk barefoot on hot coals, the devil will tell you that you can walk barefoot on hot coals.

If you know that you can't walk towards a poisonous snake without getting bit, the devil will tell you that you can walk towards a poisonous snake without getting bit.

The Lord will never tell you and me to do something that we can't do.

The Lord will not tell you to fly a plane when you know that you can't fly a plane.

The Lord will not tell you to swim in the ocean when you know that you can't swim.

The Lord will not tell you to drive a tractor trailer truck when you know that you can't drive a tractor trailer truck.

When the Lord tells us to do something, He knows that we can do it, even if we don't know that we can do it.

If the Lord tells us to do it, we should know that we can.

The Human Heart

The human heart has caused global warming.

The human heart of greedy men has built factories all around the world.

These factories produce a lot of smoke, rising way up in the sky and wearing out the ozone layers that protect us from the dangerous rays of the sun.

The ozone layers are very thin because of the hearts of greedy men who treat money as their god.

The heat from the sun warms up the ocean waters and stirs up hurricanes that can destroy a lot of things on the dry land when the hurricanes surely touch down.

The human heart has caused many diseases to spread all around the world.

The human heart has caused viruses to spread all around the world.

The human heart has caused so much death all around the world.

The human heart is so messed up to God, and a human heart has no power over God to make Him change His holy word.

The human heart can't cause God to lie.

The human heart can't cause God to fail.

The human heart has lied.

The human heart has failed.

The human heart is a global problem every day that God's Son, Jesus Christ, has already solved.

He solved it by giving up His life on the cross to save us from being lost in our sins that are within our human heart.

Jesus is above the human heart and will not condemn the human heart that condemns Him with its sins.

Only Jesus can save the human heart because He always knows how to reach out to the human heart and get it to accept Him with Joy or reject Him with no excuses or explanations that won't make any good sense.

No Baby is Born to Hate

No baby is born to hate — a baby has to be taught to hate.

No baby is born to hate — a baby has to be raised up to hate.

No baby can choose to hate, because a baby can't make any choices for oneself.

A baby doesn't know right from wrong, but mature people do.

There are many teenagers who are at a mature age and know right from wrong.

We are who we are taught to be, whether what we're taught is good or bad.

When we are at a mature age, we can choose to do either good or evil to each other.

A baby has no sins to confess and repent to God.

A mature-age man, woman, boy and girl has sins to confess and repent unto God.

A baby can't feel any hate, but a mature person can feel hate and can choose not to hate.

No baby is born to hate anyone, but a baby can grow up to hate because a baby learns hate from the environment a baby grows up in.

There is a spiritual birth that God gives to everyone so that we can be a spiritual baby that grows up to love everyone.

God's spiritual environment will never have a bad effect on spiritual babies who grow up spiritually and who God loves every day.

If a baby is not born to hate, then what about a spiritual babe who can be at a mature age where he or she can choose to love God and his or her neighbors every day.

A baby is pure and innocent to God, who doesn't hold a baby accountable for its sins.

A spiritual baby is pure and innocent to God, who will hold the spiritual adult accountable for living right in Him to set an example for the spiritual babies.

No physical baby is born to hate anyone, but a baby can be influenced to love or hate.

When you and I were babies, we didn't know love or hate but we were influenced by the love and hate of mature people.

No baby knows love or hate, but a baby can be influenced as it grows up and matures, to love or hate.

On the TV of Life

You and I are watched every day and every night on the TV of life.

The holy angels are watching our every move.

They're watching what we say, whether they are good words or bad words.

They are watching what we do, whether we are doing good deeds or bad deeds.

The fallen angels are watching you and me to try and tempt us to sin against God.

The TV of life is for the unseen to watch.

You and I are seen in the eyes of the unseen.

The TV of life is for the unseen to watch you and me, who are seen in the eyes of the unseen.

You and I can watch one another, and may not see the real you and me because we can disguise ourselves by wearing a spiritual mask.

The angels in heaven see our true condition.

The fallen angels see our true condition.

Most of all, God in heaven sees our true condition.

You and I can play act with one another, but we can't play act with the angels and God.

The TV we watch in this world can't compare to the TV of life that shows everyone's words and deeds to the angels and, most of all, to God.

God and the angels will not miss out on anything that we say and do in this life.

The TV that we watch can't show us everyone in this world.

What it shows can be fleeting and may never be shown again.

You and I and all of the world will never go off of God's TV screen.

Every living soul is watched by God and the angels, every day and every night.

God is not only watching, but He will also direct our lives if we love and obey Him every day.

The TV of life that we watch has directors for every show.

Those directors are not perfect to direct every TV show and earn a good rating.

On the TV of life, God can only give you and me a good rating.

He knows our motives and intentions to be true or false.

We can't play act with God the father, the Son and the Holy Spirit, or even the heavenly Angels and fallen Angels on the TV of life.

They are watching everything that we say and do.

Our souls are so naked to the unseen on the TV of life.

We can be saved in Jesus Christ, who covers over our naked soul in His precious blood that the unseen can't uncover.

The Righteous Will Barely Be Saved

If the righteous will barely be saved, then there is no way possible for a wicked person to be saved and go to heaven.

The fallen angels were not spared to live in heaven after they rebelled against God.

The Bible says that if we believe in Jesus Christ, we shall be saved.

It doesn't mean that once we are saved we are always saved.

We can only be saved in Jesus one day at a time.

Many people were once saved in Jesus and then they turned their backs on Him and strayed away.

How can anyone be saved in Jesus Christ and live in sin?

How can anyone be saved in Jesus while living in adultery?

How can anyone be saved in Jesus while telling lies?

How can anyone be saved in Jesus while fornicating?

How can anyone be saved in Jesus while stealing?

How can anyone be saved in Jesus while killing?

How can anyone be saved in Jesus while disobeying their parents?

We can't be saved in Jesus if we are gossiping.

We can't be saved in Jesus if we are greedy for worldly gain.

We can't be saved in Jesus if we believe that we are self-made.

We can't be saved in Jesus if we are proud and arrogant.

The righteous will barely be saved like the Bible says.

Jesus will save us, if we confess and repent and turn away from living in our sins.

God's goodness leads us to repent, but everybody will not repent and be saved in Jesus Christ.

It's easy to be saved in Jesus Christ, if we believe in Jesus Christ.

Believing in Jesus Christ is to love Him and keep His Commandments.

If the righteous will barely be saved in Jesus Christ, then there's no way possible for people who are not living right to be saved and go to heaven one day.

Righteous people are people who live right unto the Lord every day.

Don't be deceived — no unrighteous person will go to heaven.

We can't be saved in Jesus if we are living an unrighteous life.

If the righteous will barely be saved, then you and I should surely want to be saved because we love Jesus and not because we are afraid of being lost.

The righteous will barely be saved, even though many Christians live their lives like it's easy to be a Christian all the time.

There are people in the Bible who disobeyed the Lord on their Christian journey, even though they were very sincere about the Lord, they had fallen short of His glory.

This comes to show and tell us that the righteous will barely be saved.

There is no way possible for an unrepentant soul to be saved and go to heaven if the righteous will barely be saved and go to heaven.

The fallen angels refused to repent of their sins, and they fell from heaven.

Jesus loves us all and He gave up His life on the cross and rose from the grave to save us all.

It's easy for Jesus to save us if we believe in Him, even though the righteous will barely be saved and go to heaven.

This comes to show that only a few will enter into heaven when Jesus Christ comes back again.

Even though those going to heaven will be a number that no man can count, it will only be a few compared to all the people who ever lived in this world from the beginning of this world to the end of this word.

The righteous will barely be saved, and hopefully you and I will be in the few who will be made like the countless angels who number so much more than all who ever lived on this Earth and all who are living in these last days on Earth.

In Every Church

There are some true Christians in every church, even though every church doesn't preach and teach all the truth in the Bible.

There are some true Christians in every church where they love Jesus.

There are some true Christians in every church where they obey Jesus.

There are some true Christians in every church where they love all of their brothers and sisters in the Lord Jesus Christ.

There are some true Christians in every church and they put all of their trust in Jesus Christ to work things out for them.

There are some true Christians in every church where they use their spiritual gifts to build up the church.

There are some true Christians in every church where they live a holy life inside and outside the church.

There are some true Christians in every church where they live a righteous life inside and outside the church.

There are some true Christians in every church where they give all the praise and glory to the Lord Jesus Christ.

There are some true Christians in every church where they live right by example to all the world.

There are some true Christians in every church where they worship the Lord in spirit and truth.

There are some true Christians in every church even though they don't keep the holy Sabbath day of rest on the seventh day of the week.

There are some true Christians in every church where they live right like the right they know about the Lord Jesus Christ.

There are some true Christians in every church that God will judge.

There are some true Christians in every church where they please the Lord and not the world.

There are some true Christians in every church where they will go through trials for Jesus' holy name sake.

There are some true Christians in every church where they sincerely pray unto the Lord with a selfless heart.

There are some true Christians in every church where they are humble before the Lord.

There are some true Christians in every church where they are saved in Jesus Christ.

There are some true Christians in every church where they will go back to heaven with Jesus Christ when He comes back again.

There are some true Christians in every church where they are filled with the Holy Spirit.

There are some true Christians in every church, even though every church doesn't have a large congregation.

There are some true Christians in every church where they give testimonies about Jesus Christ.

A Woman Can

A woman can look so beautiful.

A woman can have the most beautiful smile.

A woman can cause a man to be successful.

A woman can make a weak man strong.

A woman can do almost anything that a man can do.

A woman can do some things that a man can't do.

A woman can take good care of her children without a man.

A woman can be very interesting to talk to.

A woman can be good to be around.

A woman can be very brilliant.

A woman can be a genius.

A woman can change a man for the better.

A woman can fight like a man.

A woman can love more deeply than a man.

A woman can cause a man to feel on top of the world.

A woman can be strong when the going gets tough.

A woman can dress up to get a lot of attention.

A woman can build a man up when he has been torn down.

A woman can encourage her children to do great things.

A woman can be a better communicator than a man.

A woman can have more feelings than a man.

A woman can sense things better than a man.

A woman is the greatest gift from God for a man to not deny.

A woman can get a man's attention on his worst day.

A woman can cause a man to go the extra mile.

A woman can cause a strong man to become weak.

A woman can cause a man to behave much better.

A woman can cause a man to dress better.

A woman can cause a man to straighten up and do right.

A woman can be a trophy to a man.

A woman can be so wonderful to love.

A woman can be so captivating to a man.

A woman can be so careful to reject a man she is not interested in.

A woman can be very clever to get what she wants from a man.

A woman can be more giving than a man.

A woman can be more forgiving than a man.

A woman can be more trustworthy than a man.

A woman can be more cheerful than a man.

A woman can love the Lord more than a man.

A woman can get up and go more than a man.

A woman can have more faith in the Lord than a man.

A woman can obey the Lord more than a man.

A woman can have more compassion than a man.

A woman can have more heart than a man.

A woman can work harder than a man.

A woman can be more educated than a man.

A woman can have better understanding than a man.

A woman can see things that a man can't see.

A woman can be more careful than a man.

A woman can be more successful than a man.

A woman can figure out things that a man can't figure out.

A woman can be more helpful than a man.

A woman can be more hopeful than a man.

When God created a woman for a man, it was no mistake.

Sin entered into this world through a man and not through a woman.

Sin entered into this world through a man who ate the forbidden fruit.

A man can't blame a woman for his own actions.

Adam and Eve's eyes were opened to sin right after Adam bit into the forbidden fruit.

We men can't live in this world without women.

We men would die out and have no existence without women giving birth to us human beings.

God said that it is not good for man to be alone.

God created a woman to give birth, and no man can do that.

This comes to show that a woman can do a miraculous, wonderful and profound thing that no man can do.

A woman can help a man to be transparent.

A woman can help a man to give his heart to the Lord.

A woman can be a man's best friend.

A woman can be everything to a man.

A woman can hurt a man's pride.

A woman can cause a man to feel like a king.

A woman can cause a man to feel very important.

A woman can cause a man to feel like nothing.

A woman can be so good to a man.

A woman can cause a man to feel powerful.

A woman can be very helpful to a man.

A woman can help a man to come back to the Lord.

A woman can look very desirable to a man.

A woman can be like a dream to a man.

A woman can cause a man to love her more than anything in this world.

A woman can be very powerful and do great things.

A woman can cause a man to do anything for her.

A woman can be who God requires her to be.

A woman can be God's wonderful friend.

A woman can be beautiful on the outside and on the inside.

Mr. Selfishness and Mr. Repent

One day, Mr. Selfishness and Mr. Repent met up with each other on the borderline of Heaven and Hell.

They both had been waiting for this moment to face each other so they could clear up their differences.

When they met up with each other, Mr. Selfishness said to Mr. Repent, "I am not going to repent unto Jesus, because I am perfect in my own eyes. I see that I can do nothing wrong."

Mr. Repent responded to Mr. Selfishness saying, "Your selfish attitude toward Jesus means there is no place in heaven for you to spread your self-centered words."

Mr. Repent continued, saying to Mr. Selfishness, "Repenting is the only way for you to come to Jesus. Give your heart to Him before it's too late for you."

Mr. Selfishness refused to believe what Mr. Repent said to him, so he crossed over the border into hell.

When Mr. Selfishness entered hell, he realized that Mr. Repent had been so right about everything and that you must repent unto Jesus Christ to cross over the border into heaven.

He realized that only those who have repented of their sins are saved in Jesus Christ, who created heaven and hell.

Jesus created heaven, where Mr. Repent will go to one day, and Jesus created hell, where Mr. Selfishness will stay because he refused to repent of his sins unto Jesus Christ.

A New Day and a New Start

A new day and a new start to love the Lord.

A new day and a new start to obey the Lord.

A new day and a new start to pray to the Lord.

A new day and a new start to read the Bible.

A new day and a new start to believe in the Lord.

A new day and a new start to trust the Lord.

A new day and a new start to depend on the Lord.

A new day and a new start to have hope in the Lord.

A new day and a new start to be a witness of the Lord.

A new day and a new start to live unto the Lord.

A new day and a new start to talk about the Lord.

A new day and a new start to give all the glory and praise to the Lord.

A new day and a new start to have a relationship with the Lord.

A new day and a new start to choose the Lord.

A new day and a new start to have faith in the Lord.

A new day and a new start to give our hearts to the Lord.

A new day and a new start to keep our minds on the Lord.

A new day and a new start to give our problems to the Lord.

A new day and a new start to give our all to the Lord.

A new day and a new start to listen to the Lord.

A new day and a new start to work for the Lord.

A new day and a new start to uplift the Lord.

A new day and a new start to not deny the Lord Jesus Christ.

The Storm that Woke Jesus Up

The disciples of Jesus got caught up in a storm with heavy falling rain and strong winds that alarmed them and make them afraid of being harmed by the storm that looked so mean to them.

Jesus Christ, the Lord, calmed down the storm, even though it didn't wake Him as He slept on His pillow down in the ship that was being tossed and whipped by the heavy rainfall and strong winds that stirred up the depts of the sea.

The tossing sea didn't wake Jesus Christ, because He walks on the storms of our lives and calms them down for you and me so we can walk on His holy ground and walk on the rugged waves of our persecutions for Jesus' holy name sake.

Jesus' disciples had to do this to be fishers of men and hook lost souls on Jesus so He could save them from being lost in sin.

Jesus' disciples committed sins against Him because they were afraid of the storm, so Jesus used it to show them that they had no faith in Him on the ship.

You and I need to remember this lesson when the storms of life rock our ships.

The storm that woke Jesus up was His disciples on the ship.

My Reward

You can cheat me and you can rob me and you can hate me and you can lie on me, but you can't take my reward that will be my gift from Jesus Christ, my God, who's coming back again to give me my reward in the end.

You, too, will answer to Jesus Christ for the way you live your life here on earth.

You can judge me, think bad about me and sink me down in your quicksand, but Jesus can raise me up in your eyes that can't see my reward that God has for me.

You can knock me down and kill me, but you cannot take my heavenly reward because it's locked around my soul and you have no key to unlock it.

Down to my last second to live on my biological time clock, God's time is always on time to let you and me know that He's in charge under the sun that shines up on the righteous and the wicked, receiving their just rewards from God.

Is Jesus a God?

For in the eighth chapter and fifty-eighth verse of John, Jesus said, "Before Abraham was, I am."

The Jews got worse than what they were before against Jesus Christ, the Lord, who looks to be equal with God, the Father.

In the third chapter and fourteenth verse of Exodus, where God spoke the words to Moses, saying, *"I am that I am,"* and Moses surely heard those words.

Is our Lord Jesus a God?

Read the fourteenth chapter and tenth verse of Romans, where Jesus is surely meant to be the only judge who will judge you and me and all men who God will judge.

In the fiftieth chapter and sixth verse of Psalms, the psalmist clearly states that God is the judge Himself, so it must be true that Jesus is equal with God, for no one else can say, "I and my Father are One."

The Jews tried to take Jesus' life after He claimed Himself to be One with God.

No man will fully understand that Jesus Christ is a God who was made flesh and became a man in outward appearance, while being God wrapped up in flesh without sin.

In the Lord's Hospital

I dreamed that I was walking through a hospital where I saw many patients lying down on their beds here and there.

I walked past some nurses in their blue and pure white uniforms.

As I walked so softly under the bright ceiling lights, I directed my footsteps down the hospital corridors.

My walk took me to some rooms where I saw no doors, so I kept on walking down the hospital hallways.

I gently walked by some nurses and I looked into their big, bright eyes.

There was a nurse who gave me a big, beautiful smile, looking brighter than her pure white uniform.

For a while I felt the power of her love as she gently walked away from me.

I followed behind her until she walked down another hallway where I could barely see her.

She disappeared into an empty room without a door for her to close behind her.

Oh, I wanted to stay close behind her as the scene changed and led me down another hallway in the hospital.

There, I saw some more patients lying down on their pure white beds as though they were dead.

They were wrapped up in pure white sheets from their heads to their feet.

I softly walked away from their beds and walked up to some men sitting down on a sofa.

One man was ready to talk to me, and he said, "You look small but you are heavy."

As we talked back and forth to each other, the man caused me to feel so free and I said, "This is one of the best hospitals I've ever seen."

Then, I woke up and realized it was only a dream.

I realized my dream was telling me how heavy my burden was and then it was lifted off of me in the Lord's hospital where I can always go to get spiritually healed in Jesus Christ, who is the best doctor I can always go to and get spiritually healed.

I am My Mountain to Climb

I am my mountain to climb day by day.

I, alone, must climb my way up the mountain.

I truly see me needing to always climb my mountain to get to Jesus Christ, the holy and precious Lamb of God sitting on top of my mountain.

I have tried to climb to the top of me and failed because I didn't choose Jesus over me because I just knew I could climb my mountain on my own.

As I fell down and broke my spiritual bones, Jesus healed me when I accepted Him as the Lord and Savior of my life.

From the bottom to the top of my mountain, I am my mountain to climb because no one can stop me but me and only Jesus can set me free from falling off the mountain of me.

I must keep my eyes on Jesus to see Him waving my freedom flag in heaven non-stop to save my soul in His holy name.

I am my mountain to climb but I must give all the glory to Jesus, my Lord God, I am that I am.

High above, I am my mountain to climb to a new creature in Jesus Christ.

It's Like Trying to Put Ourselves Above God

If we don't forgive others for doing us wrong, it's like trying to put ourselves above God who will forgive us of our sins if we confess and repent of our sins.

What if God didn't forgive us when we did God wrong in ways that we didn't realize?

We would be better off never being born if God didn't forgive us of our sins.

Who are we to believe that we are too good to not forgive others, who God will forgive if they confess and repent of their sins?

No matter what wrong thing someone does to us, God will sooner or later get vengeance that can surely cause that someone to straighten up and do right by Him.

If you and I seek revenge when someone does us wrong, it's like trying to put ourselves above God, whose vengeance is always good to save a soul from being lost, when our vengeance can surely cause a soul to be more lost in sin.

We know that it is not easy to forgive when someone does us wrong, but who are we to believe that we are better than those who hurt us?

We hurt God if we don't forgive others who He also loves and gave His son, Jesus Christ, to save them from their sins.

It's like trying to put ourselves above God if we don't forgive someone for doing us wrong.

That someone may make it to heaven someday, but we will go to hell for having an unforgiving heart that displeases God.

If you and I don't forgive someone for doing us wrong, it won't stop God from forgiving him or her because they may not know that they have done us wrong.

It's like trying to put ourselves above God if we hold onto grudges and don't forgive others.

You and I do God wrong every day in some kind of way, unseen or seen, and God has every right to not forgive us for this.

But God is forevermore better than us.

Forgiving others will set us free from hurting people and the wrong they do us won't have a lasting bad effect on us.

Who are we to not forgive oneself who God will forgive because God loves us even if we don't love ourselves.

Are Like Twin Brothers

The truth and a lie are like twin brothers who look so much alike.

Many people will believe the truth to be a lie.

Many people will believe a lie to be the truth.

A lie can sound so much like the truth.

A lie loves to imitate the truth, but the truth will never imitate a lie.

The truth and a lie are like twin brothers who can talk so much alike.

You can tell many people the truth, but they may believe it to be a lie.

You can tell many people a lie, and they may believe it to be the truth.

The truth and a lie are so close together that you can't always tell them apart.

The best way that you and I can know the difference between the truth and a lie is to read God's holy word, because that is all truth.

The truth and lie are like twin brothers who can dress alike so that you and I cannot tell them apart from each other.

The truth and a lie can be so much alike because the truth can cause us to feel good just like a lie can cause us to feel good.

The truth will look like a lie to many people, and a lie will look like the truth to many people.

In the garden of Eden, the devil's lies seemed like the truth.

Jesus Christ was the living truth in the presence of the Pharisees, who believe that Jesus was a liar when He claimed to be the son of God in their presence.

The truth and a lie are like twin brothers who can talk so much alike, but the truth's breath will never smell bad.

The truth and a lie can act so much alike, but the truth will never pretend.

Even a liar can pass a lie detector test and look like he or she is telling the truth, but God sees every lie being far from the truth.

The truth and a lie are like twin brothers, and only God will always know the difference.

When God Closes His Grace on this World

When God closes His grace on this world, He will remove His holy spirit from this world.

When God removes His holy spirit from this world, the devil will have complete control over all who are not saved in Jesus Christ.

All who are lost in their sins will have only evil thoughts, evil words and do evil deeds because they will be controlled by the devil.

When God closes His grace on this world, there won't be any more chances for anyone to choose to love and obey Jesus Christ.

The devil will have complete control over all who are lost in their sins.

There will be evil in this world like there has never been before the beginning of time.

Constantly, evil will be in the minds and hearts of everyone who is not saved in Jesus Christ.

The righteous living will not be so sure that they are saved in Jesus Christ when God removes His holy spirit from this world.

God will seal His righteous living children, even if many of them will be put to death by the wicked.

Today is the time for you and me to believe in Jesus Christ and love and obey Him, because God may close His grace on this world today.

No one knows the hour or the day when Jesus Christ is coming back again, because before He comes back, God will close His grace on this world.

Today, God is giving us borrowed time to get ourselves right with Him before it's too late.

The devil knows that his time is very short and running out, so he is trying his best to cause as many souls as he can to be lost in sin.

Jesus is very serious about saving our souls from being lost.

You and I need to be very serious about loving Jesus with all of our mind, heart, soul and strength.

When God closes His grace on all the world, God will remove His holy spirit from this world and all hell will break loose on all the souls who are lost in sin.

There will be terrible times like we've never seen in this world.

We who are alive have a chance to run to Jesus today and cross over the finish line of salvation in Him.

Tomorrow may be too late to be saved in God's grace, so today we need to be spiritually awake and see that God is moving His holy spirit from this world.

If we believe that this world is really bad today, then we haven't seen the worst that will come upon us when God closes His grace on this world.

Do You Believe?

Do you believe your thoughts?

Do you believe your words?

Do you believe your actions?

Do you believe your dreams?

Do you believe your appetite?

Do you believe your feelings?

Do you believe you?

Do you believe your eyes?

Do you believe your talents?

Do you believe your spiritual gifts?

Do you believe the bible?

Do you believe in Jesus Christ?

Do you believe truth?

Do you know what to believe?

Do you believe what you sing?

Do you believe what you read?

Believing is very powerful.

Believing is very real.

Believing is very effective, whether you believe you are right or wrong.

Believing in Jesus Christ is an eternal belief that will surely guarantee you and me to one day enter into heaven with Jesus when he comes back again.

Do you believe your ears?

Do you believe your nose?

Do you believe your body?

Believing can be an abundance of life in Jesus Christ.

Believing can be a short life for believing the devil's lies.

Believing is the key to lock the door of your destiny, because believing is the reason for the choice that you make.

Believing is the strong backbone of every choice that you make.

Do you believe your heart?

Do you believe your life?

Do you believe your health?

Do you believe your tradition?

Lucifer had believed that he could take God's place on God's holy throne, causing him to rebel against God.

You and me can believe a lot of things, and every day we believe to live if we are not ill in our mind to kill oneself.

You and me will believe something before we ever make a choice.

The choice that we make will surely affirm what you and me believe.

Do you believe that you exist to love and obey Jesus Christ?

Do you believe that you will become like who you believe in?

Do you believe that Jesus is above whoever and whatever you believe?

If you and me believe in Jesus Christ, we will be like Jesus Christ in our daily living.

If you and me believe the devil, we will be like the devil.

Do you believe that your choices in life are the results of what you believe in from day to day?

Believing is before any action that is seen because what you and me believe, we will do, whether it's good or bad.

If you believe that you must eat food to live, you will eat food to live.

If you believe that you must drink water to live, you will drink water to live.

Believing is what God has given to you and me to use for our good of believing in His Son Jesus Christ who the demons believe with fear and tremble whenever you and I call on the name of the Lord Jesus Christ.

Do you believe what is right and what is wrong that you will choose to think, say and do from the results of whoever you believe and whatever you believe from day to day.

Do you believe your knowledge?

Do you believe your intelligence?

Do you believe your common sense?

Do you believe that God gave you the freedom to believe whatever that you want to believe?

Do you believe that a robot will do something different from what you programmed it to do?

God didn't create you and me to be a robot that can't believe anyone or anything but will only do what you program it to do.

Do you believe that Jesus Christ is the son of God and the life eternal?

Do you believe that Jesus gave up his life on the cross for your sins?

Do you believe that Jesus got the victory over death and the grave?

Do you believe that if you believe in Jesus Christ he will save you from your sins?

God gave you and me the freedom to live by who we believe and what we believe.

Who we believe and what we believe can never ascent above God the Father, God the Son and God the Holy Spirit who is the origin of the bible that you and me can always believe and live by with no regrets to denounce the highest belief that is rooted and grounded in Jesus Christ.

Do you believe your trials?

Do you believe your ups and downs in life?

Do you believe your comings and goings?

Do you believe your testimonies?

Do you believe your education?

Do you believe your mistakes?

Do you believe your motives?

Do you believe your intentions?

Do you believe your purpose?

Do you believe your choices that are the results of your beliefs day after day.

Do you believe that Jesus Christ is your only salvation?

Do you believe that Jesus Christ is your only living hope?

Do you believe that Jesus Christ is your only undying love?

Do you believe that Jesus Christ is who you can always trust to love you, even if you don't love him?

Do you believe that Jesus Christ is your best friend?

Do you believe that Jesus Christ will never leave you or forsake you?

Do you believe that Jesus Christ won't give up on you, even if you give up on yourself?

Believing is in its highest and greatest place of existence in this world, if we believe in Jesus Christ who has overcome every false belief in this world.

Believing in anyone else or anything else more than believing in Jesus will be an eternal regret for us to miss out on heaven where angels believe in Jesus Christ to be the son of God and the creator of all things.

Do you believe your theories?

Do you believe your plans?

Do you believe your pretense?

Do you believe your hypothesis?

Do you believe your opinions?

Do you believe your prejudice?

Do you believe your freedom?

Do you believe your bondage?

Do you believe your love?

Do you believe your hatred?

Do you believe your difference?

Do you believe your fear?

Do you believe your courage?

Do you believe your existence in life?

Do you believe your victories?

Do you believe your defeats?

Do you believe what you have been through in your life?

Do you believe what you are going through in your life?

Do you believe your wealth?

Do you believe your poverty?

Do you believe your blessings?

Do you believe your curse?

Do you believe your destiny?

If you and I believe in ourselves or anyone else and anything else more than we believe in Jesus Christ, we are doomed to be like the wind that blows in different directions, for only Jesus to always know where we will blow to in our wayward beliefs.

Believing can be a hurricane down in the soul.

Believing can be an earthquake down in the soul.

Believing can be a wildfire down in the soul.

Believing can be a tornado down in the soul.

Believing can be a volcano to erupt down in the soul.

Believing can be a flood down in the soul.

Believing can be a train wreck down in the soul.

Believing can be a tidal wave down in the soul.

Believing can be a piled-up car wreck down in the soul.

Believing can surely be a bad thing if you and me don't believe in Jesus Christ who is the fulfillment of the bible that we can always believe to be the truth about Jesus who the devil and his fallen angels believe to come back again on the clouds of glory.

The devil believes that he can run throughout the earth to devourer whoever that he can to cause them to be lost in their sins and miss out on heaven.

Do you believe that you can get your life right with Jesus before it's too late?

Believing is the sunshine down in your soul for believing in Jesus Christ.

Believing is a peaceful river down in your soul for believing is Jesus Christ.

Believing is joy down in your soul for believing in Jesus Christ.

Believing is paradise down in your soul for believing in Jesus Christ.

Believing is a lily in the valley down in your soul for believing in Jesus Christ.

Believing is a beautiful red rose down in your soul for believing in Jesus Christ.

Believing is a beautiful garden down in your soul for believing in Jesus Christ.

Believing is a high mountain down in your soul for believing in Jesus Christ.

Believing is a treasure chest down in your soul for believing in Jesus Christ.

Believing is a gold mine down in your soul for believing in Jesus Christ.

Believing is great wealth down in your soul for believing in Jesus Christ.

Believing is beauty down in your soul for believing in Jesus Christ.

Believing is eternal life down in your soul for believing in Jesus Christ.

Believing is every good thing down in your soul for believing in Jesus Christ.

You and I can believe in Jesus Christ like it's our last day to live, that can't over-shadow our belief that will be sealed in Jesus in the grave, that Jesus will open up and raise us up in His eternal life for believing in Him.

Death and the grave believe that Jesus has all the power to raise the righteous dead when He comes back again on the clouds of glory.

Do you and I believe in Jesus Christ even more than believing that we can die anytime in the day and night that can't stop Jesus from sealing us in His eternal life if we are saved in Him.

If you believe Jesus Christ, your belief is holy.

If you believe in Jesus Christ, your belief is perfect.

Believing in Jesus Christ will get rid of every unbelief in you and me.

Do you believe that Jesus always knows what is good and best for you?

Do you believe to serve your master, whether it be money, material things, a human being or Jesus Christ?

Do you believe a surprise that is at its best in Jesus Christ who can surprise you and me better than anyone in the world?

Do you believe in luck that has no spiritual things to give to you that only Jesus can do?

Do you believe magic that has no heaven to put you in that only Jesus can do when he comes back again?

Do you believe lies that have no truth that is Jesus Christ who sets you and me free from believing lies?

Do you believe the Church that the devil can go to but Jesus Christ is the head of the church to separate the wheat from the tares, when you and me can pull up a wheat that we may believe to be a tare?

Do you believe your ministry in the church to win souls to Jesus Christ who is the only one who can judge your ministry to be about praising him or praising oneself to want to make oneself look good before others?

Do you believe your beauty that will fade away as you age old?

Believing in Jesus Christ is inner beauty that will not fade away as you age old.

Do you believe in your physical strength that will deteriorate as you age old?

Believing in Jesus Christ is inner strength that will not deteriorate as you age old.

Do you believe your mind that can change at any time?

Believing in Jesus Christ is not judging anyone who Jesus always completely knows to repent or not repent of all of one's sins.

Someone in the church can hold onto a sin for only Jesus to know and judge that someone for having a heart of unbelief in Him.

Holding onto even one unconfessed and unrepentant sin will cause you and me to not believe in Jesus who gave up His life on the cross to save us from all of our sins for us to have no excuse to hold onto even one sin that breaks God's Commandments that are holy, righteous and perfect to show unbelievers that we believe in Jesus Christ.

Do you believe your job that can overwork you and underpay you?

Do you believe your business that can go out of business?

Do you believe your clothes that can fade?

Do you believe your shoes that can wear out?

Do you believe your car that can break down?

Do you believe your government that can shut down?

Do you believe your nation that can go to war?

Do you believe your house that can need repair work?

Do you believe your pets that can give you a big veterinarian bill?

Do you believe your phone that can be corrupted with scammers?

Do you believe your computer that can get a computer virus?

Do you believe social media that can turn against you, if you say something wrong?

Do you believe fame that can turn against you, if you do something wrong?

Do you believe that the bank can protect your money from wire fraud?

Believing in Jesus Christ is surely being wise about what's going on in this world.

Believing in Jesus Christ is spiritual protection being our best protection from the wiles of the devil and his demons and his human agents who is all about causing you and me to not believe in Jesus Christ.

Do you believe your spiritual seeds will grow up into a beautiful spiritual fruit tree on God's holy ground where the Holy Spirit plants your spiritual gifts for you to harvest the field of the world to win souls to Jesus Christ?

God Created us to Socialize

God created us to socialize, and it's mostly women who love to talk.

It's mostly women who can talk to one another with ease.

A lot of women don't have to think about what they will talk about, they just do it with ease.

A lot of us men don't know how to socialize well with one another like women who can talk from sun up to sun down like breathing air in and out of our nostrils.

It's mostly women who have the gift to talk just about anything that they have no problem to talk about on any day.

When I go to church, my church sisters love to socialize and they are so good with doing that, but I have to search for words to say.

The average mother can talk a lot to her children with ease, when the average father will run out of words to say to his children.

A lot of children know that especially their mothers will have a lot of words to say to them when they get into some trouble.

Mostly women and girls are the real talkers every day in the home, on the job, in the church and in this world.

There are men who can talk a lot, but many women will out-number the men when it comes to socializing.

Most of us men can't keep up with the women in talking because the average woman has a mouth that is full of words, even when doing other things while talking.

A lot of us men have a long way to go when it comes to socializing with one another and with women, it's mostly women who can talk all day long and not get tired of talking even to their energetic children who can wear a lot of men down and cause them to run out of words to say.

Jesus' mother must have talked to Jesus more than His earthly father, Joseph.

It's mostly women who will raise up their children with a lot of words to say to them that they will cherish or not cherish for life.

Jesus must have cherished his mother Mary's every word.

The average man cannot out-talk the average woman because God has truly given women the gift to socialize and be the best communicators in this world.

God created us to socialize, but it's mostly women and girls who will usually talk the most every day.

Jesus loves everybody but Jesus probably listens to the prayers of mostly women, more so than the prayers of men.

I believe that women will talk to Jesus more than us men.

Most of us men don't talk to one another.

It's mostly the women who motivate us men to open up and talk about what is on our minds.

When it comes to speaking, most women are better talkers than we men, but the Lord Jesus Christ loves to talk to every man, woman, boy and girl every day that we can listen to Jesus talking to us in love in His holy word.

The Lord also uses many women to get a lot of good things done in this world, where without the socializing of women, most of us men would be at a loss for words to say every day.

As many people do say that behind a great man is a great woman.

I believe that a great woman is the real socializer in the home where her words are more than a few for her husband and children to hear.

God created us to socialize with one another, but mostly women and girls don't easily run out of words to say because talking is one of the greatest gifts from God.

Mr. Rush and Mr. Patient

One day in the morning, Mr. Rush and Mr. Patient met each other for the first time.

They could see how different they were when Mr.

Rush said to Mr. Patient, "I've got to go right now."

Mr. Rush said to Mr. Patient, "I've got to do it right now."

Mr. Rush said to Mr. Patient, "I've got to say it right now."

Mr. Rush said to Mr. Patient, "I've got to leave right now."

Mr. Rush said to Mr. Patient, "I just can't wait on you."

Mr. Patient finally said to Mr. Rush, "You need to take your time when going where you want to go because rushing can cause you to fall off course."

Mr. Patient said to Mr. Rush, "You need to take your time when doing what you want to do because rushing can cause you to do something that you don't intend to do."

Mr. Patient said to Mr. Rush, "You need to take your time when saying what you want to say because rushing can cause you to say what you don't mean to say."

Mr. Patient said to Mr. Rush, "You need to take your time when leaving because rushing to leave can cause you to leave something behind."

Mr. Rush said to Mr. Patient, "I am not like you because I don't take my time; I want to do things right now.

Taking my time is moving too slow for me."

Mr. Patient said to Mr. Rush, "Suppose if Jesus had rushed to come to this world before the fullness of time."

Mr. Patient said to Mr. Rush, "If Jesus had rushed to come to this world to save sinners from being lost, then His mission would not have been accomplished.

"So many people would have been left out of God's saving grace, which is His patience for all sinners to eventually be saved in Jesus Christ.

"God was patient to send His Son, Jesus Christ, into this world while the devil was rushing to cause as many people as he could to be lost in their sins.

The devil is still rushing today to cause you and me to be lost in sin, while God is patient with us all today to confess and repent of our sins and believe in His Son, Jesus Christ, to be saved.

God's patience will run out one day and that is why the devil is in a big rush to cause as many souls as he can to be lost.

The Lord is patient to save as many souls as He can before it is too late and God will close His probation on this world when Jesus stands up and says that it is finished.

When that happens, those who are righteous will be righteous still and those who are filthy with sin will be filthy still."

Mr. Patient said to Mr. Rush, "Be patient and wait on the Lord and good things will come to you."

Many People Love God's Creations

Many people love God's creations but they don't love God.

Many people love the sunshine but they don't love God, who created the sun to shine.

Many people love the full white moonlight but they don't love God, who created the moon that reflects its light onto us.

Many people love the stars that sparkle in the night sky but they don't love God, who created the stars that sparkle in the night sky.

Many people love the mountains but they don't love God, who created the mountains.

Many people love the oceans but they don't love God, who created the oceans.

Many people love the flowers but they don't love God, who created the flowers.

Many people love God's creations, but they don't love God.

Many people love the sky but they don't love God, who created the sky.

Many people love the rain but they don't love God, who created the rain.

Many people love the snow but they don't love God, who created the snow.

Many people love God's creations but they don't love God.

Many people love the trees but they don't love God, who created the trees.

Many people love the grass but they don't love God, who created the grass.

Many people love the dry land but they don't love God, who created the dry land.

Many people love animals but they don't love God who created the animals.

Many people love the birds but they don't love God who created the birds.

Many people love this world but they don't love God who created this world.

Many people love God's creations but they don't love God and don't worship God.

Benefits

There are no good benefits for being a slave for men.

There are good benefits for being a slave for Jesus Christ.

You won't have a peace of mind for being a slave for men.

You will have a peace of mind for being a slave for Jesus Christ.

You won't have any joy for being a slave for men.

You will have joy for being a slave for Jesus Christ.

You won't feel good about being a slave for men.

You will feel good about being a slave for Jesus Christ.

You won't have any freedom for being a slave for men.

You will have freedom for being a slave for Jesus Christ.

There are no good benefits for being a slave for men.

There are good benefits for being a slave for Jesus Christ.

You won't get any love for being a slave for men.

You will receive everlasting love for being a slave for Jesus Christ.

You won't be encouraged for being a slave for men.

You will be encouraged for being a slave for Jesus Christ.

You won't live a good life for being a slave for men.

You will receive an abundance of life for being a slave for Jesus Christ.

There are no good benefits for being a slave for men.

There are eternal good benefits for being a slave for Jesus Christ.

What good benefits would you and I get for being a slave for men?

If anything good comes out of being slave for men, the good is from the Lord Jesus Christ who owns everything.

Ungodly men have put many people into slavery to benefit them in obtaining what the Lord owns.

Your Talents Will

Your talents will lift you up more than they will lift anyone else up.

Your talents will bring out the best in you more than bringing out the best in anyone else.

Your talents will help you more than they will help anyone else.

Your talents will do you more good than they will do anyone else good.

Your talents will build you up more than they will build up anyone else.

Your talents will reassure you more than they will reassure anyone else.

Your talents will give you more joy than they will give joy to anyone else.

Your talents will give you more security than they will give to anyone else.

Your talents will give you more courage than they will give courage to anyone else.

Your talents will give you more peace the they will give peace to anyone else.

Your talents will give you more hope than they will give hope to anyone else.

Your talents are given to you from the Lord so you can glorify His holy name.

Your talents are from the Lord, who knows what talents you are to have.

Your talents are from the Lord, who gives you the talents you need to win souls in His name.

Your talents are from the Lord Jesus Christ, who gives you all the right talents to help you hold onto Him, even if all hell breaks loose in your life.

If you use your talents for the Lord, you won't become burdened.

You can choose to use your talents for the Lord or use your talents for your own selfish desires.

If you use your talents for the Lord, you will fulfill the true purpose in your life which belongs to the Lord.

Your talents can bless other people's lives, but they will bless your life the most, especially if you use your talents to glorify the Lord's holy name.

Education

There are people who love to show off their education.

They will show off by speaking big fancy words that can't be understood by those who are uneducated.

It's a blessing from the Lord to get a good education but don't show off your education by causing uneducated people to feel dumb.

Use your education to bless people by being down to earth and speaking in a simple fashion.

College is not for everybody to go to and get a good education.

A good education is meant to be used to help the poor and needy to better their circumstances, which can't happen when you speak down to them.

Getting a good education is not about speaking big fancy words to make yourself look good, especially before those who are not educated.

Nobody can ever be more educated than Jesus Christ, who spoke in a down to earth way without sin.

Jesus never spoke big fancy words even though He could have done that, because Jesus is the educator of the heavens and other worlds.

Jesus is the educator of educators and no educated person knows how to come down to earth and speak plain and simple words to you and me better than Jesus.

There are people who are so educated that they have a hard time being down to earth and speaking plain and simple words.

The Pharisees and religious leaders could never outsmart Jesus with their limited education that they believed to be superb in their own eyes.

Jesus was all-knowing, and knew what they would say before they spoke one word.

There are people who love to flaunt their education to look so important, especially in the eyes of uneducated people who no one can educate better than Jesus.

Jesus can surely educate simple people with His wisdom so they have good common sense to make good choices every day.

There are some educated fools who make bad choices every day.

Jesus educated us the most through His holy word because there is no higher education above God's holy word for us to live by day after day.

Getting a college education is a good thing, but it does not guarantee to make us wise; there are educated people who do foolish things.

There are people who are very well educated in God's word that has elevated, sharpened, enhanced and enriched their minds for them to do extraordinary things in their lives.

God the Father, the Son and the Holy Spirit educated all eternity for the angels and other worlds to forever know that God is all-wise and all-knowing beyond the limited education of human beings who were born in sin to die and know nothing.

The Lion's Den and Furnace Fire

We true children of God will be thrown into a spiritual lion's den and furnace fire for standing up for Jesus and not bowing down to the golden image of the world.

You and I will be thrown into the lion's den and furnace fire of criticizing words from non-Sabbath keepers who see us keeping the sabbath day holy on the seventh day of the week, which is Saturday and not Sunday.

You and I will be thrown into the lion's den and furnace fire of unbelievers' spiritualism because they believe that they can talk to the dead, but we show them the bible truth about the dead knowing nothing.

We true children of God will stand up for His Son, Jesus Christ, even though we will be thrown into the lion's den and furnace fire of unbelievers' false doctrines because we won't compromise the truth that will keep us rooted and grounded in God's holy word from the book of Genesis to the book of Revelation.

You and I can't be anything less than a true child of God for standing up for Jesus who shut the lions' mouths in the den and made it like a paradise to Daniel.

Jesus was also in the furnace fire and acted like a central cooling air conditioner to the three Hebrew boys.

Daniel and the three Hebrew boys didn't deny the true, living God, even when they faced death.

God didn't allow death to get victory over them.

You and I will be thrown into the lion's den and furnace fire of rejection by unbelievers for speaking the truth of God's holy word in love to them.

We all want to live to see Jesus come back again, but are we willing to be thrown into the lion's den and furnace fire of persecution for standing up for Jesus in this golden image of a sinful world.

If we miss out on heaven when Jesus comes back again, then it comes to show that we bowed down to worship the golden image of false pretense that is also in the church.

Daniel and the three Hebrew boys had nothing but true worship unto the true, living God, while the unbelievers in Babylon were full of false pretense worship which will one day become their lion's den and furnace fire of burning hell after the second resurrection.

I am Only Human

Many people love to say, "I am only human," so they can do what they want to do.

Many people love to say, "I am only human," so they have an excuse to not want to change for the better.

Many people love to say, "I am only human," as if the Lord can't help them to overcome their human problems.

Jesus left all of heaven to become a human being so He could relate to us human beings.

Jesus gave up all of heaven to become a human being without sin to save us human beings from our sins.

You and I can't be more human than Jesus was when He lived here on earth among sinful human beings.

Jesus knows all about being human, and He knows more than you and I will ever know because He was a human being who was tempted by all of the devil's temptations.

You and I will never be tempted by all of the devil's temptations because Jesus made a way for us to escape from the devil's worst temptations that our human lives wouldn't be able to handle.

Many people love to say, "I am only human," as if Jesus was never a human being sent to ease their minds from worrying about things that Jesus can work out and remove like they never existed.

Saying, "I am only human," is disrespecting Jesus, who we have no excuse to doubt because of all the things He can do for us in our distress.

Jesus was human and there is nothing that Jesus didn't go through to give us the strength to overcome our human deficiencies.

You and I can easily say, "I am only human," as if the Lord doesn't know that we have human weaknesses.

292 † Ricky Clemons

We cannot use "I am only human" as an excuse to not put all of our trust in the Lord to be there for us who can't trust our human ways to comfort us.

Jesus can always comfort us in our human misfortunes.

To be Exactly Like You

Would you love for someone to smack their lips at the same time that you smack your lips?

Would you love for someone to talk at the same time that you talk?

Would you love for someone to joke at the same time that you joke?

Would you love for someone to bite their nails at the same time that you bite your nails?

Would you love for someone to be exactly like you?

Would you love for someone to make a mistake at the same time that you make a mistake?

Would you love for someone to dig up their nose at the same time that you dig up your nose?

Would you love for someone to be disappointed at the same time that you are disappointed?

Would you love for someone to fall down at the same time that you fall down?

Would you love for someone to get angry at the same time that you get angry?

Would you love for someone to get choked at the same time that you get choked?

Would you love for someone to spit at the same time that you spit?

Would you love for someone to scratch their head at the same time that you scratch your head?

Would you love for someone to be afraid at the same time that you are afraid?

Would you love for someone to be exactly like you?

Would you love for someone to use the toilet at the same time that you use the toilet?

Would you love for someone's breath to smell exactly the same time as your breath?

Would you love for someone to feel some pain at the same time that you feel pain?

Would you love for someone to think all the same thoughts that you think?

Would you love for someone to say all the same words that you say?

Would you love for someone to feel all the same emotions that you feel?

Would you love for someone to do all the same things that you do?

Would you love for someone to be exactly like you?

No two people are exactly alike because God created everyone to be different with wonderful talents and gifts in the church.

If God had created everybody exactly alike, this world would be so void of being different and no one would make different choices.

Would you love for someone to be exactly like you who is not perfect and has sins to confess and repent unto the Lord Jesus Christ?

Like an Island Sitting All Alone

Our free will choice is like an island sitting all alone because God will not choose for us; we must make a choice all alone.

An island will sit all alone above the deep sea waters every day, just like you and I must make our choices all alone.

I have my mind and you have your mind to think on what choices to make.

I can choose what to say and you can choose what to say, even on the spur of the moment.

I can choose what to do and you can choose what to do, even on the spur of the moment.

God won't interfere with the choices we make all alone just like an island sitting all alone above the ocean waters.

An island will surely stand out all alone day after day that God won't make us choose to love and obey Him.

The devil can't make us choose to do evil on any day that our free will choices are like an island sitting all alone above the deep ocean waters.

No one can make anyone do anything against their free will choice, whether the choices are good choices or bad choices.

We choose to think what we want to think.

We choose to say what we want to say.

We choose to do what we want to do.

Nothing in this world is more free than our free will choices that are so all alone between God and the devil every day.

Our free will choice is like an island sitting all alone by itself while being surrounded by the deep waters, just like good and evil surrounds our free will choices that stand out and above everything in this world.

Our free will choice is like an island sitting all alone by itself.

Our destiny will greatly surround our free will choices every day that an island is sitting all alone above the deep ocean waters.

Also in the Simple Things in Life

Regardless of theologies, Jesus is also in the simple things in life.

Regardless of philosophies, Jesus is also in the simple things in life.

Regardless of religions, Jesus is also in the simple things in life.

Regardless of technologies, Jesus is also in the simple things in life.

Regardless of mysteries, Jesus is also in the simple things in life.

Regardless of education, Jesus is also in the simple things in life.

Regardless of educated guesses, Jesus is also in the simple things in life.

Regardless of phenomenons, Jesus is also in the simple things in life.

Regardless of great wisdom, Jesus is also in the simple things in life.

Regardless of miracles, Jesus is also in the simple things in life.

A simple thing in life can be a smile that Jesus is also in.

A simple thing in life can be a helping hand that Jesus is also in.

A simple thing in life can be being honest that Jesus is also in.

A simple thing in life can be a listening ear that Jesus is also in.

A simple thing in life can be not making the same mistakes that Jesus is also in.

Jesus is also in the simple things in life, regardless of intellectual words.

Jesus is also in the simple things in life, regardless of sophisticated ministries in the church.

A simple thing in life can be giving encouragement that Jesus is also in.

A simple thing in life can be laughter that Jesus is also in.

A simple thing in life can be getting a good night's sleep that Jesus is also in.

Regardless of the complicated things in life, Jesus is also in the simple things in life.

A simple thing in life can be taking good care of yourself that Jesus is also in.

A simple thing in life is being in control of yourself that Jesus is also in.

A simple thing in life is treating people right that Jesus is also in.

A simple thing in life is not forming your own opinion about anyone who only Jesus knows completely.

When Jesus Lived on Earth

When Jesus lived on earth without sin among the people back in the bible days, He knew everything about the future.

Jesus knew everything about what's in this world today, but He didn't speak to the people about it.

If Jesus had talked to the people about airplanes, trucks and cars, the people would not have understood him.

They would've probably believed that Jesus had lost His mind.

When Jesus lived on earth without sin among the people back in the bible days, He knew everything about today's technology and science but He didn't speak about that to the people then because He knew they would not understand him.

The people back in the bible days just didn't realize they were in the presence of a God who knew all the past, all the present and all the future that was and is all about Jesus being in control of all things.

The people back in the bible days didn't know they were in the presence of a God who knew all about the heavens and all about other worlds that He created.

We are no better off than the people back in the bible days because with all of our technology and science today, Jesus is still forevermore advanced in all things that He can do and has done up in heaven and in other worlds.

Jesus is far more advanced in the things we can't see.

When Jesus lived on earth without sin among people who were born in sin, they didn't know they were in the presence of eternal life because it was covered over in flesh and bone to be nailed to the cross and shed blood for the sins of all the world.

We are no better off than the people back in the bible days because we can live our lives like there is no eternal life in Jesus Christ, who we can nail on the cross all over again with disbelief in Him that causes us to live by eyesight and not by faith in Jesus.

Because of Sin

Because of sin, everyone has some kind of mental defect.

Some people have more mental defects than other people.

Because of sin, the richest man and woman can say something foolish and do something foolish.

Because of sin, the most genius man and woman can say something foolish and do something foolish.

Lucifer had a mental defect and believed he could take God's place on His holy throne up in heaven; instead, he was cast out for rebelling against God.

Lucifer caused his own mental defect because he wanted to be God when that was impossible, because God created him.

Because of sin, everyone won't think right all the time.

Because of sin, everyone won't say the right words all the time.

Because of sin, everyone won't do right all the time.

The holiest of men and women will fall short of the glory of God because of having a sinful nature that causes them to sin against God in some kind of seen and unseen way.

Jesus Christ, our Lord and Savior, foreknew that because of sin being in this world He would have to give up His sinless life and die on the cross for our sins and rise from the grave with victory over death.

The blood Jesus shed will cleanse us of our sins if we confess and repent of our sins.

Because of sin, everyone has a flaw to be recognized.

Because of sin, the righteous and the wicked go to the grave, but the righteous dead are saved in Jesus Christ.

Jesus will come back again to raise the righteous dead and give eternal life to the righteous saints, whether they were knowledgeable or not so knowledgeable of God's holy word.

What Can We Call Our Own?

What can we call our own, when tornadoes can take away everything that we have?

What can we call our own, when hurricanes can take away everything that we have?

What can we call our own, when floods can take away everything that we have?

What can we call our own, when earthquakes can take away everything that we have?

What can we call our own, when wars can take away everything that we have?

What can we call our own, when unemployment can take away everything that we have?

What can we call our own, when scammers can take away everything that we have?

What can we call our own, when illness can take away everything that we have?

What can we call our own, when misfortune can take away everything that we have?

What can we call our own, when poverty can take away everything that we have?

What can we call our own, when drugs can take away everything that we have?

What can we call our own, when alcohol can take away everything that we have?

What can we call our own, when God can take away everything that we have?

What can we call our own, when death can take you and me to the grave where we have nothing to own?

Death will own you and me until Jesus comes back again to set us free from death if we are saved in Him.

The only thing that we can truly call our own is our free will choices that no natural disasters, illness, misfortune or poverty can take away from us.

God will not take away our free will choice to choose, even if we lose everything that we have.

Spiritual Pollution

We know that air pollution is bad, but spiritual pollution is much worse in this world.

Spiritual pollution is believing that we are saved through grace and don't have to keep the Commandments of God.

Jesus says, "If you love Me, keep My Commandments."

Spiritual pollution is believing that there is no God, when the bible says that God created the heavens and the earth.

We can look at nature and see that there is a much higher intelligence than human beings.

Spiritual pollution is believing that after we die we go straight to heaven.

The bible says that Jesus Christ is coming back again to raise the righteous dead and change the righteous living from mortal to immortal and take them to heaven.

Hopefully you and I will be in that great number that no man can count.

Spiritual pollution is believing that Jesus Christ was only a prophet, when Jesus is the Son of God.

In the Garden of Eden, Jesus was in the creation of Adam and Eve because God had said, "Let us make them in Our likeness."

Spiritual pollution is believing that Sunday is the holy Sabbath day of rest, when Saturday is actually the holy Sabbath day of rest.

Saturday is the seventh day of the week when God finished all of His works and rested.

The seventh day of the week is Saturday, not Sunday.

Spiritual pollution is believing that we can eat whatever foods we want to eat.

God tells us in the bible not to eat unclean meats, which many people eat today.

Air pollution is bad, but spiritual pollution is much worst and causes our souls to be lost and one day burn up in fire and brimstone.

Debate

The devil loves to debate the bible scriptures to try to make the scriptures what he wants them to be.

The devil loves to misinterpret the scriptures to try to make the bible scriptures look like a lie.

The devil has his human agents who love to debate the bible scriptures and twist them up and turn their truth around to lies.

The devil has his human agents who will give their own interpretations of the bible scriptures because they reject the Holy Spirit who inspired holy men to write the bible scriptures given to them by God.

Debating the bible scriptures is of the devil who twisted God's words up to Eve who the devil lied to in the Garden of Eden.

People who love to debate the bible scriptures are not living by God's holy word because they reject them as truth that will set them free from the devil's lies.

The people who love to debate the bible scriptures will surely reap what they sow and it will show and tell in their lives.

Debating the bible scriptures is a normal thing for many people to do, but it is not normal to God who had given no misinterpretations to his holy men to write the bible scriptures to correct us in our errors.

Can't Take Away

People's criticism can't take away what the Lord has given to you.

People's silence can't take away what the Lord has given to you.

People's prejudice can't take away what the Lord has given to you.

People's hatred can't take away what the Lord has given to you.

People's tricks can't take away what the Lord has given to you.

People's lies can't take away what the Lord has given to you.

People's deceptions can't take away what the Lord has given to you.

People's jealousy can't take away what the Lord has given to you.

People's envy can't take away what the Lord has given to you.

People's greed can't take away what the Lord has given to you.

People's discouragement can't take away what the Lord has given to you.

People's rudeness can't take away what the Lord has given to you.

People's doubts can't take away what the Lord has given to you.

People's threats can't take away what the Lord has given to you.

People's disloyalty can't take away what the Lord has given to you.

People's carelessness can't take away what the Lord has given to you.

People's neglect can't take away what the Lord has given to you.

People's confusion can't take away what the Lord has given to you.

People's drama can't take away what the Lord has given to you.

People's pride can't take away what the Lord has given to you.

People's achievements can't take away what the Lord has given to you.

People's wealth can't take away what the Lord has given to you.

People's education can't take away what the Lord has given to you.

People's fame can't take away what the Lord has given to you.

People's pretense can't take away what the Lord has given to you.

People's false doctrines can't take away what the Lord has given to you.

People's selfishness can't take away what the Lord has given to you.

People's failures can't take away what the Lord has given to you.

People's motives can't take away what the Lord has given to you.

People's intentions can't take away what the Lord has given to you.

People's theories can't take away what the Lord has given to you.

People's plans can't take away what the Lord has given to you.

People's educated guesses can't take away what the Lord has given to you.

People's choices can't take away what the Lord has given to you.

If the Lord gives you talents, no one can take them away from you.

If the Lord gives you skills, no one can take them away from you.

If the Lord gives you genius, no one can take it away from you.

If the Lord gives you intelligence, no one can take it away from you.

If the Lord gives you common sense, no one can take it away from you.

If the Lord gives you spiritual gifts, no one can take them away from you.

You can surely take away what the Lord gives to you if you put anyone above the Lord.

You can surely take away what the Lord gives to you if you put anything above the Lord.

You and I will take away our own blessings from the Lord if we do our own will and live our lives in the foolishness of sin.

You can't blame anyone else for taking away what the Lord give to you, when you can choose to seek the Lord, who you can surely find in His holy Word.

You can only blame yourself for taking away what the Lord gives to you to use to glorify and magnify His holy name.

People's unconcerned ways can't take away what the Lord gives to you.

If the Lord is for you, who can be against you and take away what the Lord gives to you?

The Lord Jesus Christ will never give you and me anything that is bad that will cause our souls to be lost or anyone else's soul to be lost in hell.

What the Lord gives to you is for your good and for the good of others to be saved in Him.

No Better Than

You are no better than me, and I am no better than you.

You need to eat food just like me, and I need to eat food just like you.

You need to drink water just like me, and I need to drink water just like you.

You need to take a shower just like me, and I need to take a shower just like you.

You are no better than me, and I am no better than you.

You need to brush your teeth just like me, and I need to brush my teeth just like you.

You need to work just like me, and I need to work just like you.

You need a roof over your head just like me, and I need a roof over my head just like you.

You can get sick just like me, and I can get sick just like you.

You need encouragement just like me, and I need encouragement just like you.

You need a good friend just like me, and I need a good friend just like you.

You need to read the Bible just like me, and I need to read the Bible just like you.

You need to love Jesus and keep His Commandments like me, and I need to love Jesus and keep His commandments like you.

You are no better than me, and I am no better than you.

You need to put on some clothes like me, and I need to put on some clothes like you.

You need to lay down to sleep like me, and I need to lay down to sleep like you.

You need to take good care of yourself like me, and I need to take your care of myself like you.

You need to put on some shoes like me, and I need to put on some shoes like you.

When Jesus comes back again, I will go to heaven with Him like you, and you will go to heaven with Him like me if we are saved in Jesus.

I am no better than you, and you are no better than me in the all-seeing eyes of our Lord God who created you and me in His image.

I can fall down like you, and you can fall down like me.

I can feel pain like you, and you can feel pain like me.

I can have dreams in my sleep like you, and you can have dreams in your sleep like me.

I can take a chance like you, and you can take a chance like me.

I can have good and bad thoughts like you, and you can have a good and bad thoughts like me.

I have a free will to choose like you, and you have a free will to choose like me.

I have a destiny like you, and you have a destiny like me.

Even though our destinies may be different, it's only for God to know whether my destiny is heaven and your destiny is hell or if my destiny is hell and your destiny is heaven.

I am no better than you, and you are no better than me in the eyes of Jesus, who shows no respect of persons to save you and me from being lost in our sins.

The "I" Word

The "I" word is not always about being proud.

The "I" word can also be a humble word to say.

You can say, "I love my wife," and that is not being proud.

You can say, "I love my husband," and that is not being proud.

You can say, "I love my children," and that is not being proud.

You can say, "I love my friends," and that is not being proud.

You can say, "I love my pets," and that is not being proud.

You can say, "I love everybody," and that is not being proud.

You can say, "I love the Lord," and that is not being proud.

You can say, "I will do the Lord's will," and that is not being proud.

You can say, "I love going to church," and that is not being proud.

The "I" word is not always about being proud.

You can say, "I love my job," and that is not being proud.

The "I" word can also be a humble word to say.

You can say, "I will confess and repent of my sins," and that is not being proud.

You can say, "I will hold onto the Lord," and that is not being proud.

You can say, "I love to pray," and that is not being proud.

You can say, "I love to give God all the glory and praise," and that is not being proud.

The "I" word can be a humble word to say.

The "I" word is not always about being proud.

You can say, "I will humble myself into the Lord," and that is not being proud.

Many people will say the "I" word to make themselves look good.

Many people will say the "I" word to draw attention to themselves.

Lucifer said "I will ascend above the stars in heaven," and that was a proud way to use the "I" word.

The "I" word can be used for good and it can be used for evil.

A Mystery

We all would love to solve a mystery — that will surely get our attention.

We all are drawn to a mystery.

A mystery excites our minds.

A mystery can take our minds to heights of uncertainty.

A mystery can keep our minds on guard to the unknown.

A mystery has a story that we don't know about.

A mystery is something that has already happened and we just don't know how it ends.

A mystery can puzzle our minds.

All through the night, the full white moonlight can shine so mysteriously with its glow.

In the night, a shooting star can look so mysterious as it moves across the sky and disappears.

The sun can set, and look so mysterious as it seems to go down into the deep ocean waters.

A mystery didn't create its own presence.

There is something much more profound than a mystery.

There is a mysterious God who has revealed some of His mysteries to us in His holy word.

God is the greatest mystery known to all of mankind, who doesn't know where God came from.

All we know is that God is God, who existed before all things.

We believe that there is a heaven, which is also like a mystery.

We believe that we will go there one day because we believe in His Son, Jesus Christ.

Jesus Christ revealed the mystery of God because Jesus is God to be one with God and the Holy Spirit.

They are the greatest mystery that no angel and no human being can ever solve.

Lucifer tried to solve the greatest mystery when he rebelled against heaven.

The Lord is forevermore profound above the most genius mind that doesn't even know the smallest mysteries of God's eternal existence.

If the angels don't know all of God's mysteries, then there is no way for us to ever know.

God created mysteries all around us, even in some of our dreams.

We can fail to solve the smallest mystery that is so plain and simple to God.

Only God can solve all mysteries.

Imaginary

Many people imagine they are superheroes.

Many people imagine there is a Superman, Superwoman, Super Boy and Super Girl.

Many people imagine they are superhuman and have extra strength.

Many people have good imaginations and write imaginary books that get published.

Some of those imaginary books make lots of sales and become bestsellers.

Imagining things can be very powerful.

Many people imagine they are in a perfect relationship with someone.

Many people imagine they are in a perfect marriage.

Many people imagine they live in a perfect world.

Many people imagine they are all-powerful.

Many people imagine they are perfect.

Many people imagine they are god.

Many people believe that the Bible is imaginary.

Many people believe that Jesus Christ is imaginary.

Many people believe that God is imaginary.

Many people imagine they can walk on water.

Many people imagine they can calm the storm.

Many people imagine they have super powers.

Many people imagine they can rule the world.

Many people believe that heaven is imaginary.

Many people believe that angels are imaginary.

Many people believe that the devil is imaginary.

When Jesus walked on water, that was real and not imaginary to His disciples.

When Jesus calmed the storm, that was real and not imaginary to His disciples.

When Jesus fed the hungry, that was real and not imaginary to His disciples.

When Jesus cast out demons, that was real and not imaginary to His disciples.

When Jesus opened the eyes of the blind, that was real and not imaginary to His disciples.

When Jesus died on the cross, that was real and not imaginary to His disciples.

When Jesus rose from the grave, that was real and not imaginary to His disciples.

Jesus Christ was real, not imaginary to His disciples.

Many people today believe that Jesus is imaginary.

Many people today believe that eternal life is imaginary.

No one believes that they are imaginary.

We all believe that we are real, whether we live a long life or a short life.

There is nothing imaginary about God the Father, the Son and the Holy Spirit who created Adam and Eve, who were real human beings.

This world is filled with real people, not imaginary people.

Many people imagine they can do nothing wrong.

Many people imagine they can do anything they want.

Many men imagine they can get any woman they want to be with.

Many women imagine they can get any man they want to be with.

Many little girls imagine their doll babies can talk to them.

Many people imagine they are rich, and there are real rich people in the world.

Many people imagine they are flying a plane, and there are people who really are flying planes.

No one is living an imaginary life, because the lives we live are real.

No one is living an imaginary life, because our bodies can feel real pain.

No one is living an imaginary life, because we can get sick and die.

Many people imagine that they can talk to their dead loved ones but they are actually talking to Fallen Angels who appear to be their dead loved ones.

Those fallen angels are demons talking to those who believe they are talking to the dead.

Death is not imaginary for those who have lost loved ones.

Many people imagine they will never get caught doing bad things.

Who in their right mind would trade their real life for an imaginary life that doesn't exist?

Many people imagine they are saved, but they don't believe in Jesus Christ.

A Thief, a Murderer and a Liar

The devil is a thief, a murderer and a liar every day.

The devil loves to steal every day.

The devil loves to kill every day.

The devil loves to tell lies every day.

The devil hates what God gives to us and the devil loves to steal it from us.

The devil would kill you and me on any day if God allows him to.

The devil loves for us to lie every day, but the devil also loves to tell us lies.

If the devil wasn't a thief, then why would God call him a thief?

If the devil wasn't a murderer, then why would God call him a murderer?

If the devil wasn't a liar, then why would God call him a liar?

The devil would have killed Job if God had allowed the devil to kill Job, whose wife had told him to curse God and die.

Jezebel was one of the devil's human agents who wanted to kill Elijah, the prophet of God.

The devil has always been a thief, a murderer and a liar from the beginning of his rebellion against God, who many people believed to be a thief, a murderer and a liar because that's what the devil tells many people who don't believe in God's son, Jesus Christ.

Can we ever imagine how it would be if God was all about stealing, killing and lying?

We all would be better off never being born if God was an evil God.

The Bible says that the devil is a thief, a murderer and a liar and if that's not true then the Bible would be a lie.

The devil doesn't want us to believe that he will steal from us.

The devil doesn't want us to believe that he will kill us.

The devil doesn't want us to believe that he will lie to us and lie on us.

The devil wants us to believe that God is a thief, a murderer and a liar.

The devil wants us to believe that God loves to take away life, when it's the devil who loves to take away life that God loves to give.

God is life and not death.

It's the devil who loves to use death to his advantage to kill even innocent men, women, boys and girls, as well as innocent animals.

If it was God who steals from everybody, or God who takes away everybody's life, or God who lies to everybody, then why does the Bible say that the devil is a thief, a murderer and a liar?

The Bible says that God is love.

It's the devil who wants you and me to die being lost in our sins.

If God was to let the devil have his way all the time, then the devil would cause every nation to shoot off nuclear missiles to kill everybody around the world.

God is all about giving life and not taking away life, which is what the devil will do if God allows him to.

If God allows the devil to have his way all the time and lets the devil put on us more than what we can bear, no one would be saved and we will die in our sins.

The devil is all about killing us so we will be lost in our sins because he doesn't want anyone to go to heaven and live forever.

There were times in the Bible that God put people to death, but there was always a good reason for God to do this.

The devil's reasons are always evil when he puts people to death, and he puts people to death whether they are good or evil.

The devil is a thief, a murderer and a liar and he will be that way until Jesus Christ comes back again to give eternal life to all who are saved in Him.

The devil put a lot of people and animals to death because he is a murderer.

When God puts people to death it is because He wants to save their souls.

When God puts people to death is because they are too wicked.

The devil doesn't care about putting anyone to death or whether they are rich or poor, educated or not educated.

The devil doesn't care about putting people to death or whether they good or bad, because the devil is a thief, a murderer and a liar who will steal, kill and lie just being who he is every day.

The devil doesn't care about who he steals from every day.

The devil doesn't care about who he lies to and lies on every day.

A Heavenly and Universal Subject

The heart of earthly human beings is a subject in heaven for the angels to talk about amongst themselves.

The heart of earthly human beings is a very intense subject to the angels in heaven who talk to Jesus the most about man's heart rebelling against God.

Jesus talks to the angels to let them know that He has faithful people like Abel, Abraham, Jacob, Joseph, Moses, Job, Rahab, Esther, Jeremiah, King David, John the Baptist and like Mary Magdalene.

The heart of earthly human beings is a big subject in other worlds where there is no sin.

The perfect creatures in other worlds talk about the heart of earthly human beings to one another as they gather together to talk to Jesus about sinful men and women on earth.

Jesus tells them that He has faithful people like Noah, Joshua, Elijah, Hosea, Malachi, Peter, Stephen, Apostle Paul, Sarah, Jochebed, Rebekah, Ruth, Rachel, Zipporah, Hannah, Deborah, and many like Dorcas.

A heavenly and universal subject is about the heart of earthly human beings, who Jesus came into this world to save from our sins, not to condemn us earthly human beings in our sins.

The heart of earthly human beings is a heavenly and universal eternal subject for the holy angels and creatures in other worlds to talk about to you and me when Jesus Christ comes back again to take us to heaven where we will tell them that we gave our hearts to Jesus, who will defend our hearts throughout eternity in the presence of the angels and creatures in other worlds.

Jesus tells the angels and the creatures in other worlds that He has the power to not condemn the hearts of earthly human beings who He has redeemed back to God through His blood that was shed on the cross when He died and rose from the grave and this causes the angels and creatures in other worlds to rejoice in their hearts.

Real, True Beauty

Real, true beauty is beautiful words and beautiful actions beyond the beauty of the skin.

Real, true beauty is a beautiful mind that will think on the Lord.

Real, true beauty is beautiful words that will speak about the Lord.

Real, true beauty is beautiful actions that will do what the Lord says in His holy word.

The beauty of the skin will fade away in old age wrinkles.

The real, true beauty of words about the Lord will never grow old.

Real, true beauty is beneath the beauty of the skin.

A burning fire can destroy the beauty of the skin, but not the beauty of words and actions.

Bad chemicals can destroy the beauty of the skin, but not the beauty of words and actions that will surely get the attention of our Lord Jesus Christ, who spoke the most beautiful words and had the most beautiful actions when He lived His life without sin in this sinful world.

Jesus spoke the truth and those were the most beautiful words to speak.

Jesus live the truth and those were the most beautiful actions to live.

Jesus had the most beautiful mind when He lived on earth without sin.

Jesus Had the most beautiful heart when he lived on earth without sin.

The beauty of the skin will never be more beautiful than a beautiful mind.

The beauty of the skin will never be more beautiful than beautiful words.

The beauty of the skin will never be more beautiful than beautiful actions.

The beauty of the skin will never be more beautiful than a beautiful heart.

A beautiful woman can truly thank the Lord for giving her outward beauty, but a woman should never forget that the Lord can take her beauty away from her if she doesn't give Him the glory and praise for her beauty.

Real, true beauty is a beautiful character being about the Lord who is the origin of inner beauty and outer beauty.

A woman will look so rich in her outward beauty, but her inner beauty is spiritual riches that will never fade away.

A woman who has both inward beauty and outward beauty seems to be rare in this world today.

For Only a Moment

There are people who we see for only a moment and we never see them again for the rest of our lives.

There are people who we only talk to once in life and it's like only a moment that passes by and never comes back again.

We had loved ones in our lives who were only in our lives for a moment, but they will always be in our minds even though they've now gone to the grave of no return.

We drive by many people on the road for only a moment and we don't know if we will see them driving on the road ever again.

We see some people in the grocery store for only a moment and we don't know if we will see some of those people in the grocery store ever again.

We see some people in the doctor's office for only a moment and we don't know if we will see those people in the doctor's office ever again.

Life passes by like only a moment that doesn't last long at all, but Jesus Christ is coming back again one day soon to take us to heaven if we are saved in Him.

It will be like only a moment that we will be changed from mortal to immortality and the angels will take us up on the clouds of glory to be with Jesus up in the sky.

There are people who come into our lives for only a moment, like a visitor in church.

He or she might never come back again and we just don't know if they are alive or dead.

Life in this world is for only a moment and we need to live our moment loving Jesus Christ and keeping His commandments that are eternal beyond everybody's moment in life.

Only Jesus can truly turn our moment in life into eternal life when He comes back again, which will be like only a moment to God in heaven.

There are so many people who we will see for only a moment but hopefully we will see many of those people in heaven when Jesus Christ comes back again to be beyond everyone's moment in life.

We All Can Be Slow

There are people who are slow in catching onto things, but they are not stupid to know if we treat them good or bad.

You and I can be slow in catching onto things when it comes to Jesus, who knows how to work out everything for our good.

We can be slow to listen to and obey the voice of God's Holy Spirit telling us to say this and not say that.

We can be slow to listen to and obey the voice of God's Holy Spirit telling us to do this and not do that.

We all can be slow when it comes to loving everybody like Jesus loves everybody.

Jesus gave up His life on the cross to save everybody from their sins.

Jesus is not slow to answer our prayers and He always answers on time and not too slow or too fast.

Jesus is not slow to provide all of our needs, whatever they might be.

Jesus will provide everything to us on time.

There are people who are slow in learning things, but they are not stupid and know if you and I love them or don't love them.

You and I can be slow when it comes to trusting Jesus to work things out for us according to His holy will.

We all can be slow in catching onto the spiritual things of the Lord, who can send angels unaware to us who surely won't even know it because we are spiritually slow and don't recognize God's messengers from heaven.

We all can be slow in having faith as big as a mustard seed that we can stop from growing into a beautiful fruit tree for doubting what Jesus can do for us.

Back in the Bible days, the religious leaders and Pharisees believed that they were fast to try to trap Jesus into saying something wrong, but they were slow to trap Jesus who was very fast to stay ahead of them because he knew their hearts before they spoke one word to Him.

How Did God Come into Existence?

How did God come into existence?

Did God create Himself?

The bible says that God created the heavens and the earth.

If evolution brought everything into existence, then is it possible that evolution created itself from nothing?

Did God come from nothing?

No human being will ever know how God came into existence, because that is very impossible for all creations to ever know and fathom God's omnipresence and eternal existence.

We Christians depend on the bible that tells us about holy men and holy women who had an encounter with supernatural beings called angels who claimed to be sent from heaven by God.

The fullness of heaven was unseen by those holy men and holy women who believed in an unseen God who atheists see to be so useless to them because they believe that evolution created all existence.

Atheists would go insane before knowing how God came into existence.

We have eyes to see the things that exist around us.

We believe without a doubt that what we see is real and it exists to us.

We have experienced some things that we have seen, and you and I who believe in Jesus Christ have experienced God's love in Jesus who we have never seen.

We Christians believe that Jesus is extraordinary and above anyone and anything in this world.

We Christians believe that God is who He says He is and that it's God who is keeping us alive.

We exist by no coincidence, and we know we can trust this because all existence comes from God who is unseen by the naked eye.

Evolutionists are prone to claim that only the existence they can see is real, but there is so much more in existence that is eternal and that they cannot see because God created it.

Many people will put their theories above God, but their theories have no substance and are like the wind.

God has eternal substance, and the bible tells us that God created this world with substance.

Even atheists claim this world is real and they can see it with their eyes from day to day.

We Christians believe in Jesus Christ, and have seen lots of evidence that God is real.

He answers our prayers and He provides for all of our needs.

We Christians, especially, have experienced the power of Jesus Christ, who cleanses us from our sins so that we have no desire to commit those sins again.

God the Father, God the Son Jesus Christ and God the Holy Spirit is the beginning of all existence, seen and unseen.

Many atheists have returned to the dust of the earth and are nothing that God created all existence from.

We Christians don't need to know how God came into existence.

If we can't handle everything that exists to our naked eyes, then how can we handle the information about the origin of God?

Many angels fell from heaven because they took God for granted, acting as if God was beneath them and not worthy to be above their level of existing forever and ever.

How God came into existence is an eternal mystery to all of God's creations, and we will not be able to solve that mystery from eternity to eternity.

God is God who existed before all seen and unseen things that would vanish into thin air before God would tell anyone how He existed before all things.

How did God come into existence?

The existence of thousands of universes and trillions of galaxies is nothing in comparison to the existence of God.

How did God come into existence?

The angels are prone to receive eternal death and exist no more because of rebelling against God who will one day eliminate the fallen angels' existence.

How did God come into existence?

We human beings are prone to receive eternal death and exist no more because of rebelling against God, who will one day eliminate every wicked human being to prove that existence was created by God.

Evolution is only created in the minds of atheist men and women who believe that evolution created them to exist.

We Christians believe that a genius intelligence created us human beings to make choices, whether they're right or wrong.

We Christians believe that we exist because of God, but many people will create their own false gods that don't have anything to do with their existence and have no power to convict and convert a sinner to repent and turn away from living in sin.

How did God come into existence?

We don't need to know the answer to that question, but we can truly be thankful that God will exist forever and ever so that you and I can receive eternal life through His Son, Jesus Christ, who existed in the beginning with God.

Even before the fallen angels existed and rebelled against God, Jesus existed in God's eternal glory, power and majesty for all existence to worship Him who didn't force the angels to worship.

How did God come into existence?

All of existence can't come up with the slightest clue to answer this, and neither can you or I.

Our lives are like one second on the clock to an eternal God who created all existence from nothing.

Evolutionists make it seem like evolution is an eternal substance, but it only exists in their minds.

They cannot ever cause God to not exist to us Christians, or even to the animals that can sense God in their existence.

How did God come into existence?

History has existed with God in allowing the past generations to have a family tree today.

This is true especially for God-fearing Christians who pass down their faith in Jesus Christ to reach younger generations today.

How did God come into existence?

God existed in the technology back in the bible days when God gave Moses the technology to build an earthly sanctuary for him to dwell in among his people.

Evolution can't get rid of God, who existed before mortal evolutionists who knew nothing in their mother's womb when God knitted their bodies together.

When they were born, they did not know how to speak one word that makes good sense.

How did God come into existence?

Angels and mortal human beings can never figure this out because we are so low down beneath God in His eternal wisdom, knowledge and power that caused the fallen angels' temptations to be limited, especially upon all who believe in His Son, Jesus Christ.

If Lucifer had known how God came into existence, he would never have wanted to take God's place on His holy throne because he would truly know that only God is worthy to be God.

Lucifer would truly know that only God can handle being God on His holy throne.

Lucifer would have known that his existence would be so useless without God's existing eternal love for him.

How God came into existence is a question that only God can answer, and before God would answer that question all existence would pass away and be worthless to God's existence of eternal holiness, righteousness and perfection.

God's existence comes from God and the existence of eternity can't ever comprehend that.

You and I are well on our way to returning to dust as we age each day and get older in a fallen, sinful world where our lives only exist for a short time under the sun, especially in the presence of an eternal, existing God.

After we die, we can only exist again in Jesus Christ, the Son of God, who we must believe in to be saved to receive eternal life when Jesus comes back again.

For there will be no other kind of existence of life-eternal without Jesus, who existed with God and the Holy Spirit to create the heavens and earth.

How did God come into existence?

God is everlasting to everlasting, forever beyond you and me who don't know what living really is until we live in heaven with Jesus and exist forever and ever.

All the angels and unfallen worlds will know that God sealed our eternal existence in His Son, Jesus Christ, who existed before eternity, which would be very short without God's approval to exist forever and ever.

How did God come into existence?

God proves to all existence that He is love, even out of His strange act to one day destroy all the fallen angels and rebellious human beings in the lake of fire.

How did God come into existence?

God will take no desire to take pleasure in destroying the all wicked one day while forgiving you and me of our sins if we repent and turn to His Son, Jesus Christ, who gave us His life on the cross and rose from the grave to save us from our sins.

How did God come into existence?

God originated chance, and God gives us a chance to live for Him before it's too late, and that is the real, ultimate chance that only God can give to all human beings.

How did God come into existence?

Time does not exist for God, who came into existence when time had no meaning.

God created time here on earth to give us sinners like you and me no excuse to not give Him any of our time in prayer and service unto Him.

How did God come into existence?

Existence is nothing without God, who is not sitting down on His holy throne and doing nothing.

God is truly very aware and active in heaven and earth and in unfallen worlds that know God truly cares to keep His eternity sealed in obedient hearts unto Him.

How did God come into existence?

God has everyone's name in His book of life for believing in Jesus Christ, who the old books in the bible point to for His ultimate sacrifice for everybody's sins.

How did God come into existence?

No one can put themselves above God and live forever believing that existence originated from a big bang theory, which was an idea only formed in imaginative minds that are far from God's handworks of His creations.

How did God come into existence?

The naked eye can't see the unseen God in all of His glory that God had to keep away from Moses, who would have died if he'd seen God in all of His existence.

How did God come into existence?

The war in heaven could not eliminate God's existence, when mortal, wicked war mongers will strive to commit genocide against those they hate here on earth.

How did God come into existence?

Sin can never eliminate God's existence, and Jesus Christ truly proved that to all the holy angels, the unfallen worlds and to you and me who believe in Him, knowing that one day He will create a new heaven and a new world to exist forever and ever.

Jesus has truly proved that God will exist forever and ever beyond this fallen world that couldn't keep Jesus in the grave, and the grave will not exist for all the saints going with Jesus to heaven when He comes back again.

How did God come into existence?

God is the origin of existence, not evolution like foolish mortal people think.

They can't ever imagine the eternal truth of God that stretches out into the endless light years in countless unknown galaxies and universes beneath the highest heaven where God dwells on His eternal holy throne.

Astronomers are countless light years away from discovering the countless unknown in the outer space that is too small to contain God in it.

How did God come into existence?

God revealed His Son, Jesus Christ, in flesh and blood to sinners who would have dropped dead if Jesus had revealed His supreme totality to them.

How did God come into existence?

God's existence makes science look so dwarfed before the giant of God's eternal creativity that dissolves science into the capsule of this cureless world.

Jesus is our only cure in this sin-sick world where healing is permanent in Jesus, who can surely baffle the fields of science, technology and astronomy.

How did God come into existence?

We Christians won't question God about His eternal existence because His existence is love.

Regardless, many people will question God, especially if a loved one dies and doesn't exist anymore.

God is a Master Genius

God is a master genius who told Noah to build an ark to save him and his family and many animals from the flood.

God is a master genius who told Abraham to leave his native country and go to the Canaan land where his descendants would inherit the land.

God is a master genius who told Lot and his family to leave Solomon and Gomorrah before He destroy it with fire and brimstone.

God is a master genius who told Moses from the burning bush to go back to Egypt and tell his people that he will set them free.

God is a master genius who told Joshua to march his army around the Jericho walls once a day for six days and seven times on the seventh day so the walls would tumble down.

God told Elijah to meet with the false prophets of Baal at Mount Carmel to have a showdown about who is the true living God, who truly being the God of Elijah, burned up all the water in the trench around the altar.

God is a master genius who told a whale to swallow Jonah and keep him in his belly for three days because Jonah had disobeyed God and refused to go to Nineveh to tell the people to repent unto God.

God is a master genius who told Samuel to choose the shepherd boy David to fight the Philistine giant Goliath.

God is a master genius who told his son Jesus to come to this sinful world to save you and me from our sins.

No angel and no human being can be more genius than God.

Cross Over the Border of Heaven

One day, we will cross over the border of heaven and become citizens of heaven.

Heaven won't have a border patrol agent to keep you and me from crossing over the border into heaven.

There will be no spiritual illegal immigrant crossing over the border into heaven.

Only the righteous will have legal rights to cross over the border into heaven one day when Jesus Christ comes back again with our spiritual legal papers signed by Him for us to cross over the border of heaven.

There won't be any border walls to keep the righteous from crossing over.

There will be a border wall for the wicked who are spiritually illegal immigrants to Jesus.

Jesus will make you and me citizens of heaven, and there will be no prejudice, no discrimination and no injustice in the holy land of heaven.

No righteous man, woman, boy or girl will be mistreated in heaven, and there will be no spiritual illegal immigrants who could smuggle any drugs of sin into heaven.

You and I and all of God's righteous children will migrate to heaven one day to live in a heavenly mansion that Jesus built for us.

Every righteous man, woman, boy and girl is a spiritual illegal immigrant to the devil because this old sinful world is his home.

The devil loves to especially mistreat you and me with his temptations because he knows that we will one day be citizens of heaven.

Only One Body Language

There are many languages spoken all around the world, but there is only one body language spoken every day.

The body language is the only language that everyone can pretty much understand clearly.

Body language can be as clear as a crystal-clear glass.

We can hear what people say in other languages but may not know what they say, but we can read their body language and know what they do.

A smile is a body language that people all around the world can understand.

A helping hand is a body language that people all around the world can understand.

Shedding some tears is a body language that people all around the world can understand.

Eating food is a body language that people all around the world can understand.

Lying down to sleep is a body language that people all around the world can understand.

Coughing is a body language that people all around the world can understand.

People all around the world can pretty much figure out what body language is saying, when speaking different languages in words can be confusing because of not knowing what is said in a different language.

Being very angry is a body language that people all around the world can understand.

Fighting is a body language that people all around the world can understand.

Kissing is a body language that people all around the world can understand.

Holding hands as a body language that people all around the world can understand.

Laughing is a body language that people all around the world can understand.

Hugging is a body language that people all around the world can understand.

God had created the many languages for people to speak in words, but God has also given us all one body language so we can pretty much understand the nonverbal body language all around the world.

There are people who can speak different languages, but body language pretty much needs no interpreter

All around the world if we're drinking some water it is a body language that everyone can understand.

God gave us all one body language to understand, when words can be misunderstood even in the same language.

If You

If you have never been an aircraft pilot you can't relate to someone who is an aircraft pilot.

If you have never been a tractor trailer truck driver you can't relate to a tractor trailer truck driver.

If you have never been a doctor you can't relate to someone who is a doctor.

If you have never been a nurse you can't relate to someone who is a nurse.

If you have never been a soldier you can't relate to someone who is a soldier.

If you have never been a police officer you can't relate to someone who is a police officer.

If you have never been rich, you can't relate to someone who is rich.

If you have never been poor, you can't relate to someone who is poor.

If you have never been in jail, you can't relate to someone who is in jail.

If you have never been sick, you can't relate to someone who is sick.

If you have never been heart broken, you can't relate to someone who has a broken heart.

If you have never been shot, you can't relate to someone who has been shot.

If you have never been married, you can't relate to someone who is married.

If you have never been divorced, you can't relate to someone who is divorced.

If you have never been an author, you can't relate to someone who is an author.

If you have never been a pastor, you can't relate to someone who is a pastor.

If you have never been a musician, you can't relate to someone who is a musician.

If you have never been a teacher, you can't relate to someone who is a teacher.

If you have never been a mechanic, you can't relate to someone who is a mechanic.

If you have never been an actor, you cannot relate to someone who is an actor.

If you have never been a politician, you can't relate to someone who is a politician.

If you have never been a lawyer, you can't relate to someone who is a lawyer.

If you are not a man, you can't relate to another man.

If you are not a woman, you can't relate to another woman.

If you are not an adult, you can't relate to another adult.

If you are not wise, you can't relate to someone who is wise.

If you are not intelligent, you can't relate to someone who is intelligent.

If you are not brilliant, you can't relate to someone who is brilliant.

If you are not good, you can't relate to someone who is good.

If you have never been in love, you can't relate to someone who is in love.

If you can't swim, you can't relate to someone who can swim.

If you have never been an athlete, you can't relate to someone who is an athlete.

If you have never been a publisher, you can't relate to someone who is a publisher.

If you have never been a social worker, you can't relate to someone who is a social worker.

If you have never been a firefighter, you can't relate to someone who is a firefighter.

If you have never been to church, you can't relate to someone who goes to church.

If you don't believe in Jesus Christ, you can't relate to someone who believes in Jesus Christ.

If you don't keep God's Commandments, you can't relate to someone who keeps God's Commandments.

If you are not a Christian, you can't relate to someone who is a Christian.

If your life has never been in danger, you can't relate to someone whose life is in danger.

If you don't read the Bible, you can't relate to someone who reads the Bible.

If you are not content, you can't relate to someone who is content.

If you tell lies, you can't relate to someone who tells the truth.

If you live in lies, you can't relate to someone who lives the truth of God's holy word.

If you have never been a news reporter, you can't relate to someone who is a news reporter.

If you have never been an engineer, you can't relate to someone who is an engineer.

If you have never been a carpenter, you can't relate to someone who is a carpenter.

If you have never been a business owner, you can't relate to someone who is a business owner.

If you have never been disabled, you can't relate to someone who is disabled.

If you have never been in an accident, you can't relate to someone who has been in an accident.

If you have never had any children, you can't relate to someone who has children.

If you have never been homeless, you can't relate to someone who is homeless.

If you don't have a relationship with Jesus Christ, you can't relate to someone who has a relationship with Jesus Christ.

Brother Real and Brother Phony

One day in the early evening, Brother Real and Brother Phony were walking through the park together.

They were talking about the people of the world, as well as the people in the church where Brother Real and Brother Phony both worked.

Brother Real and Brother Phony look like twin brothers and it was hard to tell which of them was which.

Brother Real said to Brother Phony in the park, "We came from a different path that will not shock anyone who knows that Jesus is real and knows that the devil is a phony who will only appear to be real. Only Jesus will always see so clear.

Jesus will help Brother Real to see that Brother Phony will try his best to fool you and me who can always trust Jesus to be real in His holy word.

In Our Own

In our own eyes who we see and what we see can look so good but might not be good for us, like falling down in some deep mud.

In our own minds, we can believe that our thoughts are pure but we may think so evil and we'll never be cured.

In our own hearts what we feel can feel so good and be so wrong that we might not let it go and believe that we are so right and strong.

In our own way, we can believe that we don't' need to change, and at the same time our own way is like a heat wave moving across the terrain.

In our own eyes, we are often blind and have the nerve to believe that everything we see is so right.

As soon as we are so wrong, we look surprised and act like we can't believe that we are wrong.

Jesus knew that already forever long.

Influence

What you hear me say and what you see me do will have an influence on you in a good way or in a bad way.

What I hear you say and what I see you do will have an influence on me in a good way or in a bad way.

How I groom myself will have an influence on you and how you groom yourself will have an influence on me.

My hygiene will have an influence on you and your hygiene will have an influence on me.

The way I look at you will have an influence on you and the way you look at me will have an influence on me.

How I treat you will have an influence on you and how you treat me will have an influence on me.

I will influence you in a good way or in a bad way.

You will influence me in a good way or in a bad way.

There are many people who believe that what they say and what they do will have no influence on anyone.

Children are the best imitators to let you and me know how we influence them to speak good words or evil words and to do good things or evil things.

Influence is a remote control that can change the channels on someone's behavior.

Influence is a swinging door that we can walk into and get knocked down because we didn't see it coming our way.

Influence is like smoke in the air that can burn our eyes and make us cough because influence is real and can have a bad effect on you and me.

Influence is like a beautiful, sunny, warm spring day that can have a good effect on you and me.

There is good influence and there is bad influence every day in the world.

People who believe that they have no influence on people are living their lives in denial, and those same people will be influenced by someone in a good way or in a bad way to keep good company or bad company.

Influence is like a magnet that can pull you and me into its forcefield where we can feel the effects of influence that is like an open window on a rainy day because our mind can get wet with bad influence coming through that open window.

The church is the greatest influence to anyone who loves Jesus Christ, who is influenced by a repentant heart.

This world is the greatest influence to people who put their trust in this world from day to day.

The power of influence is so great that it can move anyone's behavior to be good or bad.

Comparing Yourself to Someone Else

Comparing yourself to someone else is like telling someone that it is wrong to be who you are when you can only be you and no one else.

Making comparisons can divide people and make them hate one another.

Making comparisons can ruin a child for life.

Comparing yourself to someone else is like telling God He didn't create everyone to be wonderfully made in His image.

Comparing yourself to someone else is like calling God a liar, because we are all equal in the presence of God.

Making comparisons can start a war within the family circle.

Making comparisons can end a good relationship with the dearest of people.

Making comparisons can build up a mountain of mistrust.

Comparing yourself to someone else is the root of your low self-esteem.

Comparing yourself to someone else is trouble about to happen soon.

Comparing yourself to someone else will cause the devil to laugh hard at us with his false pride.

Comparing someone to someone else can cause people to keep their distance from one another.

Making comparisons can corrupt people and make them believe their better than other people.

Making comparisons can cause good hereditary tendencies to look so ill.

Making comparisons can cause children to bully other children.

Making comparisons can cause jealousy to bite someone like getting bitten by a pit bull dog.

Comparing yourself to someone else is like sentencing someone to prison for a crime that he or she didn't commit.

Comparing yourself to someone else is like putting a dark veil over someone's eyes and taking the shoes of their feet so they'll step on some rusted nails they can't see.

Comparing yourself to someone else is like stealing someone's wealth and saying it belongs to you.

Comparing yourself to someone else is like wanting God's approval to knock down and kick around someone else's self-esteem.

Making comparisons is telling God indirectly, "Step aside and let me make someone be my footstool to step all over."

Jesus Christ will never compare you to me, because He loves us all the same every day.

Jesus knows no comparisons and would never say that you are better than me in His holy presence.

You are I are equal with different spiritual gifts, talents and skills.

People who compare themselves to other people will not love anyone with a whole heart.

A Changing World

We are living in a changing world where things can change us if we don't keep our trust in Jesus Christ, the living word of God, who will never change.

This changing world will be strange and dim to us for not changing on Jesus, who's all about changing our lives to be saved in this changing world.

This world is changing all the time because of technology, which is changing for our good, but morality is changing into immorality for the worst.

The church needs a makeover to change itself into a multicultural church.

The youth need to see a change in the church because the church needs young people to inspire ideas and youth leadership to bring every age group of people closer to the Lord.

We will be victorious in these last days and changing times if we don't compromise our religious believe in Jesus Christ.

Many distractions are migrating into the church and many church folks are changing their way of thinking in the church.

We are living in a changing world where people's moods are changing like the wind blowing in different directions.

Changing one's mind to do God's will is an abundance of life in Jesus Christ.

Changing one's mind to live in sin after experiencing the power of the Holy Ghost in one's life means it's better off never being born into this changing world.

We can choose not to change and do evil, deny ourselves and follow Jesus to a changing new heaven and earth one day, regardless of people changing on one another in the church.

Jesus equipped the church to withstand this changing world that will never change God's mind or make Him change His holy word.

In this changing world we can change our lives and someone else's life for the better or for the worst.

We will see a change or no change in one another, especially in the church where love can change people's lives for the better.

Love changes more than all the other spiritual gifts that are so vain without love for one another in this changing world.

People need to see you and me being like Jesus, who's all about changing lives to be saved in this changing world.

Ignorance

Ignorance is more deadly than the most poisonous snake because what we don't know can kill us.

So many people are dying because they are ignorant and don't want to obtain the knowledge of what is good and right for their lives.

Living a life in ignorance of the fact that the Lord created all men, women, boys and girls for greatness can set anyone back from years and years of success.

Ignorance is like a deadly disease that can kill you and me dead.

Ignorance is like an evil plot against life.

What we don't know can do us a lot more harm than good.

So many people don't know the word of God and don't want to know the Lord's will for them that is written in the Bible.

When people reject Bible truth, the Lord will not wink at their lack of knowledge.

Ignorance will kill more people dead than any war or atomic bomb.

Ignorance is the worst killer on earth.

When people reject medical knowledge for their health, it's like committing suicide.

Ignorance is the enemy of knowledge that is a good friend to you and me.

Ignorance is like making a bad excuse to say, "I didn't know when the Lord was giving me every good opportunity to search for knowledge that is like good medicine to cure an illness."

Ignorance can show its ugly face in every class of people.

There are ignorant people in every race, creed and color of people.

Ignorance can separate people and ignorance can give people ill feelings toward anyone they don't know.

Ignorance can masquerade as knowledge, even in the church where many church folks will use their ignorance like it's knowledge.

Ignorance is not knowing one's own body language that can speak negative words before speaking one word from the tip of the tongue.

Ignorance is temporary, but Jesus is eternal.

There is a Righteous Behavior

Can we form our own opinion about one another's behavior?

An evil man can behave himself in a good way to get what he wants without one spoken word to the contrary.

A good man can behave in a bad way on the spur of the moment, making someone think he's a bad man.

I can form my opinion about your behavior, but I can be so wrong about you because I don't know your heart.

You can form your opinion about my behavior, but you can be so wrong because you don't know my heart.

Many people in the church can behave in a nice way to get their own way, and that can be so wrong and have a lasting effect on someone's life.

The devil can appear to have good behavior in the church where he can ruin peoples' lives and make them leave the church and never want to come back again.

There is a righteous behavior to act right with a pure heart.

Someone can behave the right way with bad motives, day after day.

Only Jesus Christ can judge our behavior, even when we go through the motions of putting on a good act for outward appearances but deep down in our hearts our emotions may be shipwrecked on the hard rocks of holding grudges.

There are many church folks who are masters at showing good behavior after they know they have done others wrong with their "I don't care" attitude that is spreading like cancer within the church.

You and I are very good at making bad choices with a good behavior as if no one can ever see how transparent we are.

Only Jesus Christ, our Lord and Savior, can judge your behavior and judge my behavior by His righteous behavior.

Our behavior can be like filthy rags and can play tricks on us who don't always understand our own behavior and can't tell if it's righteous or unrighteous.

There is a righteous behavior that will cause us to suffer for Jesus Christ's name sake.

There is an unrighteous behavior that has caused many people to die at a young age because of their bad behaviors.

Our Lord Jesus' behavior was righteous when He chased the money exchangers out of His house of prayer.

Those money exchangers must have believed Jesus' behavior was bad in their eyes.

We can be like those money exchangers, using the Bible to have a combat fight with one another in the house of prayer that belongs to Jesus to be worthy to give His Holy Spirit to anyone who has a righteous behavior and walks away from contention?

Your Youth Ministry

Your youth ministry begins with you ministering to your parents by doing what your parents tell you to do.

You can carry your youth ministry with you to school to minister to your teachers and classmates by obeying your teachers' rules in the classroom.

Your youth ministry beings with you respecting those who don't respect themselves and don't care to know how to respect you, whose youth ministry work begins with you ministering the love of God to your kinfolks and friends.

Everyone in the church is not your friend to be blessed by your youth ministry being all about Jesus Christ, who will supply all of your needs.

Your life should be a living ministry in peoples' eyes so they see you being real about loving Jesus with all of your heart, giving you favor with God who created you young people to be like Jesus.

Jesus ministered to doctors to be about His Father's business at the age of twelve years old, for you young people to know that wisdom doesn't come with age.

There are many young and old fools who will reject your youth ministry that the Holy Spirit has given to you to spread the gospel of Jesus Christ.

Do you have a relationship with Jesus in your youth ministry and do you young visionaries keep your eyes on Jesus?

Until Someone Rocks Our Boat

It's easy to say "I love you," until someone rocks our boat and rubs us the wrong way, especially on the spur of the moment when we had no plan to say something bad or do something bad to hurt someone's feelings.

We've all done that.

We can talk too much at the wrong time and say words to try to gain control of others.

We can love to dish out negative words, but can't take in negative words.

Love is an action word to be fitly spoken in our body language.

These body language words are a lot more powerful than speaking words of love from the tip of our tongues.

We all are guilty of saying one thing and doing another thing.

We all are good at hiding how we truly feel about one another, but my true self and your true self can't hide from God.

It's so easy for me to see your flaws and it's so easy for you to see my flaws, but we don't like to see our own flaws.

We all have some bad hereditary tendencies that can look so righteous in our own eyes, until someone steps on our toes and then they experience our wrath that can discourage anyone.

We are all in the same boat and need Jesus, our Lord, to help us love one another with our whole hearts, because we cannot love one another with half a heart.

If we don't' love one another with a whole heart, we will rock Jesus' boat.

If we don't love one another with a whole heart, we don't love Jesus.

Love is not a spur of the moment good feeling that can vanish as soon as someone disagrees with you and me.

We can say "I love you" and not mean it, which shows in our body language that will always speak the truth a lot more than words of love.

Is it possible to give love and be afraid to receive love?

Action love is real love that sails our boat on a smooth ride, even through the storms.

Day by day we can go through the feel-good motion of giving love, but may only want to receive love from a distance.

Love is love and there is no halfway love and no keep-at-a-distance love.

Love words and action love are like a husband and wife being one flesh that God joined together for no man to put asunder.

We are all in the same boat to love one another on the high and low tides of life, through the storms where we can be life rafts for one another like when sickness, disappointments and grief knock us out of our boats.

If we truly love Jesus Christ, we will love one another so we reach the seashores of spiritual maturity in the Lord, who will rock our boat and rub us the wrong way to strengthen our faith in Him.

You and I can give up on one another and be like a sinking boat until Jesus shows us that He is for us and not against us.

Jesus tells us that He loves us in His holy word.

Jesus shows us His love through His blessings upon our lives that we can live giving love with a whole heart to rock the devil's boat and turn it over.

Your Youth is What You Make It

Your youth is what you make it, so be real to yourself even if no one else is real with you.

You can take control of your youth so you can enjoy your youth in the Lord, who didn't create your youth to be worthless — only you can choose to make it worthless if you live a rebellious life.

Youth is what you make it.

You can be victorious over stressful situations or be defeated by stressful situations.

You can choose to make your youth a blessing in your home, community, school and in the church where the Lord has put you in charge of your youth that no mid-life or old person can take away from you.

Only you can choose to be a blessing or be a curse to your neighbors.

Many mid-life and old people will rob you of your youth by putting you down as if it's a crime to be young.

Don't betray your youth by marrying someone who is old enough to be your mother or father.

Time doesn't care about your youth, since time will make you old if you live long enough in this world.

You are young and can choose to care about your moment in time and give Jesus Christ your quality time.

Your youth will not exempt you from going through some bad experiences in your life.

You can choose to live for Jesus, who was young without sin to make Him your perfect role model to give you victory over self so you can pick up your cross and follow Jesus to wherever He leads you in life.

Your young life belongs to Jesus and not to you.

You don't own your youthful life and should not live it wild and dangerous.

Your true reality check is Jesus Christ, who can allow sickness and death to take you to an early grave if you disobey your parents when they tell you things to add many years to your life.

Your youth is what you make it and it can be a wealth of joy unto the Lord, or you can sell your youth to the devil, who will devalue it so that it's worthless in this world.

Your youth is what you make it — it can be a treasure of precious gems or a play toy that can break into pieces.

Be true to your youth that is true to you in mind and body because you were born in a sinful world that will age you fast and make you look older than your age.

Being young is a high cost that you must pay to the Lord who has given you youth to do His will and not your own will.

The most beautiful appearance on earth is your youth, which makes many mid-life and old people covet it.

Youth is great wealth and can cause people to get makeovers to try to recapture it for themselves.

Don't make your youth something cheap by living a reckless lifestyle as though you will stay young forever.

The Christian youth is a living internet website for the mid-life and old people to search and find inspiring treasure and wonderful things.

Your youthful minds can choose to not let peer pressure wax you cold in this world where many young people's hearts are waxing cold for choosing to do evil against the Lord Jesus Christ who is setting the Christian youths' hearts on fire to win souls unto Him.

Your youth is the yesterday, today and tomorrow of the church that is young today in order to relate to you about God's holy word being forever young from generation to generation.

Young repentant souls are an inspiration to God, and He made the youth who can choose to repent and make Jesus their youth Leader who will never fail.

Your youth can fail you if you put your trust in who you see and what you see, because that is temporary.

Your youth is what you make it by your own free will that will sooner or later prove you to be a mature or immature youth, regardless of what you have already accomplished in your young life.

Your youth is what you make it, like a virgin keeping his or her body pure from sex until marriage, or you can make your youth like a broken mirror that can't show you how beautiful you look.

Young people can choose to beautify their character in the mirror of God's golden rules.

Right with Jesus Christ

If my heart is not right with you, my heart is not right with Jesus Christ, day after day and night after night.

If your heart is not right with me, your heart is not right with Jesus, from the start of the week to the end of the week.

The heart of Jesus Christ is always right with you and me to give us God's gift of eternal life.

I can't pass by your heart and you can't pass by my heart to get to the heart of Jesus who is always faithful and true to you and me.

If you and I don't love one another, we don't love Jesus who is the love of God to help me love you and to help you love me above and beyond my flaws.

My heart must be right with you and your heart must be right with me in order for us to be right with Jesus, who loves us all the same with His whole heart.

If I don't love you, I don't love Jesus, and if you don't love me, you don't love Jesus.

The real, true church is in our hearts and our hearts must be right with the Son of God, who is Jesus Christ.

Jesus is forever and ever right with God.

You and I can't walk, skip or run past one another's hearts to get to the heart of Jesus.

I will lie to myself and you will lie to yourself if we believe that we can love Jesus without loving one another.

The truth is Jesus Christ, who is always right with you and me to set us free from lying to ourselves.

The truth is Jesus Christ, who is always right with you and me who don't know what love is if our hearts are not right with Jesus today.

For Who We Are

Do we truly accept one another for who we are or do we just say those nice words but not really mean them?

We all have a habit of wanting to be accepted by everyone, especially in the household of faith where the Lord Jesus Christ is not accepted by everyone.

So, who are we to be accepted for who we are when there were pretenders in the church during Jesus' lifetime on earth?

Everybody in the church will not accept you and me for who we are.

Even Jesus Christ was rejected by many so-called Christians, who rejected Him for accepting the sick, blind, lunatic, hungry, deaf and disabled people.

What they did not understand is Jesus loves with no respect of persons.

Many church folks will not accept Jesus for being who He is over the church body because they want to be lord.

They will not accept that they have to surrender all of themselves to Jesus Christ, who is worthy to be Lord over the church body.

If we truly accept one another for who we are, no one would have the need to hold their church positions over people's heads as if they made it to the top so they could accuse others of being wrong and speaking out about errors that anyone can make.

Do we accept everyone for who they are or do we pick and choose who we will accept to try to manipulate them?

Are we servants to status that can create a monarchy and cause disunion in the church where we all do fall short of accepting one another for our accomplishments and our failures?

If we truly accepted everyone for who they are, we wouldn't try to cause anyone to look bad and we would not try to get revenge when people hurt our feelings.

We all can be vindictive and try to smooth things over with our own made up justice to look so right when we sentence and execute people for being who they are.

We all can talk a good talk, but when it comes to accepting one another for who we are, we all have a problem with it as soon as someone says or does something that we don't like, as if no one has any right to oppose what we say and do.

None of us is word perfect and none of us is action perfect.

Only Jesus Christ is word perfect and action perfect and will accept you and me for who we are in our sinful nature that only the blood of Jesus can cleanse us from to help us accept one another for who we are, which is so worthless without Jesus Christ.

Community Service

Community service is not only about giving out food and clothes to the poor and needy people.

Community service is also about giving people our emotional support and socializing the love of Jesus Christ with people who need to see Jesus living in our lives from day to day.

Community service is the heart of a loving a ministry in every church that is about the love of God.

The community of the Lord's church will serve the virgins without oil, the lost son, the lost sheep, the hungry and the sick that still exist in the church today.

Jesus Christ was the greatest community service worker when He was living here on earth.

Jesus fed the hungry, healed the sick, cast out demons and raised the dead to glorify His heavenly Father.

Jesus sat down and ate food with the publicans and sinners.

He socialized with them so he could lead their hearts to repentance.

Community service is the strength of the church.

Jesus not only preached and taught the love of God to people, He was also a servant to the poor and provided for their spiritual and physical needs.

The true conditions of the church body will very often show and tell through the community service in the church where you and I will be tested to see if we are about self or about Jesus whose motives were always pure to serve the poor with humility.

Whatever we do, it is to glorify Jesus Christ, not ourselves.

We cannot work our way to being saved.

If we love Jesus, our hearts will be pure to work for Jesus whose community service is heaven on earth.

The Truth

If you and I tell the truth about ourselves to the wrong kind of people, the truth can be a bad thing to them.

Anyone who loves to cover up the truth about themselves might believe that it's wrong to tell the truth.

Many people would rather read and believe a book of lies than to read and believe a book of truth that can set anyone free from being a phony to themselves.

There is nothing phony about the truth, but anyone who hates the truth is a phony.

It's always best to tell the truth in love, because a real friend will accept that.

If you and I lose friends for telling them the truth, then they were never really a friend to you and me.

Many people will tell lies to gain popularity with people, but telling the truth will gain us popularity with God.

There is truth in love that won't confuse and deceive anyone who knows how to read the body language in the book of actions where actions are more true than words.

The truth will always help us to make the right verdict in the courtroom of our hearts.

If being a Christian is the truth to only one person out of a million, then every Christian's faith in Jesus Christ is not in vain, even if a million people are against one Christian for believing in Jesus.

Telling the truth can give life and take away life.

Telling lies is a bad disease to life and a horror show to life.

Living the truth is really living a Christian life beyond words of truth that can sound so mean if the love of God is not dwelling in our hearts.

God created our hearts for the truth to live in every day of our lives.

Lies will show and tell on a liar for someone to know sooner or later.

The Fifty-Plus Christian

Life will get more pure to the fifty-plus Christian who has overcome many obstacles by holding onto Jesus Christ.

Pure like clear water is a fifty-plus Christian who is not polluted with deception and pretense.

The sky is not the limit for a fifty-plus Christian whose prayers will travel beyond the sky to enter into heaven.

Receiving the fifty-plus Christians' prayers is a beautiful gift box for Jesus to unwrap.

A fifty-plus Christian living right by example in the presence of the youth is a stairway for the youth to walk up onto and reach spiritual maturity in the Lord.

A fifty-plus Christian giving God all the glory and praise on good days and bad days is a mountain of wisdom and a deep valley of experience.

A calendar will start a new year and bring a new year to an end, but God's grace is a calendar for the fifty-plus Christian to spiritually age in countless blessings from the Lord.

Silence has no sound to listen to, but silence is eager to speak loud to foolish people of all ages.

So, listen to and take heed to the counsel of the wise fifty-plus Christian man and woman.

No one wants to publish a book with blank pages that no one can read, but a fifty-plus Christian man and woman can be a living book to read about God's goodness on every page published by our Lord and Savior Jesus Christ.

Love

If we can't squeeze water out of a turnip, then we surely can't squeeze love out of doing something wrong.

If there is no cold air in a hot dryer, there is no love in using people and hurting people.

If water doesn't leak out of a bottle filled with holes, then love can't cause anyone to have a broken heart.

Only the right shoe size will fit our foot every day, and only love will be the right fit to keep relationships good and strong.

Our breath will smell and our teeth will stain after every meal, but the breath of love will never smell bad to our hearts or stain our hearts with deceit.

We can erase an error off notebook paper, but there are no errors to erase in the hearts of loving people.

A beautiful flower can dry up and look ugly in the winter season, but the beauty of a man and woman being in love with each other will not dry up and look ugly in their winter season of sorrow and grief if they love Jesus more than each other.

If we can't squeeze air out of smoke, we can't squeeze love out of selfishness.

If we can't live without a heart pumping blood through our veins, then we surely can't live without God's love keeping this world from self-destructing.

Silence

Silence can be a good friend to you and me, especially in our time of sickness that loves quietness.

When we are well, we move around and come and go as we please while making some noise.

We really don't appreciate silence until we are sick or studying for a test and don't want to be disturbed by any noise.

Silence can heal a broken heart, when the sound of the tongue can make a mean and loud noise and do more damage to a broken heart.

A thief loves silence when he is tiptoeing through someone's house in the late midnight hour to steal anything that has great value.

Silence is like good medicine to take to get well again.

Silence is a good companion to a writer who needs his or her quiet time to think about what to write about to give readers laughter, encouragement, a peace of mind and some hope to see a better day.

We can listen to God talking to us when we are silent, even though God can still talk to us around a lot of noise that God would not choose over silence being the best way for us to hear Him so clear.

The grave is filled with silence and we are so blessed that God made it that way.

Silence will always listen to us when no one else cares to listen.

Silence is a gift to us from God.

Family and Friends

Family and friends are like a beautifully decorated Christmas tree with gifts all around it.

A radiant smile on the face of a beautiful woman cannot shine more radiant than having good family and friends.

Loving family and loving friends is great wealth to a rich man who has no loving family and friends.

Family and friends are like a beautiful rainbow arching up in the sky after the rain.

Happy people have good family and good friends.

Poverty has failed to vanish away family and friends from every home, and hate has failed to destroy family and friends from a family reunion in every culture, creed and race of people.

Having a lot of material things and good education cannot give anyone real joy like having good, loving family and friends.

Having a small, loving family and a few loving friends can have a greater positive effect on someone than a whole city of rich, selfish people only living for the moment.

Having blood family in the church is like a treasure chest filled with precious gemstones and having friends in the church is so refreshing, like drinking some water to quench our thirst.

Jesus Christ, our Lord and Savior, is always family and friend to you and me who is not always family and friend to Jesus who family and friends should be all about in the church.

Jesus is always a real, loving family and loving friend, even if our church family and friends turn against us.

Should it Matter?

Should it matter to you and me what someone says or does, as long as the words are right and the actions are right?

Should it matter to you and me if someone is rich or poor when we like to be treated right by anyone whether they're rich or poor?

Should it matter to you and me when someone voices their true feelings as long as it's not kept inside until it explodes in a big ball of anger?

Should it matter to you and me what someone thinks of us, when we can choose to control ourselves?

Should it matter to you and me who is educated or not so educated when it has nothing to do with someone's personality and anyone can be mean?

Should it matter to you and me if someone loves us or doesn't love us when we can give love that no one can take away from us?

Should it matter to you and me who wins or loses when the grave doesn't care?

Should it matter to you and me if children grow up when the educational system is failing many children making it difficult for them to grow up and be productive?

Should it matter to you and me if earthquakes, hurricanes, floods, fires, heat waves and disease attack this world more and more when many people are treating God like a criminal and trying to lock God up in the jailhouse of their wicked ways?

Should it matter to you and me if there is a God living above this world when sorrow, sickness and death seem to have the authority to take our lives today that exists because of God who owes us no apology for our life choices?

Jesus Cannot Fail

Our intellect can fail us, but the Lord can't fail to take our intellect to a higher reasoning.

We can trust Jesus to lead and guide our common sense that can fail to be of some good use to us when we need to use our common sense to make the right choices.

Jesus knows no failure like you and me, who have failed to speak the right words and do the right thing at one time or another in our lives.

Our good works can fail us and our good names can be ruined by one mistake, but Jesus cannot fail or make mistakes.

Greatness can fail us and we can be brought down to only a social security number, but greatness will not fail to give Jesus Christ the glory and praise to exalt Him as the King of Kings and Lord of Lords who can't fail to make you and me great if it's in God's will.

Our experiences can fail us and cause us to misunderstand our purpose for being here if we never had an experience with Jesus to know that He cannot fail to be our greatest experience in life.

Our knowledge can fail us and we will not know the unknown, but Jesus Christ knows the highest heavens being eternal beyond our knowledge that can vanish away so quickly from a bad accident or a bad illness.

Our love can fail us, but love cannot fail to save our souls from being lost if we love Jesus who will not use our love and abuse our love for His benefit.

Our feelings can fail us and confuse us so that we move too slowly or move too fast in the choices we make, but Jesus will never fail to be on time to give us His Holy Ghost for us to feel caught up in with our whole hearts to love Jesus, who will never play on our feelings.

From the First Day

From the first day that we were born into this world, life has been on our side and death has been against us.

The first day that we could hear, feel, see, taste and touch, destiny shook our cribs and rocked our cradles twenty-four hours, around the clock.

From the first day that we were born, time began to build a bridge of hope for us to cross over into the days of repentance.

The first day that we spoke our first words, sorry, disappointments and lies wanted to choke us with troubles.

The first day that we began to crawl on our knees, idols began to call our names for us to bow down on our knees to worship the things of this world.

The first day that we were born into this world, evil has been against us even into the first day that we began to stand up and take our first baby steps to walk.

Sin has been against us and Jesus Christ has been for us since the first day that we were born into this world.

There is a second birth that is supernatural beyond our first birth that was natural.

The first day that we were born, all hell was against us wanting us to be lost in sin, but God is for us to be born again in His newness of life.

Spiritual babes can grow up to be spiritual adults in the Lord God, who loved us first from our first day to our last day to live on earth.

We all are like a little newborn baby to God who is eternal beyond our days which are like a speck of dust floating in the air and disappearing without a trace beneath the beautiful sunlight rays.

Only the Lord can number our days from our first birth when we learned to speak the words of this world.

Jesus has made a way for everyone in this world to be born again to speak His holy words in the bible verses that lead us to life eternal beyond natural birth.

From the first day that we were born, temptation began to set up evil traps against our free will that sin hates because we can choose to pick up our crosses and follow Jesus in our second birth.

You and Me

Our dark shadow is ashamed of you and me for claiming to be a child of God while setting up traps for someone to fall into.

Time will believe it has made a mistake by giving you and me borrowed time if we use our time to despise people and trick people to make them look bad.

Life will want to run away from you and me who can make life miserable by lying to people and being a phony, especially in the church that belongs to the Lord.

Deceit is happy to lead us and guide us to the path of illusions that you and I will walk on if we're artificial with one another who the Lord loves to be real with every day.

Pain will see no wrong to cause our bodies to ache if you and I see no wrong to cause people's hearts to hurt with our poison tongue that can grieve the Holy Spirit.

The visible things want no part of us if you and I cause souls to be lost because of holding grudges against anyone who the Lord loves and will forgive.

The invisible things will see you and me as being betrayers against the Lord who we don't see and will say that we believe in Him with our mouths, but our deceitful ways are visible for anyone to see the daylight showing everything in the light.

The invisible things will not want to look upon us to see you and me living by our visible, deceitful ways that can easily discourage people from wanting to come back to the Lord.

Our own reasoning will hasten to dig a deep pit for you and me to fall into if we don't trust the Lord's reasons to work out any problems that we can make worse if we try to get ahead of the Lord.

Our destiny is like smoke rising up in the sky if we hold onto me, myself and I, who must deny self to one day rise up in the sky to be with Jesus Christ, who will smoke this whole world one day in a hot oven.

Our limit will leave us if we insult the free will choice and use our choices as an excuse to do evil against the Lord.

Compared To

Memories are great to give us something to live for compared to anyone who accepted Jesus as their Lord and Savior and back slid as if there is no Jesus Christ who gave His life up on the cross for their sins.

Being alone is great wealth compared to the people who once walked with Jesus and said goodbye to Jesus with thier actions being so spiritually poor.

Silence is royalty compared to the people who once trusted Jesus and made a U-turn to complain about what they don't have; their complaints are a cheap, loud noise that Jesus will not listen to.

A broken heart can be great strength compared to the people who once were strong in Jesus and fell into corruption, making them weak and worship material things they believe will make them strong in their own minds.

Dreams are real compared to the people who once lived in the light of Jesus and then decided to live in darkness, while the children of light give their stress to Jesus who has no darkness in Him because His is pure light from heaven.

Our shadow is a good friend to us compared to the people who were once growing up in God's grace but then decided to reject the truth about Jesus in the Bible as they walk in their own ways that lead them into the pathway of the shadow of death.

Looking at yourself in the mirror can give you great joy to be alive compared to the people who once looked in the mirror of Jesus' ten Commandments and chose not to ever look again, allowing their sins to deceive them into thinking they are perfect in their own eyes when they are actually blind and do not see how they are grieving the Holy Spirit.

Physical pain gives us hope to take some medicine to kill the pain in our bodies, compared to the people who were once temperate unto Jesus in their bodies before they chose to defile their bodies and cause spiritual pain to their souls because they are lost in sin where there is no hope for anyone because they will die in sin.

A newborn baby is pure with innocence compared to the people who were once spiritual babes in Jesus and then decided to throw away their precious innocence to grow up in selfish pride and not in the humility of Jesus who is forever pure in His holy promising word that He cannot break to us while our words can be broken and trick people into stumbling and make people feel like giving up on Jesus.

Anyone can do right in the church but holding a church office position doesn't make anyone a spiritual adult in Jesus.

Jesus loves a pure heart that finds favor with Him compared to our outward appearances that can find favor with the people of the world who are no friend to Jesus.

The Holy Scriptures

Many of the scriptures in the old and new testament are about rebellious human beings sinning against God.

The scriptures in the Bible make it clear to you and me about God the Father, the Son and the Holy Spirit inspiring ordinary people to be a dedicated sort of people living among the people of the world.

From the book of Genesis to the book of Revelation, God has inspired willing men and women to be His mouthpiece to speak the truth in love to a rebellious people who are only living their lives to please themselves.

All through the bible scriptures God gets involved with all of His children, great and small.

In the scriptures, God has allowed many of His prophets, priests and judges to live to reach old age, while some of God's messengers died at an early age, like Steven who was a young man who was stoned to death for Jesus Christ's name sake.

God didn't use a bunch of lazy people who sat around and did nothing; they were already active before God called them to work for Him to win lost souls to be saved.

All the scriptures in the bible point to God speaking to you and me through ordinary people like us.

Only God the Father, the Son and the Holy Spirit are extraordinary and inspire human beings to communicate with a supernatural God who is the highest spirit forever true to His words of life.

The bible scriptures are holy, righteous, pure and true, and God also gave them to ordinary men and women who were willing to let Him use them because they believed in God by faith and they obeyed His Commandments with joy in their hearts.

We may never understand every scripture in the bible, no matter how much we study it.

What we do understand is that God the Father, the Son and Holy Spirit speak truth in love to us to set us free from being lost in the rebellion of sin that Jesus Christ became on the cross.

Jesus is the Builder Of

A day can bring us the sunlight, clouds, rain, snow, hail, fog, dew, heat, strong winds, a warm breeze and ice-cold temperatures.

We need to bring a day of love, not envy strife, lust, greed, abuse, deceit, conceit, confusion, bloodshed, war, cold temperatures of injustice, lying and hate, which are the builders of death.

Time can be the builder of joy or anguish, and time can send us a big bill of prosperity or poverty.

Our lifetime is only a moment that disappears under the sun as our footsteps are like a shade wandering away under a tree on a hot, sunny day to be the builder of no trace of our existence.

Our memories can soar beyond the full, white moonlight and leave us behind in a bad state of mind, like a dark shadow can stand still on a wall and look so content.

We can be in our contentment and look so still on the walls of our selfish ways that we can dishonor and rip up into bad choices to be the builder of corruption and rebellion.

The pure, white snowflakes will fall from the sky, like the purity of God's purpose will fall on our lives to be the builder of living to do God's will.

A book can't read our minds and turn the pages of our thoughts, but our minds can read a book and create a book of words from our thoughts to be a builder of sharing inspiring words with one another.

To not be a sketch of anyone's character is to be real to self and be the builder of being genuine.

Glass can break into many pieces as soon as it hits the hard floor, and sickness can break our spirits as soon as it hits the hard floor of no cure to be the builder of no hope to get well.

The origin of existence is insulted by the minds of vaporized theories only rising up in smoke one day soon when all the children of God will be elevated up in the air to be with Jesus Christ on the clouds of glory one day soon.

Life in this uncertain and temporary world is the builder of broken, lost sinners needing to repent unto Jesus.

Jesus Christ is the builder of new creatures born again in the spirit of God.

Our choices are the builder of our destinies when there is nothing under the sun and beyond the sun to choose our destinies for us.

Jesus will not force us to love and obey Him.

Jesus is the builder of life and our free will choices that allows selfish people to build their false beliefs on.

When I Go to Church

When I go to church, I believe I'm going to the right place to learn more and more about Jesus Christ who I believe to be the head of the church, regardless of who comes in and leaves the church.

When I go to church, I believe that I will receive more and more of the Holy Ghost to help me to deny more and more of myself.

When I go to church, I believe that I am in the house of God who will bless me more and more, no matter who is against me.

When I go to church, I believe that I will get more and more spiritual strength to hold onto Jesus Christ's almighty hand that can hold my life together, no matter what I go through.

When I go to church, I believe that I can be a witness of Jesus in my testimonies and I believe that I will spiritually grow to love Jesus more and more as I love my neighbors more and more, even in the church where my brothers and sisters in the Lord are my neighbors.

Going to church gives me joy and allows me to share with my neighbors what Jesus is giving to me.

When I go to church, I believe that I am in a holy place that is extraordinary to me; it's where I think on God's goodness and God's favor in my life, regardless of the unpredictable bad days that come my way.

Going to church gives me some peace, even when there are times that peace seems to be pressed down in the church that I love to go to and be a blessing to my brothers and sisters that I am trying my best to love in Jesus' holy name.

When I go to church, I love to take the Holy Spirit with me, and I believe the Holy Spirit will be with my brothers and sisters too.

When I go to church, I believe that the Holy Spirit is already there, waiting on me to plant my unworthy feet down on God's holy ground.

Going to church gives me physical and spiritual rest in the Lord, who makes my burdens light as a feather so that I know that Jesus loves me too.

Oppression

What good is being intelligent without the freedom of speech?

What good is being wise if all the laws of the land are corrupt?

Being educated can look so vain in a nation that locks people up in chains of oppression.

What good is having a dream if dreams are pressed down under authoritative people who want no change?

Maturity is like a dry well in the eyes of immature government officials who will dry up the nation's economy due to drinking the water of greed.

The beauty upon a woman's face is like a fugitive on the run in a nation that oppresses women and gives them no rights to be who they want to be.

Children who are born in oppression will cause time to grieve and not want to exist to keep children from dying in oppression.

Hope will feel the discouragement of people who have given up on their nation because it crushed their hopes and caused them to feel like they'd be better off never being born.

If oppression had the power to wipe away the smiles off everyone's face, it would be happy to do so in order to break our spirit.

The worst oppression is within the church where intelligent minds will get insulted by ignorant minds.

The children of light will be oppressed by the children of darkness.

Those who keep their eyes on Jesus Christ will be surrounded by more and more appearances of evil that will beat up our good character and give us a bad name if we don't ask Jesus to help us shun away from all appearances of evil that are running to and fro, from the pulpit to the usher doors in the church.

Oppression is not something bad all the time, because the Lord Jesus will oppress us with guilt to repent and turn away from the oppression of being lost in our sins.

Believe or Not Believe

Looking good is a good promotion to reach up high in life, but looking good can be despised, even in the church.

Being sensitive might be a bad thing to some people who will get sensitive and assume things with no actual proof.

Being a senior citizen is heading toward no more retirement for raising their children's children.

Talking to the opposite sex is getting more and more stereotyped, marking you as a cheater.

Age has no number to many people who are dating and marrying people half their age, as if Eve was only half of Adam's age when God created Adam and Eve so very close to the same age.

Many church folks don't like to hear the truth stepping all over your toes and my toes.

We can believe the truth or not believe the truth, but common sense will always be a good friend to anyone who uses it.

Can knowledge be an enemy if we use it for evil?

Can ignorance be a friend if we're better off not knowing something that we don't need to know.

Can having knowledge ruin peoples' lives?

We can say that we believe in Jesus and act like we don't believe in Jesus by believing in our own words and our own actions that can sound so right and look so right in our own eyes.

There is true freedom in God's ten Commandments that will add years to our lives.

Do we have true freedom in the church where God's golden rules are not a burden, but church folks can burden one another when they're not loving one another in Jesus' name?

Believe or not believe is a choice that everyone can make when Jesus Christ is the best one to always believe for us to not believe the devil.

To Make Believe

To make believe something and think it's real is a very power deception that can captivate our minds and make us believe a lie to be the truth.

The truth is real, but a lie is deceptive.

You and I can live a deceptive life if we don't have a relationship with Jesus Christ, who is the only one who can make your life and my life real so that you and I can live being real with one another.

Speaking polished-up words and doing good deeds doesn't make anyone be true about being real.

A man can have a wife and not be real and true to her in his heart where a man can be unfaithful to his wife.

A woman can have a husband and not be real and true to him in her heart, beyond her outward kindness and loving smiles.

Holding church positions, returning tithes and offerings and using our spiritual gifts doesn't make us true to Jesus Christ if our hearts are lying to Jesus.

Jesus always knows a pure heart of love is filled with real love for everyone, no matter what race, creed, color and culture of people are living in our neighborhood every day.

There is a make-believe love that shows and tells on anyone for only talking feel-good words of love and not showing love, especially to the loveless who are broken up and holding grudges and hating.

You and I, regardless of our outward appearances can look so holy and divine.

Jesus is faithful and true, but make-believe pretenders will sooner or later reveal their true colors of conceit, covetousness, deceit, ignorance, pride, seductive mind controlling techniques, polished-up jealousy, camouflaged grudges, artificial worship and counterfeit service unto the Lord.

Who would make believe to be dead and get buried alive down in the grave when there is a spiritual grave for the spiritual dead to be buried alive in for living a make-believe life in the household of faith?

To make-believe a friendship and relationship is not real and is like digging a deep pit to fall into that only the Lord alone can pull us out of.

You and I can truly experience God's real love that is beyond anyone's make-believe love that will fail in troubled times.

Open Our Eyes to See

O Lord, open our eyes to see what's going on all around us.

Don't let us get hung up on self, as if this world revolves around us.

O Lord, open our eyes to see misery cursing our homeless people and the shame of laughing at women who are being abused and raped.

Open our eyes, O Lord, to see violation happening to children who are being abused and molested.

Many church folks will forget where they come from, as though they never lived in darkness.

O Lord, open our eyes to see the bully of poverty pushing around ignorant people in the poor house.

Open our eyes, O Lord, to see the selfish ways of educated morons who are oppressing common people.

Open our eyes, O Lord, to see the servants masquerading in the church, pretending to be your servants.

O Lord, open our eyes to see programmed robot church folks who are only going through the motions of working for You with no love for You.

Loving you, O Lord, can deprogram anyone's heart and make them confess, repent and turn away from being a hypocrite.

Open our eyes, O Lord, to see us bringing hardships upon ourselves because we're not doing what's right when we know to do what's right by Your holy word.

O Lord, open our eyes to see that we are always the last ones to see that we need to point the finger at ourselves.

Open our eyes to see what's going on all around us who will usually live our lives for self-survival as if we don't see other people struggling to keep a roof over their heads and food on the table.

O Lord, open our eyes to see judgmental people who believe they are entitled to curse people as though they are gods reigning over other peoples' lives.

Open our eyes, Lord Jesus, to see this world being very ill to one day die in a hot furnace fire that the daily news stations will not broadcast.

The children of God are broadcasting the good gospel news about Jesus Christ coming back one day soon on the clouds of glory for every eye to see.

Being Full of Self

If I'm not blessed by the ministry work that Jesus has given to you, then I am full of self.

If you are not blessed by the ministry work that Jesus gave to me, then you are full of self.

Jesus will not give you a ministry work that I will not be blessed by, and Jesus will not give me a ministry work that you will not be blessed by.

Jesus doesn't make mistakes in what He gives to us to edify His church, but members of the church can be full of self and believe that they are the man or the woman to minister their spiritual gifts to edify the church.

Being full of self will cause me to learn nothing good from your inspired sermon, song, testimony, teaching and showing me some love in the Lord, who has inspired you to bless me in this church.

If you are full of self, you will learn nothing good from Jesus who has inspired with me a ministry to bless you.

Your ministry work and my ministry work is equal in the presence of God, who shows no respect of spiritual gifts and ministry work in the church.

Anyone who believes that their ministry work is better than someone else's ministry work is being full of self and is putting a stop to their own spiritual growth in the Lord, regardless of how long they have been in the church.

Being full of self is being an enemy against the Lord, and we are all guilty of being full of self in the eyes of Jesus Christ.

We cannot be in the presence of the Lord and believe that we have no flaws of self.

The church is not about you and me, who can put a block on our own blessings from the Lord if we believe we have a superior ministry and are entitled to receive God's favor above others.

Your Reason, O Lord

Your reason, O Lord, is not for human beings to question because human beings are born in sin and fall short of Your glory.

Your reason, O Lord, is keeping me in the land of the living because you, O Lord, didn't let my own ignorant reasons kill me dead in my sins.

No human being can reason with You, O Lord, and understand Your wisdom that is higher than the heavens.

Every human being who is alive right now is alive because of Your reason alone, O Lord, while many righteous people and wicked people are dead in the grave.

Your reason, O Lord, is allowing many wicked people to gain wealth and will allow many of Your righteous people to remain poor.

Your reason, O Lord, is good therapy to the most insane winds that will calm down and blow so sane for Your right reason.

Your reason, O Lord, will give justice to the waters of the deep that is being treated so unfairly by the mighty tidal waves that will bring judgment upon dry land if Your reason, O Lord, allows the mighty water floods to be judge and rule over the dry land.

The earthquakes are very violent criminals serving time and being anxious to release another violent break up of the ground.

Fire would be alive and run to and fro through the earth, burning up everything if Your reason, O Lord, allows the fire to be an escaped fugitive on the run.

Your reason, O Lord, is omnipotent and infinite, surpassing the immeasurable universe that is too short to reach up and touch Your reason, O Lord.

Time can't figure out Your reason, O Lord, to give human beings time to repent before it's too late.

Like The

Like the sun's rays shining through the clouds, God's love is shining through this dark world.

Like the clouds moving across the sky, God's Holy Spirit is moving across hearts to repent.

Like the rain falling from the clouds in the sky, God's mercy is falling from heaven down on sinners.

Like the wind that blows in different directions, the mystery of God is blowing in different generations.

Like the waves that roar upon the seas, God's chastisement is roaring upon those He loves.

Like the ocean waters that flow, God's goodness is flowing into our lives.

Like the sun that rises in the sky, spiritual gifts of God are rising in the lives of the youth.

Like the sun that sets in the sky, the gospel of Jesus Christ is setting over the entire world.

Like the full, white moon that glows in the night sky, the prophecies of God are glowing majestically in these last days.

Like the stars that sparkle all night long, the children of God sparkle their little lights in the nighttime of this world.

Like the pure, white snow falling from the clouds in the sky, the righteousness of Jesus Christ is falling so pure from heaven to cover our righteousness that's like filthy rags.

Like the thick fog that is hard to see through, the tests of God can be hard to pass sometimes.

Like the mountain cliffs that are high, the cliffs of God's reasoning are too high for us to reason with.

Like the valleys that run deep, the deep, profound therapy of God's Holy Spirit reaches the truth of God's word down in the deep illness of the mind and body so it can be healed if it's God's will because His will is unchangeable when our will can be broken by changing times in this changing world.

Revealed to Me

The storms revealed to me that I am a storm raging in the presence of the Lord because I did not heed the voice of His Holy Spirit.

The waters of the deep oceans revealed to me that my troubles will be ocean deep if I don't give all of my heart to the Lord.

The dark nights revealed to me that I will spiritually sleepwalk in the day if I don't talk to Jesus with sincerity.

Love revealed to me that love will leave me if I love the creature more than my Lord God, the creator of love.

Fear revealed to me that fear is a friend to me if I fear God and keep His Commandments.

Fear revealed to me that I need to be afraid to keep company with seducers.

Silence revealed to me that I am like a silent night to the sound of my thoughts, which sound like a rugged, running river if I don't think on pure thoughts and meditate on the Lord's word.

My five senses revealed to me that I am all alone on my walk with the Lord as I pick up and carry my own cross, even into situations that don't make any good sense to me.

The free will choice revealed to me how I enslave myself and con myself with my own selfish desires instead of waiting on the Lord who can supply all of my needs.

What I see all around me revealed to me that my heart should not hang around temporary things that the Lord will one day pass away.

My body revealed to me that I can't trust my flesh because it's weak and will sin against the Lord if I don't pray and ask the Lord to give me the strength to keep my body under control according to God's holy word.

Temptations revealed to me that sin can be so desirable and can seem to be so right to do, especially on the spur of the moment, but the Lord desires my obedience that is so right to do unto the Lord.

The Bible revealed to me that God the Father, Son and Holy Spirit is talking directly to me as if I was the only sinner, instructing me how to know God's will for me to live by.

The Closer We Get to Jesus

The closer we get to Jesus the more things in this world will move further away from our hearts.

The closer we get to Jesus, the more our heart's desire will be for spiritual things that are eternal.

The temporary things will look so vain to us as we get closer to Jesus Christ, our Lord and Savior.

We will hate more and more sin as we get closer and closer to Jesus, who loves sinners and hates sin.

We will have no desire to live in sin if we get closer to Jesus.

The closer we get to Jesus, the more we will shun the evil we know in order to draw closer to the goodness of Jesus.

The closer we get to Jesus, the more we will know that this world is not our home and we will not stay here.

We will have no desire to do evil things as we get closer to Jesus Christ, who is good all the time to you and me.

The closer we get to Jesus, the more we will forgive those who do us wrong.

We will be good to those who hate us as we get closer to Jesus.

The closer we get to Jesus, the more good choices we will make in life.

We will get closer to one another in the church as we get closer and closer to Jesus.

We will not put our trust in the government as we get closer and closer to Jesus, who is coming back one day soon to create a new heaven and earth.

The closer we get to Jesus, the more the days and nights will be our pathway to lead us closer to the streets of gold.

We will let go of the things that can weigh us down as we get closer and closer to Jesus.

402 † *Ricky Clemons*

We will win more and more victories over our problems as we get closer and closer to Jesus.

The closer and closer we get to Jesus, the more we will be wise and not make the same mistakes.

The closer we get to Jesus, we will love Jesus more and more.

We will love people for who they are as we get closer to Jesus.

The closer we get to Jesus, the more we will love our enemies and want their souls to be saved in Jesus before it's too late.

We will be good to our loved ones in our own household as we get closer and closer to Jesus.

Our Time is this Present Day

We can watch a movie about prehistoric times and it can cause us to feel like we should have existed back then instead of existing in our time.

We can watch a good Bible story movie and it can cause us to feel like we should have been born back in the days when Jesus Christ lived on earth.

The Lord God predestined you and me to be born in this present time because He foreknew it was the right point in time for you and me to be born into this world.

God didn't make a mistake by not letting you exist in the days of noel.

If God had allowed you and me to exist in the time of noel, we might have been among the people who died in the world's greatest flood.

Our time is this present day, and we were born into this time because God predestined you and me to exist on earth today to serve His holy purpose and to be saved in His Son, Jesus and obey His Commandments.

We can easily believe that the people who once lived on earth over a thousand years ago had it so good, and not want to exist in this present time that God knew was right for us.

The time when Abraham, Isaac and Jacob were born was not our time to be born, no matter how heavenly divine the Bible makes that time sound, telling the stories about the prophets of old being the voice of God and talking to the angels of the Lord face to face.

If you and I had existed back in the ancient days, we would probably have been like King Pharaoh, Jezebel, King Saul and the Pharisees.

God didn't allow you and me to exist back in the Bible days because God is good to every human being and will not put on us more than we can bear.

We would be better off never having been born than to be born in the wrong time, as if God has no control over time and would allow time to have its way with our existence to appear and disappear like a shadow.

God is the ancient of days and appoints every human being a time to be born, though we can shorten our time and die through poor choices.

God is the past, present and future, for God is all-present beyond existence.

We should not take this too lightly, as if we have control over this present time and pretend to make ourselves immortal

Pretending immortality can be easy to do if we are climbing up the ladder of prosperity in this present day and time.

This present day is causing many people to doubt God's perfection.

We Can Be Quick and We Can Be Slow

We can be quick to say how someone has done us wrong, and be slow to say how we have done someone wrong.

We can be quick to talk bad about someone, and be slow to talk good about someone.

We can be quick to get jealous of someone, and be slow to be happy for someone moving up in life.

WE can be quick to get a swelled head, and be slow to humble ourselves.

We can be quick to tell a life, and be slow to tell the truth.

We can be quick to hurt some feelings, and be slow to apologize to someone.

We can be quick to form opinions about someone, and be slow to get to know someone.

We can be quick to lay traps for someone to fall into, and be slow to save someone from falling into a trap.

We can be quick to get revenge, and be slow to trust the Lord to get vengeance.

We can be quick to only look out for ourselves, and be slow to look out for someone else's well being.

We can be quick to outsmart someone else, and be slow to accept that someone is smarter than you and me.

We can be quick to feel rejected by someone, and be slow to see how we have rejected someone.

We can be quick to pretend with someone, and be slow to be real with someone.

We can be quick to give someone an evil eye look, and slow to give someone a kind look.

We can be quick to say I love you, and slow to put love into action.

We can be quick to say that I'm saved and sanctified, and be slow to come on one accord in the church of the Lord Jesus.

We can be quick to go to church, and be slow to reverence the Lord in His holy sanctuary.

We can be quick to say what we will do today or tomorrow, and be slow to say if it's the Lord's will that we do this or that.

We are all Definitions

We are all definitions for only Jesus Christ to always define us so very correctly.

The words that we say are not always our true definition to define you and me as telling the truth when we can say some words that aren't true even if we believe what we are saying is true.

In moments of anger, we can say words that we don't mean to say that can be defined as mean, when the true definition of us might be a nice person who is easy to get along with.

We can live under the same roof with someone for years and years and not know the true definition of that person as they go through the motions of doing daily chores, which do not truly define them.

Only Jesus Christ, our Lord, can always define what is real.

We are all definitions that are true or false, and we can't define our own hearts; only Jesus Christ can do that.

You are a definition that I will never truly define because we don't know each other's hearts, which is truly a good thing.

If I knew your heart and you knew my heart, we would probably run and hide from one another after we see some evil things that would probably give us a heart attack.

We all are definitions and can be desperately wicked when the choices we make can define you and me in many ways.

Only Jesus can give you and me a new definition for repenting of our sins and turning away from our sins to love and obey Him.

Jesus Christ is the true definition of God, who defines us with a free will to choose to be saved in His Son, Jesus Christ.

Beneath the Color of Our Skin

Beneath the color of our skin, we are all the same and can feel good or bad.

We all can have good and bad motives beneath the color of our skin.

We all can plot to do evil against someone.

Beneath the color of our skin, we all can lust and we all can get jealous.

We all can hide our real, true feelings beneath the color of our skin, and we all can pretend to be who we are not beneath the color of our skin.

We all can be covetous and we all can have greed in our hearts beneath the color of our skin.

Beneath the color of our skin, we all can think good thoughts and evil thoughts.

Beneath the color of our skin, we are all the same and feel so free or feel like we're in bondage.

We all can feel good about ourselves and feel bad about ourselves beneath the color of our skin.

We all can feel happy and we all can feel sad beneath the color of our skin because we are all the same beneath the color of our skin.

We all can be afraid of something and we all can feel bold beneath the color of our skin.

We all can feel empty and we all can feel ill, and we all can feel so well beneath the color of our skin where we are all the same whether we feel proud or humble.

We all can be kind and we all can be mean beneath the color of our skin, because beneath the color of our skin we all can feel guilty and we all can feel so not guilty.

Beneath the color of our skin, we can feel love and feel hate.

We all are the same and can choose to repent and follow Jesus Christ beneath the color of our skin where the real you and me can never deceive Jesus.

We are all the same beneath the color of our skin and we can either choose life in Christ or death.

Who are We?

Who are we to be like a canoe drifting on the deep ocean waters, if we drift away from Jesus Christ?

Who are we to be like only a moment to live and be so worthless to life, if we don't love Jesus more than our own life that Jesus owns?

Who are we to be like a dream passing through the night to be gone without a trace in the morning light, if we don't have a relationship with Jesus?

Who are we to be like the invisible wind if we don't be a witness of Jesus?

Who are we to be like an empty can to be kicked around by time if we are not a living example of Jesus?

Who are we to be like a dead fish in a fish tank full of polluted water if we are not excited about using our spiritual gifts to win souls to Jesus?

Who are we to be like a nagging back pain if we live our lives like Jesus has not given us the victory to sooth the nagging pain of problems that will occur in our lives?

Who are we to only be a particle of dust floating around in the air and have no substance if we believe that we are self-made when it was Jesus who spared our lives from death more times than we can count.

Who are we to be like an unsolved mystery to nature if we know to do what is right by the Bible and don't do it and shame Jesus' name?

Who are we to be so unpredictable to all the other earthly creatures that see us human beings changing on Jesus like the seasons when Jesus will never change on us for the worst?

Who are we to be blindfolded by the charms of pride that leads us into the dark traps of illusions and flatters us, when we are nothing without Jesus?

Who are we to be so naked in our shame that we can't cover up the motives and intentions in our hearts when Jesus sees us looking naked in all of our words and deeds?

Who are we to originate anything when Jesus Christ is the origin of all existence when foolish people will try to make God's creations to be a hoax?

Who are we to be a servant to a forceful cause when Jesus originated the free will choice for angels and human beings to know that He will not force anyone to love Him and keep His Commandments?

Who are we to fulfill our own purpose in life when we all were preordained by Jesus to fulfill His holy purpose on earth?

Who are we to convince our destiny to trust us to make no mistakes when only Jesus Christ was born in the flesh without sin?

Who are we to be like a rug on the floor to get walked over by not knowing what a day will bring us when the day will treat us right or treat us wrong according to Jesus' reason that will overthrow our reasoning that can be a burden to the day.

Real Life is Not Rehearsed

Real life is not rehearsed like making a movie.

Real life is not rehearsed like a TV show.

Real life is not rehearsed like a TV commercial.

Real life is not rehearsed like a church choir.

Real life is not rehearsed like a Broadway show.

Actors must rehearse their scripts to make a movie.

Actors must rehearse their scripts to make a TV show.

Actors must rehearse their scripts to make a TV commercial.

The church choir must rehearse their songs to sing in the choir.

Musicians must rehearse their instruments to play their music in a musical show.

Singers and dancers must rehearse their voice and body movements to perform in a Broadway show.

Actors can rehearse to make a mistake in a movie.

Actors can rehearse to have a flaw in a movie.

Actors can rehearse to have a bad habit in a movie.

Actors can rehearse to be evil in a movie.

Real life is not rehearsed because we don't rehearse to eat food.

Real life is not rehearsed because we don't rehearse to take a shower.

Real life is not rehearsed because we don't rehearse to get in our cars and drive, we just do it.

Besides being an actor, who in their right mind would rehearse to make a mistake?

Besides being an actor, who in their right mind would rehearse a flaw?

Besides being an actor, who in their right mind would rehearse a bad habit?

Besides being an actor, who in their right mind would rehearse to say bad words

Besides being an actor, who in their right mind would rehearse to do evil?

Real life is not rehearsed, because Jesus Christ never rehearsed anything in the presence of anyone when He lived here on earth without sin in his flesh.

Life can't get more real than Jesus, who never had to rehearse what He would say to anyone.

Life can't get more real than Jesus, who never had to rehearse the miracles that He did in the presence of people.

Real life can never be rehearsed to have no errors like a rehearsed movie with every scene looking so perfect and projecting its story to the audience.

What goes on in real life is no rehearsal to make life look perfect like a movie with actors pretending to make the movie look perfect.

Real life is not rehearsed, because we will do good or we will do evil with no thoughts about rehearsing it.

Even After I Mess Things Up

Even after I mess things up, God is still good to me.

Even after I mess things up, God is still merciful to me.

Even after I mess things up, God is still patient with me.

Even after I mess things up, God is still for me.

Even after I mess things up, God still loves me.

Even after I mess things up, God still forgives me.

God is God.

So, no matter how many times you and I mess things up, God can make something good out of what we messed up.

Adam and Eve messed us all up with sin, but God gave us His only begotten Son to save us from our sins.

Even after I mess things up, God is still God to make my life better if I confess and repent of my sins unto His Son, Jesus Christ.

Even after I mess things up, God is still on His holy throne looking down on me from heaven to make me to be His child, regardless of what I messed up.

Even after I mess things up because I am messed up in sin, God is still God to send His Son, Jesus Christ, back to this world to take me to heaven if I am saved in Jesus.

Even after I mess things up, God still has my back to get me out of things I mess up.

You're Supposed to Love Everybody

You're supposed to love everybody, but don't let anybody use you.

You're supposed to love everybody, but don't let anybody put you down.

You're supposed to love everybody, but don't let anybody push you around.

You're supposed to love everybody, but don't let anybody take advantage of you.

You're supposed to love everybody, but don't let anybody cause you to be dishonest.

You're supposed to love everybody, but don't let anybody cause you to stoop down to their level of foolishness.

You're supposed to love everybody, but don't let anybody cause you to lose your dignity.

You're supposed to love everybody, but don't let anybody make you do something wrong.

You're supposed to love everybody, but don't let anybody make you do what you don't want to do.

You're supposed to love everybody, but don't let anybody get between you and your spouse.

You're supposed to love everybody, but don't let anybody get between you and your children.

You're supposed to love everybody, but don't let anybody get between you and Jesus.

You're supposed to love everybody, but don't let anybody cause you to turn your back on Jesus.

You're supposed to love everybody, but don't let anybody cause you to be lost.

You're supposed to love everybody, but don't let anybody cause you to go to hell.

You're supposed to love everybody, but don't let anybody cause you to rebel against God.

You're supposed to love everybody, but don't let anybody cause you to live in sin.

You're supposed to love everybody, but don't let anybody cause you to be like the devil.

The Greatest Travel

Many people in this world love to travel to their favorite places.

Many people love to travel to places they've never been before.

Many people will save up their money to travel.

Many people will travel to another city to look for a job.

Many people will travel to another state to buy a new house.

Many people will travel to another country to go on a tour and sightsee.

Many people will travel across the sky in an aircraft.

Many people will travel on the road.

Many people will travel across the ocean.

Many people love to travel all around the world.

There are people who love to travel beyond the sky.

The greatest travel will one day be for all the righteous children of Jesus Christ, who will be our eternal guide to heaven when He comes back again.

If we are saved in Jesus, we will travel with Him, passing by this sinful world.

If we are saved in Jesus, we will travel with Him, passing by the sun and moon.

If we are saved in Jesus, we will travel with Him, passing by the stars.

If we are saved in Jesus, we will travel with Him, passing by the Milky Way.

If we are saved in Jesus, we will travel with Him, passing by the galaxy.

If we are saved in Jesus, we will travel with Him, passing by the black holes.

If we are saved in Jesus, we will travel with Him, passing by other worlds on our way to heaven with Jesus.

Traveling with Jesus will be the greatest travel to make the travel guide in this world to be forever below Jesus' travel guide to heaven.

The greatest travel will one day be for all the holy saints to travel with Jesus and all the angels back to heaven.

We will not get worn out on our way back to heaven.

If we are saved in Jesus Christ, we will one day soon go on the greatest travel with Jesus.

We will travel with Jesus, passing by every universe that is below the highest heaven where we will go to and celebrate our eternal destination.

As we travel through the outer space with Jesus Christ and all the holy angels, Jesus will illuminate the outer space with His glory of eternal light to pass us by all the black holes in the eternal outer space that Jesus created and can travel through any time He wants to.

The greatest travel will one day come to all the children of God to travel with Jesus back to heaven.

We will have a perfect eyesight to see other worlds and endless solar systems that we will pass by with eternal joy on our way back to heaven with Jesus Christ and all His angels.

Many people will travel to other countries that is a great travel to them, astronauts will travel to the moon that is great travel to them, but it's no comparison to traveling with Jesus one day across all the galaxies and other worlds that is very limited to the highest heaven where Jesus will take us to without us getting tired and worn out on our greatest travel.

Many people will travel in airplanes, trains, buses, motorcycles, cars, trucks, SUVs, RVs, and will travel on ships to be great to them, but if we are saved in Jesus we will one day go on the greatest travel to heaven and won't need to use any restrooms or drink any water to feel refreshed on our greatest travel to heaven.

The greatest travel will be no charge from Jesus who forever knows that no amount of money will ever be enough to pay for the greatest travel to heaven.

You and I and all of God's righteous children will have free airfare to travel with Jesus Christ and all the holy angels to heaven when Jesus comes back again on the clouds of glory.

There will be a number of righteous people that no one can count on the greatest travel to heaven one day.

All the airplanes will be of no use to take the place of Jesus, who will charge us no airfare on the greatest travel of our lives changing from mortal to immortality in Jesus Christ who is eternal life.

No airplanes and no spacecrafts can take us to heaven, that only Jesus can do on the greatest travel.

The Limelight People

Many people love to be in the limelight of things to draw attention themselves.

You and I can get addicted to the limelight and wanting to be popular, even in the church where many church folks love to be in the limelight with their ministry work in the church.

It's so easy to want to make a popular name in the church for yourself, maybe because your name might have been unpopular in your home, school, on the job or in your neighborhood for years and years.

Many church folks are becoming addicted to popularity in the church, where many church folks love to be around those they believe to be popular in the household of faith.

There any popularity contests going on in the church where there are people who love to be seen in the limelight and make a popular name for themselves to draw people to themselves and away from Jesus.

Even in the church, many church folks don't like to be around unpopular church folks who the Lord can use to speak the truth in love.

The limelight people's lives are so void of Jesus Christ and so full of themselves, and they use the name of Jesus to cover up their self-ambitions as they strive to gain influence and be popular in the church.

The limelight people love popularity and gathering many people around them who believe in them, when God says "put no confidence in man."

Only Jesus truly knows who is in the limelight for His holy name that is not a popular name to the people of the world and the selfish church folks who are only going through the motions of acknowledging the name of Jesus with no transformation in their hearts.

The limelight church folks are quick to cast anyone out of the church for smearing their light-only shining rays of pretense.

There is Freedom in Love

There is freedom in love, but there is no fear and no doubt in love.

There is freedom in love, but there are no grudges and no envy in love.

There is freedom in love, but there is no manipulation and no strife in love.

There is freedom in love, but there is no confusion and no rivalry in love.

There is freedom in love, but there are no cliques and no divisions in love.

There is freedom in love, but there is no fussing and no fighting in love.

There is freedom in love, but there is no inequality and no injustice in love.

There is freedom in love, but there is no abuse and no danger in love.

There is freedom in love, but there is no disrespect and no trickery in love.

There is freedom in love, but there is no selfishness and no lying in love.

There is freedom in love, but there is no mocking and no hate in love.

There is freedom in love, but there is no race and no skin color in love.

There is freedom in love, but there is no revenge and no foolishness in love.

There is freedom in love, but there is no illness and no stress in love.

There is freedom in love, but there is no nothing unnatural in love.

There is freedom in love, but there is no lust and no greed in love.

There is freedom in love, but there is no covetousness and no jealousy in love.

There is freedom in love, but there is no stealing and no killing in love.

There is freedom in love, but there is no disobedience and no favoritism in love.

There is freedom in love, but God's jealousy is a righteous act of God's love.

God's favoritism is a righteous act of God's love to give us more time to get our hearts right with Him.

There is freedom only in God's love through His Son, Jesus Christ, who is our freedom in love where there is no freedom in our love that can get twisted up.

Only Jesus

Only Jesus is giving us life and only Jesus can give us eternal life.

Life is not about you and me, who can pick and choose who we want to love and don't want to love, but we can only love one another if we love Jesus Christ.

Life is all about Jesus, even when we act like we are keeping ourselves alive and being the creator of our own lives.

We can carry ourselves as though we have the power to give life and take life away from anyone who we believe to be against us.

We can so often be too hard on one another in the church, as if we own one another and can give one another eternal life or eternal death when only Jesus can do this.

If eternal life was in us to have the power to raise the dead, we would raise many wicked people from the grave and give them eternal life.

We would leave many righteous people in the grave.

Eternal life is not you and eternal life is not me, because we are sinful and form cliques and cause divisions in the household of faith where we can cause a wheat to leave the church and believe that it's a tare.

You and I are not the King of Glory, even though we can pretend like we can't fall short of the glory of God in our home, on the job, in our community, in the church services, board meetings and in the church business meetings.

We can carry ourselves like we have eternal life to give, especially to those who we love the most, and we can puff ourselves up to have the power to speak eternal death upon anyone who we believe to be our enemy, especially in the church.

If eternal life was in you and me, we would fill the new heaven and new earth with partiality and injustice because we are selfish in ways that only Jesus will always see.

We can set bad examples and not care to see how people can be badly affected by what we say and what we do.

We can believe that we have eternal life and can ruin people's lives right in the church and pretend like our hands are so clean and have no blood on them.

Only Jesus can charge us with spiritual murder for killing someone's spirit.

Many People

Many people have locked up their ears from hearing the truth, but unlock their ears to hear lies.

Many people are writing best-seller books, when their life is writing blank pages of emptiness.

Many people want to be loved, but they have shut down their emotions and feel no love in their hearts.

Many people are quick to show off their intelligence and slow to think what is logical.

Youth is a treasure chest of great wealth, but peer pressure from many bad people can bring youth down to immoral poverty.

The limelight will shine down on the stage floor when the tongue is like the curtains to open up hell and perform a mesmerizing dance of words to spellbound many people's minds and make them believe a lie is the truth and the truth is a lie.

Many people have eyes that see other people's faults but cannot see even one fault in themselves.

Many people are being a friend to evil things and being an enemy to good things.

Living right is a sham to many people who have bad morals.

A thousand pieces of broken glass have a better chance of being glued back together than a broken heart that many people have.

If one church leader is a bad apple, that church leader can rot the unity of many people.

Many people who are young, middle aged and old reject the truth of God's holy word to be lost in their sins to meet their fate in Hell.

Only Jesus

The night can shine bright in visions and dreams about Jesus Christ coming back, making the night so happy to disappear from this sinful world.

The day can look so dark in evil practices upon the land, and only Jesus can light up anyone's life and shine the goodness of God throughout the day.

We can think high-minded thoughts and think low-minded thoughts that are so unbalanced, but only Jesus can keep our minds balanced in divine thoughts for keeping our minds on Him.

Hope can be labeled as being good luck or a wish to anyone who is only living for the moment.

Jesus Christ is the living hope to be faithful and true to you and me, while luck and a wish are like the wind that no one can hold onto.

Being alive is freedom and a chance to heal the body and spirit that only Jesus can create to be immortal when He comes back again one day soon.

Living from birth to old age is an insult to time if we live our lives rejecting the Holy Spirit who connects us to Jesus, who is the only one who can give us eternal life beyond this world that shows no respect of age to return us to the dust of the earth.

Only Jesus Christ can save us all.

Our free will choice is the one step that we can take to choose to want to be saved in Jesus Christ who we must believe in and obey, even if the only thing we have is the clothes on our backs.

Only Jesus knows whose back is turned against Him because he sees our spiritual nakedness all around our souls.

Only Passing Through

Are you making this world your home or just passing through this temporary home to be caught up with Jesus Christ on the clouds of glory one day soon?

Like a ship passing through the seashore docks, you and I are passing through this temporary world that will one day pass away under the sun.

Every one of us has a free will choice to make this world our home or to make heaven our home.

We are all stuck here on earth and can't leave without Jesus Christ coming back to take all of His children to paradise in heaven where eternal life has no end, unlike our temporary life here.

We all will make a conscious choice day after day to pick up our crosses and follow Jesus or leave our crosses down on the ground and follow this fallen world.

If you are only passing through this temporary home, then you should know that the road will get rough sometimes and cause you to feel so all alone, but Jesus is close to you and will pick you up and carry you through problems that won't always last because you hold onto Jesus.

This whole world is a temporary home to Jesus, who is the only doctor who can make us spiritually well down in our souls, no matter how many aches and pains our physical body may feel.

Jesus owns our bodies and souls and helps us to pass through our trials that we all have for not making this world our home to pass through temporary things under the sun.

God, Jesus and the Holy Spirit

Opinions are out of date to Jesus Christ, who is the word of God beyond our sophisticated opinions that can get us into some trouble.

Love is an action word that can be expressed in our body language that can always be positive in the love of God.

Words of love can be like rain water running down a drain without showing love in Jesus' name.

A car is not designed and manufactured by only words alone.

Foolish people will refuse to believe that there is a god who designed and created a man and woman in His own image.

For God used His own hands to mold and shape a man and woman, and God used His own breath to give a man and woman a living soul.

A true fact can be for us or against us, but God can be for us or against us and no facts will override God's decisions for us.

Nothing good can be born out of the womb of evil unless God permits it, and no one can fully understand evil except God alone.

A mind is a terrible thing to waste, and no one can have a pure mind if it's not focused on Jesus Christ.

The earth, wind, water and fire will not assume that God the Father, Son and Holy Spirit is not one trinity godhead, but man can assume he's a god all by himself and that he needs no other person.

We can't separate ourselves from the air we breathe, because we would all die without oxygen.

We can't separate Jesus Christ and the Holy Spirit from God.

Lucifer and his fallen angels tried to do this and failed, causing their eternal damnation.

Our moment in time is in a battle against our fate, and only Jesus Christ can make a peace treaty with one accord.

We can be at war with one another and be morons during our moment in time and morons to our fates because we have no love for Jesus to not love God to reject the Holy Spirit.

God's Mercy

God's mercy makes us well in mind and body.

God's mercy keeps us alive when we deserve to die.

God's mercy renews our strength against temptation that can make us weak.

God's mercy protects us from harm and danger that we can be unaware of.

God's mercy gives us another minute to get our hearts right with Jesus Christ.

God's mercy leads us to conviction and repentance.

God's mercy reveals to us the love of God for us.

God's mercy carries us through our own mistakes that can turn against us.

God's mercy keeps us from falling into the traps that can cause our souls to be lost.

God's mercy gives us a second chance to humble ourselves before God and one another.

God's mercy will open our eyes to see ourselves being better off not being born than to live a rebellious life against Jesus Christ who is the Son of God.

God's mercy will remove the dark clouds from our lives so we can rejoice in the sunny days of His blessings upon our souls.

God's mercy will energize us to give God all the glory and praise that He deserves from us for as long as we shall live.

God's mercy holds back the angel of death from taking our breath away.

God's mercy loves to bring us back to Jesus who we can stray from and not even realize it, regardless of our good works that can't save us.

God's mercy is a good friend to us when we can be our own enemy any time and any day.

Can Be

A woman can look so beautiful in her outward appearance, but can project an ugly look of selfishness on the inside.

Good criticism can be bad criticism to anyone who believes they don't need to make a change for the better.

Someone who has been wounded a lot in life can turn into a very judgmental person.

A man who is full of himself can be so empty and lack good character.

Rain will fall from the clouds up in the sky and hit the ground, but when stupidity falls from the mind of fools they can be so foolish that their ideas hit the ground of desperation.

A heart that has no love can be like a bad disease.

The eyes can look so honest but the voice can be so dishonest.

Cool air can flow through an open window and cool off the hottest room in the house, but anger can be like hot air flowing through an open mouth.

Life is an open book to read about the living, but death can be like a page ripped out of that book that will not have a complete story because of that missing page.

A lie from the tip of the tongue can make a liar happy, but the Lord cannot lie to anyone who can be untrue to themselves.

A father and son and a mother and daughter are the same genders, and one can be good and the other can be bad, but God the Father and His Son can never be different and no one can separate what death failed to do when Jesus Christ rose from the grave.

A Woman Represents the Church

A woman was the first creature on earth to rebel against God, but the man has taken his rebellion to the extreme.

All the wars on earth have been about men fighting against men and killing men.

Men have proved to the world that they can be so loveless when it comes to women, who seem to be the peacemakers in this world.

No war has ever been about one nation of women fighting against another nation of women.

Women are the most loving creatures here on earth, and many women have proved this to be a true fact.

All through the Bible stories, wars, bloodshed and death have been caused by men killing men.

A woman was the first to disobey God, but a man was the first murderer who killed another man for being so jealous.

Women are few in number compared to men when it comes to murders, and the prisons are filled with mostly men.

Could it be that God has been using women to be the peacemakers in this world where it's very often the man being quick to get angry and want to kill?

Jesus Christ was the only man without sin, and He is the Prince of Peace.

It had to take a sinless man to be more loving than women, who are the most beautiful and most loving creatures on earth where a woman represents the church that the devil hates and makes war against because she loves Jesus with all of her heart.

The World Heavyweight Bout

The World Heavyweight Bout that I'm about to reveal to you is the match between the truth and the deception of lies.

That truth will knock you out because God is the truth that we can't afford to ever doubt.

For in the right-hand corner of God, weighing in at the weight of our victory is the Truth which protects our souls from the devil who is like a poisonous snake with his venom being nothing but lies.

In the left-hand corner of the world, weighing in at the weight of deception is the Liar, who only appears to look like the truth that's always real.

The match is ready to begin, with the referee named Ignorance standing in between the Truth and the Liar in his uniform that God winks His eye at, regardless of the fight sounding like a thunderstorm.

The bell rung for round one was when God told Adam and Eve the Truth that they didn't believe, and they let the Liar beat the Truth in round one.

The bell rung for round two was when Noah was building the ark and only eight people believed the Truth that truly shocked everyone else when they saw the rain falling down.

Round three was when the Truth finally knocked the Liar out when the Son of God was made flesh and rocked the whole world in the cradle of His love, especially when Jesus Christ gave his life on the cross for the sins of the world and rose from the grave with a knockout punch to win and pay our cost.

The referee of Ignorance just didn't understand this at all, until the Truth opened his eyes to show him the Liar's broken tooth that Jesus knocked out with an eternal knockout punch.

God is the Truth and the Truth is God who cannot lie.

Lying is surely impossible for God to do sitting on His everlasting holy throne on hight.

One Blood and by the Blood

Here on earth we all have blood running through our veins, whether we're rich or poor, good or bad, sane or insane.

Everyone's blood is the color red, no matter what the color of our skin is or the color of the hair on our heads.

We are all one blood in a world that will be destroyed by fire, not another flood.

We all will bleed blood when we get a cut, and no baby was ever born without blood while coming into this world to live and one day die, only God knows when.

Man's first sacrifice to God was blood, and God was pleased by this while He sat above the highest mountain cliff and looked down on this world that could only be cleansed of its sins by the blood of Jesus Christ who shed blood for the sins of all men.

No animal blood could ever do anything like this back during and after the days of Cain and Abel.

The Grass in Our Lives

We will eat nothing but the grass in our lives if we don't bow down unto Jesus, the Lord of Lords, who will pass His decree of chastisement down on you and me.

We are the living dust of the earth that will agree and can't set us free from worshipping the golden image of the world.

King Nebuchadnezzar ate grass like an ox that God allowed to last long enough to humble the king so that he would see himself being nothing but a fool in the presence of God when he tried to exalt himself above God.

He failed and was sent right into the wilderness that became his hell.

King Nebuchadnezzar also learned the hard way about the grass not being greener on the other side when he disobeyed God, who the grass will obey and never deny.

What Ms. Riding High Said to Ms. Riding Low

Up in the twilight zone, Ms. Riding High looked down on Ms. Riding low and said, "I'm having the ride of my life over the sun and moonlight glow and over all the shining starts of this world where you, Ms. Riding Low, have fallen down so low in your own scars.

"Who do you think you are, Ms. Riding Low, to tell me that I will one day fall flat on my face if I don't let Jesus live in my heart?

"I don't care about that and surely won't sweat it.

"You, Ms. Riding Low, just don't know what a high ride you are missing over the rainbow."

Right after Ms. Riding High said those words to Ms. Riding Low, a heavy dark cloud appeared with a roaring sound of thunder and out of nowhere a lightning bolt knocked Ms. Riding High down to the ground.

Ms. Riding Low comforted Ms. Riding High and said, "Now you know and should be glad that Jesus chastises all who He loves."

There is No One Like You

There is no one like you, My Lord, who can make me feel like I'm in heaven on earth that's below Your heavenly hills.

No other one can mend my broken heart and soothe my mind and remove the dark clouds like You, O Lord, who is my sunshine on a rainy day and my north star who can find me when I get lost.

You can find me, even in the household of faith where I can easily go astray and not keep my eyes on You, My Lord Jesus Christ.

You are the way, the truth and the only life because there's no one else like You, my Lord Jesus Christ.

You can pick me up when I fall and raise me up when others kill me with their words of spite.

There is no one like You, Jesus, who will never size me up and compare me with someone else who is not always wise.

It Was Jesus

One day in the afternoon, my platoon Sergeant and I decided to search for a log cabin after walking to the top of the mountain, which had worked the rest of the troops overtime.

As they laid down to rest on the floor of the laboratory that was on top of the mounting, words couldn't express the awesomeness of the view; it was so breathtaking to me.

The whole Charlie Company of the 65th Engineer Battalion had walked for miles up that mountain and everybody was so glad when we made it to the laboratory at the very top of the mountain because we had walked nonstop.

When we all reached the top, we got a bite to eat.

It was a good, hot meal that soothed everyone's tired feet.

My platoon Sergeant and I decided to go and look for a log cabin that was five miles away from the laboratory.

We ended up at a place where we were lost and got caught in a snow blizzard that was looking like a wizard.

My platoon Sergeant and I turned back around because it was getting dark, when suddenly something took charge of me and directed my footsteps to lead the way back to the laboratory.

To this very day, I truly know that it was Jesus who led me and my platoon Sergeant back to the laboratory that was so far away we couldn't see it.

When we made it back, my platoon Sergeant gave me the glory in the presence of the other troops for leading him back, but I truly know the real, true story today.

Jesus directed my footsteps back to that laboratory when there was no one else around to help.

Time and Chance

Time looked straight at me and said, "Since the day you were born, you couldn't afford to take the change to not join God's faithful children.

"You can choose to want to join and follow Jesus, who is always good and fair and doesn't pull any stunts on you and me, unlike the devil who wants to destroy you on his bounty hunt."

I looked back at Time and Chance and asked Time, "What chance do I have to make it to heaven, way beyond the sun that shines over me who can't pay sinful fines that only Jesus can pay?

"Jesus is surely my only chance to be saved and truly advance to heaven one day soon.

"Jesus is giving me my time today and this is my only chance to love and obey Him, since time and chance bow down and worship Him in every way."

Time looked straight at me again and said, "I can catch up with you, but you can't catch up with me.

"Who will fill and empty your cup?"

There is a chance you can take to help prolong your life or help shorten your life — the choice of your own footsteps will decide.

Jesus gives you time to take a chance with Him and it's always a good chance to take during your time that's hanging on a limb.

Jesus Will Never Divorce His Wife

Jesus will never divorce His wife even when she plays the whore taking on many other lovers as soon as she kicks Jesus out the door.

Even if she locks Jesus out of her house while telling her other lovers she has no spouse.

There is a wealthy man named money who Jesus' wife loves to make love to, calling him her honey.

O, what a tall, muscular built man named materialism.

He gives her a beautiful silk see-through gown to wear to seduce him so he'll make love to her and she can bear his child named Idol.

She bows down to Idol and worships him while caring less about how vital it is to love and obey her husband Jesus, who forgives her in her shame and nakedness that all of her lovers look upon and see her like a skinned cat with no fur.

Jesus' wife is the church, and she is so blessed to be the wife of Jesus Christ.

Stop by Jesus' House

You and I are only passing through this temporary world that will one day pass away through the universe that has no ending.

You and I can come to an end on any day while we pass by one another, whether we're good or bad, while we walk by and drive by one another on the road.

We also pass by many businesses and houses as we go here and there, and sometimes we stop by the store or stop by a friend's house just to say hi.

We go about our business from day to day, passing by some people who may pass away today.

We may stop by their grave, where you and I don't want to go before stopping by Jesus' house to be saved in Jesus Christ whose house is the church that so many people pass by on their way to work.

They don't care to know that they are passing by the best work to prosper their souls to spiritual wealth.

Our greatest success is achieved by stopping by Jesus' house to spend some time with Jesus Christ, who stops by the house in our hearts and knocks on our doors to give us an abundance of life.

Jesus will also give this abundance to the maimed person who wants to be saved in His name.

Jesus will bless the house of our bodies from being an instrument of sin that can stop by Jesus' house and pretend to be a friend to you and me.

The Technicalities of God's Word

When we get into the technicalities of God's word, more than obeying God's word by faith, we will be self-righteous and become like the Pharisees, examining every little detail to make God's word to be a burden instead of a blessing to hail Jesus Christ as the Son of God as the bible tells us so well.

Many people like to examine all the technicalities more than examining their own hearts that can do nothing good without the grace of God giving us another day to be saved.

We should not analyze our blessings; they are sometimes too complicated to understand because we do not deserve God's blessings that He gives to all great and small in this world.

Technicalities have caused many people to put their lives on pause because of not having faith in Jesus Christ who can do supernatural things and perform a miracle in anyone's life.

So, get beyond all the technicalities that are like holding back a good sneeze that feels so good to let go, leaving us feeling so refreshed.

Jesus can always do this for us above the technicalities that can make me and you so weary.

Why are We Here in this Church?

Why are we here in this church on the holy Sabbath day?

We are all different and should be glad to be here to worship Jesus Christ.

We come together in this church looking for something good to happen to us on our soul search to experience a supernatural and holy divine Lord and Savior who knows how to comfort our minds and hearts.

We are here today because we have a good reason to believe that Jesus Christ is the faithful and true living story in the best inspiriting book on earth.

Many people will believe the bible to be a fiction story and will love to get the glory that belongs to Jesus who created this world.

We are here today to remember our creator, God, who remembered you and me and set us free from our sinful words and deeds.

We are in the best place to get away from material things and away from the scribes and Pharisee people who love to judge us for being here in this church today.

We are here because we made our choice to worship the holy great One who gives us holy pleasures and heavenly things to think on in this world that Jesus owns every day.

We are here on the holy Sabbath day of rest to come together in love for one another, because if we love one another, we love the holy great God who is love all the time.

Jesus knows why we are here better than you and I will ever know on our good days and bad days.

We are here to worship the One and only real Jesus Christ, who is invisible and wants us to love and obey Him who is visible in His holy word and can be visible in our hearts if we believe in Jesus as the bible says.

We are here because we all have chosen to be here in this church today.

Jesus doesn't force anyone to worship Him on the holy Sabbath day of rest, but we come together by our free will choice to get blessed by the Lord, whose Holy Spirit takes two steps to our one step to lead us here.

We Can Live Our Lives

We can live our lives as if Jesus owes us God's love.

We can live our lives as if Jesus owes us the church that we can use to run people out of, as if the church belongs to us to separate the wheat from the tares.

We can live our lives as if we are entitled to be blessed by Jesus, who owes us nothing, while you and I owe Jesus all the glory and praise for the rest of our lives.

Jesus doesn't owe us even one second of His blessings, no matter how much tithes and offerings we return, as if we think we're worthy and Jesus should pat us on the shoulder.

We can live our lives as if Jesus owes us what we want and what we need.

We can live our lives as if Jesus owes us His Holy Spirit to teach us all truth.

We can live our lives as if we don't owe death a penny, even though we were born in sin and die as if our living is so worthless.

We can live our lives as if Jesus Christ owes us spiritual gifts and talents that we can use to glorify ourselves.

We can live our lives as if Jesus owes us success and prosperity that we can use to pretend to be self-made.

We will always owe God the Father, the Son and the Holy Spirit our body and soul for being made in the likeness of God as if we were never born in sin.

We can live our lives as if Jesus owes us freedom to say what we want to say and do what we want to do, when in reality we owe Jesus our repentance and our obedience that He deserves every day that we owe our faith and works to Jesus.

We can live our lives as if Jesus owes us the Bible that we don't always interpret the right way, when we actually owe Jesus our daily bible study.

We can live our lives as if Jesus owes us His listening ear to hear our prayers that should always be honest and selfless that we owe to Jesus Christ.

We owe Jesus our strength and our weaknesses, as well as our successes and our failures.

We owe Jesus our good days and our bad days.

Jesus doesn't owe us anything but death unto us.

Jesus suffered and died on the cross and rose from the grave that owes Jesus the victory over death to give you and me eternal life as if we live our lives without sin and are entitled to heaven one day soon.

We can live our lives as if Jesus owes us this day to live, when we really owe our thanks to Jesus for giving us this day to live as if there is no tomorrow.

We can live our lives as if Jesus owes us youth, mid-life and old age, but we actually owe Jesus for yesterday, today and tomorrow is only a moment in time to Him.

Socializing with Nature

Nature can teach us how to socialize with God and one another.

Nature can teach us how to be real with one another because nature is always real with you and me who can be so rigid sometimes and not socialize with each other.

Nature knows no antisocial behaviors that you and I are very familiar with.

Nature knows how to relate to you and me who don't always know how to relate to one another.

Nature knows how to relate to God's love so crystal clear as we walk down nature's trail roads to see the beautiful flowers, green grass and tall trees being social to us and expressing God's tranquility.

The great blue skies, sun, moon, stars and clouds can socialize and show us what a friend we have in God's only begotten Son, Jesus Christ, who is our Lord and Savior and the Lord over nature.

The oceans, seas, rivers, lakes and ponds can socialize with us and show the ways of God flowing so gentle on the surface of our lives, even during our hurricane trials when the hurricane eye of God's love will gently flow God's compassion around our souls.

The mountains, hills and deep valleys can socialize with us and show God's greatness and excellence that can relate to you and me.

God created us to do great things in His holy name that is greater than life.

We can always socialize with nature and it can relate to us peace and give us a peace of mind in this hustle and bustle world.

Nature is a good friend to you and me and gives us some good, wise advice.

Nature can teach us how to be quiet and listen to one another to understand what we say to one another.

You and I will very often invite each other to gather together, but nature needs no official notice from us to socialize with us and relate God's love to us.

Our Medicine Cabinet

If we put Jesus Christ in our medicine cabinet, a lot of the medical doctors will sooner or later vanish because Jesus is better medicine than the doctor's medicine in our medicine cabinet.

Good doctors are God's healing remedy to make us well and keep us well.

Medicine cabinets can get over-crowded with different kinds of doctors' medicines, but Jesus is the only doctor who can heal our sin-sick souls that need to be healed for our minds and bodies to prosper in good health.

There is spiritual healing in Jesus, but the doctors' medicine will only heal the body and not the broken spirit.

When the spirit is well, the body has a greater chance of getting well.

The only way we can worship God is in spirit and truth that brings great healing to our souls.

Having a strong will to live beyond crippling illnesses is mostly a spiritual thing, being higher than physical pain and suffering.

Many people who survive terrible suffering have a connection with the Lord whose healing power is in His holy word that is our good medicine from Jesus to decrease the doctors' medicines in our cabinet.

My Flesh

I can go to church and get more power of the Holy Ghost until I leave the church the next few hours to face up to this flesh of mine all over again.

I must pray without ceasing, even when time seems to be against me whose flesh is weak when my spirit is willing to meet Jesus Christ at the cross where He died in my place and rose from the grave to give me victory over my flesh that can hasten to give into temptation if I don't stay prayed up and grounded in God's holy word day after day as my flesh makes war with my spirit.

No matter what good I say and do, that can't give me the victory over my flesh when my righteousness is like filthy rags that have no fresh scent to breathe in and out of my nostrils.

I can go to church and leave the church being the best place for me who can get more power of the Holy Ghost to give me the strength to resist the devil's temptations.

I live my life here on earth, where my flesh is weak but my spirit is willing to do God's will that will never ill my soul in this sinful world.

What Do We Own?

What do we own when our emotions can own us and play with our minds like a child playing with his or her toys?

Can we own a smile that can run away from us during our troubled times?

What do we own when death can put its arms around us and hug us close to the grave?

Can we own a relationship with anyone when time can cause us to make a U-turn and go back to our old selfish ways?

What do we own when our flesh can get weak and desire the wrong things that can own our hearts for giving into the wrong things?

Can we own our minds that can think evil, as if we can't think of anything that is good?

What do we own when our bodies can get ill and our health and strength can be paralyzed and confine us to the bed?

Can we own our eyes that can look too long in the wrong places and not look long enough in the right places?

What do we own when our ears can only hear words of gossip and lies that can cause us to stray away from the Lord?

Can we own our hands and touch only the things that will do us good and well, when our hands can own us and touch nothing but trouble that can ruin our good name or may even our lives?

Can we own our feet and not step on the devil's balcony that we will fall from and break our spiritual walk with Jesus Christ if we don't keep our feet planted on God's holy ground?

What do we own and hold onto even when people can change on us and turn their backs on us for no good reason.

No one likes to own up to their faults, but it makes good sense to not claim anything that God owns, which is all things.

Someone in Hell

Someone in hell asked someone in heaven, "How is it you got to heaven and I didn't when I was bowed on my knees before God? If there's anybody who doesn't belong in heaven, it's you. You disobeyed the Lord and robbed and killed people over the dollar bill."

Then the soul in heaven replied, "Did you confess and repent of your sins to the Son of God? If you had done that, He would have cleansed you of your sins and forgiven you, just as Jesus has forgiven me and taken me into heaven so kindly.

Then someone in hell remembered that he never repented during all the years he had lived.

There are Mosquito People

There are mosquito people who can bite us with their words and with their actions and can cause us to itch with doubts about them not being Christians, even though they go to church and clap their hands.

Mosquitoes will surely suck our blood out of our veins, and mosquito people will suck away our innocence and make us feel guilty about the conclusions they draw about us.

Without a doubt, the devil's temptations are spiritual mosquitoes trying to suck out our spiritual walk with the Lord.

God's word is our spiritual mosquito repellent and it protects us from the mosquito bites of the devil.

A mosquito can buzz in our ears to make a sound that's so annoying, but Jesus will kill spiritual mosquitoes with the truth of His holy word.

A mosquito bite can surely itch and it can spread, but Jesus can stop the spiritual itch and keep it from spreading in the church among his sheep.

Mosquitoes can carry the West Nile virus, but Jesus can carry the cure to get rid of spiritual itch and make our hearts pure.

There is No Weight

There is no weight to a fly that can land on us, who may not know it.

Our tongue can carry a weight of words to knock someone down on the ground of hatred.

The holy bible will carry a heavy weight of the truth that is always reliable to lead us to Jesus, who has no weight of sins.

There is no weight to the air that we breathe and there is no weight in our eye vision to see.

You and I can blow hot air in the form of words and create a heavy weight of strife.

The truth of God's word has no heavy weight on anyone who lives his or her life by the truth that is light like the air to anyone being set free by the truth.

There is no weight to a feather that can float through the air. Jesus can float our minds on the air of his peace.

There is no weight in a bubble that will burst so silent in the air. We should love Jesus first because He wants to burst our bubbles of selfishness.

Many People Will

Many people will move away from their country, state, city or town where they grew up because many people love to live on the ground of prosperity and gain some financial wealth that no one can put down.

Many women are looked at as being weak because of being feminine.

Many men are looked at as bad boys because of being masculine.

God created feminine and masculine to remain in their correct gender.

Many people will pay time no mind and put time up on a shelf to collect dust until they get sick and need to find some time to get well again. Time is on no one's side.

If God wants to, He can unwind our biological clocks and makes them stop ticking.

Today many people have a good start in life and end up with a bad finish. They keep company with trouble that is no friend.

Many people will have a bad start in life and end up with a good finish. They keep company with the Lord as if He is in body form.

Only a few people will be real about examining themselves to surely know that Jesus Christ is real in their lives.

Many people will feel so proud for being so intelligent, creative and skillful, when they will overlook how to get in tune with their natural senses that don't foul anyone's conscious to especially love and obey Jesus.

My Receipt

One day, I went to drop off bags of clothing to an organization collecting such items for the needy.

When I pulled up to the booth, a man stepped out and took the bags.

He then asked a routine question, "Would you like a receipt?" while pulling out his pen.

I declined and as I drove away, the Lord spoke to me, *"It is I who writes out all of your receipts, ones that no man could ever add or subtract, dating back to the day you were born. This is the receipt I gave to all the world to be saved."*

Everyone's Shoes

Sitting in my bedroom, I noticed the different styles of shows I've been wearing through thick and thin.

Suddenly, the Lord spoke to me, *"I have walked in all of your shoes to set you free from a life of sin that will never be your friend nor a friend to any man throughout the land."*

People may say Jesus hasn't walked in their shoes, but rest assured, our Lord has felt the blues and the joys of walking so strong and steady in everyone's shoes.

The Ladder

The Lord put a ladder before me and told me to climb up the ladder because He wanted to see how high I would climb up beyond the joys and scars of life.

I began to climb up the ladder, making it midway before the ladder began to sway to and fro, side to side, leaving me in a fearful way.

As I reached the top rung, I saw that the ladder was broken, something of which Jesus had never spoken.

Now I know that ladder was a mere illusion meant to help strengthen my faith as I climbed, up the ladder step by step, day after day.

The Second Resurrection

There was a man who preached God's holy word with all his heart.

This man returned his tithes and offerings unto the Lord.

He was so full of love that he could sing, write and play musical instruments, and of course, pray.

Many people just knew this man had earned a place in the eternal heavenly land.

But, unlike God, they did not know this man's heart.

God knew all too well that this man was holding onto some sins that caused him to wake up in the second resurrection, which was no surprise to God, who knew him too well below the heavens.

It's Always Love

It's always love that draws people into the church to find Jesus on their holy soul search.

It's always love that keeps people in the church where faith and love grow together in the good and bad weather.

So many people are hurting and they yearn to be loved more than they want to hear the truth and get the knowledge and wisdom that can so quickly slip away.

Yes, it is love that people need most, especially from God above.

What good is a sermon, a Bible lesson or a song praising the Lord if we don't love one another and live on one accord?

Yes, it's always love—the greatest gift of all—that you and I will fall short of.

What My Spirit Said to My Flesh

My spirit said to my flesh, *"You must follow Jesus all the way and He will carry you far above all that makes you weak and bleak."*

My flesh said to my spirit, *"Living in pleasure feels so very good, like discovering a chest full of treasure."*

My spirit wisely replied, *"Oh, before long, that treasure chest will be empty for not loving Jesus, who keeps it filled."*

Next thing I knew, the spirit of the Lord convicted my soul with the two-edge sword of God's holy word.

Now, my spirit and my flesh speak in glorious unison, always the same words: *"Jesus loves me."*

Which Man Would God Respect the Most?

When a rich man visited the church wearing his expensive three-piece suit and a Rolex on his wrist, every brow stood at attention with a steadfast salute.

The rich man was the highlight, the talk of the church.

This man was fully degreed —bachelors, masters and a doctorate — and he slipped behind the wheel of a shining Rolls Royce for all to see when he left out of the church.

When a poor man visited the church wearing faded jeans and a dingy shirt with the odor of liquor reeking on his breath, the eyebrows dropped.

Many stared at him with open disgust.

Which man would God respect the most?

Which is neither one, because God loves them both the same but hates their sins, but whoever that repents and turns to God, he will be saved.

Believe in Me
and You Shall be Saved

Jesus says, "If you believe in Me you shall be saved."

Jesus didn't say that you must get rid of all your faults in this world before you can believe in Me.

If you and I had to get rid of all of our flaws to believe in Jesus, we would never get rid of them on our own.

Jesus would not have to do a background check on you or me to see if we are good enough to believe in Him to be saved.

Jesus Christ our Lord never had to form a meeting with his disciples to vote on souls to save to add to His church.

Jesus says you must repent of your sins unto Me and believe in Me to be saved by being born again and baptized in the name of the Father, Son and Holy Ghost.

Believing in Jesus is loving Jesus and keeping His holy laws from coast to coast.

Anyone will be saved for believing in Jesus Christ as long as they truly deny self, beyond question and comment.

Baptism, church membership, church positions and keeping the law of God can't save us from our sins. We must believe in Jesus Christ with all our hearts for Jesus to save our souls.

Jesus will never force anyone to choose to believe in Him. Many fallen, sinful creatures will believe in creatures and get deceived.

Believing in Jesus has no deceptions.

I Want to Keep My Eyes on Jesus

I don't want to keep my eyes on people who make mistakes.

I want to keep my eyes on Jesus; He makes no mistakes.

I don't want to keep my eyes on people who have flaws.

I want to keep my eyes on Jesus, who has no flaws.

I don't want to keep my eyes on people who can say something wrong.

I want to keep my eyes on Jesus, who can't say anything wrong.

I don't want to keep my eyes on people who can do something wrong.

I want to keep my eyes on Jesus, who can't do anything wrong.

I don't want to keep my eyes on people who I can't put all my trust in.

I want to keep my eyes on Jesus, who I can put all my trust in.

I don't want to keep my eyes on people who can let me down.

I want to keep my eyes on Jesus, who will never let me down.

I don't want to keep my eyes on people who can tell me a lie.

I want to keep my eyes on Jesus, who can't lie to me.

I don't want to keep my eyes on people who can deceive me.

I want to keep my eyes on Jesus, who will never deceive me.

I don't want to keep my eyes on people who can disappoint me.

I want to keep my eyes on Jesus, who will never disappoint me.

I don't want to keep my eyes on people who can talk bad about me.

I want to keep my eyes on Jesus, who will never talk bad about me.

I don't want to keep my eyes on people who can lie about me.

I want to keep my eyes on Jesus, who will never lie about me.

I don't want to keep my eyes on people who can cheat me.

I want to keep my eyes on Jesus, who will never cheat me.

I don't want to keep my eyes on people who can use me.

I want to keep my eyes on Jesus, who will never use me.

I don't want to keep my eyes on people who can hate me.

I want to keep my eyes on Jesus, who will never hate me.

I don't want to keep my eyes on people who can dislike me.

I want to keep my eyes on Jesus, who will never dislike me.

I don't want to keep my eyes on people who can fail me.

I want to keep my eyes on Jesus, who will never fail me.

I don't want to keep my eyes on people who can give me injustice.

I want to keep my eyes on Jesus, who will always give me justice.

I don't want to keep my eyes on people who can misunderstand me.

I want to keep my eyes on Jesus, who will never misunderstand me.

I don't want to keep my eyes on people who can kill me.

I want to keep my eyes on Jesus, who will never kill me.

I don't want to keep my eyes on people who can steal from me.

I want to keep my eyes on Jesus who will never steal from me.

I don't want to keep my eyes on people who can hurt me.

I want to keep my eyes on Jesus who will never hurt me.

I don't want to keep my eyes on people who can be opinionated about me.

I want to keep my eyes on Jesus, who will never be opinionated about me.

I don't want to keep my eyes on people who can change on me.

I want to keep my eyes on Jesus, who will never change on me.

I don't want to keep my eyes on people who can leave me or forsake me.

I want to keep my eyes on Jesus, who will never leave me or forsake me.

I don't want to keep my eyes on people who can reject me.

I want to keep my eyes on Jesus, who will never reject me.

I don't want to keep my eyes on people who can take me the wrong way.

I want to keep my eyes on Jesus, who will never take me the wrong way.

I don't want to keep my eyes on people who can ignore me.

I want to keep my eyes on Jesus, who will never ignore me.

I don't want to keep my eyes on people who can trick me.

I want to keep my eyes on Jesus, who will never trick me.

I don't want to keep my eyes on people who can want to control me.

I want to keep my eyes on Jesus, who will never control me.

I don't want to keep my eyes on people who can want to fight me.

I want to keep my eyes on Jesus, who will never fight me.

I don't want to keep my eyes on people who may not be real with me.

I want to keep my eyes on Jesus, who is always real with me.

I don't want to keep my eyes on people who can see me and can act like they don't see me.

I want to keep my eyes on Jesus, who sees me and lets me know that He sees me.

I don't want to keep my eyes on people who can hear me and can act like they don't hear me.

I want to keep my eyes on Jesus, who hears me and lets me know that He hears me.

I don't want to keep my eyes on people who can oppress me.

I want to keep my eyes on Jesus, who will never oppress me.

I don't want to keep my eyes on people who can depress me.

I want to keep my eyes on Jesus, who can never depress me.

I don't want to keep my eyes on people who can cause me to get sick.

I want to keep my eyes on Jesus, who will never cause me to get sick.

I don't want to keep my eyes on people who are not perfect.

I want to keep my eyes on Jesus, who is perfect and without sin.

I don't want to keep my eyes on people who have sins to confess and repent of.

I want to keep my eyes on Jesus, who can save me from my sins.

I don't want to keep my eyes on people who have no heaven to put me in.

I want to keep my eyes on Jesus, who has a heaven to put me in.

I don't want to keep my eyes on people who can mess things up.

I want to keep my eyes on Jesus, who will never mess anything up.

I don't want to keep my eyes on people who can set me up for a fall.

I want to keep my eyes on Jesus, who will never set me up for a fall.

I don't want to keep my eyes on people who can be jealous of me.

I want to keep my eyes on Jesus, who wants to give me the best.

I don't want to keep my eyes on people who can act like they're better than me.

I want to keep my eyes on Jesus, who created me wonderfully made in His image.

I want to always keep my eyes on Jesus Christ, my Lord and Savior.

I don't want to keep my eyes on people who can pretend to be something they are not.

I don't want to keep my eyes on people who can mock me.

I want to keep my eyes on Jesus, who will never mock me.

I don't want to keep my eyes on people who can break my heart.

I want to keep my eyes on Jesus, who will never break my heart.

I don't want to keep my eyes on people who can tell me one thing and then do another thing.

I want to keep my eyes on Jesus, who will do what He tells me He will do.

I don't want to keep my eyes on people who can try to make me look bad.

I want to keep my eyes on Jesus, who makes me look good for doing His will.

I don't want to keep my eyes on people who can give me evil eye looks.

I want to keep my eyes on Jesus, who gives me His kind looks of mercy.

I don't want to keep my eyes on people who can ruin my reputation.

I want to keep my eyes on Jesus, who gives me a good reputation for loving Him and keeping His Commandments.

I don't want to keep my eyes on people who may not care anything about what I'm doing for the Lord.

I want to keep my eyes on Jesus, who always cares about what I am doing in His holy name.

I don't want to keep my eyes on people who can condemn me to Hell.

I want to keep my eyes on Jesus, who wants to save me from being lost in Hell.

I don't want to keep my eyes on people who can betray me.

I want to keep my eyes on Jesus, who will never betray me.

I don't want to keep my eyes on people who can laugh at me.

I want to keep my eyes on Jesus, who will never laugh at me.

I don't want to keep my eyes on people who can cause me to sin.

I want to keep my eyes on Jesus, who wants to cleanse me from my sins.

I don't want to keep my eyes on people who can twist their words up on me.

I want to keep my eyes on Jesus, who makes His words straight with me.

I don't want to keep my eyes on people who can confuse me.

I want to keep my eyes on Jesus, who will never confuse me.

I don't want to keep my eyes on people who can plot evil things against me.

I want to keep my eyes on Jesus, who is good to me all the time.

I don't want to keep my eyes on people who may not be true to me.

I want to keep my eyes on Jesus, who is always true to me.

I don't want to keep my eyes on people who may try to butter me up to do what they want me to do

I want to keep my eyes on Jesus, who will tell me like it is and let me choose to do what He wants me to do.

O Lord, Help Me

O Lord, help me to not lie to anyone.

O Lord, help me to not lie on anyone.

O Lord, help me to not steal from anyone.

O Lord, help me to not kill anyone.

O Lord, help me to not to cheat anyone.

O Lord, help me to not hurt anyone.

O Lord, help me to not abuse anyone.

O Lord, help me to not use anyone.

O Lord, help me to not to be jealous of anyone.

O Lord, help me to not to envy anyone.

O Lord, help me to not want what belongs to someone else.

O Lord, help me to not put anyone down.

O Lord, help me to not talk bad about anyone.

O Lord, help me to not treat anyone bad.

O Lord, help me to not hate anyone.

O Lord, help me to not disrespect anyone.

O Lord, help me to not be rude to anyone.

O Lord, help me to not give anyone a bad name.

O Lord, help me to not ruin anyone's name.

O Lord, help me to not discourage anyone.

O Lord, help me to not disappoint anyone.

O Lord, help me to not judge anyone.

O Lord, help me to not deceive anyone.

O Lord, help me to not give anyone an evil eye look.

O Lord, help me to not get revenge back at anyone.

O Lord, help me to not hold grudges against anyone.

O Lord, help me to not trick anyone.

O Lord, help me to not try to control anyone.

O Lord, help me to not care less about anyone.

O Lord, help me to not be mean to anyone.

O Lord, help me to not make trouble for anyone.

O Lord, help me to not quarrel with anyone.

O Lord, help me to not fight with anyone.

O Lord, help me to not treat anyone unfairly.

O Lord, help me to not neglect anyone.

O Lord, help me to not show favoritism to anyone.

O Lord, help me to not cause anyone to stumble into sin.

O Lord, help me to not cause anyone to leave the church.

O Lord, help me to not cause anyone to be lost in their sins.

O Lord, you command me to love my neighbor, as I love myself.

Everybody in the church is my neighbor and everybody in this world is my neighbor, who you, O Lord, command me to love.

O Lord, help me to not be impolite to anyone.

O Lord, help me to not believe that I am better than anyone else.

O Lord, help me to not cause anyone to get ill.

O Lord, help me to love you and love my neighbors for me to love myself.

This Day

O Lord, I think You for blessing me to live to see this day that thousands of years ago can't compare to.

O Lord, I think You for blessing me to live to see this day that hundreds of years ago can't compare to.

O Lord, I think You for blessing me to live to see this day that decades ago can't compare to.

O Lord, I think You for blessing me to live to see this day that a year ago can't compare to.

O Lord, I think You for blessing me to live to see this day that a month ago can't compare to.

O Lord, I think You for blessing me to live to see this day that a week ago can't compare to.

O Lord, I think You for blessing me to live to see this day that yesterday can't compare to.

This day may be a thousand years away from the end of this world.

This day may be a hundred years away from the end of this world.

This day may be a decade away from the end of this world.

This day may be a year away from the close of God's probation on this world.

This day may be a month away from the close of God's probation on this world.

This day may be a week away from the close of God's probation on this world.

This day may be one day away from the close of God's probation on this world.

O Lord, I think you for blessing me to live to see this day that my past sinful life can't compare to.

O Lord, I think you for blessing me to live to see this day that my yesterdays can't compare to.

O Lord, I think you for blessing me to live to see this day that my past ignorance can't compare to this day that I don't deserve to know the truth of Your holy word that has set me free from the devil's lies.

This day is like eternity to me, whose alive above the grave where there is no consciousness of life to know anything.

O Lord, I thank You for blessing me to be alive this day that my destiny is sealed in the choices that I make today.

It only takes this day for me to choose life or death.

It only takes this day for me to choose Jesus or the devil.

O Lord, I thank You for blessing me to be alive this day that I can die, because I know that a thousand years are like just one day to You, O Lord.

You will wake me up again in the first resurrection or in the second resurrection which can be like only tomorrow to you, O Lord.

O Lord, I think you for blessing me to be alive this day that I can choose to love You and keep Your Commandments that will destine me to enter into heaven when You come back again, which will be a day that only God knows when this day is unpredictable to me and not to God.

O Lord, I thank you for blessing me to live to see this day, and only You will know how this day will be for me who can give You, O Lord, my all this day.

O Lord, I thank You for blessing me to live to see this day that is a miracle from You, O Lord, for me to see.

O Lord, I thank You for blessing me to live to see this day that all the living surround me and know that life is from You, who gives it to me to enjoy living my life unto You, my Lord, no matter what this day will bring to me.

O Lord, I thank You for blessing me to live to see this day that no one can take away from me without Your approval that is guaranteed to be for my good, even unto my death.

O Lord, I thank You for blessing me to live to see this day that is more real than all of my yesterdays that are gone like they never happened, because this day is what really matters to my soul's salvation for me to be saved in You, O Lord.

O Lord, I thank You for blessing me to live to see this day that is so far away from thousands of years ago, even though this day surely has the same sunshine as it did thousands of years ago.

O Lord, I thank You for blessing me to live to see this day that has the same sky like thousands of years ago.

O Lord, I thank You for blessing me to live to see this day that has the same invisible air like thousands of years ago.

O Lord, I thank You for blessing me to live to see this day that is presence of life like thousands of years ago.

O Lord, I thank You for blessing me to live to see this day that lets me know that You, O Lord, are not finished with me yet and I won't be going to the land of the dead this day.

This day is like eternity to me for being alive to choose to live for You, my Lord and Savior Jesus Christ, who this day I love and obey even through deep distresses that can't overrule Your supreme authority over this day, O Lord.

In Every Skin Color

There are beautiful women in every skin color.

There are strong men in every skin color.

There are intelligent women in every skin color.

There are intelligent men in every skin color.

There are good women in every skin color.

There are good men in every skin color.

There are honest women in every skin color.

There are honest men in every skin color.

There are trustworthy women in every skin color.

There are trustworthy men in every skin color.

There are faithful women in every skin color.

There are faithful men in every skin color.

There are respectful women in every skin color.

There are respectful men in every skin color.

There are educated women in every skin color.

There are educated men in every skin color.

There are tall women in every skin color.

There are tall men in every skin color.

There are short women in every skin color.

There are short men in every skin color.

There are big women in every skin color.

There are big men in every skin color.

There are bad women in every skin color.

There are bad men in every skin color.

There are talkative women in every skin color.

There are talkative men in every skin color.

There are quiet women in every skin color.

There are quiet men in every skin color.

There are great women in every skin color.

There are great men in every skin color.

God loves everybody in every skin color.

God loves little children and he loves teenagers in every skin color.

We all are God's beautiful rainbow colors of people who the devil hates in every skin color.

Racism is of the devil who hates the human race.

There are brave women in every skin color.

There are brave men in every skin color.

There are funny women in every skin color.

There are funny men in every skin color.

There are deceptive women in every skin color.

There are deceptive men in every skin color.

There are working women in every skin color.

There are working men in every skin color.

There are lazy women in every skin color.

There are lazy men in every skin color.

There are proud women in every skin color.

There are proud men in every skin color.

The devil hates every skin color.

He knows that every skin color will enter into heaven one day when Jesus Christ comes back again.

Every skin color of people will be saved in Jesus Christ and go to heaven where that racist devil was kicked out of forever and ever.

O Lord, You Kept Today's Technology Away

O Lord, you kept today's technology away from those people back in the Bible days.

O Lord, if you had allowed today's technology to exist back in the Bible days, many people would have worshipped this technology.

Many people would have believed in today's technology and not believed in You, O Lord.

O Lord, you have created many people who were brilliant and skillful back in the Bible days.

Many of them would have used their brilliance and skillfulness to greatly advance this technology so that they could rule the world with it.

O Lord, you kept today's technology away from the people back in the Bible days.

Many kings back in the Bible days would have used today's technology to greatly oppress many people.

The technology back in the Bible days caused many kings to be very proud.

If they had today's technology, they would have been a lot prouder about building up their kingdoms.

Many kings back in the Bible days would have probably used today's technology to annihilate every nation that was against them.

Jesus Christ came to this world during the darkest days on earth, when so many people were rebellious against God.

If they had today's technology back in the Bible days, they would have been a lot more rebellious.

They would have probably believed that they were more powerful than God if they had today's technology.

Many people back in the Bible days would probably not have believed in Jesus Christ if they had today's technology.

Many people back in the Bible days would have probably believed that there is no God if they had today's technology.

Many people today believe that there is no God because they put their trust in today's technology.

Many people today worship technology like it's God.

Many people back in the Bible days would have probably been much worse off and living their lives unto today's technology just like many people live their lives today.

Oh Lord, you kept today's technology away from the people back in the Bible days.

If this world will still be here another thousand years, the Lord will keep that thousand years technology away from you and me today because the Lord knows that we would probably worship that new thousand years technology if we had it now.

The Lord doesn't overdo anything that would cause this world's past, present and future to be out of order with time.

It wasn't the time for the people back in the Bible days to have today's technology and it's not our time to have the technology of one thousand years in the future.

The Lord kept today's technology away from the people back in the Bible days because the Lord keeps technology, as well as science, in its rightful place.

The Highest Beauty

The highest beauty is not the lilies in the valley.

The highest beauty is not a shadow moving over the landscape.

The highest beauty is not a diamond ring.

The highest beauty is not a treasure chest.

The highest beauty is not jewelry.

The highest beauty is not the sunrise.

The highest beauty is not the sunset.

The highest beauty is not the full, white moonlight's glow.

The highest beauty is not the sparkling stars.

The highest beauty is not the glaciers on the mountain tops.

The highest beauty is not the puffy white clouds.

The highest beauty is not the great blue skies.

The highest beauty is not nature.

The highest beauty is not the oceans.

The highest beauty is not the tropical islands.

The highest beauty in this world is a beautiful woman on the inside and on the outside.

God created Eve to be the highest beauty in this world, where even the Garden of Eden wasn't more beautiful than Eve.

The serpent that tempted Eve was beautiful, but not more beautiful than Eve.

Adam couldn't resist Eve because she was so beautiful to him, and he ate the forbidden fruit she gave to him.

The highest beauty is a beautiful woman on the inside and on the outside that God had created from the beginning of time on earth.

There is nothing more beautiful than a beautiful Christian woman on the inside and on the outside, just like Queen Ester was in the bible.

The highest beauty is not a beautiful house.

The highest beauty is not a beautiful vehicle.

The highest beauty is not a beautiful building

The highest beauty is not a beautiful yard.

The highest beauty is not beautiful clothes.

The highest beauty is a beautiful woman on the inside and on the outside.

Even if she is poor, that can't take away her beauty that God gave to her.

Our Shadow Will See Us

Our shadow will see us as a Christian or a hypocrite.

We can be dishonest to our shadow but it will not be dishonest to us and will do whatever we do.

Our shadow will see us as good or evil.

We can be untrustworthy to our shadow, even though we can trust our shadow wherever we go.

Our shadow will see us do right or do wrong.

We can be unstable in our ways but our shadow won't be unstable and won't do something different from what we do, whether we do right or wrong.

Our shadow will see us for who we are.

We can pretend to be who we are not, but our shadow will not pretend with us.

Our shadow moves when we move and will stand still when we stand still.

Our shadow will see us even when we run and hide away from someone.

No matter what we do wrong, our shadow will not run and hide away from someone.

Our shadow is held captive by us and is a slave to whatever we do, even on the spur of the moment.

Our shadow will see us making mistakes, but our shadow won't make any mistakes and will do just what we do.

Our shadow will go wherever we go, and we will see our shadow beside us, below us or in front of us especially at night.

Our shadow will always see us and reflect whatever we do because we can't fool our shadow and our shadow wont' fool us and will always be truthful to us.

Our shadow will stay close, connected to us and we will never think about getting rid of our shadow.

Many people want to get rid of God, who is more connected to us than our shadow for loving Him and doing His will in whatever we do for the Lord.

There were many sick people who believed that they would be healed by even Peter's shadow if he just walked by them.

Our shadow will see us when we are being like Jesus Christ or not like Jesus Christ.

We have a God-given free will to choose in the presence of our shadow that can't choose to do anything different from what we do.

If our shadow could choose to do something different from what we do, then our shadow would scare us to death.

God created us and gave us a shadow to remind us that we are alive to move around here and there as we do God's holy will and not our own will.

Many people are deceitful when their shadow will not deceive them.

Many people are afraid to do what is right when their shadow is never afraid to do what is right by doing whatever they do.

No one's shadow will stand still when they are moving around here and there, but we can stand still when God tells us to move around to spread the gospel of Jesus Christ who created our shadows to move when we move around here and there.

Our shadow will see us not always paying close attention to what we're doing, but our shadow will do whatever we do.

Our shadow can truly show us that Jesus is forevermore true to us than our shadow.

A Spiritual Closet

Everybody has a spiritual closet and only Jesus always knows what is inside it.

Every day we have a spiritual closet that we need to pray to Jesus to clean out because only Jesus can do that for you and me.

We can't clean out our spiritual closets that have some sins in them that we don't even know about because they are unseen to us.

We have seen sins and unseen sins in our spiritual closets that we need to open up and let Jesus come in and clean out.

We have closets in our houses that we can fill up with things to hold onto.

We have a spiritual closet where we need to get rid of the junk of our sins that Jesus sees when no one else can see them.

Our spiritual closets will hold us captive due to our secret sins if we don't confess and repent of them unto Jesus Christ.

A closet is a very closed-in place where we don't want to be because it will make us feel uncomfortable.

We know that a closet is not a good place to be in on any day.

We know that a closet will isolate us from going anywhere.

Our spiritual closet will isolate us from going anywhere with Jesus who wants to take us to spiritual heights in His holy word that is no secret closet for the world to not see the truth that will set us free from the devil's lies.

We can go into our spiritual closet and not even realize it until the Holy Spirit opens the door and pulls us out to see that only Jesus can cleanse us even from our secret sins.

A closet is nothing to cherish because no one likes being locked up in a closet.

We will lock ourselves up in our spiritual closets if we live in sin that throws away the key.

Only Jesus can find the key and unlock our spiritual closets and let us out with His mercy and grace to give us a second chance to deny ourselves and pick up our crosses and follow Him to where there are no spiritual secret closets to hold us captive in the darkness of sin.

We know that it can be dark in a closet and there's not much space to move around.

A spiritual closet is much worse because our secret sins will close its four walls very tight on us and suffocate us so we spiritually die.

Nobody in their right mind would want to be locked up in a closet, but many people cherish their spiritual closets filled with secret sins like they're the best thing that can happen to them because they enjoy living in their secret sins.

We create our own spiritual secret closets if we hold onto even one unconfessed sin that Jesus wants to save us from.

We must choose to let Jesus clean out our spiritual closets that will sooner or later pile up with the junk of sin.

The Bible Truth

The things that go on in this world are from the truth of the bible prophecy that God's prophets predicted would happen.

The bible truth is what goes on in this world every day that philosophies, theories, educated guesses, science, opinions, phenomenon, spiritualism, luck, magic, wishes and lies cannot rise above.

The bible truth is the real deal about everything that is going on in this world where philosophies are so artificial compared to the bible truth.

The bible truth is the real deal about everything that is going on in this world where theories are so artificial compared to the bible truth.

The bible truth is the real deal about everything that is going on in this world where educated guesses are so artificial compared to the bible truth.

The bible truth is the real deal about everything that is going on in this world where science is so artificial compared to the bible truth.

The bible truth is the real deal about everything that is going on in this world where opinions are so artificial compared to the bible truth.

The bible truth is the real deal about everything that is going on in this world where phenomena are so artificial compared to the bible truth.

The bible truth is the real deal about everything that is going on in this world where spiritualism is so artificial compared to the bible truth.

The bible truth is the real deal about everything that is going on in this world where luck is so artificial compared to the bible truth.

The bible truth is the real deal about everything that is going on in this world where magic is so artificial compared to the bible truth.

The bible truth is the real deal about everything that is going on in this world where wishes are so artificial compared to the bible truth.

The bible truth is the real deal about everything that is going on in this world where lies are so artificial compared to the bible truth.

The bible truth hovers over this world every day like the sky hovers over the world.

The bible truth hovers over the heavens because Jesus Christ is the bible truth that is eternal in heaven above this world that will one day pass away with every artificial thing.

Our Actions will Talk a Lot More

Our actions will talk a lot more than the words that we say.

We can shut our mouths and be silent, but our actions are not silent and talk a lot through our body language.

Our actions will talk to people when we run out of words to say.

Our actions will talk all the time and will very often tell the truth about me and you.

We don't usually pretend with our actions, because they are very often real and tell the truth a lot more than our words.

Many actors will pretend with their actions as they portray things to be real, and feeble-minded people may have a hard time telling the difference between what is real and what is pretend.

Our actions don't run out of words to say, whether they are good actions or bad actions that will very often tell the truth even with our mouth is shut.

Jesus' actions talked a lot more than His divine words, because all of Jesus' actions were perfect with no pretending.

Jesus was always real with no playacting involved when He lived here in this world where our actions will talk a lot more than what we say out of our mouths.

Actors love to live a normal life with real true actions, but they are with their family and friends who they will not pretend with in their words and actions.

The actions of every Christian are closely watched, a lot more than the actions of the people of the world who can also go to church and profess to be a Christian with pretend actions that can look holy and righteous while holding office positions in the church.

Our actions will talk a lot more than what we say out of our mouths.

Real, true Christians have real, true good actions, a lot more than words about Jesus Christ.

When Jesus lived here on earth without sin, He had no pretend words and no pretend actions.

Jesus' perfect actions talked a lot more than His perfect words.

Actors are very good at making their actions look real, but they are not real.

Whether our actions are real or pretend, our actions will talk a lot more than what we say out of our mouths.

God's Ambassadors

We Christians are God's ambassadors on earth where we are supposed to spread the gospel of Jesus Christ and win souls to Him.

We Christians are God's ambassadors on earth where we are supposed to love Jesus and keep His Commandments in the presence of the people of the world.

We Christians are God's ambassadors on earth where we are supposed to live right by example.

The sun is God's ambassador in the universe.

The moon is God's ambassador in the universe.

The stars are God's ambassadors in the universe.

The galaxies are God's ambassadors in the universe.

The black holes are God's ambassadors in the universe.

The planets are God's ambassadors in the universe.

The solar system is God's ambassador in the universe.

The meteors are God's ambassadors in the universe.

The universe is God's ambassador in the universe.

Other worlds are God's ambassadors.

They all represent God's creation beyond this world.

The holy angels are God's ambassadors in heaven above the universe.

Ambassadors are the highest-ranking representatives of their country.

Ambassadors are the greatest representatives of their country's policies.

God's ambassadors represent God's Son, Jesus Christ, in this world that is foreign to you and me for being a Christian.

God's ambassadors in heaven and the universe and in other worlds and on earth are God's joyous representatives, giving God's Son, Jesus

Christ, all the glory and praise and worship because He is worthy to sit on the right-hand side of God's holy throne forever and ever.

The sky is God's ambassador to represent this world.

Nature is God's ambassador to represent this world.

The elements in the earth are God's ambassadors to represent this world.

Ambassadors are the highest representatives for any nation.

We Christians are ambassadors of God.

We Christians are the highest representatives of God here on earth.

Jesus Christ, our Lord and Savior, is the ambassador of God in heaven where Jesus once came from to represent God's love here on earth as he was bruised for our iniquities and wounded for our transgressions.

Jesus is God's ambassador who had shed His blood and died on the cross to become sin in our place.

Jesus is God's ambassador who rose from the grave with the victory over death and the grave.

There is no greater ambassador than Jesus Christ, who represents God's love to all the world, to all the other worlds, to all the universes and to all existence seen and unseen.

Jesus Christ is God's ambassador in heaven where all the angels bow down before Him and give Him all the glory and praise for creating them and all things visible and invisible.

For what have human beings created that Jesus can't destroy when He will create a new heaven and new earth beyond this world that will pass away one day along with everything in it.

Jesus is God's ambassador to represent God's supreme power and rulership over all creatures that Jesus created.

Each of us is an ambassador of our own free will choices that we represent every day in our words and actions before one another and Jesus.

Only Jesus always knows the motives and intentions of our hearts, because Jesus is the ambassador of our hearts and represents you and me in the presence of God.

Conspiracy is of the Devil

One nation can conspire against another nation to bring it down to ruin.

Conspiracy can come in all kinds of ways.

Smuggling drugs in a nation is a conspiracy to kill many people and weaken a nation.

Cyberattacks against a nation are a conspiracy to bankrupt that nation and make it fall into ruin.

Deadly viruses coming into a nation is a conspiracy to make many people sick and kill them to discourage a nation.

Spying on a nation is a conspiracy to steal very vital information from a nation to make that nation vulnerable.

Conspiracy is of the devil, who has his human agents to conspire especially against God's holy children.

The devil and his human agents will conspire against you and me and try to make us look like hypocrites for living right unto the Lord.

The devil also has human agents in the church where so-called Christians will not live right by God's holy word and will cause you and me to look bad for not doing the wrong things that they are doing.

Conspiracy is nothing new today.

Lucifer had conspired against God in heaven, where he caused one-third of the angels in heaven to rebel against God.

The Pharisees and religious leaders conspired against Jesus to try to trap Him into saying something wrong and doing something wrong.

Anyone who loves to conspire is of the devil.

Conspiring against a nation is all about trying to find a way to gain power and control over a nation.

Many people will conspire against people in their own family, especially when it comes to trying to get control of a lot of money.

Conspiracy had no victory over the Lord Jesus Christ, who saw through all of His enemies' conspiracies when He lived here on earth without sin.

You and I Will Be

You and I will be criticized for living right unto the Lord Jesus Christ.

You and I will be disliked for living right unto the Lord Jesus Christ.

You and I will be disrespected for living right unto the Lord Jesus Christ.

You and I will be lied on for living right unto the Lord Jesus Christ.

You and I will be put down for living right unto the Lord Jesus Christ.

You and I will be scorned for living right unto the Lord Jesus Christ.

You and I will be talked bad about for living right unto the Lord Jesus Christ.

You and I will be looked down on with contempt for living right unto the Lord Jesus Christ.

You and I will be misunderstood for living right unto the Lord Jesus Christ.

You and I will be falsely accused for living right unto the Lord Jesus Christ.

You and I will be hated for living right unto the Lord Jesus Christ, who was hated by His enemies because Jesus lived right with no sins in His flesh to be the Son of God.

You and I will have enemies for living right unto the Lord Jesus Christ.

You and I will be persecuted for living right unto the Lord Jesus Christ.

You and I will be taken in the wrong way for living right unto the Lord Jesus Christ.

You and I will be despised even by so-called Christians for living right unto the Lord Jesus Christ.

So who can be against You and I who the Lord Jesus Christ is for because of living right unto Him who the devil and his fallen angels and human agents can't ever defeat with all of their evil schemes and deeds?

If We Look At

If we look at our problems and don't look at what the Lord can do for us, then our problems will get the best of us.

If we look at people and not what the Lord can do for us, then people will get the best of us.

If we look at our finances and not what the Lord can do for us, then our finances will get the best of us.

If we look at our mistakes and not what the Lord can do for us, then our mistakes will get the best of us.

If we look at our bad habits and not what the Lord can do for us, then our bad habits will get the best of us.

If we look at our bad situations and not what the Lord can do for us, then our bad situations will get the best of us.

If we look at our failures and not what the Lord can do for us, then our failures will get the best of us.

If we look at our discouragements and not what the Lord can do for us, then our discouragements will get the best of us.

If we look at our grief and not what the Lord can do for us, then our grief will get the best of us.

If we look at our doubts and not what the Lord can do for us, then our doubts will get the best of us.

If we look at our enemies and not what the Lord can do for us, then our enemies will get the best of us.

If we look at ourselves and not what the Lord can do for us, then ourselves will get the best of us.

We need to always look at what the Lord can do for us who can't do ourselves or anyone else any good if we don't keep our eyes on the Lord, whose goodness leads us to repent of our sins and turn to Him.

No Matter Where You Go

No matter where you go, your thoughts will go with you.

No matter where you go, your words will go with you.

No matter where you go, your good deeds will go with you.

No matter where you go, your bad deeds will go with you.

No matter where you go, your joy will go with you.

No matter where you go, your sadness will go with you.

No matter where you go, your love will go with you.

No matter where you go, your hatred will go with you.

No matter where you go, your peace will go with you.

No matter where you go, your strife will go with you.

No matter where you go, your brilliance will go with you.

No matter where you go, your intelligence will go with you.

No matter where you go, your common sense will go with you.

No matter where you go, your talents will go with you.

No matter where you go, your skills will go with you.

No matter where you go, your mind will go with you.

No matter where you go, your heart will go with you.

No matter where you go, your feelings will go with you.

No matter where you go, your kindness will go with you.

No matter where you go, your respect will go with you.

No matter where you go, your truth will go with you.

No matter where you go, your lies will go with you.

No matter where you go, your lifestyle will go with you.

No matter where you go, your sins will go with you.

No matter where you go, your greed will go with you.

No matter where you go, your corruption will go with you.

No matter where you go, your realness will go with you.

No matter where you go, your pretense will go with you.

No matter where you go, your rebellion will go with you.

No matter where you go, your habits will go with you.

No matter where you go, your health will go with you.

No matter where you go, your lust will go with you.

No matter where you go, your pride will go with you.

No matter where you go, your self-esteem will go with you.

No matter where you go, your jealousy will go with you.

No matter where you go, your prejudice will go with you.

No matter where you go, your evil will go with you.

No matter where you go, your education will go with you.

No matter where you go, your knowledge will go with you.

No matter where you go, your ignorance will go with you.

No matter where you go, your religion will go with you.

No matter where you go, your faith in Jesus Christ will go with you.

No matter where you go, your spiritual gifts will go with you.

No matter where you go, your obedience unto Jesus will go with you.

No matter where you go, your love for Jesus will go with you.

We Can Usually Understand the Truth

We can usually understand the truth because there is only one way to tell the truth.

Trying to understand a lie can be confusing because a lie can be told in many different ways.

We can usually understand the truth and that can give us a peace of mind.

Trying to understand a lie can trouble our minds.

We can usually understand the truth, which can heal our broken hearts.

Trying to understand a lie can hurt our hearts.

We can usually understand the truth that will set us free from lies.

Trying to understand a lie can put us in the bondage of sin and we can't fully understand how sin will mess us up if we don't confess and repent of our sins unto Jesus Christ, who can save us from our sins.

We can usually understand the truth of God's holy word.

Trying to fully understand sin can surely give us no hope in this sinful world where every lie comes from sin that originated from the devil.

No one can fully understand the sin that Jesus was up against in the wilderness for forty days and forty nights.

That sin fully understood the mission of Jesus to minister to sinners.

Sin fully understood and hated that only Jesus was the living truth to set the captives free from living in sin.

Jesus came to this world to save us from our sins because He fully understood that sin brings death and eternal death upon all sinners.

We all are sinners who don't fully understand that sin can catch us off guard at any time of the day and night and leave us so helpless.

We can usually understand the truth that a child can understand to obey their parents.

A child can feel guilty for lying to their parents, but a child doesn't understand that sin is the root of every lie.

We can usually understand the truth that a fool can understand to not be a lie that comes from sin that we have in our natures every day.

Only Jesus fully understands sin that is in our genes and hereditary tendencies.

We can usually understand the truth that is easy to accept for everyone who loves the truth.

Who in this world can fully understand sin that God hates because He knows that Lucifer misunderstood Him and believed that he was right about God not being worthy to be God?

We can usually understand the truth because there is no misunderstanding about God's love that the devil and his fallen angels and his human agents will try to make to be a lie.

So who can fully understand sin that Jesus fully understood on the cross where He became sin?

That sin fully understood that it failed to conqueror Jesus, who rose from the grave with victory over death.

We can usually understand the truth that is Jesus Christ, who is the way, the truth and the life that is never complicated if we live our lives unto Jesus.

We cannot fully understand sin that will twist and turn us in every wrong direction and will blind our eyes to not see the truth.

We can usually understand the truth when the truth is told to us.

But, who can fully understand sin that every lie comes from?

Jesus fully understood sin and defeated it on the cross to redeem us back to God.

We can't fully understand sin that can come at us in all kinds of ways, but the truth will come at us in only one way and that is Jesus, who is the truth to set us free from the devil's lies.

You and I can't fully understand sin that is the origin of false doctrines and false theories that foolish people believe to be the truth about how we come into existence.

We can usually understand the truth that is at its best in God's holy word, but we can't fully understand sin that Adam and Eve committed against God for believing a lie.

Many people today will misunderstand the truth to be a lie, even with God's holy word that we can't fully understand without the Holy Spirit teaching us all truth.

We can usually understand the truth that can surely cause us to feel so relieved of lies and deceptions that come from sin that brilliant minds can't fully understand for being stained with sin that only the blood of Jesus can wash clean when we confess and repent unto Jesus.

We can usually understand the truth because of Jesus being the light of the world to shine His eternal truth all through our minds and hearts in this dark, sinful world.

If the devil could get rid of all of the truth, he would do that without any hesitation so he could fill this world with nothing but lies.

Lies were Lucifer's biggest sin he committed against God, because he told the angels in heaven that God was unfair to not let him in on the creation of human beings who God created in His likeness.

We can't fully understand sin, even in its smallest form viewed under a microscope.

Sin can spread like the Corona virus that killed millions of people because the corona virus comes from sin and we just didn't understand how it began as we lived in our ignorance of not knowing if we would get the virus.

We can usually understand the truth that can truly give us some comfort because the scientists had comforted our minds when they found an antidote for the corona virus, but we can't fully understand sin that is all about troubling our minds every day.

We can usually understand the truth that was originated by God the Father, the Son and the Holy Spirit, giving understanding to prophets to speak the truth in this dark, sinful world.

We can't fully understand how sin can work its bad effects in us until we reap what we sow from that sin catching up with us.

Sin can surely lead us even to our death if we don't confess and repent of that sin unto Jesus Christ.

We can usually understand the truth that sin has no power over for no one to misunderstand the truth about Jesus Christ who shed His blood and gave up His life on the cross to save us from our sins.

The devil knew that Adam and Eve wouldn't understand the bad effects of their sins that would greatly affect all life and nature in this world that would groan from the absence of God's perfect creation upon this world.

We can usually understand the truth that God told Adam and Eve in the Garden of Eden where they understood the truth but rejected the truth in favor of what they believed to be the truth from the devil who originated sin.

Lucifer didn't even understand sin that he created for rebelling against God who could have vanished Lucifer into thin air, but God didn't do that and gave Lucifer a chance to repent.

Lucifer didn't take the chance God gave him to repent because he didn't understand that he would be lost in his sins forever and ever and burn up in the lake of fire.

Lucifer didn't understand that God means what He says, and Lucifer took God's words for granted and didn't understand all of the truth of God.

We can usually understand the truth when we hear the truth of God's holy word in sermons and Sabbath school lessons in the church that is for every race of people to enter into and worship the Lord Jesus Christ.

No one can fully understand the lies of sin that hates all the truth, especially all the truth of God's holy word that can detect every sin under the microscope of this sinful world.

We can't fully understand sin that can camouflage itself behind billions of faces every day that the truth of God's holy word will sooner or later reveal in everyone's life.

We can usually understand the truth that has no assumptions or opinions about anyone who the truth completely knows every day whether we have mood changes or remain the same way in our life day after day.

We can't ever fully understand sin that has over a thousand ways to distract us from the Lord Jesus Christ if we don't stay in prayer without ceasing to keep our eyes on Jesus day after day.

Only Jesus fully understands sin that He overcame in this world where He humbled Himself unto death to save us from our sins.

The devil doesn't understand the love of God who he rebelled against in heaven.

Lucifer took God's love for him to be weak, so he tried to walk over God which he could not do and was cast out of heaven with one third of the angels following behind him.

You and I can usually understand the truth that will never put us in any kind of bondage, but we will never fully understand sin that makes up all kinds of lies that the truth will set us free from for believing in Jesus Christ.

Jesus is all-powerful to cleanse us from our sins and save us from our sins if we repent and turn to Him.

Jesus understands all things that He created that can't ever rise above Him or His God-given authority over all things seen and unseen.

We can usually understand the truth that is all about Jesus Christ who is the Son of God and the word of God that was made flesh and lived among sinners without sin in His flesh.

We can't fully understand sin that hates people and brings on wars and rumors of wars against God's peaceful nations that sin covets.

We can usually understand the truth that sin can never get rid of with its lies.

Only Jesus fully understands the devil's evil schemes and knows that the devil can change on us so fast on the spur of the moment.

We can't fully understand the wiles of the devil's sins that only Jesus can truly protect us from in many ways that we don't see.

We can usually understand the truth that can be so crystal clear when the Holy Spirit speaks the truth to us, but we can't fully understand sin that will twist up our minds with the devil's lies if we don't spend any time reading the bible to know the truth about Jesus Christ, our only living hope and true lover of our souls to save us from our sins.

We can usually understand the truth that we true Christians love to tell and love to live.

We don't fully understand sin that we can commit against God over and over again.

God's grace is much greater than our sins and gives us undeserved favor with God.

The devil doesn't understand this undeserved favor we get from God who gives us all the opportunity to accept the truth or reject the truth of His holy word.

We can usually understand the truth that God put in even the hearts of children to feel guilty for telling their parents a lie and break the truth of God's Commandments in their hearts.

We don't fully understand sin that has no shame or guilt about murdering our souls, leaving us lost in our sins.

Sin takes great pleasure in trying to confuse and deceive everybody with its lies every day without giving us a break.

We can usually understand the truth that we can't afford to take a break from on any day because sin loves to cause us to misunderstand the truth of God's holy word.

We can usually understand the truth that is all about Jesus Christ who can make us to be a real, true Christian if we love Him with all of our minds, hearts, souls and strength.

We can't fully understand sin that will make us be a phony in many ways if we live in sin that will never be real with us because sin loves to tell us lies every day.

We can usually understand the truth that we can always be sure about to set us free from lying to ourselves so that we can always be true to ourselves.

We can't fully understand sin that is all about lies and death all around the world where God is present to give us good understanding of His truth that is everlasting beyond all sin that God will one day burn up in the lake of fire and brimstone right here on earth.

We can usually understand the truth that shines like the sun in our minds and hearts so that we can discern the truth from a lie.

We can't fully understand that sin is total darkness and can appear to be the light of God's truth that the devil knows so much better than you and me.

Adam and Eve didn't understand sin that disguised itself to be the truth in that unforbidden fruit that Eve and Adam ate in the Garden of Eden.

They were perfect in every way but the devil caused them to misunderstand that with his lie.

We can thank God for His Son, Jesus Christ, who didn't give into sin to save us from our sins because Jesus fully understands the deadly effects of all sin that He became on the cross and was forsaken by God.

Jesus probably felt eternally lost when God had forsaken Him who became the totality of the darkness of all sin that we will never fully understand until we enter into heaven when Jesus comes back again to take us to heaven if we are saved in Him.

We can usually understand the truth that treats everybody right to be set free from lies.

We can't fully understand sin that takes great pleasure in lying on the truth and abusing love to try to cause us to believe that God is not love, especially if God doesn't answer our prayers on our time that can be too soon or too late.

We can't fully understand sin's waywardness that is very destructive over a billion ways, but we can usually understand the truth that loves to heal us from the brokenness of lies that are the crown on the head of sin as it wears the robe of death.

We can usually understand the truth that is our Lord God and Savior Jesus Christ, who we can only worship in spirit and truth.

We can't fully understand sin that fools will worship and not know that sin will laugh really hard and make fun of their fate.

We can usually understand the truth that will stay the same no matter how many times we tell the truth, but we can't fully understand sin that every lie comes from and can change its story more than a thousand times.

We can usually understand the truth that can be so accurate and clear for even a child to understand, but we can't fully understand sin that can surely confuse and deceive the most genius minds to doubt and scorn the truth of God's holy word.

We can usually understand the truth that Jesus Christ is the origin of to set us free from believing lies and living a lie, but we can't fully understand sin that the devil is the origin of to try to bind us up in his bondage of lies.

God gave us a free will for us to choose to believe and live the truth that is all about loving and obeying Jesus Christ, or we can choose to believe and live in sin that is all about the devil and his lies that we can't fully understand.

We can't fully understand how many ways sin can deceive us and kill us who the devil hates.

We can usually understand the truth that only liars will fear because the truth will expose them for who they really are, but we can't fully understand sin that will imitate the truth so many times that we can't count.

We can usually understand the truth that Jesus Christ proclaimed to all the world in God's totality of truth and love that Jesus demonstrated on the cross to save us from our sins.

Nothing in this world can be more truth than the love of God.

The devil and his fallen angels and human agents don't understand this because they are lost in their sins.

We can usually understand the truth that a true Christian will speak and live in love every day.

We can't fully understand sin that takes pleasure in causing us to say and do something wrong, especially on the spur of the moment.

Sin can come at us so swiftly that we can't fully understand, but we can usually understand the truth that is swifter than sin because of Jesus Christ who can answer our prayers faster than our guardian angel can protect us.

We can't fully understand sin that the devil parades in his appearance as an angel of light before us to distract us away from God.

We can usually understand the truth that God gave us a free will to choose to love and obey Jesus Christ or live in sin.

We can't fully understand how deep that sin can take us down into its depths of darkness.

We can usually understand the truth that will sooner or later reveal who we really are being like Jesus or being like the devil.

We can't fully understand sin that came from Lucifer who was the most beautiful and highest angel in heaven.

Lucifer became full of himself and rebelled against God over what was impossible for him to achieve — to be like the most-high God.

We can't fully understand why a perfect angel would flaw his perfection over what was impossible for him to achieve in heaven.

We can usually understand the truth that we will reap what we sow, but we can't fully understand sin that is locked in chains of eternal denial before God.

We can usually understand the truth that we can choose to deny ourselves and pick up our crosses and follow Jesus Christ, who is the way, the truth and the life for us to live every day.

We can't fully understand sin that takes pleasure in causing us to dig our own graves, regardless of whether we're good or bad, because sin will take us down in its darkness of eternal death if we don't repent of our sins and live for Jesus every day.

We can usually understand the truth that can surely keep us on the right course, but we can't fully understand sin that is very shady and will ruin anyone's good reputation even in the church where the wheat and tares grow together for only Jesus to separate.

Jesus fully understands that only He knows how not to pull up a wheat to be a tare, and He can fully understand sin's endless motives that are nothing but nonsense to God.

We can usually understand the truth that is all about Jesus Christ who is merciful to carry us even through the hardships that we can bring on ourselves.

We can't fully understand sin that thrives on making anyone miserable, but we can usually understand the truth that can give us joy to spread the truth of the gospel of Jesus Christ to all the world.

We can usually understand the truth that is always good to speak in love to make this world a much better place to live in.

We can't fully understand that lying evil sin that is all about making this world hard to live in, like what we see and hear on the world news that is rampant with unpleasant words to say and bad things that we see.

We can usually understand the truth that can sharpen and elevate the minds of uneducated people to become bible scholars.

We can't fully understand sin that can cause an educated man and woman to act like fools, as if they don't have a brain in their heads.

We can usually understand the truth that can ease our minds, but we can't fully understand sin that many people will praise and feel no uneasiness in living in their sins that God hates, even as God loves their souls to be saved in His Son, Jesus Christ.

We can usually understand the truth that liars will get very offended by because the truth will reveal their true identities.

We can't fully understand sin that can cause us to not fully understand ourselves who can think, say or do something that we don't understand.

We can usually understand the truth that can be motivating, encouraging and plain for us to hold onto very tight every day.

We can't fully understand sin that takes great pleasure to especially complicate the truth of God's holy word that was written to us in love by holy men who God inspired to write the truth that scoffers very strongly criticize and reject.

We can usually understand the truth that can straighten things out, we can't fully understand sin that can cause us to mess things up.

We can usually understand the truth that enhances and enlightens the mind, but we can't fully understand sin that can ill the body and mind.

We can usually understand the truth that can surely convince the members in our family that you and I are Christians who they have seen down through the years up to this day.

We can't fully understand sin that can wear a mask on its face for years and years and can cause anyone to live proudly and die proudly in an illusion.

We can usually understand the truth that is Jesus Christ our Lord who is the origin of all truth in the heavens and here on earth where the truth is for the good of everyone to worship God in spirit and truth.

We can't fully understand sin that is the origin of adversities, lies, foolishness, demoralizing things and the origin of death that can come upon us so unaware at any time.

We can usually understand the truth that the judge and jury loves to hear in the courtroom, but we can't fully understand sin that can make a lying criminal to be found innocent in the courtroom.

We can usually understand the truth that is Bible prophesy that will be fulfilled, but we can't fully understand sin that mocks all Bible prophecy and loves to degrade humanity.

We can usually understand the truth that will surely be seen in our actions, but we can't fully understand sin that has nothing but bad motives and can be only full of hot air from the tip of the tongue.

We can usually understand the truth that loving people tell in love to have no bad intentions of hurting anyone's feelings with the truth, but we can't fully understand sin that has nothing but bad intentions to hurt anyone's feelings with its lies.

We can usually understand the truth that is the judge of our thoughts, words and actions, but we can't fully understand sin that takes great pride in making a good person look bad and a bad person to look good.

We can usually understand the truth that can surely keep us spiritually awake in this dark, sinful world, but we can't fully understand sin that can cause anyone to spiritually sleep walk in this dark, sinful world where the devil loves to ambush spiritual sleepwalkers who are spiritually unconscious to the truth of God's holy word.

We can usually understand the truth that a prosecutor and a defense lawyer would try to prove their case with the truth in the courtroom where one of them doesn't have the truth but will pretend to have the truth and may still win their case in the courtroom.

We can usually understand the truth that will surely stay the same way every day, but we can't fully understand sin that is prone to change on anyone for the worse in every evil way.

We can usually understand the truth that is very real with no deceptions and pretense, but we can't fully understand sin that can deceive anyone and can cause a brilliant deceptive person to deceive millions of people.

We can usually understand the truth that will always make very good sense to anyone who loves to hear the truth and live the truth of God's holy word, but we can't fully understand sin that is surely evil and nonsense, especially to God.

We can usually understand the truth that the day will change over into the night and the night will change over into the day in its purity, but we can't fully understand sin that is filled with impurity to cause good weather to change into bad weather and can cause a Christian to change like Dr. Jekyll and Mr. Hyde.

We can usually understand the truth that is all about correcting us when we are wrong and teaching us what is right by God, but we can't fully understand sin that is all about schemes, violence, lust, strife, prejudice, greed, betrayal, unfairness, lawlessness and death because sin breaks God's ten golden rules.

We can usually understand the truth that defines and elevates the courts, but we can't fully understand sin that can downgrade the highest courts of justice that are supposed to fall in line with the truth of God's holy word.

We can usually understand the truth that can ease our minds, but we can't fully understand sin that many people will praise and feel no uneasiness in living in their sins that God hates but loves souls to be saved in His Son, Jesus Christ.

Has a Big Effect on God

What we think has a big effect on God.

What we say has a big effect on God.

What we believe has a big effect on God.

What we eat has a big effect on God.

What we drink has a big effect on God.

How we dress has a big effect on God.

How we treat one another has a big effect on God.

How we treat ourselves has a big effect on God.

How we treat the animals has a big effect on God.

How we treat nature has a big effect on God.

How we treat this world has a big effect on God.

Whatever we do has a big effect on God.

Every choice we make has a big effect on God.

The way we live our lives has a big effect on God every day.

When Lucifer and one third of the angels in heaven rebelled against God, it had a big effect on God who cast them out of heaven.

When Adam and Eve sinned against God, it had a big effect on God who put them out of the Garden of Eden.

When Cain killed his brother Abel, it had a big effect on God who made Cain a fugitive.

When God's Son Jesus Christ was betrayed, it had a big effect on God and meant that Judas would have been better off to never have been born.

When Jesus was spit on, bruised and beaten, it had a big effect on God.

When Jesus was nailed on the cross and died on the cross, it had a big effect on God who felt the pain of the death of His only begotten Son.

The bloodshed of war has a big effect on God, who created us all to love one another and not hurt and kill one another.

Every living soul has a big effect on God, who gave us His Son to save us from our sins.

How we feel has a big effect on God, who will heal our broken hearts.

Every day that we live our lives has an effect on God, who can shorten our lives or prolong our lives according to His reasons that are always right.

There is nothing that doesn't have a big effect on God, who sees all things seen and unseen and knows all things that have a big effect on God who had wonderfully made all things from the beginning of time on earth.

If we believe that whatever we think, say and do doesn't have a big effect on God, then we are only fooling ourselves.

The devil and his fallen angels know too well that our soul salvation has a big effect on God, so the devil tries his best to cause our souls to be lost like he is forever lost.

The devil had no true repentance unto God after he rebelled against God and had a big, negative effect on God who will one day cast him and all of his fallen angels and human agents into the lake of fire.

We can read all through the bible about what people did that had a big effect on God and caused him to bless people or punish people according to the choices they made that God didn't overlook or let slip by Him.

Death has a bigger effect on God than on you and me who God created from the beginning to live forever.

Adam and Eve brought death upon themselves for disobeying God and they brought death upon us all, which has a big effect on God who gave us His Son Jesus Christ to give us eternal life if we believe in Jesus Christ.

Nothing has a big effect on us more than it does God, because everything that exists has a big effect on God, even when we lay down to sleep and don't know what is going on around us.

Every breathing, living creature has a big effect on God, and every living thing has a big effect on God who didn't create any junk from the beginning.

All creatures great and small have their purpose in life that has a big effect on God.

Even the smallest thing has a big effect on God, who doesn't overlook anyone or anything that He can use for His good but the devil will try to use anyone or anything for evil.

Our destiny has a big effect on God, who doesn't choose our destiny for us because He gave us a free will to choose our own destiny, whether we believe in Jesus or believe in the devil.

This whole world has a big effect on God who will one day create a new world of righteous living.

If God is Imaginary

If God is imaginary, then we can burn up all the bibles.

If God is imaginary, then we all can become atheists.

If God is imaginary, then we all wouldn't exist.

If God is imaginary, then we all would be better off never having been born.

If God is imaginary, then every church would be so worthless.

If God is imaginary, then life would be so dead.

If God is imaginary, then hope would be so out of date.

If God is imaginary, then time would be so hopeless.

If God is imaginary, then nothing would be possible.

If God is imaginary, then religion would be so useless.

If God is imaginary, then lies would be so true.

If God is imaginary, then the devil would have the power to kill us all.

If God is imaginary, then we all would be so possessed by the devil.

If God is imaginary, then Jesus Christ would be a fraud.

If God is imaginary, then the truth would be so void.

If God is imaginary, then every human being would be so suicidal.

If God is imaginary, then this whole world would be so inhumane.

If God is imaginary, then the whole universe would be so momentary.

If God is imaginary, then all existence would be so fictional.

If God is imaginary, then all things seen and unseen are only a bluff.

God is forever far from being imaginary because nature itself is also a bible that we can study to know that God is read.

There are many church folks who project God to be imaginary because they live their lives like God is not real.

They live their lives with no renewed life in Jesus Christ, who was a real, sinless man and God in the flesh.

There are many so-called Christians who cause God to be imaginary before unbelievers who see many church folks living in their sins against God.

Many unbelievers see no real change in many so-called Christians making God to be only imaginary because they have no real godly change in their lives and are playing church.

There are many so-called Christians, but they don't stand a chance against a real, true, all-powerful God who is not imaginary to anyone who believes in His Son, Jesus Christ.

Living for Jesus is real and not imaginary in His holy word that is the real, everlasting truth about God the Father, the Son and the Holy Spirit.

If God is imaginary, then every word that comes from the tips of our tongues would be meaningless.

If God is imaginary, then everything that we do would have no substance like the air that we breathe in and out of our nostrils.

If God is imaginary, then heaven is not real, the universe is not real and this world is not real for us to be so imaginary that anyone in their right frame of mind won't claim to be because we love being real in our real bodies that a real God gave to us, even though atheists and evolutionists pretty much doubt this.

Jesus' Bride is His Church

Jesus' bride is His church.

Her love covers a multitude of sins every day that she speaks the love of Jesus and gives that love to everybody.

Her beauty shines like the sun to brighten up everybody's lives in the name of her husband, Jesus Christ.

She goes through the wilderness of life with her eyes stayed on Jesus, who gives her the strength and encouragement that she needs to make it through this life.

Jesus' bride is His church.

Her faith in Jesus withstands the test of time that she cherishes each day in this world to spread the gospel of Jesus Christ.

She falls down at times on the ground of being misunderstood and falsely accused, but her loving husband, Jesus, will waste no time to be there for her and stand her back up with her head up high.

Jesus' bride is His church.

She discerns this world with the word of God that she knows and lives by before the world every day.

She loves Jesus with all of her heart, soul, mind and strength and will never deny her husband, Jesus, before anyone in this world.

She dresses up in holiness and righteousness to draw the right kind of attention which she uses to honor her husband, Jesus, with the utmost respect every day.

Jesus' bride is His Church.

She will joyfully talk about the love of Jesus and how He is always there for her in this sinful and troubled world.

She puts all of her trust in her husband, Jesus, who she knows will give her joy and a peace of mind to live in this world of changing times.

She is very sure and content that Jesus will never take her through any changes for the worse, but will surely do so for the better so she can be more and more like Jesus.

Jesus' bride is His church.

Her prayers unto Jesus are true and sincere with humility of confession and repentance and healing that she knows she needs to empty herself to be filled with the Holy Spirit.

She makes her calling to be very sure that she works out her soul's salvation by examining herself to be like Jesus every day.

She has no doubt that her husband, Jesus, is holy, righteous and perfect in every word that He says and everything that He does for her to win souls to Him who is always so faithful and true to her that she has no reason to ever doubt.

Jesus' bride is His church.

She sometimes stumbles and gets weary for living in this sinful world that she takes no pleasure in because she believes that Jesus is coming back again to take her to heaven to live with Him forever and ever.

She knows that Jesus will put stars on her crown for winning souls to Him, even souls who she never sees in this world.

She knows that she can always fall back on Jesus who is there to catch her when she is blinded by many of her own spiritual brothers and sisters who proclaim to be a Christian and don't bear fruit of the Holy Spirit.

Jesus' bride is His church.

She loves to stay spiritually awake in this sinful world that loves to try to cause her to fall spiritually asleep when her husband, Jesus, is coming back to this world like a thief in the night.

She knows that she is all secured in Jesus' almighty hands that will hold her together no matter what trials and persecutions come her way.

She knows that her strong foundation is Jesus, who she can always stand on because Jesus will never lose His strong foundation in any storm that will come her way.

She knows without a doubt that she is happily married to the Son of God who gave this world His only begotten Son to redeem everyone back to God.

Jesus' bride is His church.

She invites everyone into her house and feeds them with the bread of life, who is her husband, Jesus, who supplies all of her needs to win souls to Him.

She knows what it means to love Jesus and keep His Commandments that won't burden her down but will set her free from spiritual adultery.

Jesus' bride is His glorious church that He adorns in His heavenly Father's everlasting love.

She gladly makes her choice to deny herself and pick up her cross to follow Jesus all the way through the thick and thin of her life and through the good days and bad days of her life that she knows is in Jesus' almighty hands.

She can never say and believe that Jesus let her slip out of His hands that keep a tight grip on her every day, no matter when she can't see where she is going like a blind person.

When she gets weary, Jesus strengthens her to stay on the strait and narrow road to keep her from getting on the road of destruction.

She loves everybody like Jesus loves everybody.

She is the greatest wife and the greatest mother and the greatest friend to spiritually nurture souls to believe in her husband, Jesus, who will save any soul who confesses and repents and turns to Him before it's too late.

Jesus' bride is His faithful and loving church that is not in vain because of Jesus, who took away the devil's power over this world when he died on the cross for our sins and rose from the grave with victory over death and the grave.

Jesus has made His bride to be victorious in Him who said in His holy word that the world will hate His church because the world hated Him for speaking the truth of God and living the truth of God.

Jesus' bride is His remnant church.

She knows not to judge anyone before Jesus comes back again because she knows that her mission in this life is to love souls and win souls to Jesus.

When Jesus takes her to heaven for a thousand years, Jesus will allow her to judge the fallen angels and every lost soul for her to truly know that God is an everlasting and fair God to all of His creations.

She knows what it means to pray without ceasing and to be watchful for Jesus coming back again like the five wise virgins who kept their lamps burning to meet their bridegrooms.

With His Everlasting Love

God loves you and me with His everlasting love no matter how much we mess up in life.

No matter how bad off we are, God loves you and me with His everlasting love.

God doesn't hold grudges against you and me for doing Him wrong, which we all do in one way or another way.

God loves you and me with His everlasting love that God gives to us through His Son, Jesus Christ.

Even if you and I tell lie after lie and pretend to be who we are not, God loves you and me with His everlasting love.

God's everlasting love hovers over you and me every day like the great blue sky showing you and me how special we are to Him.

It hurts God's heart when we are hurting from life's disappointments and griefs that are no comparison to God's everlasting love for you and me.

God doesn't want you and me to be lost in our sins — that breaks God's heart.

You and I can't ever imagine how much God loves us with His everlasting love that you and I can hold onto real tight every day.

God loves you and me with His everlasting love that will get us through any hardships in this life.

We must trust God, who is every good thing to us because God will never let us down.

If we repent and turn to God's Son, Jesus Christ, Jesus will fill our lives with unspeakable love.

Nothing will Evolve Beyond God

Things will evolve in this world because of sin that evolves every evil thing.

From the beginning of God's creation in this world, everything was perfect to stay the same way with no existence of any kind of evolvements in this world.

Whatever evolves comes from sin and not from God, who stays the same forever and ever.

Only here on earth things will evolve from the deadly effects of sin that don't exist in heaven and in other worlds where everyone and everything is perfect and will never evolve into the uncertain, temporary changes in life that are only here on earth.

Nothing will evolve beyond God, who gave us His only begotten Son, Jesus Christ, to save us from our sins that instantly evolved in our nature because of Adam disobeying God.

God held Adam so much more accountable for eating that unforbidden fruit.

Nothing will ever evolve beyond God the Father, the Son and the Holy Spirit, who said, "Let us make man and woman in our likeness," before Adam and Eve sinned against God.

After they sinned against God, it affected this whole world and began the process of evolving everything that was created by God.

Many things have evolved in this world because of sin, which caused many things to gradually change and develop into the things that God didn't create from the beginning.

Nothing will ever evolve beyond God, who will one day destroy all sin for nothing to evolve in the new world that God will create to be perfect and nothing will ever evolve there.

We Can Say, "What did I get myself into with the Lord?"

We can say, "What did I get myself into with the Lord?" by asking Him to bless us with what we pray to Him for.

We can say, "What did I get myself into with the Lord?" by asking the Lord to give us more faith in Him.

We may not be prepared to receive more faith that can surely put us to the test to pass or not pass with a high grade of the trials that can come our way.

We can say to the Lord, "What did I get myself into for asking You to give me what I may not be strong enough to receive from You?"

The Lord always knows what we can handle, but you and I don't always know if we will be ready to do whatever He tells us to do to uplift and glorify His holy name before brilliant unbelievers.

We can say, "What did I get myself into with the Lord who won't put on us more than what we can bear?"

We can pray to the Lord to bless us to achieve in representing Him and using our spiritual gifts to build up the church.

There is a high cost we must pay for following the Lord on the strait and narrow path that will surely let us know what we get ourselves into with the Lord.

We can very well go beyond our limits in asking the Lord for things that the Lord knows we are not prepared to receive from Him.

The Lord may very well at times answer our prayers and give us what we want and don't need so that we can truly see what we got ourselves into with Him.

We can say and ask ourselves, "What did I get myself into with the Lord who is perfect in all of His ways of doing things in our lives?"

We sinners saved through God's grace can surely regret some things for asking human beings to give us things that can ruin our lives, but the

Lord will never ruin our lives by giving us some things that we want and don't need.

We can say, "What did I get myself into with the Lord when He gives us what we ask Him for, even in our ignorance?"

The Lord will never go overboard in giving us anything that will cause our souls to be lost.

The Lord will give us just enough for us to learn a good lesson so we wise up and trust Him to give us what we need so that we don't have to ask ourselves, "What did I get myself into with the Lord?"

The Lord always knows what is best for us.

Every Generation is Different

Every generation is different and will not see eye to eye on everything.

Every generation of people will do some things in a different way.

The generation before our generation didn't have the technology that our generation has today.

The next generation will have even better technology than our generation today.

Every generation of people will not have the same fashions; those change in every generation.

Every generation of people will not have the same lifestyles; those change in every generation.

Every generation of people will not have the same ideas; those change in every generation.

Even in the church, every generation of Christians will come up with some new ideas to win souls to our Lord and Savior Jesus Christ.

Even though every generation is different in some ways, God will not change His holy word — that will stay the same in every generation of people.

Generations will change, but the Lord God is the same yesterday, today and tomorrow.

The past generations, the present generation and the future generations can't change God's mind and make Him change His holy ten Commandments.

God's Commandments are for every generation of people to keep and we will keep them if we love Jesus Christ.

Everybody in the Church

Everybody in the church has their personal struggles, but we should not let them keep us from worshipping the Lord and being rooted and grounded in the Lord.

Everybody in the church has their personal struggles, but we should not let them stop us from respecting one another and loving one another.

Everybody in the church has their personal struggles, but we all can give them to our Lord and Savior Jesus Christ, who overcame every struggle in this world where He once lived without sin in His flesh.

Everybody in the church has their personal struggles, but Jesus can give us the strength to bear them from day to day.

Everybody in the church has their personal struggles, but they are not too hard for Jesus to lighten our burdens and make us strong so we can stand on top of our struggles.

Everybody in the church has their personal struggles, but we should not let them get between us and Jesus.

Everybody in the church has their personal struggles, but we should not let them keep us from giving Jesus our best efforts to love Him and keep His Commandments.

Everybody in the church has their personal struggles that Jesus foreknew before we were born and knew nothing about the things we would go through, especially for His holy name's sake.

Everybody in the church has their personal struggles that Jesus can use for our good to draw us closer and closer to Him, even in some ways that we don't see.

Everybody in the church has their personal struggles that have no power to get us off the pathway to Jesus if we have faith in Jesus to use our personal struggles to encourage us to depend on Him and not on ourselves to overcome our personal struggles that Jesus can truly help us to overcome.

Everybody in the church has their personal struggles, but we can pray to Jesus without ceasing and live for Jesus who our personal struggles can't ever take the place of in our lives if we choose to believe in Jesus Christ over our personal struggles.

Our personal struggles are not more believable than Jesus, who has all power and authority over everybody's personal struggles and public struggles through His blood that was shed on the cross to cleanse us from our sins and save us from our sins.

Everybody in the church and outside the church has their personal struggles and some public struggles, but every true Christian knows what it means to give them all to Jesus who can do all things but fail us.

Everybody in the church has their personal struggles whether they're married or single, young or old, educated or not educated, rich or poor, but Jesus is the head of the church and gives everybody in the church the power to trample over every personal struggle and public struggle to shame the devil who loves to cause everybody in the church to struggle more than anyone who is not in the church.

Everybody in the church has their personal struggles and public struggles, but if we put our hope and trust in Jesus Christ even our struggles will look so peaceful in this troubled world that foolish people put their trust in to give them the victory over their personal struggles and public struggles.

To the Full Extent

No one can keep the law of God to the full extent.

We will break the law of God in a knowing or ignorant way.

The purpose of God's holy law is to show us our sins.

The law of God can't save us from our sins.

Jesus foreknew that the law of God would not save anyone from their sins.

Jesus foreknew that He would have to leave all of heaven to be made flesh without sin and live a sinless life among sinners to show them that He was the only one who could keep the law of God to the full extent.

We sinners were born in sin to break God's holy law even unintentionally on the spur of the moment is something we Christians can do.

Without the law of God, we wouldn't know what sin is and wouldn't know that we disrespected God's character.

God's holy law is the character of God, who can do no evil and no wrong to anyone.

No one in this world can keep the law of God to the full extent, for as long as we live in this sinful world, we will break God's holy law in some kind of way.

We can break God's holy law in our thoughts, words and actions and may not realize it until the Holy Spirit convicts us that we broke God's holy law.

Only Jesus Christ, our Lord and Savior, kept God's holy law to the full extent because He was perfect to have no sins for Him to be truth and grace given to us who don't deserve it.

We are saved through God's grace because of Jesus Christ who gave up His life on the cross to save us from our sins which is something the law of God can't do for us.

Just because the law of God can't save us doesn't meant we have an excuse to not want to try to keep the ten Commandments of God.

We need the Holy Spirit to help us to keep the ten Commandments of God because we cannot keep them on our own strength that will fail us and we will break the law of God in some kind of seen and unseen way.

It's truly God's grace that keeps us from dropping dead as soon as we break God's holy law that points out our sins to us.

Even for people who don't know God's law, God put His law in their hearts so that even a child will feel guilty after telling his or her parents a lie.

Back in the bible days, the Pharisees believed that they were keeping the law of God to the full extent even as they broke them for especially not believing in Jesus Christ, who fulfilled the law of God.

Jesus says, "If you love Me, you will keep My Commandments," but Jesus is not saying that we will never break His Commandments.

We Christians can greatly desire to keep God's Commandments but we will fall short of the glory of God and sin against God even in some ways that we don't see.

Jesus truly knows all who love Him, regardless of having a sinful nature that God's grace hovers over like the sky hovers over all the world.

No one can keep the law of God to the full extent and never break it.

We will have a sinful nature to break God's law.

Our righteousness is like filthy rags because we were born in sin that breaks God's law.

Only the righteousness of Jesus can make us right with God.

The law of God can't make us right with God because the purpose of the law is to show us that sin exists in us to break God's law, which we can do even in an ignorant way no matter how much we know the word of God.

No one has ever kept the full extent of God's law except Jesus Christ, who had no sin in thoughts, words or actions when He lived in this sinful world among sinners like you and me.

Jesus gave us His life on the cross to save us from our sins, and He rose from the grave to give us eternal life that is the full extent of God's love for us.

The purpose of confessing our sins and repenting of our sins is because we have sins to break God's law and not keep the full extent of God's law.

We can thank God for His Son, Jesus Christ, who kept the full extent of God's law for you and me to be saved in Him.

We cannot save ourselves because we are cursed by the law of God if there is no grace given to us through Jesus Christ, who is truth and grace from God.

Only Jesus can save us from our sins to the full extent if we love Jesus and want to keep His Commandments — the law of God can't do this.

No matter how much every Christian loves Jesus, you and I will still fall short of the glory of God and have sins to confess and repent of to prove that we break God's holy law.

We true Christians have no desire to want to break God's holy law because we want to love Jesus Christ to the full extent that pleases God, who gives us His Holy Spirit to the full extent.

Jesus says that if we love Him, we will keep His Commandments, but Jesus is not saying that we will never sin against Him ever again.

If we love Him, we must confess our sins unto Him because of breaking God's holy law that is the full extent of God's character.

Our love for Jesus is a lifetime of spiritual growth because there is always more room for us to love Jesus more and more to the full extent.

We can break God's holy law in our thoughts, words, and actions without being aware we're doing it, but that doesn't mean that we don't love Jesus who will wink his eye at our ignorance of what we don't know.

No true Christian will love and obey Jesus to the full extent because we are unaware of sins we don't see that break God's holy law.

Only the righteousness of Jesus Christ will make us right in God's eyesight.

All the right thoughts we think, all the right words we say and all the right deeds we do don't come close to keeping the full extent of God's holy law.

Only the blood of Jesus will cleanse us of our sins that only Jesus can save us from to the full extent.

Jesus is our only living truth and grace to the full extent.

No one's imagination or false theories can override God's holy law, and no one has an excuse to knowingly break Gods' holy law.

No one can keep God's holy law to the full extent, especially if you believe that you can save yourself and enter heaven without believing in Jesus Christ, who can save us from our sins which the law of God can't do.

If we love Jesus, we will want to keep His Commandments.

Only the Holy Spirit can help us to keep God's holy law one day at a time.

We must pray to the full extent and live for Jesus, whose righteousness covers over our best righteousness, which is like filthy rags before God every day.

Because of our sinful nature, we will break God's holy law in some kind of way for the Holy Spirit to convict us to confess and repent of our sins.

As Though We

We can eat food as though we can't gain weight.

We can talk as though we are alone for no one to hear us.

We can hear as though we are deaf to what someone says to us.

We can see as though someone is invisible to us.

We can wear clothes as though we have no clothes to wear.

We can sleep as though we are conscious to see our dreams and grab onto them.

We can smile as though no one will notice it.

We can do something as though we didn't move at all.

We can be silent as though we spoke many words.

We can find something as though we never lost it.

We can lose something as though we never had it.

We can clap our hands as though we have no joy.

We can spend money as though we never had it.

We can have knowledge as though we are ignorant.

We can have common sense as though it is no good use to us.

We can go to church as though it doesn't exist.

We can know the truth of God's holy word as though it has no good effect on us.

We can misrepresent Jesus Christ as though Jesus won't hold us accountable.

We can live our lives and one day die as though we were never born to live.

We can live our lives as though we own them and not Jesus, who also owns the afterlife in heaven.

Jesus will take all of His righteous children to heaven when He comes back again on the clouds of glory as though we never lived in this sinful world.

Our Dreams are Like Watching a Movie

Our dreams are like watching a movie in the unconscious world of our dreams in the night time that we sleep and dream away.

Our dreams are like watching a movie and we don't know what we will see in the next scene of our dream.

Our dreams are like watching a good movie or a bad movie that we can be in to see ourselves having no control over the unconscious world of our dreams that can control us to be in every scene of our dreams.

Our dreams are like watching a movie that can seem like eternity, taking us from one place to another place in our dreams in the night that we sleep and dream away into the morning light.

The movies that film producers make are rehearsed and take a lot of work to produce.

Our dreams are like watching a movie that has no film producers and no rehearsals in the unconscious world of our dreams that we have no clues about what we will dream about in our sleep.

Only the Lord can direct every scene in our dreams to be in His holy will.

Our dreams are like watching a movie but only the Lord knows what we will dream about before we lay down to sleep in the unconscious world of our dreams that also belong to the Lord because no dream is too impossible for the Lord to not understand and give us the true meaning to our dreams.

Jesus Christ is the Truth to Set Us Free from Living in Sin

Jesus Christ is the truth to set us free from living in sin.

Luck is not the truth to set us free from living in sin.

Magic is not the truth to set us free from living in sin.

Jesus Christ is the truth to set us free from living in sin.

Witchcraft is not the truth to set us free from living in sin.

Horoscopes are not the truth to set us free from living in sin.

Jesus Christ is the truth to set us free from living in sin.

Mediums are not the truth to set us free from living in sin.

Sorcery is not the truth to set us free from living in sin.

Jesus Christ is the truth to set us free from living in sin.

Omens are not the truth to set us free from living in sin.

Spiritualism is not the truth to set us free from living in sin.

Jesus Christ is the truth to set us free from living in sin.

False doctrines are not the truth to set us free from living in sin.

Politics are not the truth to set us free from living in sin.

Jesus Christ is the truth to set us free from living in sin.

Religion is not the truth to set us free from living in sin.

Miracles are not the truth to set us free from living in sin.

Jesus Christ is the truth to set us free from living in sin.

Wealth is not the truth to set us free from living in sin.

Prosperity is not the truth to set us free from living in sin.

Jesus Christ is the truth to set us free from living in sin.

War is not the truth to set us free from living in sin.

Theories are not the truth to set us free from living in sin.

Jesus Christ is the truth to set us free from living in sin.

Philosophies are not the truth to set us free from living in sin.

Phenomena are not the truth to set us free from living in sin.

Jesus Christ is the truth to set us free from living in sin.

Technologies are not the truth to set us free from living in sin.

Science is not the truth to set us free from living in sin.

Jesus Christ is the truth to set us free from living in sin.

Money is not the truth to set us free from living in sin.

Sex is not the truth to set us free from living in sin.

Jesus Christ is the truth to set us free from living in sin.

Human beings are not the truth to set us free from living in sin.

Animals are not the truth to set us free from living in sin.

Jesus Christ is the truth to set us free from living in sin.

Skills are not the truth to set us free from living in sin.

Talents are not the truth to set us free from living in sin.

Jesus Christ is the truth to set us free from living in sin.

Laws are not the truth to set us free from living in sin.

Choices are not the truth to set us free from living in sin.

Jesus Christ is the truth to set us free from living in sin.

Marriage is not the truth to set us free from living in sin.

The church is not the truth to set us free from living in sin.

Jesus Christ is the truth to set us free from living in our sins that Jesus became on the cross He died on to save us from our sins.

Success is not the truth to set us free from living in sin.

Education is not the truth to set us free from living in sin.

Jesus Christ is the living truth to set us free from living in sin that has corrupted everybody to have a sinful nature to sin against God in thoughts, words and in our actions.

Jesus Christ is the living truth to set us free from living in our sins that originated from the devil who hates God and every human being who God created in His likeness

This is the truth that the devil has been trying to make a lie by planting the idea of evolution in the minds of educated and uneducated fools.

It's Not Me, It's the Lord

It's not me, it's the Lord who brought me this far in my life.

I know that I didn't bring myself this far in my life.

It's not me, it's the Lord who is keeping me alive.

I know that I am not keeping myself alive.

It's not me, it's the Lord who supplies all of my needs.

I know that I don't supply all of my needs.

It's not me, it's the Lord who gives me good thoughts.

I know that I don't give myself good thoughts.

It's not me, it's the Lord who gives me good words to say.

I know that I don't give myself good words to say.

It's not me, it's the Lord who gives me good deeds.

I know that I don't give myself good deeds.

It's not me, it's the Lord who gives me air to breathe.

I know that I don't give myself air to breathe.

It's not me, it's the Lord who gives me strength in my body.

I know that I don't give myself strength in my body.

It's not me, it's the Lord who protects me from unknown harm and danger.

I know that I don't protect myself from unknown harm and danger.

It's not me, it's the Lord who gives me the victory.

I know that I don't give myself the victory.

It's not me, it's the Lord who gives me wisdom.

I know that I don't' give myself wisdom.

It's not me, it's the Lord who gives me common sense.

I know that I don't' give myself common sense.

It's not me, it's the Lord who gives me discernment.

I know that I don't give myself discernment.

It's not me, it's the Lord who gives me peace of mind.

I know that I don't give myself peace of mind.

It's not me, it's the Lord who owns me.

I know that I don't own myself.

It's not me, it's the Lord who gave me knowledge.

I know I didn't give myself knowledge.

It's not me, it's the Lord who gave me a mind

I didn't give myself a mind.

It's not me, it's the Lord who gave me a heart.

I know I didn't give myself a heart.

It's not me, it's the Lord who gave me the free will to choose.

I know I didn't give myself the free will to choose.

It's not me, it's the Lord who gave me His Holy Spirit.

I know I didn't give myself the Holy Spirit.

It's not me, it's the Lord who gave me salvation.

I know I didn't give myself salvation.

It's not me, it's the Lord who has given me the truth.

I know that I didn't give myself the truth.

It's not me, it's the Lord who has given me grace.

I know that I didn't give myself grace.

It's not me, it's the Lord who has given me unspeakable joy.

I know that I didn't give myself unspeakable joy.

It's not me, it's the Lord Jesus Christ who has given me God's love.

I know that I didn't give myself God's love.

It's not me, it's the Lord who winked his eye at my ignorance.

I know that I didn't wink my eye at my ignorance.

It's not me, it's the Lord who never failed me.

I know that I have failed myself.

It's not me, it's the Lord who will always love me.

I know that I didn't always love myself.

It's not me, it's the Lord who can work everything out for my good.

I know that I can't work everything out for my good.

It's not me, it's the Lord who opened my eyes to see the devil's lies.

I know that I didn't open my eyes to see the devil's lies.

It's not me, it's the Lord who is keeping me going strong in Him.

I know that I can't keep myself going strong in the Lord.

It's not me, it's the Lord who has a heaven to put me in.

I know that I don't have a heaven to put myself in.

It's not me, it's the Lord Jesus Christ who will give me eternal life for being saved in Him.

I know that I can't save myself through good works that I do because they can't give me eternal life.

It's not me, it's the Lord who can cleanse me of my sins.

I know that I can't cleanse myself of my sins.

It's not me, it's the Lord who can forgive me of my sins.

I know that I can't forgive myself of my sins.

It's not me, it's the Lord who can save me from my sins.

I know that I can't save myself from my sins.

It's not me, it's the Lord who is worthy to be praised.

I know that I am not worthy to be praised.

It's not me, it's the Lord who has no sins.

I know that I have sins to confess and repent unto the Lord.

It's not me, it's the Lord who cannot lie.

I know that I can tell a lie and live a lie.

It's not me, it's the Lord who knows all things.

I know that I don't know anything compared to everything that the Lord knows.

It's not me, it's the Lord who sees all things.

I know that I am blind compared to the all-seeing Lord.

It's not me, it's the Lord who never fails.

I know that I can fail to do even some simple little things.

It's not me, it's the Lord who lives forever and ever.

I know that I will one day die, and that could be any day before the Lord Jesus Christ comes back again on the clouds of glory.

It's not me, it's the Lord who will raise me from the dead if I am saved in Him.

I know that when I die I can't raise myself from the dead and I can't take myself to heaven because that's something only the Lord can do.

Is a Success

Many people will only believe that getting rich is a success.

Many people will only believe that getting a college degree is a success.

Many people will only believe that having a great job is a success.

Many people will only believe that making achievements is a success.

Many people will only believe that winning a championship is a success.

Many people will only believe that winning the lottery is a success.

Many people will only believe that writing a best-seller book is a success.

Many people will only believe that winning an Oscar is a success.

Many people will only believe that winning an Emmy is a success.

Not making the same mistake again is a success.

Keeping your vehicle and your house clean is a success.

Not over-working yourself is a success.

Paying your bills is a success.

Eating right is a success.

Having good hygiene is a success.

Helping someone in need is a success.

Saying the right words is a success.

Dressing decent is a success.

Treating yourself right is a success.

Telling the truth is a success.

Keeping the laws in the land is a success.

Having a good marriage is a success.

Having good friends is a success.

Raising up your children in the right way is a success.

An author getting only one book sold is a success.

Having a good outlook on life is a success.

Saving someone's life is a success.

Doing good things is a success.

If you only win one soul to the Lord Jesus Christ, it is a success for all the angels in heaven to rejoice about.

Loving Jesus and keeping His Commandments is a success.

Being saved in Jesus Christ is a success.

Success can happen in so many ways, but the greatest success is going with Jesus Christ back to heaven when He comes back again on the clouds of glory.

Everyone will not be successful in going with Jesus back to heaven when He comes back again.

No one can ever be more successful than Jesus Christ, who got the victory over death and the grave to give you and me His free gift of eternal life.

No one can ever be more successful than Jesus Christ, who overpowered the devil for never sinning against God when He lived here on earth among sinners and did not ever sin to take this world back from the devil who Adam and Eve gave their dominion over to for sinning against God in the Garden of Eden.

No one can ever be more successful than Jesus Christ, who will successfully write everyone's name in the book of life for being saved in Him.

No one can ever be more successful than Jesus Christ, who will be very successful in showing all the holy saints in heaven why some didn't make it to heaven, especially those who did good works in Jesus' name but had no true conversion to repent and love Jesus and keep His Commandments.

No One is Alone in this World

No one is alone in this world because the choices that we make will affect one another in some kind of way.

No one is alone in this world because everyone will be in the presence of someone sooner or later, no matter being good or bad.

No one is alone in this world where everyone has a mother and father who procreated and caused them to live in this world where everyone needs some kind of help from someone no matter being good or bad.

The Lord didn't create human beings to be alone because God is the origin of relationships and community that everyone in this world needs every day.

Anyone in their right mind won't be happy about wanting to be all alone because that truly won't prosper anyone to be in a relationship with the Lord.

God is never alone up in heaven where the holy angels surround Him as He sits on His holy throne.

God doesn't leave us alone to ourselves, even though we are prone to make a bad choice whether we know it or not.

God always reaches out to us first to let us know that we are not alone in this world to wander through life with no purpose, because our purpose is to love God and keep His Commandments.

No one is alone in this world and left to themselves because God's love is for everyone to receive and share with one another, which we can only do through Jesus Christ.

No one can ever be so alone like Jesus was on the cross to say to His heavenly Father, "God, why has thou forsaken me?"

Jesus experienced the worst kind of being alone to save us from our sins that Jesus became on the cross and could not bear His heavenly Father turning His back on Him.

No one is alone in this world to say or believe that God doesn't love them, because God gave us His only begotten Son to redeem us back to Him who has an eternal community in heaven.

No one is so alone in this world that God doesn't see and reach out to have a relationship with you.

God is always joyful to be in a relationship with us if we just choose to trust Him to fill our lives with love for one another so we don't feel alone.

No one is alone in the world because God gives His grace to everyone to be saved in His Son, Jesus Christ.

Everyone in their right mind can choose Jesus over the false belief of being alone and all by themselves.

Everyone is loved by God and will answer to God, who leaves no one alone by themselves for as long as we live.

Giving Jesus Your Best

As long as you know you are giving Jesus your best, you don't need to worry about how other people feel and what they say about you.

There will always be some church folks who won't believe you are giving Jesus your best.

No one knows you like you and Jesus day after day, and Jesus knows your weaknesses and strengths.

Only Jesus always knows what is your best, certainly much better than anyone else can know.

You pretty much know what you can do and can't do day after day.

You might give your spouse, children and friends your best and they may not appreciate it.

You might give your best to your boss on your job and he or she may not appreciate it.

If you give Jesus your best, Jesus and all the angels in heaven will appreciate it.

Jesus will truly bless you for giving Him your best.

You might give your church family your best, but there may be some church folks who will criticize and degrade your best efforts.

They don't know you like Jesus knows you completely, because only Jesus is worthy to judge your best.

Giving Jesus your best will surely please Him and will keep you going strong in Him.

You can give people your best but there are always some people who will be displeased by your best.

There are people who know that you are giving them your best and they will take advantage of you and cause you to overwork yourself.

Jesus will never overwork you for giving Him your best.

Jesus will truly bless you for doing your best, but there are people who will use your best against you.

Your motives and intentions can be good for giving people your best, but there are people who will take you doing your best as a threat to them.

You can always give Jesus your best and He will never take it in the wrong way like people can do and give you a bad name.

Giving Jesus your best from your heart is a great thing that no one can take away from you no matter how much they take your best in the wrong way.

As long as Jesus is pleased with your best, that is all that really matters because Jesus has a heaven to take you to when He comes back again.

What is Best for Us

The Lord knows what is best for us, even though it can hurt us sometimes when the Lord doesn't give us what we ask Him for.

The Lord knows what is best for us, because the Lord will not give us false hopes like people can do to be our discouragement on any day.

The Lord knows what is best for us, who can ask the Lord for things that the Lord knows we don't need.

The Lord knows what is best for us, because the Lord will always see what we don't see down the road that the Lord knows to be a dead-end when we don't know that.

The Lord knows what is best for us, who don't always know what we are asking the Lord to give us.

The Lord knows if we are ready and strong enough to receive what we ask Him for.

You and I may not have the slightest clue what we ask the Lord to give us, but the Lord always knows what is best for us.

There are times when we put our foot in our mouth and ask the Lord to give us things that the Lord knows wouldn't be good for us.

The Lord always knows what is best for you and me, who don't know what the Lord always knows to protect us from harming and ruining ourselves.

The Lord always knows what is best for us and won't always give us what we ask Him for.

The Lord knows that we don't always pay attention to His warnings about the hidden dangers of not always realizing what we pray and ask Him for.

The Lord always knows what is best for us, even though we can feel like the Lord is wrong for not giving us what we ask Him for.

We are truly wrong for insulting the Lord by feeling like He is wrong when the Lord always knows what is best for us.

If the Lord Jesus Christ gave us everything we pray and ask Him for, then we might very well believe that He is our puppet on a string that we can maneuver any kind of way we want.

The Lord always knows what is best for us, who can easily believe that we are always asking the Lord for the right things.

We can be so wrong for doubting the Lord about anything that He refuses to give to us who don't always know what is best for us.

When We Really Get Down to the Truth

When we really get down to the truth, a lot of people don't want to hear the truth.

When we really get down to the truth, a lot of people won't accept the truth.

When we really get down to the truth, a lot of people hate the truth.

When we really get down to the truth, it can hurt our hearts.

When we really get down to the truth, a lot of people are threatened by the truth.

When we really get down to the truth, a lot of people are afraid of the truth.

When we really get down to the truth, a lot of people will cover up the truth.

When we really get down to the truth, a lot of people will criticize the truth.

When we really get down to the truth, a lot of people won't own up to the truth.

When we really get down to the truth, a lot of people will degrade the truth.

When we really get down to the truth, a lot of people will corrupt the truth.

When we really get down to the truth, a lot of people will get rid of the truth.

When we really get down to the truth, a lot of people will downsize the truth.

When we really get down to the truth, a lot of people will mock the truth.

When we really get down to the truth, a lot of people will lie on the truth.

When we really get down to the truth, a lot of people will lie to the truth.

When we really get down to the truth, a lot of people will underestimate the truth.

When we really get down to the truth, a lot of people will make excuses to the truth.

When we really get down to the truth, a lot of people will misunderstand the truth.

When we really get down to the truth, a lot of people will disqualify the truth.

When we really get down to the truth, a lot of people will scorn the truth.

When we really get down to the truth, a lot of people will disrespect the truth.

When we really get down to the truth, a lot of people will terrorize the truth.

When we really get down to the truth, a lot of people will interrupt the truth.

When we really get down to the truth, a lot of people will put down the truth.

When we really get down to the truth, a lot of people will not face up to the truth.

When we really get down to the truth, a lot of people will opinionate the truth.

When we really get down to the truth, a lot of people will be prejudiced against the truth.

When we really get down to the truth, a lot of people will enslave the truth.

When we really get down to the truth, a lot of people will despise the truth.

When we really get down to the truth, a lot of people will pollute the truth.

When we really get down to the truth, a lot of people will delusion the truth.

When we really get down to the truth of God's holy word, the truth will set us free.

When we really get down to the truth of God's holy word, the Holy Spirit will teach us all the truth about Jesus Christ, who is the everlasting truth.

When we really get down to the truth of God's holy word, all the truth in this world is secured in God's holy word that will never change because of Jesus Christ, who is the word of God.

When we really get down to the truth of God's holy word, a lot of people will add their lies to the truth of God's holy word.

When we really get down to the truth of God's holy word, only a few Christian people out of billions of people will live the truth of God's holy word for believing in Jesus Christ, who is the way, the truth and the life to live.

Common sense is from the Lord Jesus Christ who spoke to people with common sense to reach them on their level to understand Him with no excuse to not believe in Him who was without sin when He lived in this world where no one would never be more genius than Jesus.

The True Church
and the False Church

The true church preaches all the truth and the false church preaches truth mixed with lies.

The true church teaches all the truth and the false church teaches truth mixed with lies.

The true church keeps all the ten Commandments of God and the false church preaches and teaches that we are saved through God's grace and don't have to keep all the ten Commandments of God.

The true church preaches and teaches salvation through Jesus Christ and the false church preaches and teaches salvation through our works.

The true church preaches and teaches Jesus Christ is coming back again on the clouds of glory to raise the righteous dead and change the righteous living from mortal to immortal in the twinkling of an eye.

The false church preaches and teaches that people die and go straight to heaven and they can see you and me and appear before you and me to comfort us.

The true church lives all the truth in the bible, but the false church compromises the truth and does not live all the truth.

The true church preaches and teaches humility unto Jesus Christ, but the false church preaches and teaches prosperity should be the primary goal in a Christian's life.

The true church preaches and teaches God the Father, the Son and the Holy Spirit being the Trinity Godhead, but the false church only preaches and teaches God the Father, leaving out the Son, Jesus Christ, and the Holy Spirit.

The true church preaches and teaches that there is a heaven where Jesus will take us to if we are saved in Him.

The true church also preaches and teaches there is a hell where the devil and his angels and human agents will burn up.

The false church preaches and teaches that there is a purgatory where we will go to if all of our sins are not forgiven by God.

The true church preaches and teaches that sanctification is a lifetime process, but the false church preaches and teaches that once we are saved we are always saved in Jesus.

The true church preaches and teaches that we are made right in God's eyesight through the righteousness of Jesus Christ.

The false church preaches and teaches that we can get ourselves right with God on our own effort.

The true church preaches and teaches that we must believe in Jesus Christ to receive eternal life, but the false church preaches and teaches that we can die and go to heaven and receive eternal life before Jesus comes back again.

Jesus' main reason for coming back again is to give us eternal life in heaven, where we can't go to before Jesus comes back again.

The true church preaches and teaches Jesus Christ, but the false church preaches and teaches the false doctrines of rebellious human beings.

If You Talk Right to People and Treat People Right

If you talk right to people and treat people right, it can cause people to feel good about themselves.

If you talk right to people and treat people right, it can cause you to feel good about yourself.

If you talk right to people and treat people right, it can cause people to think twice about doing something wrong.

If you talk right to people and treat people right, it can cause you to always want to do what is right.

If you talk right to people and treat people right, it can cause people to want to treat themselves right.

If you talk right to people and treat people right, it can cause you to wise up.

If you talk right to people and treat people right, it can cause people to want to talk right and do what is right.

If you talk right to people and treat people right, it can cause you to be a better person.

If you talk right to people and treat people right, it can cause people to feel bad for talking bad to people and treating people bad.

If you talk right to people and treat people right, it can cause you to always want to be good to people.

If you talk right to people and treat people right, it can cause people to want to get the help they need.

If you talk right to people and treat people right, it can cause you to always want to help yourself.

If you talk right to people and treat people right, it can cause people to think right in their minds.

If you talk right to people and treat people right, it can cause you to always want to be positive.

If you talk right to people and treat people right, it can cause people to want to be honest.

If you talk right to people and treat people right, it can cause you to always want to be honest with yourself.

If you talk right to people and treat people right, it can cause people to love and trust you.

If you talk right to people and treat people right, it can cause you to always want to love and trust yourself.

If you talk right to people and treat people right, it can cause people to believe that there is a God.

If you talk right to people and treat people right, it can cause you to believe that there is a God watching over you.

If you talk right to people and treat people right, it can cause people to have some hope to get them through their hardships.

If you talk right to people and treat people right, it can cause you to not give up on hope.

If you talk right to people and treat people right, even some bad people will want to straighten up and live right unto the Lord Jesus Christ.

If you talk right to people and treat people right, it can cause you to want to believe in Jesus Christ, whose righteousness makes you right before God.

If you talk right to people and treat people right, it can cause people to cheer up and not look back on their misfortunes.

If you talk right to people and treat people right, it can cause you to be joyful in being content.

If you talk right to people and treat people right, it can cause people to forgive those who have done them wrong.

If you talk right to people and treat people right, it can cause you to not want to hold grudges.

If you talk right to people and treat people right, it can cause people to feel guilty for talking bad to you and treating you bad.

If you talk right to people and treat people right, it can cause people to feel ashamed for talking bad about you and disrespecting you.

If you talk right to people and treat people right, it can cause people to respect themselves.

If you talk right to people and treat people right, it can cause you to always want to have good motives and intentions.

If you talk right to people and treat people right, it can cause people to want to confess their sins and repent and turn to Jesus Christ.

If you talk right to people and treat people right, it can cause you to want to put Jesus first in your life and give Him all the glory and praise for loving you and helping you to talk right to people and treat people right.

Every word that you and I say right and everything that you and I do right is from the Lord Jesus Christ, not from you and me whose righteousness is like filthy rags before the Lord our God.

If you talk right to people and treat people right, it can cause people to not give you the evil eye look.

If you talk right to people and treat people right, it can cause you to not want to give people the evil eye look.

If you talk right to people and treat people right, it can cause people to be jealous of you for not being like them and showing favoritism to certain people.

If you talk right to people and treat people right, it can cause you to want to be protective like God, who is protective of every soul that belongs to Him.

God loves all souls to be saved in His Son, Jesus Christ, and God doesn't want anyone to be lost in their sins and join the devil and his fallen angels who are on their way to an eternal doom of fire and brimstone.

If you talk right to people and treat people right, it can cause people to want to take good care of themselves.

If you talk right to people and treat people right, it can cause you to want to take good care of yourself.

If you talk right to people and treat people right, it can cause people to want to change for the better.

If you talk right to people and treat people right, it can cause you to want to think good of people.

If you talk right to people and treat people right, it can cause people to want to be like you because you are wise to give God the glory and praise for all the right words that you say and all the right things that you do.

All of the good things we do and say come from the Lord God, not you and me because we are sinners who will sooner or later say something wrong and do something wrong.

God's grace is sufficient in Jesus Christ to save us from our sins and the devil hates for you and me to talk right to people and treat people right.

Voting is Showing that You

Voting is showing that you truly care about who you want to run this nation.

Voting is showing that you are very concerned about other people.

Voting is showing others that you are present in this nation.

Voting is showing that you have a voice.

Voting is showing that you believe addressing your concerns is important.

Voting is showing that you want what is best for your nation.

Voting is showing that you don't live in isolation.

Voting is showing that you are strong in what you believe.

Voting is showing that you have some trust in who you vote for.

Voting is showing that you are bold to express yourself.

Voting is showing that you have hope in your nation.

Voting is showing that you exist in the nation.

Voting is showing your presence in the voting box.

Voting is showing that you care about the welfare of your nation.

Voting is showing that you love your freedom.

It's in God's will for you to vote for loving and honest leaders to govern this nation.

It's in God's will for you to vote for good and trustworthy leaders to govern this nation.

It's God's will for you to vote for God-fearing leaders to govern this nation.

Voting is showing the real you, because who you vote for to represent you in this great nation is who you are, and this nation is great today because God allowed the United States of America to be great.

Voting is showing that you love your nation that only God can truly make better if it's His holy will.

The Lord Can Truly Look Out for Us

If the Lord can look out for billions of galaxies, then the Lord can truly look out for us.

If the Lord can look out for billions of universes, then the Lord can truly look out for us.

If the Lord can look out for billions of creatures, then the Lord can truly look out for us.

If the Lord can look out for trillions of stars, then the Lord can truly look out for us.

If the Lord can look out for all of the holy angels, then the Lord can truly look out for us.

If the Lord can look out for all of the unfallen worlds, then the Lord can truly look out for us.

The Lord can truly look out for us so much better than we can ever look out for ourselves.

The Lord can truly look out for us in our homes.

The Lord can truly look out for us in our neighborhood.

The Lord can truly look out for us on the road.

The Lord can truly look out for us in the stores.

The Lord can truly look out for us on our job.

The Lord can truly look out for us in the church.

The Lord can truly look out for us wherever we go.

If something bad happens to us, the Lord can truly look out for us to keep that bad situation from being so much worse on us.

The Lord can truly look out for us who don't have the slightest clue about how the Lord is moving an evil thing out of our way.

The Lord can truly look out for us who can forget something that we truly need, but the Lord can truly bring it back to our memory right on time.

The Lord can truly look out for us who can't always look out for ourselves, even in the safest places that the devil can appear in.

The Lord can truly look out for us even in ways that we can't imagine until the Lord opens our eyes to see that it was Him who truly protected us from the evils of the unknown.

The Lord Jesus Christ can truly look out for us who are like a lost sheep in the wilderness for the Lord to call us to hear His voice.

The Lord can truly look out for us who are like a wanderer having no focus on where to go without Jesus leading us to Calvary to redeem us back to God through His death on the cross for our sins.

Jesus rose the third day to truly look out for us to receive eternal life if we repent and turn to Him who is coming back on the clouds of glory.

I Want to be Caught Up in You, My Lord

I want to be caught up in You, my Lord Jesus Christ, who gives me the strength to keep going on day after day.

O Lord, I thank You for Your blessings upon my life, but I don't want to be caught up in Your blessings upon my life.

I want to be caught up in You, my Lord Jesus Christ, who answers my prayers that I don't deserve for not always waiting on You who is always on time to be there for me.

I don't want to be caught up in Your blessings, my Lord, because your blessings can't forgive me of my sins.

My Lord, Your blessings can't save me from my sins.

My Lord, Your blessings can't cleanse me of my sins.

I want to be caught up in You, my Lord and Savior Jesus Christ, who can forgive me of my sins, save me from my sins and cleanse me of my sins if I confess and repent and turn to You, my Lord Jesus Christ, which I can only do one day at a time.

I want to be caught up in You, my Lord Jesus Christ, who I need to keep my eyes on every day.

I don't want to keep my eyes on Your blessings, my Lord Jesus Christ, because Your blessings can blind my spiritual eyes to not see that I need to always keep my relationship with you, my Lord.

I don't want to be caught up in Your blessings, my Lord, because Your blessings can't relate to me like You, my Lord, who can always relate to me no matter what I go through in my life.

I want to always be caught up in You, my Lord Jesus Christ, because only You can give me Your Holy Spirit to convict me of my sins and convert my life for me to live it unto You.

I don't want to be caught up in Your blessings, my Lord, because Your blessings can't give me Your Holy Spirit.

It's so easy for anyone to get caught up in Your blessings, my Lord, while not giving You the glory and praise.

All good things come from You, my Lord, and all blessings are from You.

Every true saint will not put their blessings above You, my Lord.

Every true saint knows what it means to be caught up in You, my Lord Jesus Christ, because Your blessings are only a shadow moving where You tell it to go.

I want to be caught up in You, my Lord Jesus Christ, because You can give me a peace of mind, while being caught up in Your blessings will surely be dissatisfying to me and make me not be content with the blessings you give to me, my Lord and Savior Jesus Christ.

Love is More

Love is more intelligent than anyone in this world.

Love is more brilliant than anyone in this world.

Love is more genius than anyone in this world.

Love is more convincing than anyone in this world.

Love is more beautiful than any woman in this world.

Love is more strong than any man in this world.

Love is more free than anyone in this world.

Love is more captivating than anything in this world.

Love is more rich than anyone in this world.

Love is more solid than anything in this world.

Love is more rewarding than anything in this world.

Love is more obedient than anyone in this world.

Love is more energetic than anyone in this world.

Love is more serious than anyone in this world.

Love is more healthy than anyone in this world.

Love is more forgiving than anyone in this world.

Love is more friendly than anyone in this world.

Love is more honest than anyone in this world.

Love is more helpful than anyone in this world.

Love is more youthful than anyone in this world.

Love is more smart than anyone in this world.

Love is more genuine than anyone in this world.

Love is more joyful than anyone in this world.

Love is more simple than anyone or anything in this world.

Love is more patient than anyone in this world.

Love is more balanced than anyone in this world.

Love is more good than anyone in this world.

Love is more brave than anyone in this world.

Love is more protective than anyone in this world.

Love is more put together than anyone in this world.

Love is more spiritual than anyone in this world.

Love is more thoughtful than anyone in this world.

Love is more faithful than anyone in this world.

Love is more healing than anyone in this world.

Love is more kind than anyone in this world.

Love is more alive than anyone in this world.

Love is more eye-catching than anyone or anything in this world.

Love is more organized than anyone in this world.

Love is more fast than anyone in this world.

Love is more attentive than anyone in this world.

Love is more careful than anyone in this world.

Love is more wise than anyone in this world.

Love is more active than anyone in this world.

Love is more trustworthy than anyone in this world.

Love is more hopeful than anyone in this world.

Love is more straightforward than anyone in this world.

Love is more interesting than anyone or anything in this world.

Love is more understanding than anyone in this world.

Love is more lasting than anyone or anything in this world.

Love is more humble than anyone in this world.

Love is more peaceful than anyone in this world.

Love is more right than anyone in this world.

Love is more communicating than anyone in this world.

Love comes from God who is love.

Nobody in this world can love anyone more than God, who so loved this world that He gave us His only begotten Son and whosoever believeth in Him shall not perish but have eternal life.

You and I Will Be

You and I will be criticized for living right unto the Lord Jesus Christ.

You and I will be disliked for living right unto the Lord Jesus Christ.

You and I will be disrespected for living right unto the Lord Jesus Christ.

You and I will be lied on for living right unto the Lord Jesus Christ.

You and I will be put down for living right unto the Lord Jesus Christ.

You and I will be scorned for living right unto the Lord Jesus Christ.

You and I will be talked bad about for living right unto the Lord Jesus Christ.

You and I will be looked down on with contempt for living right unto the Lord Jesus Christ.

You and I will be misunderstood for living right unto the Lord Jesus Christ.

You and I will be falsely accused for living right unto the Lord Jesus Christ.

You and I will be hated for living right unto the Lord Jesus Christ, who was hated by His enemies because Jesus lived right with no sins in His flesh to be the Son of God.

You and I will have enemies for living right unto the Lord Jesus Christ.

You and I will be persecuted for living right unto the Lord Jesus Christ.

You and I will be taken in the wrong way for living right unto the Lord Jesus Christ.

You and I will be despised even by so-called Christians for living right unto the Lord Jesus Christ.

So, who can be against You and I who the Lord Jesus Christ is for because of living right unto Him who the devil and his fallen angels and human agents can't ever defeat with all of their evil schemes and deeds?

If It's Foolish To

If it's foolish to believe in Jesus Christ, then why should we have even been born?

If it's foolish to put our trust in Jesus Christ, then why should we even be visible to one another?

If it's foolish to worship Jesus Christ, then why should we even live?

If it's foolish to give Jesus the glory and praise, then why should we even prosper in any king of way?

If it's foolish to live for Jesus Christ, then why should we even have a free will?

If it's foolish to have a relationship with Jesus Christ, then why should we even have a heart?

If it's foolish to love Jesus Christ, then why should we even have breath to breathe?

If it's foolish to keep God's Commandments, then why should we even have freedom and justice?

If it's foolish to get to know Jesus Christ, then why should we even open the bible?

If it's foolish to spread the gospel of Jesus Christ, then why should we even have a voice?

If it's foolish to want to be like Jesus Christ, then why should we even believe that there is an afterlife?

If it's foolish to put our hope in Jesus Christ, then why should we even pray?

If it's foolish to be saved in Jesus Christ, then why should we even exist?

If it's foolish to be a Christian, then why should we waste our time going to church that Jesus Christ is the head of to separate the wheat from the tares within the church?

If it's foolish to go through hardships for Jesus' name sake, then why should we even have a conscious to secure our minds to stay on Jesus in our hardships?

Will Not Reappear

Rebellion against God will not reappear among the angels in heaven because two-thirds of the angels in heaven did not rebel against God like the one third of the fallen angels did.

Pride will not reappear in heaven among the angels because it was those fallen angels who were proud of themselves and believed that they could rule over God.

They failed and were cast out of heaven forever and ever.

One day, God will destroy all the fallen angels in fire and brimstone, and He will also destroy all the wicked human beings who joined in with the fallen angels' rebellion against God.

Rebellion against God will not reappear in the new heaven and new earth that God will create for all of His obedient angels and all of his obedient children who will be made like the angels having no sins that will not reappear because of Jesus Christ who is cleansing the heavenly sanctuary with His blood that was shed on the cross to save us from our sins.

All of the angels in heaven are forever converted in Jesus Christ, who was Michael the Archangel being the commander who led the victory over all the fallen angels from heaven.

Rebellion against God will not reappear in heaven where all of God's righteous children will go when Jesus comes back again with all of His angels.

Rebellion and disobedience will never exist again after God creates a new heaven and new earth where no sin will exist among the angels and every human being who makes it to heaven.

There will be no reappearance of any kind of sin because no angel in heaven will make the mistake that Lucifer and the other fallen angels made when they rebelled against God in heaven.

No righteous child of God who enters into heaven will repeat any wickedness in heaven because Jesus Christ saved them from their sins that they confessed and repented of unto Jesus.

You and I must be saved in Jesus in this sinful world because God will not allow us to take or sins with us to heaven where Lucifer and his angels were cast out.

God is love, and sin is evil that God will not allow to reappear in the new heaven and new earth.

God will one day destroy the rebellion of sin forever and ever, making it impossible for sin to ever exist again.

No one will go to heaven with even one sin, no matter how many good and righteous deeds we do.

Jesus has paid it all to cleanse us and save. Us from our sins that cannot enter into heaven.

Many people live their lives rebelling against God, and will believe that they will enter into heaven along with their sins.

It doesn't work that way with God, who foreknew that His Son, Jesus Christ, was the only one who could save us from our sins.

Rebellion and disobedience will not reappear in the presence of God, because all the fallen angels and wicked human beings will one day be destroyed in fire and brimstone.

Sin will not reappear in the new heaven and new earth.

It will be like a bubble that bursts and can't reform its shape, so it will be gone forever from our eyesight.

No angel in heaven and no human being who makes it to heaven will have a thought, desire or inclination to want to rebel against God like Lucifer did.

It is like a mystery that Lucifer had everything except God's supreme authority on his holy throne, and threw it all away.

For some reason, what God had given Lucifer wasn't enough for him.

He wanted to be God, and that caused him to sin against God who will not allow sin to reappear in heaven ever again.

God will not allow sin to exist forever so. It spreads throughout the universe and other worlds because God is not an evil God.

Rebellion and disobedience against God is evil and it will not reappear in the new heaven and new earth that God will create after He destroys all the fallen angels and every wicked human being in fire and brimstone.

This will make it impossible for sin to reappear again in another world.

There will be no other worlds of sin to exist because God has bound the fallen angels in the bottomless pit here on earth that God will make new one day with no reappearance of any kind or form of sin.

The only time that the rebellion of sin against God will reappear is in the second resurrection, where all the wicked dead will be raised up to join the fallen angels as they surround the new Jerusalem holy city to attack it.

This attack will fail because God will rain down fire and brimstone on them all and destroy them so they can never reappear with their sins.

If we confess and repent of our sins, Jesus will forgive us and cast our sins into the bottom of the sea to never reappear in our lives here on earth because we become a new creature in Him whose righteousness makes us right in God's holy eyesight.

When Jesus cleanses us of our sins, we are cleansed so that our sins won't reappear in our lives that we live unto Him who has no sins to appear before God to represent our case in heaven.

Jesus will not allow sins to appear in heaven.

Lucifer and his fallen angels were case out of heaven because of their sins of rebellion against God.

There will be no repeat of this because sin will never exist again to reappear in any angel in heaven or any human being who makes it to heaven for being saved in Jesus Christ who defeated the devil on the cross and when he rose from the grave to break the chains of sin from us.

No matter how much we claim to be a child of God in our daily living we must also appear that way before our neighbors and show them we are saved in Jesus.

If we hold onto even one sin, we will not enter into heaven with Jesus when He comes back again.

There will be no other devil and fallen angels and wicked human beings after they are destroyed in fire and brimstone by God, who will not fail to keep sin from reappearing in His holy and righteous presence.

When God eliminates sin, it will be gone forever and it will never reappear in the new heaven and new earth that God will create.

There will be no appearances of rebellion against God there.

If our sins reappear in our lives after we have been in communion with Jesus, then we never truly repented of our sins unto Jesus with a heart of deep remorse and desire to change from our sinful ways.

There will be no reappearance of any sins on our way back to heaven with Jesus who will take no one's sins with Him back to heaven.

Now is the time for us to confess and repent of all of our sins unto Jesus who will not reappear on the cross to save anyone from their sins.

What Jesus has done is for all existence and will not reappear with any sins ever again from anyone in heaven, where free will originate to worship God and no other in His presence.

A movie will betray that the good guys destroyed the monsters, but the monsters will reappear and be worse than what they were before committing their evil destruction.

It will be no movie when God destroys the rebellion of wickedness that will not reappear and will never exist again after destroys it all in fire and brimstone.

God will not allow sin to reappear in the new heaven and new earth where all the angels and all the saints will truly know what it means to love and obey our Creator.

You Are

You are the biggest problem to solve.

You are the deepest valley to walk down into.

You are the deepest ocean to dive down into.

You are the highest mountain to climb.

You are the deepest mystery.

You are the most untrustworthy.

You are the most in denial.

You are the most delusional.

You are the most deceptive.

You are the most encouraging.

You are the most discouraging.

You are the most motivating.

You are the worst critic.

You are the most difficult.

You are the most confusing.

You are the most joyful.

You are the most filled with grief.

You are the most flawed.

You are the most prideful.

You are the most fearful.

You are the boldest.

You are the best friend.

You are the worst friend.

You are the best challenge.

You are the destroyer.

You are in bondage.

You are the most let down.

You are the most put down.

You are the most unhappy.

You are the most insecure.

You are in the best control.

You are out of control.

You are the most determined.

You are ready to give up.

You are the most civilized.

You are the most uncivilized.

You are the most blind.

You are the most defeated.

You are the disappointed.

You are the most victorious.

You are heading for a downfall.

You are the most curious.

You are the most surprised.

You are the most offended.

You are the most defensive.

You are the most offensive.

You are the most wrong.

You are the most right.

You are on a dead-end road.

You are the worst slave.

You are the most troublesome.

You are the most peaceful.

You are the most content.

You are the most discontent.

You are the most competitive.

You are the most dependable.

You are the most undependable.

You are the most comfortable.

You are the most uncomfortable.

You have the longest path to walk down.

You are the fire burning out of control.

You are the water putting out the fire.

You are the fuel thrown on the fire.

You are the love song.

You are a sad song.

You are a textbook.

You are an educated guess.

You are a learning process.

You are a stairway to walk up and down.

You are an opportunity.

You are a possibility.

You are the most free.

You are a sinner.

You must repent and turn to Jesus Christ who is the self-existent One with God and the Holy Spirit.

You have a free will to choose to believe anything.

You can't ever rise above Jesus Christ because you didn't create yourself to be self-existent like Jesus.

You and I must deny ourselves and pick up our crosses to follow Jesus beyond ourselves who have no heaven to put ourselves in and live forever.

You are the most realistic.

You are the biggest pretender.

You need Jesus the most above and beyond yourself, who is limited to the self-existent One who is eternal in the trinity Godhead.

You will return to dust if Jesus doesn't come back again during your lifetime and your time is short under the heavens.

You will answer to God on judgement day when your destiny is revealed.

You must get it right with Jesus today, before it's too late for you to be saved in Jesus Christ.

You can't save yourself because there is no salvation in you, who can't slip by Jesus and enter into heaven that Jesus created before time existed on earth.

You are living on borrowed time that holds the hand of God's grace and walks with God's grace throughout the land of the living.

You will use it or lose it because whatever talent, skill or spiritual gift you receive from God will do you a lot of good if you use it, especially for the glory of God.

You are the shortest route to take to cut yourself short in life.

You are the longest journey to take, especially to get to the heart of God who so loved the world that He gave His only begotten Son that whosoever believeth in Him shall not perish but have eternal life.

You are the most perished for being selfish, which will bring on eternal death upon you if you don't repent and turn to Jesus Christ before it's too late to repent.

You are the most honest.

You are the most dishonest to yourself.

You are the most loyal to yourself.

You are the most disloyal to yourself.

You are the only you.

You have the most friends within yourself to treat yourself well in a lot of different ways.

You have the most enemies within yourself to treat yourself bad in a lot of different ways.

You are hard to know all of.

You will not fully know yourself who God fully knows every day.

You are the most unforgiving to yourself.

You need to forgive yourself for doing yourself wrong.

You will love everybody if you love God.

You also love yourself with no desire to be self-centered.

You will be a lover of yourself if you love Jesus Christ, who is the lover of all souls to save for loving Him with all of your mind, heart, soul and strength day after day.

It Doesn't Take Much at All

It doesn't take much at all to get into an accident.

It doesn't take much at all to fall down.

It doesn't take much at all to forget something.

It doesn't take much at all to get sick.

It doesn't take much at all to get disappointed.

It doesn't take much at all to say something wrong.

It doesn't take much at all to feel bad.

It doesn't take much at all to feel proud.

It doesn't take much at all to get hurt.

It doesn't take much at all to make a mistake.

It doesn't take much at all to get angry.

It doesn't take much at all to think wrong.

It doesn't take much at all to be selfish.

It doesn't take much at all to not see one's own flaws.

It doesn't take much at all to not see one's own sins.

It doesn't take much at all to quench the Holy Spirit.

It doesn't take much at all to deny Jesus Christ.

It doesn't take much at all to sin against God.

It doesn't take much at all to doubt what Jesus can do for us.

It doesn't take much at all to be lost in our sins.

It doesn't take much at all to choose to do right or wrong.

It doesn't take much at all to lie to oneself.

It doesn't take much at all to live a lie.

It doesn't take much at all to die.

It doesn't take much at all for Jesus to save us from our sins if we confess and repent and turn away from our sins.

It doesn't take much at all for Jesus to give anyone a second chance to deny self and pick up one's cross and follow Him before it's too late.

Sin Will Show
No Respect of Persons

Sin doesn't care about you being a doctor because sin will cause you to be lost if you live in sin.

Sin doesn't care about you being a scientist because sin will cause you to be lost if you live in sin.

Sin doesn't care about you being an engineer because sin will cause you to be lost if you live in sin.

Sin will show no respect of persons.

Sin doesn't care about you being a model because sin will cause you to be lost if you live in sin.

Sin doesn't care about you being a actor because sin will cause you to be lost if you you live in sin.

Sin doesn't care about you being a aircraft pilot because sin will cause you to be lost if you live in sin.

Sin will show no respect of persons.

Sin doesn't care about you being a mother because sin will cause you to be lost if you live in sin.

Sin doesn't care about you being a father because sin will cause you to be lost if you live in sin.

Sin doesn't care about you being a husband because sin will cause you to be lost if you live in sin.

Sin doesn't care about you being a wife because sin will cause you to be lost if you live in sin.

Sin will show no respect of persons.

Sin doesn't care about you being a musician because sin will cause you to be lost if you live in sin.

Sin doesn't care about you being a singer because sin will cause you to be lost if you live in sin.

Sin doesn't care about you being a judge because sin will cause you to be lost if you you live in sin.

Sin doesn't care about you being a police officer because sin will cause you to be lost if you live in sin.

Sin will show no respect of persons.

Sin doesn't care about you being an athlete because sin will cause you to be lost if you live in sin.

Sin doesn't care about you being rich because sin will cause you to be lost if you live in sin.

Sin doesn't care about you being poor because sin will cause you to be lost if you live in sin.

Sin doesn't care about you being the president of the United States because sin will cause you to be lost if you live in sin.

Sin doesn't care about you being a pastor because sin will cause you to be lost if you live in sin.

Sin doesn't care about you being a teacher because sin will cause you to be lost if you live in sin.

Sin will show no respect of persons.

Sin doesn't care about you being a pope because sin will cause you to be lost if you live in sin.

Sin doesn't care about you being young because sin will cause you to be lost if you live in sin.

Sin doesn't care about you being old because sin will cause you to be lost if you live in sin.

Sin doesn't care about you being an author because sin will cause you to be lost if you live in sin.

Sin doesn't care about you being a lawyer because sin will cause you to be lost if you live in sin.

Sin doesn't care about you being a soldier because sin will cause you to be lost if you live in sin.

Sin doesn't care about you being a body builder because sin will cause you to be lost if you live in sin.

Sin doesn't care about you being a martial artist because sin will cause you to be lost if you live in sin.

Sin will show no respect of persons.

Sin doesn't care about you being a publisher because sin will cause you to be lost if you live in sin.

Sin doesn't care about you being a business owner because sin will cause you to be lost if you live in sin.

Sin doesn't care about you being a motivator because sin will cause you to be lost if you live in sin.

Sin doesn't care about you being a supervisor because sin will cause you to be lost if you live in sin.

Sin will show no respect of persons.

Sin doesn't care about you being a nurse because sin will cause you to be lost if you live in sin.

Sin doesn't care about you being a psychiatrist because sin will cause you to be lost if you live in sin.

Sin doesn't care about you being a genius because sin will cause you to be lost if you live in sin.

Sin doesn't care about you being educated because sin will cause you to be lost if you live in sin.

Sin doesn't care about you being ignorant because sin will cause you to be lost if you live in sin.

Sin will show no respect of persons and Jesus Christ will show no respect of persons to save anyone from being lost in sin if we confess and repent of our sins and live a renewed life in loving Him and keeping His Commandments that point out our sins to us.

Some Things are Best Left Behind in the Past

Some things are best left behind in the past and not talked about at all because that may cause someone to stumble or fall into disappointment.

Some things are best left behind in the past and not written about because that may cause someone to stumble or fall into discouragement.

Some things are best left behind in the past and not revealed because that may cause someone to stumble or fall into wanting revenge.

Some things are best left behind in the past and not brought back up because that may cause someone to stumble or fall into unforgiveness.

Some things are best left behind in the past and not gossiped about because that may cause someone to stumble or fall into sadness.

Some things are best left behind in the past and not joked about because that may cause someone to have animosity.

Some things are best left behind in the past and not broadcasted because that may cause someone to stumble or fall into hatred.

Some things are best left behind in the past and not think about because that may cause you and me to stumble or fall into not moving on.

If the Lord can wipe away past committed sins, then who are we to bring up the bad things that happened in the past?

If the Lord can forgive us our past committed sins, then who are we to not forgive anyone who did us wrong in the past?

Some things are best left behind in the past, not used as an excuse to judge those who especially knew what was right to do and didn't do it.

The Lord truly knows all who confessed and repented of their past sins that Jesus left behind when He rose from the grave.

Some things are best left behind in the past and everybody doesn't need to know them because it may cause someone to stumble or fall into holding onto their past mistakes that God had covered with His mercy and grave that brought us all this far to see this day when we all deserved to have died in the past.

When it Comes to Winning Souls

When it comes to winning souls to the Lord, we believe that we are only supposed to reach out to the people who are not in the church.

We usually believe that the only lost souls are the people who don't go to church to worship the Lord and give Him all the glory and praise.

When it comes to winning souls to the Lord, it's for the people in the church too because there are people who go to church and are still of the world.

When it comes to winning souls to the Lord, it's also for the people in the church where there are people who are not saved in Jesus Christ, our Lord.

There are people in the church who are not of the church and you and I need to minister to them with our spiritual gifts from the Lord.

Everybody who goes to church doesn't believe in Jesus Christ, and they're only going through the motions of going to church with no true newness of life in Jesus Christ.

When it comes to winning souls to the Lord, we usually believe that just because there are people in the church then they must already be saved in Jesus from the pulpit to the church pews, but many souls are not rooted and grounded in Jesus Christ.

Winning souls is for church folks too because we need to give all of our minds, hearts, and souls to Jesus every day, not just one day out of the week that we usually go to church.

You and I will usually believe that the people who don't go to a church at all are the ones for us to win to the Lord.

There are people who have been going to church all of their lives but they are not converted and need to be won to the Lord.

Winning souls to the Lord is also for us church folks who need to deny self and pick up our crosses to follow Jesus, who we need to be like every day.

God Will Not Change His Holy Word

The seasons will change, but God will not change His holy word.

Our moods can change, but God will not change His holy word.

Our behavior can change, but God will not change His holy word.

Our voices can change, but God will not change His holy word.

Our feelings can change, but God will not change His holy word.

We can change our minds, but God will not change His holy word.

We can change our clothes, but God will not change His holy word.

The wind can change and blow in a different direction, but God will not change His holy word.

We can change our plans, but God will not change His holy word.

Our lives can change, but God will not change His holy word.

Time will change, but God will not change His holy word.

We can go through changes in our lives, but God will not change His holy word.

Our bodies can change, but God will not change His holy word.

We can change what we say, but God will not change His holy word.

This world will change, but God will not change His holy word.

God will not change the truth of His holy word.

The heavens and earth will pass away before God would change His holy word.

Technology can change, but God will not change His holy word.

Science can change, but God will not change His holy word.

Luck can change, but God will not change His holy word.

People can change, but God will not change His holy word.

All existence would disappear before God would change His holy word.

We can change our theories, but God will not change His holy word.

We can change the way we look, but God will not change His holy word.

God will not change His holy word for anyone, no matter how rich and great they are.

God will not change His holy word that is all about God sending His only begotten Son, Jesus Christ, to this sinful world to redeem all human beings back to God.

God had predestined His holy word to never change, even before God created the angels in heaven.

No fallen angel and no human being can change God's holy word that didn't change in the Garden of Eden where Adam and Eve's lives changed from total perfection to totally flawed in sin for disobeying God who spoke the truth of His holy word to them to live by in the Garden of Eden.

Can Seem to be Eternal

A bad storm can seem to be eternal until the storm is over.

A sickness can seem to be eternal until you get well.

A war can seem to be eternal until the war is over.

Being overweight can seem to be eternal until you lose some weight.

A heartache can seem to be eternal until you find love again.

Grief can seem to be eternal until time heals your broken spirit.

Trouble can seem to be eternal until you get out of trouble.

Gossip can seem to be eternal until you don't listen to it.

Injustice can seem to be eternal until you get justice.

Anger can seem to be eternal until you calm down.

The rain can seem to be eternal until it stops raining.

A hurricane can seem to be eternal until it is over.

A tornado can seem to be eternal until it is over.

An earthquake can seem to be eternal until it is over.

The day can seem to be eternal until the night comes in.

The night can seem to be eternal until the morning light comes in.

A broken bone can seem to be eternal until it heals.

A divorce can seem to be eternal until you get married again.

A mistake can seem to be eternal until you are forgiven.

A crime can seem to be eternal until you stop committing the crime.

Being in danger can seem to be eternal until you are out of danger.

Guilt can seem to be eternal until you confess and repent of your sins unto the Lord Jesus Christ who will save you from being lost in your sins for believing in Him, who is eternal life beyond anything that can seem to be eternal to you and me.

What can seem to be eternal to you and me is only a brief moment to Jesus, who can send an angel from heaven to earth quicker than a blink of an eye.

Death can seem to be eternal until Jesus Christ comes back again and raises the righteous dead to live with Him in heaven as if death never existed.

Will Waste No Time

The sun will waste no time to shine.

The moon will waste no time to glow.

The stars will waste no time to sparkle.

The birds will waste no time to fly.

The rivers will waste no time to flow.

The wind will waste no time to blow.

The grass will waste no time to grow.

The sky will waste no time to hover over us.

The clouds will waste no time to form.

The rain will waste no time to pour down on us.

The leaves will waste no time to fall on the ground.

Children will waste no time to play.

Trouble will waste no time to come our way.

Tornadoes will waste no time to destroy anything in their pathway.

Criminals will waste no time to do wrong.

The government will waste no time to conduct its policies.

Jesus will waste no time to save anyone from their sins if they confess and repent of their sins unto Him.

Jesus will waste no time to come back again on His own time when it will be too late for many people to be saved after rejecting Jesus.

Many people will waste no time to live in their sins but will waste a lot of time denying themselves and picking up their crosses to follow Jesus.

Many people will waste no time to do things of their own will but will waste a lot of time when it comes to doing things of the Lord's will.

The devil will waste no time to cause souls to be lost, but the Lord will waste no time to give His Holy Spirit to anyone who believes in Him.

God didn't waste any time sending His only begotten Son, Jesus Christ, to this sinful world to save us from our sins.

You and I will waste no time wanting to live if our life is in danger, but we can waste some time shunning away from the appearances of evil that are a danger to our spiritual life every day.

A baby will waste no time to cry out loud because of feeling some discomfort, but you and I can waste some time crying out loud unto the Lord with tears of joy about what the Lord brought us through for us to see this day.

We should waste no time to love and obey the Lord like it is our last day to live.

Don't Underestimate

Don't underestimate what the Lord can do for anyone who loves and obeys Him.

Many people will underestimate people who are less talented than they are.

Many people will underestimate people who are less educated than they are.

Many people will underestimate people who are less fortunate than they are.

Many people will underestimate people who are less intelligent than they are.

Don't underestimate what the Lord can do for anyone who the Lord can allow to be great.

Don't underestimate who the Lord can allow to rise up above you and me.

Many people will underestimate those who are less healthy than they are.

Many people will underestimate those who are less financially stable than they are.

Many people will underestimate those who are less outgoing than they are.

Many people will underestimate those who are less prosperous than they are.

Don't underestimate what the Lord can do for anyone who is saved in Him.

Many people will underestimate those who are less skillful than they are.

Many people will underestimate those who are less alert than they are.

Many people will underestimate those who are less active than they are.

Many people will underestimate those who are less determined than they are.

Many people will underestimate those who are less attractive than they are.

Many people will underestimate those who are less talkative than they are.

Many people will underestimate those who are less wise than they are.

Many people will underestimate those who the Lord sees to be no less than you who the Lord will open the windows of heaven for and pour out His blessings upon for returning faithful tithes and offerings from even a small income that the Lord can greatly increase.

Don't underestimate yourself who can repent and live for the Lord Jesus Christ who the birds won't underestimate to feed them every day.

Youth Comes Around Once in Life

Youth comes around once in life so youth is like pure gold.

Youth comes around once in life so youth is like a precious pearl.

Youth comes around once in life so youth is like a sparkling diamond.

Youth comes around once in life so youth is like a red ruby.

Youth comes around once in life so youth is like a beautiful love song.

Youth comes around once in life so youth is like the sun that shines.

Youth comes around once in life so youth is like the full moonlight's glow.

Youth comes around once in life so youth is like a bird flying so free across the sky.

Youth comes around once in life so youth is like the fresh air that we breathe in and out of our nostrils.

Youth comes around once in life so youth is like a beautiful red rose.

Youth comes around once in life so youth is like the shade under a tree on a hot summer day.

Youth comes around once in life so youth is like a high mountain.

Youth comes around once in life so youth is like a lily in the valley.

Youth comes around once in life so youth is like the stars that sparkle all night long.

Youth comes around once in life so youth is like a chest full of treasures.

Youth comes around once in life so youth is like riches and wealth.

Youth comes around in life in every generation, and then youth comes and goes into the guilty plea of old age.

When Jesus comes back again to take us to heaven, we will be young forever and ever in our immortal bodies.

We will never age and grow old in heaven because our youth will be eternal.

Youth comes around once in life, and so many of us took our youth for granted when we were young and foolish.

Youth comes around once in life but many young people today take their youth lightly and live a dangerous life.

Youth comes around once in life, so wise young people take it seriously so they don't make the same mistakes their parents and grandparents made.

Youth comes around once in life, so Jesus especially loves to use the youth to win souls to Him.

Youth comes around once in life so the youth have a true purpose to love Jesus and keep His Commandments.

Youth comes around once in life so the youth are so loved by Jesus who told His disciples that they must be humble like little children to enter into the kingdom of heaven.

Words are Very Powerful

Words are very powerful because words can have a good effect on us and words can have a bad effect on us.

Words are very powerful because words can build up our self-esteem and words can tear down our self-esteem.

Words are very powerful because words can make us happy and words can make us sad.

Words are very powerful because words can make us laugh and words can make us cry.

Words are very powerful because words can encourage us and words can discourage us.

Words are very powerful because words can make us feel good and words can make us angry.

Words are very powerful because words can be positive and words can be negative.

Words are very powerful because words can heal our heart and words can break our heart.

Words are very powerful because words can be true and words can be lies.

Words are very powerful because words can be loving and words can be hateful.

Words are very powerful because words can make us strong and words can make us weak.

Words are very powerful because words can be straightforward and words can beat around the bush.

Words are very powerful because words can be beautiful and words can be ugly.

Words are very powerful because words can be direct and words can be indirect.

Words are very powerful because words can be victorious and words can be a defeat.

Words are very powerful because words can be exciting and words can be boring.

Words are very powerful because words can prolong our lives and words can shorten our lives.

Words are very powerful because words can be healthy and words can be unhealthy.

Words are very powerful because God's holy word can encourage us to believe in Jesus Christ and the devil's wicked words can discourage us to be lost in our sins.

Words are very powerful because God's holy word is all the truth about Jesus Christ who shed His precious blood and gave up His life on the cross to save us from our sins.

The devil's wicked words are nothing but lies to send us to hell if we believe his lying words.

Words are very powerful because Jesus Christ is the word of God who became flesh and lived without sin among sinners speaking many sinful words against Jesus and only degrading themselves in the presence of God.

Just Because We

Just because we go to church it doesn't mean that everything will be smooth all the time.

Just because we worship the Lord doesn't mean that everything will be smooth all the time.

Just because we are working for the Lord doesn't mean that everything will be smooth all the time.

Just because we have a relationship with the Lord doesn't mean that everything will be smooth all the time.

Just because we hold office positions in the church doesn't mean that everything will be smooth all the time.

Just because we have spiritual gifts in the church doesn't mean that everything will be smooth all the time.

Just because we pray to the Lord doesn't mean that everything will be smooth all the time.

Just because we are blessed by the Lord doesn't mean that everything will be smooth all the time.

Just because we return faithful tithes and offerings doesn't mean that everything will be smooth all the time.

Just because we read the bible doesn't mean that everything will be smooth all the time.

Just because we have faith in the Lord Jesus Christ doesn't mean that everything will be smooth all the time.

Just because we love Jesus and keep His Commandments doesn't mean that everything will be smooth all the time.

Just because we confess and repents of our sins unto the Lord doesn't mean that everything will be smooth all the time.

Just because we are saved in Jesus Christ doesn't mean that everything will be smooth all the time.

When Jesus lived here on earth without sin everything wasn't smooth all the time for Him.

Jesus had many rough times.

Every day, the devil tried to cause Jesus to sin against God.

The devil used every temptation he had to try to cause Jesus to fail His great mission from God, but Jesus got the victory overall the devil's temptations.

Many People
Don't Talk About Jesus

Many people will talk about who they see.

Many people will talk about how they feel.

Many people will talk about what they did.

Many people will talk about what they can do.

Many people don't talk about Jesus.

Many people will talk about their car.

Many people will talk about their truck.

Many people will talk about their pets.

Many people will talk about their success.

Many people will talk about their job.

Many people don't talk about Jesus.

Many people will talk about their education.

Many people will talk about their children.

Many people will talk about their spouse.

Many people will talk about sports.

Many people will talk about where they've been.

Many people will talk about where they want to go.

Many people will talk about how many awards they have.

Many people will talk about how many trophies they have.

Many people will talk about their problems.

Many people don't talk about Jesus.

Many people will talk about how much money they make.

Many people will talk about what they heard.

Many people will talk about the news.

Many people will talk about politics.

Many people will talk about technology.

Many people will talk about science.

Many people don't talk about Jesus.

Many people will talk about food.

Many people will talk about clothes.

Many people will talk about jewelry.

Many people will talk about makeup.

Many people will talk about hairstyles.

Many people don't talk about Jesus.

Many people will talk about movie stars.

Many people will talk about entertainers.

Many people will talk about the government.

Many people don't talk about Jesus.

Many people will talk about crimes.

Many people will talk about romance.

Many people will talk about sex.

Many people will talk about luck.

Many people will talk about magic.

Many people will talk about nature.

Many people don't talk about Jesus.

Many people will talk about history.

Many people will talk about human beings.

Many people will talk about their talents.

Many people will talk about their skills.

Many people will talk about the military.

Many people will talk about war.

Many people will talk about their prosperity.

Many people will talk about their poverty.

Many people don't talk about Jesus.

Many people will talk about who treated them bad.

Many people will talk about what they want to do.

Many people will talk about who they helped.

Many people will talk about what they have.

Many people will talk about what they believe.

Many people will talk about the weather.

Many people will talk about climate change.

Many people will talk about horoscopes.

Many people will talk about their health.

Many people will talk about their rights.

Many people don't talk about Jesus.

Many people will talk about injustice.

Many people will talk about their accomplishments.

Many people will talk about their pride.

Many people will talk about their mistakes.

Many people will talk about their loved ones.

Many people will talk about their friends.

Many people will talk about their life.

Many people will talk about death.

Many people will talk about their enemies.

Many people don't talk about Jesus Christ who talks about us human beings to His heavenly Father God up in the heavenly courtroom where Jesus is pleading our cases before God.

Many people don't talk about Jesus who gives us all life, health and strength, which we can take for granted.

Many people don't talk about Jesus who blesses us all, even when we mistake His blessings for our own belief that we are self-made and caused our own prosperity.

Many people don't talk about Jesus Christ who is the head of the church.

Many church folks don't talk about Jesus much at all to the people of the world.

Many people will talk about things that have no substance like air.

Jesus will talk to us in His holy words that give us the full description of the greatest and most powerful words of truth for us all to live by every day.

There is eternal, holy, righteous and divine substance in Jesus' talk.

Many people will talk about everybody else except Jesus.

Many people will talk about everything else except Jesus Christ who every real, true Christian loves to talk about and loves to obey.

Light Cannot Agree with Darkness

Light cannot agree with darkness twenty-four hours around the clock.

Good cannot agree with evil.

Wisdom cannot agree with foolishness.

Light and darkness cannot agree with anything.

The law cannot agree with crimes.

The truth cannot agree with lies.

Light cannot agree with darkness.

Peace cannot agree with war.

Love cannot agree with hate.

Wellness cannot agree with sickness.

Light cannot agree with darkness on any day.

Good hygiene cannot agree with body odor.

Kindness cannot agree with meanness.

Knowledge cannot agree with ignorance.

Light cannot agree with darkness, not even for one second.

A smile cannot agree with a frown.

A good name cannot agree with a bad reputation.

Working cannot agree with laziness.

Contentment cannot agree with greed.

Light cannot agree with darkness in the presence of God.

Right cannot agree with wrong.

Freedom cannot agree with slavery.

Equality cannot agree with discrimination.

Justice cannot agree with unfairness.

Light cannot agree with darkness, because God is light and the devil is darkness.

God cannot agree with the devil.

God cannot agree with sin and that is why God sent His only begotten Son to this dark world so He can save us from our sins.

God cannot agree with anyone who doesn't love Him and keep His Commandments.

God cannot agree with anyone who doesn't believe in His Son, Jesus Christ.

God cannot agree with those who are lost in their sins.

Light cannot agree with darkness because Jesus Christ is the light of the world to shine God's love all around the world, but darkness is of the devil who is like a roaring lion ready to devour you and me on any day.

Humility cannot agree with pride.

Courage cannot agree with fear.

Giving cannot agree with selfishness.

Faith cannot agree with living by eyesight.

Light cannot agree with darkness because God is light to reveal everything that we do, even in secret, and the devil is darkness who loves to spiritually blind anyone who walks in the darkness of sin.

The Church cannot agree with pretense.

God's holy word cannot agree with false doctrines.

A Christian cannot agree with a fool.

Light cannot agree with darkness because the light will shine through the dark.

Light cannot agree with darkness because the light will eliminate the dark.

Light cannot agree with darkness because God is everlasting light shining on this dark temporary world, and God will one day eliminate the darkness of sin in fire and brimstone.

The darkness of all wickedness will be destroyed beneath the eternal light of God who the devil is no match for.

The devil cannot overshadow even a dim light of God.

When We Fall Asleep

When we fall asleep, we are not aware of anything going on around us.

When we fall asleep, we don't see anything.

When we fall asleep, we don't feel anything.

When we fall asleep, we don't know anything, like we're dead.

When we fall asleep, it's like we're dead to the world.

Many people are spiritually asleep and aren't aware of the spiritual things of the Lord.

Many people are spiritually asleep and aren't aware of having faith in Jesus Christ.

Many people are spiritually asleep and aren't aware of praying to Jesus.

Many people are spiritually asleep and aren't aware of trusting Jesus.

Many people are spiritually asleep and aren't aware of calling on Jesus' holy name.

Many people are spiritually asleep and aren't aware of confessing and repenting of their sins unto Jesus.

Many people are spiritually asleep and aren't aware denying self and picking up one's cross to follow Jesus.

Many people are spiritually asleep and spiritually dead to the Lord Jesus Christ.

Jesus wakes us up in the morning out of our physical sleep so we can be conscious and aware of what is going on around us.

Jesus can wake up anyone out of their spiritual sleep for choosing to believe in Him who is forever alive beyond and above our conscious awareness and deep sleep.

When we fall asleep we are not even consciously aware enough to know if we are snoring in our sleep.

Many people are spiritually snoring out loud with the temporary things in their lives.

Jesus surely hears their snores in their spiritual sleep.

When we fall asleep, we have no conscious awareness of whether we will wake up again.

There are church folks who are falling asleep spiritually and they're spiritually snoring out loud about their desires for this sinful world.

Studying God's holy word and living by God's holy word will give anyone a spiritual awakening out of the spiritual sleep in this world.

One day, there will be a great spiritual awakening for all the world when Jesus comes back again on the clouds of glory for every eye to see Him, but that spiritual awakening will be too late for all who will fall dead at the brightness of Jesus' holy light.

The Lord's great spiritual awakening will be too much for the wicked to bear because they refused to believe in Jesus Christ to be saved.

Over the Rainbow

Over the rainbow is the sun, moon and all the stars.

Over the rainbow are billions of galaxies.

Over the rainbow are endless black holes.

Over the rainbow are endless of other universes.

Over the rainbow are other worlds.

Over the rainbow are the heavens.

Over the rainbow are the holy angels.

Over the rainbow is Jesus Christ.

Over the rainbow is God.

Over the rainbow is eternal life.

Over the rainbow is everlasting love.

Over the rainbow is immortality.

Over the rainbow is perfect peace.

Over the rainbow is paradise.

Over the rainbow is no time.

Over the rainbow is no war.

Over the rainbow is no hate.

Over the rainbow is no jealously.

Over the rainbow is no disunity.

Over the rainbow is no favoritism.

Over the rainbow is no grudge.

Over the rainbow is no strife.

Over the rainbow is no heartache.

Over the rainbow is no grief.

Over the rainbow is no injustice.

Over the rainbow is no inequality.

Over the rainbow is no sickness.

Over the rainbow is no lie.

Over the rainbow is everlasting truth.

Over the rainbow is no pain.

Over the rainbow is no deformity.

Over the rainbow is no misfortune.

Over the rainbow is no age.

Over the rainbow is no retirement.

Over the rainbow is everlasting joy.

Over the rainbow is God sitting on His holy throne.

Over the rainbow is Jesus Christ on the right-hand side of God's holy throne.

Over the rainbow is Jesus in the heavenly sanctuary representing our case before God.

Over the rainbow is the book of life that is open with our names written in it, if we are saved in Jesus Christ.

Over the rainbow is heaven where we all want to go to with Jesus who created the rainbow as a sign for us to know that this world will not be destroyed by water again.

The rainbow is a sign of God's promise to us.

There is a perfect place over the rainbow where we want to go with all of our hopes and dreams that only Jesus can fulfill under the rainbow and over the rainbow.

Over the rainbow is no trouble.

Over the rainbow is no worry.

Over the rainbow is no fear.

Over the rainbow is no death.

Over the rainbow is no envy.

Over the rainbow is no sin.

Over the rainbow is heaven beyond this sinful world where a wish and luck are no foundation for anyone to stand on.

Over the rainbow is where Jesus is building us a heavenly mansion to live in forever and ever.

Over the rainbow is where all who are saved in Jesus will enter into heaven when Jesus comes back again.

Over the rainbow is where heaven is real beyond imaginary and made up wishes and dreams that can make us feel so good but have no real truth.

Only Jesus is forever and ever beyond the imaginary not existing over the rainbow where the unseen heaven is real.

Over the rainbow is no fairytale of make believe; that is only under the rainbow, which gives us false hopes and dreams.

Astronauts can fly into the outer space over the rainbow, but they can't enter into heaven with their sins that only Jesus can save them from so they can one day enter into heaven when He comes back again over the rainbow.

Under the Sun

Under the sun, we move around here and there and usually ask no questions about where we should go.

Under the sun, many people write books and get them published but there is only one book of life that is published by God beyond the sun.

Under the sun, we have motives and intentions that will sooner or later reveal the real you and me.

Under the sun, all great people are not good people.

Under the sun, religion can twist and turn many people's minds until they think nothing about God.

Under the sun, many people make up their own religion that is far from being in line with God's holy word.

Under the sun, we will make some mistakes.

Under the sun, we will learn some things the easy way and we will learn some things the hard way.

Under the sun, many people will wash the dirt off of their hands and believe that they haven't done anything wrong.

Under the sun, many people will do evil and believe that it is good.

Under the sun, we are all alike when it comes to being a human being.

Under the sun, we are all alike when it comes to being alive.

Under the sun, we are all alike when it comes to dying.

Under the sun, we all have a sinful nature.

Under the sun, we all need to love and obey Jesus Christ.

Under the sun, we all can be saved in Jesus Christ.

Under the sun, we all fall short of the glory of God.

Under the sun, we all have sins to confess and repent of unto the Lord Jesus Christ.

Under the sun, we all can eat the spiritual food of God's holy word that will never dull our senses.

Under the sun, we all have one thing in common and that is God created us all in His image.

Under the sun, we all are people living here on earth together every day.

Under the sun, we all have a destiny that can't pass by God.

Under the sun, we all have a destiny that God knows about.

Under the sun, we all have a destiny that God will judge.

Under the sun, many people will pass by you and me every day, but no one can pass by God who is everywhere in heaven and everywhere under the sun.

There are many people who you and I will cross paths with only once under the sun.

There are many people who will drive past you and me on the highway and local roads, but no one can drive past God who is everywhere in heaven and everywhere under the sun.

There are many people who will walk past you and me in the stores and in the shopping malls, but no one can walk past God who is everywhere in heaven and everywhere under the sun.

Under the sun, we are born into this world and we will one day die in this world, but God lives forever in heaven and lives forever under the sun.

Under the sun, many people believe that there is no God, but many other people believe that there is a God who is with us under the sun.

Under the sun, we all don't know the day that we will die, but while we live we can choose to live unto Jesus Christ who can save us from our sins under the sun.

Under the sun, we all have free will choice given to us by God.

No one can overpower you and me and make us not choose doing right instead of wrong under the sun.

Under the sun, we all must eat food and drink water to live day after day.

Under the sun, we all must breathe air in and out of our nostrils to live day after day.

Under the sun, we all must take a bath or take a shower to keep our bodies clean.

Under the sun, we all must brush our teeth to keep our breath fresh.

Under the sun, we all will have some kind of influence on one another.

Under the sun, we all have some flaws.

Under the sun, we all need to be loved.

Under the sun, none of us wants to be lied to.

Under the sun, we all want to be accepted.

Under the sun, we all want to be loved and not be hated.

Under the sun, we all are human and feel some pain.

We can say this and say that under the sun, but God's word will never change.

We can do this and do that under the sun, but God will keep His oath to us under the sun.

Under the sun, we all have a limit, but many people will go over their limit and shorten their own lives under the sun.

Under the sun, we all have a purpose for being here in this world and everybody has a good purpose given to them by God.

Under the sun, we all can choose to fulfill our purpose, which is to love and obey Jesus Christ.

Under the Sky

Under the sky is where love is not so sure to grow up and mature.

Under the sky, life experiences can be like riding on a roller coaster.

Under the sky, time is not so sure to be on our side when we need it.

Under the sky is where we can't be so sure about anything in this world.

Under the sky, the great and small have problems that are not always solved.

Under the sky, life is not so sure to give us another day to live.

Under the sky is where change can be painful.

Under the sky is where logic can be degraded.

Under the sky is where hope can be helpless.

Under the sky is where friends can turn their backs on you and me.

Under the sky is where we can't be so sure about ourselves.

Under the sky is where ignorance can be praised.

Under the sky is where knowledge can be combative.

Under the sky is where wisdom can be foolish to a fool.

Under the sky is where Jesus Christ once lived to show to the world God's love.

Under the sky is where Jesus Christ once lived to save us from our sins.

Under the sky is where sin can look like an angel from heaven.

Under the sky is where the wicked have made their homes.

Under the sky is where the natural can be like an uncommon thing to the unnatural.

Under the sky is where a marriage can seem like it's for sale at a cheap price.

Under the sky is where doing something bad is like a good thing to do.

Under the sky is where religion can be like a hustler who gambles with people's souls that Jesus loves to save.

Under the sky is where Jesus Christ once lived among sinners like you and me to show the world that there is a true Living God who wants to have a relationship with the human race.

Under the sky is where death can be like a king sitting on his throne where everyone can see him joking and laughing at life.

Under the sky is where we were born to one day die, which is like throwing water on a campfire to make it burn out on a cold night.

Under the sky is where Jesus Christ once lived without sin as He took on our trespasses and inequities and was like a lamb in a den of hungry wolves.

Under the sky a good day is for us, and a bad day is against us, which is like a split personality that changes on us.

Under the sky is where Jesus Christ once lived and never changed on anyone because Jesus is the same yesterday, today and tomorrow.

Jesus is like a good day every day, and only Jesus can make the day be a blessing for us in some kind of way.

Under the sky is where feelings can get trampled down like a crushed egg.

Under the sky is where beauty can fade away like it never existed before old age.

Under the sky is where a war can look so meaningless when it's all over, like it was never fought.

Under the sky is where an actor can be a good pretender and captivate an audience to make someone believe the pretense is real.

Under the sky is where Jesus Christ once lived with no pretense and was real like the deep waters under a bridge that make the bridge very useful to cross over.

Under the sky is where accomplishments can break into pieces, like when a good name is ruined.

Under the sky is where wealth can be a burden to a rich person, like being lost in a forest.

Under the sky is where faith in the Lord Jesus Christ can be out of date for unbelievers who believe and live by their eyesight day after day.

Under the sky is where history can be like wallowing in mud that only clean water can wash off of our bodies.

Under the sky is like trying to clean up the past, and dress it up for the present.

Under the sky is where violence and killings can be like a lifestyle that is accepted into society.

Under the sky is where dreams can be questioned and might not give you the right answer.

Under the sky is where Jesus Christ once lived and was like a good dream passing through every generation.

Under the sky is where education can be the right answer to every problem, to be like a vault in a bank that is under tight security.

A professional criminal may very well break into that vault, which shows that education can also be used for evil practices.

Under the sky is where Jesus Christ once lived to minister to and educate His disciples with the word of God, who is good all the time with the right answer to every problem.

Jesus educated His disciples to do good deeds, but Judas chose to do an evil deed by betraying Jesus Christ.

Judas used his education for evil.

Jesus educated Judas with his ministry and then Judas used that against Him for evil.

Under the sky is where limits exist because we were born in sin.

This is like if we see a poisonous snake in our pathway it would be best to wait until the snake crawls far away out of our eyesight before we walk down the pathway.

The poisonous snake is our limit for us to not go near to it in our pathway.

Under the sky is where we have limits to add more years to our lives.

Jesus Sees Who You Can Become in Him

People will normally see your mistakes.

People will normally see your bad habits.

People will normally see your weaknesses.

People will normally see your flaws.

Jesus sees who you can become in Him if you confess and repent of your sins and live your life unto Him.

People will normally see your misfortunes.

People will normally see your insecurities.

People will normally see your fears.

People will normally see your problems.

People will normally see your faults.

People will normally see your worries.

Jesus sees who you can become in Him if you believe in Him.

People will normally see your wrongs.

People will normally see your selfishness.

People will normally see your pretenses.

People will normally see your enviousness.

People will normally see your jealousies.

People will normally see your brokenness.

Jesus sees who you can become in Him if you have a relationship with Him.

People will normally see your unfriendliness.

People will normally see your carelessness.

People will normally see your unconcern.

People will normally see your inadequacies.

People will normally see your inexperience.

People will normally see your lack of intelligence.

Jesus sees who you can become in Him If you deny yourself and pick up your cross and follow Him.

People will normally see your pride.

People will normally see your shyness.

People will normally see your impatience.

People will normally see your indifference.

Jesus sees who you can become in Him if you give all of your mind, heart and soul to Him.

People will normally see your outward appearance.

Jesus sees who you can become in Him even if your spiritual brothers and sisters in the church don't see how far Jesus can take you in your life for uplifting His holy name and living right unto Him every day.

An Illusion

Someone can believe they are a doctor, when they really are not a doctor — it's just an illusion in their mind.

Someone can believe they have the talent to sing, when he or she can't really sing — it's an illusion in their mind.

Someone can believe they are intelligent, when they are not intelligent — it's just an illusion in their mind.

Some men can believe they are handsome, when they are not handsome — it's just an illusion in their mind.

Some women can believe they are beautiful, when they are not beautiful — it's just an illusion in their mind.

A man can believe he can get any woman he wants, but he can't —it's just an illusion in his mind.

A woman can believe she can get any man she wants, but she can't — it's just an illusion in her mind.

Some men and women can believe they are great, but they aren't great — it's just an illusion in their mind.

Someone can believe they are well, but they are really sick — it's just an illusion in their mind.

Someone can believe they are rich, but they aren't rich — it's just an illusion in their mind.

Someone can believe they are good, but they aren't good — it's just an illusion in their mind.

Someone can believe they can fly a plane, but they aren't a pilot — it's just an illusion in their mind.

Someone can believe they know everything, but they don't know everything — it's just an illusion in their mind.

Someone can believe they are right about what they say, but they aren't right — it's just an illusion in their mind.

Someone can believe they doing the right thing, but they aren't doing the right thing — it's just an illusion in their mind.

Someone in the church can believe they are strong in the Lord, but they aren't strong — it's just an illusion in their mind.

Someone in the church can believe they have no sins, but everyone has sins — it's just an illusion in their mind.

Someone in the church can believe they are filled with the Holy Spirit, but they aren't filled with the Holy Spirit — it's just an illusion in their mind.

Someone in the church can believe they have a relationship with Jesus, but they don't — it's just an illusion in their mind.

Someone in the church can believe they are dressed in modest apparel, but they aren't dressed in modest apparel — it's just an illusion in their mind.

Someone in the church can believe they are a preacher, but God didn't give them the gift to preach — it's just an illusion in their mind.

Someone in the church can believe they love everybody, but they put certain people up on a pedestal — so that equal love is just an illusion in their mind.

Someone in the church can believe they are like Jesus, but they aren't like Jesus — it's just an illusion in their mind.

Illusions are very powerful, but they will never be more powerful than God's holy word that reveals to true reality over every illusion in our minds, in the church and in this world.

Someone can live in an illusion and be happy, they can even die happy in an illusion.

Jesus is real, true happiness for loving Him and keeping His Commandments until we die with the happiness and joy of going to heaven with Jesus when he comes back again on the clouds of glory with all the holy angels.

Someone Said that God Uses the Devil

Someone said that God uses the devil, who is evil all the time.

Why would God want to use the devil for anything, when God is good all the time?

God allows the devil to tempt us, but God doesn't use the devil to tempt us.

God can't use the devil for anything that's good, because the devil can only appear to do good things but there are always evil reasons behind them.

There is nothing good about the devil for God to use, but God uses His holy angels and can use you and me to do good things.

The devil can't do anything good without an evil motive behind it.

There is nothing good in doing evil, which is what the devil loves to do and he will try to put God into his evil deeds.

Someone said that God uses the devil, but God will never let the devil use Him because He is a holy and righteous God who hates evil.

There is nothing evil about God, but the devil and his fallen angels and his human agents will try to make God look evil.

God doesn't use the devil to serve His holy purpose for you and me, but the devil's purpose is to cause our souls to be lost in hell where he will go one day.

Life Said to Death

Life said to Death, you can't get rid of me — I've was around before you ever existed.

Life said to Death, I kicked you out of heaven, which I filled with eternal life to be forever youthful beyond you, O Death.

Life said to Death, no matter how hard you try to get rid of me that will never happen because I am life that will be here until Jesus Christ comes back again.

Life said to Death, no sickness will be able to get rid of me.

No war will be able to get rid of me.

No virus or disease will be able to get rid of me.

No crime will be able to get rid of me.

No flood will be able to get rid of me.

No hurricane will be able to get rid of me.

No earthquake will be able to get rid of me.

No tornado or wildfire will be able to get rid of me.

Life said to Death, no nuclear bombs will be able to get rid of me.

No accident will be able to get rid of me.

No riot will be able to get rid of me.

Life said to Death, I will throw you in the Lake of fire one day, and you will burn up and turn to ash while I live on forever and ever.

Life said to Death, you can't ever get rid of me, but I will get rid of you through Jesus Christ, who gives me the victory over you, O Death.

Life said to Death, you have lied to and deceived so many people who I give life to live for Jesus Christ.

Life said to Death, I have my people who will not believe your lies and deceptions because they love to live their lives unto Jesus Christ, who is my life eternal.

Life said to Death, I will still exist when you, O Death, will one day disappear from the planet earth like you never existed.

Life said to Death, you will not exist in the new earth where I will live in all of God's children who will trample all over death like crushing up dried leaves that have fallen from the trees.

Life said to Death, I am eternal and you, O Death, are temporary and will be gone forever and ever one day.

Life said to Death, I am from God, no matter how many people you take with you to the grave.

Life said to Death, I have my people who you can't deceive into believing that their lives are so vain.

They know that living for Jesus Christ is an abundance of life that will lead them to receive eternal life one day.

Life said to Death, so many people are afraid of you all around the world, but my people are not afraid of you because they know that they will live again when Jesus Christ comes back.

Life said to Death, my people know how to pray away their fear of you, O Death.

Life said to Death, you can take my people to the grave, but you can't keep them there because Jesus will raise them from the grave as if you never existed, O Death.

Life said to Death, your time will soon be up and you will be thrown in the lake of fire and brimstone where even all the wicked will know too late that life lives on in Jesus Christ.

Life said to Death, you tried to get rid of me thousands of years ago and you failed to do so in the Garden of Eden.

Adam and Eve chose you, O Death over me, but God didn't let them die without populating the earth with their lifeblood children.

Life said to Death, I was here yesterday, I am here today and I will still be here tomorrow, beyond whoever will die.

Life said to Death, you can't get rid of me, no matter how many times you, O Death, dodge in and out of the lanes of time that will eventually crush you.

Life said to Death, I existed before your evolution and Big Bang Theory that didn't create me — I am a theory only in the minds of atheists who I give life to live with their lies.

Life said to Death, I am looking forward to giving eternal life to all who are saved in Jesus Christ, who gives me life eternal over you, who can't fill up the grave like God filling up the Heavens with life that the holy angels know to be real forever and ever.

Life said to Death, I will give life to many more babies, no matter how many people you swallow down in the grave.

Life said to Death, you can't outdo God, who is eternal life beyond you, O Death, you are doomed to never walk through the gates of heaven that my holy and righteous people will one day walk through because of Jesus Christ.

Life said to Death, none of your schemes and devices will be able to get rid of me because I am life, who is still here through thousands of years of your presence, O Death.

Your presence, O Death, is not strong enough to get rid of me.

Life said to Death, you can't get rid of me, no matter how ignorant, unjust and negligent you are, O Death.

Life said to Death, you will never overpower me and get rid of me off the face of this world.

The devil and his fallen angels and his human agents believe that you, O Death, can get rid of me.

Life said to Death, you were already defeated when Jesus Christ died on the cross and rose from the grave with victory over you.

Life said to death, you couldn't keep Jesus in the grave because Jesus is eternal life and will destroy you, O Death, one day in the lake of fire and brimstone.

The Truth is Not Popular

The truth is not popular with many people who don't like the truth.

The truth will not make many friends, even though the truth is very friendly to everyone.

The truth is not popular and will not get many followers.

The truth will make more enemies than friends.

The truth is not popular.

In the courtroom, a judge and the jury love the truth to be popular in the courtroom, but lies have won the popularity contest in some courtrooms.

The truth is Jesus Christ, who is not popular in this sinful world.

The truth never has been popular in this world where lies are very popular every day.

The truth is not popular in the government.

The truth is not popular in many bookstores.

The truth is not popular in many marriages.

The truth is not popular in many colleges.

The truth is not popular in many schools.

Lucifer tried to make his lies popular in heaven.

The devil has made his lies very popular in this world.

The truth is not popular to anyone who doesn't love the truth.

The truth is not popular to anyone who won't accept the truth.

The truth is like a nerd to many people who look down on nerds because they're not popular.

The truth is a warrior, not a nerd.

The truth is a warrior in genius, brilliance and social skills every day.

The truth is a warrior that a lie can't kill.

The truth is not popular in this world, but the truth is always victorious.

Jesus Christ gave us proof of this when He rose from the grave, triumphing over lying death and the lying grave.

Eternal life is the truth in Jesus Christ, and death and the grave know that to be the truth.

The truth is not popular in this world where lies love to wrestle with the truth, but lies will never pin down the truth.

First Impressions Shouldn't Always Be Lasting Impressions

No one can smile all of the time.

No one can be happy all the time

No one can be cheerful all the time.

People who love to smile can have a bad day, and then they may not smile at anyone.

Someone who sees them for the first time and doesn't know that they love to smile a lot might believe that they never smile.

That may be their first impression and lasting impression, even though it's wrong and that person is just having a bad day that caused them to not smile.

An evil person can make a good first impression on someone who doesn't know them.

That evil person can pretend to be so good and kind that someone who doesn't know them won't realize they're actually a serial killer.

Many women have fallen prey to serial killers because their first impressions told them they were dealing with a good person, when that person actually wants to kill them.

First impressions shouldn't always be lasting impressions about anyone.

Cheerful people can grieve sometimes, and might not be in a friendly frame of mind towards you and me.

We can meet these people for the first time and believe that they are not friendly because they didn't show themselves as friendly when we met them.

That man or woman might actually be friendly and easy to talk to when they are not feeling grief.

There is no way for you and me to know this based upon our first impressions.

To make our first impression our lasting impression can be a mistake.

Only Jesus Christ can always make a first impression be a lasting impression, because He knows the heart behind the outward appearance that can sometimes be mistaken by imperfect people.

No one is perfect, and no one can always make a good first impression.

Many people have made their first impression the lasting impression about someone and have been deceived.

Some first impressions are true, but many times the first impression is not true and should not be the lasting impression you have about someone.

There are many wolves in sheep's clothing.

They can make a good first impression on you and me, and we may believe that they are good, when in fact they are wolves and predators who love to prey on the sheep.

Common People

It's mostly common people who have caused other people to get rich.

It's mostly common people who built this nation and made it great.

It's mostly common people who are in the military.

It's mostly common people who fight in wars.

It's mostly common people who are disrespected.

It's mostly common people who are employees on the job.

It's mostly common people who go out to vote.

It's mostly common people who elect people to high office.

It's mostly common people who commit crimes.

It's mostly common people who get killed.

It's mostly common people who have common sense.

It's mostly common people who go to church.

It's mostly common people who believe in Jesus Christ.

It was mostly common people who were in the large crowds following Jesus Christ.

It was mostly common people who Jesus Christ ministered to.

It was mostly common people who loved Jesus Christ when He lived on earth.

It was mostly common people who Jesus healed.

It was mostly common people who Jesus preached to when He lived on earth.

It was mostly common people who were Jesus's disciples when He was here on earth.

It's mostly common people who live in this world.

It's mostly common people who help their fellow man.

It's mostly common people who don't believe they are better than others.

It's mostly common people who take the coats off of their backs and give them to you and me.

It's mostly common people who treat you and me right.

It's mostly common people who are friendly.

It's mostly common people who are not stuck up.

It's mostly common people who are saved in Jesus Christ.

It's mostly common people who are content.

It's mostly common people who are not greedy for worldly gain.

It's mostly common people who accept you and me for who we are.

It's mostly common people who will join Jesus Christ in heaven when He comes back again.

It's mostly common people who are treated unfairly.

It's mostly common people who get overlooked.

It's mostly common people who are poor.

It's mostly common people who work hard.

It's mostly common people who fear the Lord God.

Convicted

We don't usually like to be convicted of thinking something wrong.

We don't usually like to be convicted of saying something wrong.

We don't usually like to be convicted of doing something wrong.

We have a sinful nature that can deceive us into believing that we are so right in our own eyes all of the time.

If we have the Holy Spirit, we will be convicted if we think something wrong.

If we have the Holy Spirit, we will be convicted of saying something wrong.

If we have the Holy Spirit, we will be convicted of doing something wrong.

If we never ever feel convicted about anything in our hearts, then we don't have the Holy Spirit dwelling in us.

Many people will reject being convicted of their wrongdoings.

They are truly rejecting the Holy Spirit who convicts us all of our sins.

No one in this world is without sin to never be convicted of saying something wrong and doing something wrong.

We are all guilty in the presence of the Lord Jesus Christ, who will forgive us of our sins if we confess and repent.

No Christian is too righteous and holy to never be convicted by the Holy Spirit.

Conviction is always a good thing to let you and me know that only Jesus Christ is worthy to get all the glory and all the praise every day.

Conviction lets us know that we are all sinners saved through Jesus' grace.

Conviction lets us know that we are no better than anyone else.

Conviction lets us know that we fall short of the glory of God.

Conviction lets us know that we all need Jesus Christ to cleanse us and save us from our sins.

If we never feel conviction about anything in our hearts, then the Holy Spirit is not in us, regardless of holding positions in the church.

If we never feel convicted about anything in our hearts, then the Holy Spirit is not in us, regardless of good works that we do.

If we never feel convicted in our hearts, then the Holy Spirit is not in us, regardless of looking like a Christian in the eyes of others.

Conviction lets us know that we need to repent of our sins.

We all have some sins to repent of.

Some of us have more sins than others to repent of unto the Lord.

Conviction will set us free from believing that we're perfect in our own eyes.

Throughout the Day and Throughout the Night

Throughout the day we are very often upon our feet doing this and doing that.

We don't often think about what could go wrong, unless we are living in a warzone neighborhood.

Throughout the day, we see the sun that shines and we don't give a second thought about the sun shining down on us throughout the day.

Throughout the day, we go through the motions of doing this and doing that and we don't ask God why we must do those things because we know in our hearts that doing those things are embedded in our lives throughout the day.

Throughout the night we are very often more relaxed and much less active to lay down on our beds and go to sleep.

We need that sleep to rest our minds and bodies throughout the night that many of us will dream away throughout the night.

It is embedded in our lives because God created it to be that way.

God created the day and God created the night to be a blessing to you and me.

We are so blessed to see the day and the night that many blind people don't see and can't tell the difference between the day and night.

Throughout the day and throughout the night, God is all around us.

He gives us life that death can't wait to take away from us throughout the day and throughout the night.

Life is present throughout the day, and life is present throughout the night because of our Lord and Savior Jesus Christ, who is Lord of the day and the night.

Death is present throughout the day and death is present throughout the night because of us being born in sin to die on any day and on any night.

Throughout the day and throughout the night, Jesus truly knows what it's like to be tempted by the devil.

Throughout the day and throughout the night, Jesus knows what it's like to be hungry.

Throughout the day and throughout the night, Jesus knows what it's like to face up to death.

Throughout the day and throughout the night, Jesus knows what it's like to pray to His heavenly Father, God.

Jesus Christ, our Lord and Savior, lived here on earth so He would know what it's like to love everyone throughout the day and throughout the night.

Jesus can save us from our sins, but many people won't confess and repent throughout the day and throughout the night.

Jesus is the judge over life and death throughout the day and throughout the night.

No one can question Jesus about allowing death to come our way throughout the day and throughout the night

Jesus is in charge of all things.

The Truth

How can the truth be negative, no matter what the truth is about?

The truth is always positive to let us know what is really going on.

The truth is always positive to be real with us.

How can the truth be negative if it sets us free from lies?

The truth is always positive to help us wise up.

The truth is always positive to help us do better.

How can the truth be negative and make us say something wrong?

How can the truth be negative and make us do something wrong?

The truth is always positive to convince us to say something right.

The truth is always positive to let us know how wrong we are.

The truth is always positive to let us know how right we are.

Jesus Christ is the truth and there is nothing negative about Jesus Christ.

The truth is always positive to let you and me know that we can be negative about the truth being told to us.

How can the truth be negative when somebody tells us the truth that we know is the truth?

The truth can be negative to a liar.

The truth can only be negative to someone who doesn't want to believe the truth.

The truth can only be negative to someone who doesn't like hearing the truth.

There are many church folks who don't like hearing the truth, especially if the truth is not spoken from the pastor in the church.

They believe that if you and I are not the pastor then what we say may not be the truth.

The truth can only be negative to people who run away from the truth.

The truth is always positive to anyone who loves the truth.

The truth is always positive, no matter what the truth is about.

The truth is always positive to keep us from lying to ourselves.

The truth is always positive in the Bible.

How can the truth be negative to whoever loves the truth, no matter what the truth is about and regardless of who tells the truth?

Many people don't like to hear the truth if the truth is stomping down on their guilty conscience.

The Years of Our Lives

The years of our lives are like one drop of water in the bucket of time.

We know that one drop of water can't fill up a bucket.

Time has been here on earth since the beginning of this world, but you and I haven't been here since the beginning of this world.

The years of our lives will run out and time will still exist.

We were born to live through the days, weeks, months and years that are like one drop of water in the bucket of time.

We live our lives not always realizing how fast the years are going by in our lives.

We may be so surprised today that we have aged and can't walk and run as fast as we did when we were young.

Time doesn't age as you and I live to old age.

The years of our lives are a blessing from the Lord.

So many people didn't live to reach your age or my age, even so, the years of our lives have a limit to retire us from our days on earth.

One drop of water can surely dry up in a bucket that has plenty more space for water to fill it up.

Only the Lord can give time plenty more space for other generations to come and live the years of their lives that are a blessing from the Lord who is all for us to live a long life of many years.

Everyone will not live a long life here on earth, and we do not always know why someone's life is cut short.

Many people will cut their own lives short by living a reckless lifestyle.

Even for the oldest people who ever lived on this earth, their lives were like one drop of water in the bucket of time.

They probably didn't always realize that their days, weeks, months, and years would go by so fast, like a buzzing fly flying so fast by our ears.

One drop of water can dry up fast in a big bucket.

The years of our lives can dry up so fast with old age in that big bucket of time that only the Lord can fill up with generations to come if it's in His holy will.

Only Jesus Christ, our Lord, knows the number of young people who will grow old and be like one drop of water in the bucket of time.

Jesus Can Use Ordinary People

Jesus can use ordinary people like me and you to spread the good news about Him to the world.

You and I don't have to be geniuses for Jesus to use us with the spiritual gifts that He gives us to build up the church.

You and I don't have to be brilliant for Jesus to use us to be a witness for Him every day.

You and I don't need a college degree for Jesus to give us His Holy Spirit.

Jesus can use ordinary people like you and me to uplift His holy and precious name.

You and I don't have to be a pastor for Jesus to use us.

You and I don't have to be an elder for Jesus to use us.

You and I don't have to be an evangelist for Jesus to use us.

You and I don't have to be a Bible school teacher for Jesus to use us.

You and I don't have to be a musician in the church for Jesus to use us.

Jesus Christ's disciples were ordinary men who Jesus used to spread the good news about Him, who is the love of God to all the world.

Jesus can use you, even if you have dropped out of high school.

Many of Jesus' disciples were ordinary people.

Many ordinary men have fought on the front lines in the battlefields.

Many ordinary men have built buildings that reached way up in the sky.

Many ordinary women have stood up for women's rights.

Many ordinary people have worked very hard to make this nation great today.

Jesus' disciples were ordinary men.

Jesus gave them the power to heal the sick and cast out demons.

Jesus can use ordinary people to do some extraordinary things.

Many educated people can be amazed to see a rich ordinary person.

Many ordinary people have good common sense to prosper in this world.

Jesus can use ordinary people every day to set the right example for educated fools who make bad choices in their lives.

Many ordinary people make good choices day after day.

Jesus can use ordinary people to win souls to be saved in Him.

Many ordinary people like me and you are saved in Jesus Christ, our Lord and Savior, who doesn't discriminate in who he saves from their sins.

Jesus also loves ordinary people who he can use to help many educated people be down to earth with their words that are not too intellectual for Jesus to understand.

Actions

There are people who will do something good by their actions for the wrong reasons.

There are people who will do good deeds through their actions, just to draw attention to themselves.

Do actions always tell the truth?

Is killing someone a bad action if it's in self-defense?

There are people who go through the action of going to church, but their hearts are filled with ill feelings towards someone.

Their action of going to church can look so true but be so false because they have ill feelings towards someone whether they're in the church or outside the church.

Judas's actions looked so true before the other disciples of Jesus Christ, but Jesus knew that Judas's actions were false.

Jesus knew that Judas would betray him when the other disciples didn't know that.

Do actions always tell the truth?

Someone can do something good to try to make themselves look good so that people will talk nicely about them.

Many people do good things, but the reasons for their actions are false and selfish before the Lord.

The Lord always knows our true hearts and can see beyond our actions to know whether they are true or false.

Only the Lord can judge our actions.

He knows our motives and intentions and whether they are good or bad, even when our actions may fool other people.

Actions can never fool God, but actions can sometimes fool people.

Many people will do good things, but their actions won't give God the glory and praise.

Those actions look so worthless to God, even though they might look good to people.

Do actions always tell the truth?

When Jacob pretended to be his brother Esau so his father Isaac would bless him, Jacob's actions were not true.

God knew Isaac blessed Jacob, but Isaac believed that he had blessed Esau.

Someone can do something good for you and me with his or her actions, but they can want something in return for what they have done, which is selfish.

Many people will say you know people by their actions.

Do we always know people by their actions?

Some people will do good things and then boast about it to make their actions look even better.

People whose actions are true don't have to boast about them to bless others.

Someone can do something bad on the spur of the moment, and this action is not as bad as a bad action that is planned by someone.

There are spur-of-the-moment actions and there are planned actions.

If you mistakenly do something bad, it is not as serious as planning to do something bad.

If we do something good for the wrong reasons, then our actions are not true.

Only the Lord will always know if our actions are true or false.

Common Sense

Common sense will tell us to help somebody if we can help him or her.

Common sense will tell us to slow down.

Common sense will tell us not to tailgate anyone on the road.

Common sense will tell us to drive the speed limit.

Common sense will tell us to not talk too much.

Common sense will tell us to listen.

Common sense will tell us to be nice to people.

Common sense will tell us to treat people right.

Common sense will tell us to get our rest.

Common sense will tell us to tell the truth.

Common sense will tell us to not over do things.

Common sense will tell us to pay our bills.

Common sense will tell us to return what belongs to the Lord.

Common sense will tell us to not form opinions about others.

Common sense will tell us to take a shower.

Common sense will tell us to brush our teeth.

Common sense will tell us to comb our hair.

Common sense will tell us to take care of ourselves.

Common sense will tell us to put on our cloths.

Common sense will tell us to be faithful to our spouse.

Common sense will tell us to not make our children angry.

Common sense will tell us to keep our distance from angry people.

Common sense will tell us to treat our pets right.

Common sense will tell us to not use anyone.

Common sense will tell us to not want what belongs to others.

Common sense will tell us to not trust foolish people.

Common sense will tell us to love and obey Jesus Christ.

Common sense will tell us to love our neighbors.

Common sense will tell us to not eat too much food.

Common sense will tell us to eat the right food.

Common sense will tell us to cover our mouths when we cough.

Common sense will tell us to wash our hands.

Common sense will tell us to drink plenty of water.

Common sense will tell us to not get overweight.

Common sense will tell us to exercise.

Common sense will tell us to get some sunshine.

Common sense will tell us to not work too hard.

Common sense will tell us to not be overly righteous.

Common sense will tell us to be at church on time.

Common sense will tell us to read the bible for ourselves.

Common sense will tell us to not to worry.

Common sense will tell us to get some help if we need it.

Common sense will tell us to see a doctor if we are sick.

Common sense will tell us to not brag about ourselves.

Common sense will tell us to not brag about anyone else.

Common sense is from the Lord, who gives us common sense to survive in this world.

Common sense will tell us to not touch the hot fire.

Common sense will tell us to lock our doors.

Common sense will tell us to wash our clothes.

Common sense will tell us to be careful about what we say.

Common sense will tell us to be careful about what we do.

Common sense will tell us to trust the Lord.

Common sense will tell us to pray to the Lord.

Common sense will tell us to live our lives unto the Lord.

Not everyone uses their common sense.

Many people will act like they don't have any common sense at all.

Common sense makes things clear to us.

Common sense will tell us to be real with people.

We Take a Chance with Our Lives

We take a chance with our lives by living in our houses.

We don't know if the ground will cave in beneath our houses.

We take a chance with our lives when we leave our houses.

We don't know if something will fall on us out of the sky.

We take a chance with our lives when we drive on the roads.

We don't know if another driver will crash into us.

We take a chance with our lives when we drive on a bridge.

We don't know if the bridge will collapse.

We take a chance with our lives when we go to the store.

We don't know if a mass shooter will walk in the store and start shooting everybody.

We take a chance with our lives when we fall asleep.

We don't know if we will wake up again.

We take a chance with our lives even when we go to church.

We don't know if someone will walk in the church and start shooting.

We take a chance with our lives wherever we may go.

We don't know what kind of trouble will come our way.

We take a chance with our lives every day in this sinful world where it's so easy to get killed.

We take a chance with our lives, but Jesus Christ is our only hope to spare our lives for us to see another day.

We take a chance with our lives, but Jesus is our only real, true protection to command our guardian angels to secure our lives.

We take a chance with our lives without always realizing that the devil is always seeking anyone who he can devour.

We take a chance with our lives if we do our own will.

God's will can truly prolong our lives far beyond the chance that we take with our lives day after day.

The Greatest Deception

The greatest deception is to deceive yourself into believing that you are someone you are not.

To deceive yourself is wanting to be worshipped instead of worshipping God.

Lucifer deceived himself and wanted to be worshipped above God.

To deceive ourselves is wanting to be lord over the flock in the church.

There is only one Lord Jesus Christ, who is the head of the church.

To deceive ourselves is to believe that we are perfect without any sins to confess and repent of.

Only Jesus Christ was perfect without any sins to confess and repent of.

The greatest deception is to deceive ourselves into believing that we are always right about what we say.

The greatest deception is to deceive yourself into believing that you are always right about what you do.

To deceive yourself is to believe that you can say nothing wrong.

To deceive yourself is to believe that you can do nothing wrong.

To deceive yourself is to make excuses for your sins.

To deceive yourself is to not believe that you are a sinner.

To deceive yourself is to believe that you don't have to keep God's Commandments.

To deceive yourself is to believe that you can live in your sins and still go to heaven.

The greatest deception is to deceive yourself into thinking you are holy when you're living your life being of the world.

To deceive yourself is to believe that you are good when you're doing bad things.

To deceive yourself is to believe that you know everything, when even a child can ask you a question that you may not have the answer to.

The greatest deception is to deceive yourself into believing what Lucifer believed up in heaven where he was cast out of for trying to exalt himself above God for believing that he could be God.

To deceive yourself is to believe that your good works can save you.

To deceive yourself is to believe that you can live your life any kind of way and still be saved.

To deceive yourself is to believe that you are self-made, when the Lord made it possible for you to be successful today.

The greatest deception is to deceive yourself to believe that you can do all things, when the Lord may give you a simple thing that you can fail to do.

To deceive yourself is the greatest deception that Lucifer and the fallen angels truly know, because they fear and tremble before the Lord who cast them out of Heaven.

To deceive yourself is to believe that there is no God.

To deceive yourself is to believe that you can die and go to heaven without Jesus Christ coming back again to take you there if you are saved in Him.

To deceive yourself is to believe that you own your body and can do as you please with it, when your body is Jesus' Holy Temple that He owns every day.

To deceive yourself is to believe that you love God, who you don't see, but hate your neighbor who you do see.

The greatest deception is to believe that you are a Christian while not going through any suffering for Jesus' name sake.

The greatest deception is to deceive yourself into believing that you are innocent when you are guilty.

To deceive yourself is to believe that you made the right choice, when you made the wrong choice.

To deceive yourself is to believe that you are strong, when you are weak.

The greatest deception is to believe that you are God who cannot lie, when you are lying to yourself because you believe that you are God.

To deceive yourself is to believe that you love Jesus Christ, while you don't keep all of His Ten Commandments.

To deceive yourself is to believe that you won't reap what you sow.

To deceive yourself is to believe that what you say and do won't have an effect on others.

The greatest deception is to deceive yourself into believing that you are God's most favored one in the church body of Jesus Christ, when the church body has many members that Jesus favors all the same to build up His church.

No one member is more favored than another member in the eyes of God.

The greatest deception is to deceive yourself into believing that you are living a moral life, when you are not living your life unto the Lord who is eternally moral.

The greatest deception is to deceive ourselves into believing that we can say bad words to others and do bad things to others and get away with it.

The Lord says that we will reap what we sow, for sooner or later we will get back what we dish out to others.

We may not get it back in the exact same way, but we will get it back in some kind of way.

The greatest deception is to deceive ourselves into believing that we are saved in Jesus Christ and that we don't have to go through any hardships for Jesus' holy name sake.

The greatest deception is to deceive ourselves that we are only human to give in to the devil's temptations that Jesus overcame and can give you and me the power to resist if we live our lives unto Him.

Jesus is our divine Lord and Savior who took on our humanity to give us the power to take on His divine nature that is unlimited to us for believing in Jesus Christ.

The greatest deception is to deceive ourselves into believing that we are true to ourselves and don't have to be true to Jesus, who is the truth to set us free from anything that's not like Him.

Purpose

My pictures on the wall said to me, "My purpose is to hang here and never change."

My chairs and sofas said to me, "My purpose is to let you sit down on me and rest."

My oven said to me, "My purpose is to cook your food."

My refrigerator said to me, "My purpose is to keep your food fresh.'

My dishwasher said to me, "My purpose is to wash your dirty dishes."

My mirror said to me, "My purpose is to let you see how you look."

My TV said to me, "My purpose is to entertain you."

The doors said to me, "Our purpose is to let you in and out of your house."

My clock said to me, "My purpose is to let you know what time it is."

My bed said to me, "My purpose is for you to lay down on me and go to sleep."

My shower said to me, "My purpose is to keep you clean."

My cabinets in my house said to me, "My purpose is to keep your plates, glasses, cups, spoons, knives, forks, pots and pans in order."

The windows in my house said to me, "My purpose is to let you look through me."

My washing machine said to me, "My purpose is to wash your clothes clean."

My dryer said to me, "My purpose is to dry your wet clothes."

The broom said to me, "My purpose is to sweep your floor."

The dustpan said to me, "My purpose is to pick up the trash off of your floor."

My mop said to me, "My purpose is to clean your floor."

The trash cans said to me, "My purpose is to keep your trash in its right place."

The blinds and curtains on my window said to me, "My purpose is to open in the day and close in the night."

My central air unit said to me, "My purpose is to keep you warm in the winter and keep you cool in the summer."

My house said to me, "My purpose is to shelter you."

The fence in my backyard said to me, "My purpose is to keep out Intruders and trespassers."

The closets in my house said to me, "Our purpose is to keep your clothes in their right places."

One day they all got together and asked me what my purpose was and waited to see what I would say.

They already knew my purpose by my actions that they witnessed day after day and night after night.

They knew me very well and saw Jesus Christ in my life every day and every night.

Everything in my house, as well as my dogs, are blessed by the Lord who gives me the purpose of loving Him and keeping His Commandments.

Everything in my house has a purpose to serve me in some kind of way.

God created me in His image and gave me a much greater purpose, which is for me to live my life to serve Him.

Everything in my house has a fixed purpose that is permanent, but I have a free will choice and I choose to fulfill my purpose unto the Lord.

The Lord gave me a much greater purpose for my life than the things in my house, which can't do a thing for the Lord.

There is a God

The waterfalls tell us that there is a God.

The mountains tell us that there is a God.

The deep valleys tell us that there is a God.

The sun tells us that there is a God.

The moon tells us that there is a God.

The stars tell us that there is a God.

The universe tells us that there is a God.

The rainbows tell us that there is a God.

The lunar eclipses tell us that there is a God.

The solar eclipses tell us that there is a God.

The oceans tell us that there is a God.

The rivers tell us that there is a God.

The sky tells us that there is a God.

The rain tells us that there is a God.

The snow tells us that there is a God.

The seasons tell us that there is a God.

The nature tells us that there is a God.

The animals tell us that there is a God.

The human beings tell us that there is a God.

God created human beings in His likeness

God gave human beings a mind to reason like Him.

The bible tells us that there is a God.

A Christian will tell us that there is a God living in his or her heart.

Time tells us that there is a God who sent His only begotten Son to this world in the fullness of time here on earth.

Love tells us that there is a God who is love.

Peace tells us that there is a God.

Justice tells us that there is a God.

Faith tells us that there is a God.

Hope tells us that there is a God.

Truth tells us that there is a God.

Good mental and physical health tells us that there is a God.

Life tells us that there is a God keeping us alive right now.

A fool can tell us that there is no God until death closes in on him or her and makes them want to call on God to spare their life from death.

The spur of the moment tells us that there is a God who is always in control, even when things get out of control for us on the spur of the moment and leave us feeling so helpless.

God will intervene on the spur of the moment that we have no control over.

Wisdom tells us that there is a God.

Healing tells us that there is a God.

Joy tells us that there is a God.

Humility tells us that there is a God.

Patience tells us that there is a God.

Temperance tells us that there is a God.

Righteousness tells us that there is a God who is righteous and right about everything that He says and does.

Holiness tells us that there is a God who is holy and is different from the devil who is evil all the time.

Goodness tells us that there is a God whose goodness leads us to repentance.

The birds tell us that there is a God who feeds them so that they don't worry about where they will get their food from.

Wisdom and knowledge tell us that there is a God who is all-wise and all-knowing.

No Matter Who is Living It

A hard life is a hard life, no matter who is living it.

A hard life doesn't care about who we are.

A hard life doesn't care about the color of our skin.

A hard life doesn't care about our age.

A hard life doesn't care about favoritism.

A hard life doesn't care about who is living it.

A good life is a good life, no matter who is living it.

A good life doesn't care about who we are.

A good life doesn't care about the color of our skin.

A good life doesn't care about what age we are.

A good life doesn't care about favoritism.

A hard life is a hard life, no matter who is living it.

Moses gave up a good life to live a hard life for God.

Saul, who became the Apostle Paul, gave up a good life to live a hard life for Jesus' name sake.

Jesus gave up a good eternal life in heaven to live a hard life here on earth to save us from our sins.

A hard life is a hard life, no matter who is living it.

A good life is a good life, no matter who is living it.

A Christian can live a good life in Jesus Christ, no matter what hardships come in that Christian's life.

A Christian can still have joy in the Lord through his or her hardships in life because Jesus won't allow you and me to go through any hardships that are more than what we can bear for His holy name's sake.

A good life is a good life to many people who do their own will and are going through nothing hard for Jesus' name sake.

The hard life that we go through for Jesus' name sake is only temporary and will pass away when Jesus comes back again to take you and me with Him when He goes back to heaven if we are saved in Him who got the victory over the hard life that He lived to save our souls.

The good life here on earth is only temporary for those who do their own will thinking they have heaven on earth, but they will pass away in fire and brimstone.

The good life will be eternal in heaven for all the holy saints who will not remember the hard life on earth that every Christian will live in some kind of way for Jesus' holy name sake.

Many people who do their own will are going through a hard life that they bring on themselves and regret it.

Living a hard life for the Lord will have no regrets for anyone who is saved in Jesus Christ.

No matter who is living a hard life or living a good life, we all will answer to God who gives life to all great and small to live our lives unto Him.

The Lord Will Move Aside

If we are walking down a crowded street, there are people who will walk right into us if we don't move aside out of their way.

If we are in the grocery store or in any store that has shopping carts, there are people who will push their shopping carts right into us if we don't move aside out of their way.

If we are driving on the road, there are people who will drive right into us and hit our vehicle if we don't move aside out of their way, whether we see them or don't see them driving fast up on us from the rear end of our vehicle.

There are times when you have to move aside out of someone's way so that he or she can learn things for themselves, maybe the hard way.

The Lord will move aside out of our way to let us choose, even if we choose something wrong.

The Lord will move aside out of our way and let us choose, even if we choose to do wrong.

The Lord will move aside out of our way and let us reap what we sow.

There are people who will not move aside out of someone's way because they want to be in control.

The Lord Jesus Christ will not control anyone and make them love and obey Him, he will just move aside out of our way and let us choose to love and obey Him.

The devil will not move aside out of our way, he'll tempt us to sin against God at any time of the day and night.

The Lord will move aside our sins out of our way if we confess and repent and turn to Him.

It is Impossible

It is impossible for the creature to be the creator God.

It is impossible for the creature to be the creator God like it is impossible for a child to give birth to his or her parents.

It is impossible for the creature to be the creator God, like it is impossible for a son to be older than his father.

It is impossible for the creature to be the creator God, like it is impossible for a baby to rock his or her parents in a cradle.

It is impossible for the creature to be the creator God, like it is impossible for anyone to live without breathing air in and out of their nostrils.

It is impossible for the creature to be the creator God, like it is impossible for a man to have a womb and birth a baby.

It is impossible for the creature to be the creator God, like it is impossible for a woman to not have a womb and give birth to a baby.

It is impossible for the creature to be the creator God, like it is impossible for a dog to build a house.

It is impossible for the creature to be the creator God, like it is impossible for a cat to bark like a dog.

It is impossible for the creature to be the creator God, like it is impossible for water to be fire.

It is impossible for the creature to be the creator God, like it is impossible to talk without a tongue in your mouth.

It is impossible for the creature to be the creator God, like it is impossible for blood to be water.

It is impossible for the creature to be the creator God, like it is impossible for God to lie.

It is impossible for the creature to be the creator God who is the only self-existing One from the beginning when no procreation existed.

It is impossible for the creature to be the creator God, like it is impossible for anything in this world to hold in place without gravity that God created to keep everything on the ground from floating up into the outer space.

It is impossible for the creature to be the creator God, like it is impossible for any angel to procreate because God didn't create angels to give birth.

It is impossible for the creature to be the creator God, because the creature didn't create the only true, living God.

The creature can only create false gods that find it impossible to give us life, health and strength and answer our prayers.

Good People are Not Exempted

Good people are not exempted from the evilness of sin.

The evilness of sin has caused many good people to suffer in pain.

The evilness of sin has caused many good people to die at a very young age.

Every good child will feel some physical pain from the evilness of sin.

Every good adult, young, middle-aged and old person will feel some physical pain from the evilness of sin.

Every God-fearing Christian will have to face up to some kind of suffering because of the evilness of sin that hates everybody, especially good people who are not exempted from the evilness of sin.

All through the bible there were good Christian men and women who were not exempted from the evilness of sin.

All of God's prophets of old suffered in some kind of way for representing God to wicked people who rebelled against god.

Every good man, woman, boy and girl will go through some kind of hardship because the evilness of sin hates all good things that come from God.

No good person, great or small, is exempted from the evilness of sin that is of the devil who especially hates good people all around the world.

Good people are not exempted from heartaches, pain, trouble, misfortunes and crimes that can come upon good people at any time.

Good people are not exempted from mental illness, sicknesses, diseases and natural disasters.

Good people are not exempted from the evilness of sin that doesn't care about how young or old you are and will take you to the grave no matter how good you are.

No matter how good we Christians are, we are not exempted from the evilness of sin that favors evil over good every day that God's goodness prevails over evil.

This is Just the Way I Am

Many people will say, "This is just the way I am and I can't change that."

Everybody chooses to be the way they are, whether they are good or bad.

Many people will say, "This is just the way I am because I was born to be this way."

God gives everybody a free will to choose to be who they want to be.

Many people will say, "I can't help myself because this is the way I am."

That's like telling the Lord Jesus Christ, "You have no power to change me from my wicked ways, even if I confess and repent of my sins."

It's like telling Jesus, "Your death on the cross was so worthless to me, and I don't believe I'll be raised up in newness of life through Your resurrection from the grave with the victory over death and the grave."

It's like telling Jesus, "You wasted your time leaving heaven and coming to this sinful world to save me from my sins."

It's like telling Jesus, "Your blood that you shed on the cross can't cleanse me from my sins so I can live a righteous life and have good morals every day."

When you say, "This is just the way I am and I can't change," it's like telling Jesus that His ten Commandments are useless and have no good effect on your life.

Saying, "This is just the way I am and I don't want to change for the better," is like telling Jesus He can't help you and He has to accept you for who you are because there is no need to change what is right in your eyes.

Many people will say, "This is just the way I am," and feel everything they do is all right.

What they don't realize is the Lord has a judgement day that will reveal the truth of everybody, especially those making up their own excuses to hold onto thinking their way is right rather than repenting and turning to Jesus.

"This is just the way I am" is telling Jesus your selfish desires come before Him.

Saying, "This is just the way I am," tells Jesus that you direct your own path and walk in your own ways that are better than denying yourself and picking up your cross to follow the Lord.

Many people will way, "This is just the way I am," but they will never have unspeakable joy and an abundance of life that only Jesus can give to all who believe in Him beyond themselves.

Just "being the way I am" is sinning against the Lord, especially if it's done willfully and knowingly.

Nobody is a Mistake

I was born into this world out of wedlock and I grew up without my father in my life.

Does that make me a mistake?

I made many mistakes in my life.

Does that make me a mistake?

There are children who have been told by their parents that they are a mistake.

Many of those children grew up broken because they believed what their parents told them.

Because a child is born out of wedlock does that make them a mistake?

If that is true, then so many of us adults would be a mistake today in this sinful world where the devil loves to make us all believe that it is a mistake that we're alive.

Nobody is a mistake to the Lord Jesus Christ who would not have shed His blood on the cross if we were mistakes to Him.

Nobody is a mistake to the Lord Jesus Christ who would not have died on the cross for us if we were mistakes to Him.

God in heaven would not have given His only begotten Son, Jesus Christ, to save us from our sins if we were a mistake to God.

We all are here today by no mistake.

God didn't make a mistake when we were born into this world where our purpose for being here is to love Jesus and keep His Commandments, which is no mistake.

Nobody is a mistake to Jesus who redeemed us back to God when He rose from the grave with the victory over death that is a very big mistake to life every day.

Nobody is a mistake to live, regardless of the mistakes that we can make even unto our death.

Nobody is a mistake to God, who gave everybody the freedom to choose right from wrong using their mature minds.

It is no mistake to God to fill up our minds with His holy word for us to live by day after day.

Even Judas, who betrayed Jesus, wasn't a mistake to God who loved Judas even though he made the biggest mistake of his life by betraying Jesus and it would have been better if he'd never been born.

Nobody is a mistake and permanently lost in their sins, because there is no mistake about Jesus forgiving us of our sins and saving us from them if we repent and turn to Him who had once lived in this world without sin in His flesh to be no mistake to all who believe in Him to be saved.

There is No Time in Eternity

Jesus was eternal in heaven before He stepped down in time here on earth.

Adam and Eve were eternal, but gave that up when they believed the devil's lies and they fell down into time that God created to give to them to repent and turn to Him.

There is no time in eternity that has no seconds, minutes, hours, days, weeks, months or years; those only exist here on earth because of Adam falling down into sin.

Sin came into this world through Adam and not Eve, so God gave borrowed time to all human beings to believe in His Son, Jesus Christ, in this life on earth where time will run out one day soon.

As long as we live, we have time to repent and turn to Jesus who is eternal up in heaven where He went back to when His time on earth was up and he'd completed His mission for God.

Jesus stepped down into time to save sinners who God gave borrowed time to so they could deny themselves and pick up their crosses and follow Jesus Christ before their time runs out.

Time does not exist in the grave.

There is no time in eternity, but many people will waste a lot of time being absorbed into temporary things that will rust and erode in time.

There is no time in eternity that you and I will one day enter into if we are saved in Jesus Christ who time will give all the glory and praise to for giving you and me time to choose who we will worship.

Jesus is worthy to worship throughout eternity, and the holy angels bow down to worship Jesus forever and ever.

Lord Jesus, You are the Truth

It's You, Lord Jesus, who have given Your truth to the prophets of old to tell the truth about You to all the people back in the bible days.

It's You, Lord Jesus, who gave Your truth to the disciples to tell everyone the truth about You to all the people back in the bible days.

It's You, Lord Jesus, who are the truth that you gave to Your Holy Spirit who inspired the prophets of old and the disciples to write the holy scriptures in the bible for all people today to read the bible and know that You, O Lord Jesus Christ, are the origin of all truth.

No matter who tells the truth about You, You are the everlasting truth that the holy angels and all the unfallen worlds know about beyond this fallen world where many people don't believe that You, O Lord, are the way, the truth and the life to live day after day.

Lord Jesus, You are the truth that the devil and his fallen angels knew about and were cast out of heaven for rejecting God.

You are the truth of God and the Son of God and the Word of God.

Lord Jesus, You are the root of all truth that especially Christians love to tell and love to hear and love to live, that the devil hates because he is the father of every lie that many people love to tell and love to hear and love to live like the devil day after day.

It's You, Lord Jesus, beyond every lie that You will one day burn up in hell's fire and brimstone that liars don't believe to be the truth in the bible.

Lord Jesus, You are the truth that no one can make to be a lie and get away with it forever.

There is a judgement day that the truth will reveal showing all the holy saints saved in Jesus and all the wicked lost in their sins that God is fair.

My Lord Jesus Christ, You are the truth that got the victory over death and the grave, making the grave a liar to the righteous dead who You will raise from the dead when You come back again on the clouds of glory to avenge every lie that was told from the beginning of time on earth down to the end of time on earth.

There Comes a Time

There comes a time when we have to break off our friendship with someone who will be quick to get angry with us for just asking him or her a simple question.

There comes a time when we must move on beyond someone who only sees wrong in you and me but sees no wrong in themselves.

There comes a time when we must stay away from someone who sees no need to change for the better.

There comes a time when we have to stop talking to someone who loves to over-talk you and me to make themselves look to be so right about what he or she says.

There comes a time when we cut off all connection with someone to keep our sanity.

There comes a time when we must cut off all communication with someone who will take our kindness for weakness and try to manipulate you and me.

There comes a time when we must leave someone all alone for the Lord to work on his or her heart.

There comes a time when we must tell someone the truth about himself or herself while telling the truth in love.

There comes a time when we must move forward and not look back at the hurt that someone caused us to feel, because hurt people will hurt you and me and can claim to be a Christian to wash his or her hands clean like they never did anything wrong.

There comes a time when we must have a serious talk with Jesus about someone who just doesn't want to see that he or she needs to repent and turn to Jesus.

Someone, even in the church, may not want to repent because they believe that they are so right with God.

There comes a time when we have to truly let go of someone who loves to find fault in you and me to try to cover up his or her own faults.

The Pharisees and religious leaders tried to find fault in Jesus to try to make themselves look so holy and righteous, but Jesus called them hypocrites and a brood of vipers.

Love Has No

Love has no fear.

Love has no strife.

Love has no hatred.

Love has no prejudice.

Love has no inequality.

Love has no bondage.

Love has no trouble.

Love has no favoritism.

Love has no disrespect.

Love has no pride.

Love has no weakness.

Love has no injustice.

Love has no discrimination.

Love has no negativity.

Love has no neglect.

Love has no revenge.

Love has no war.

Love has no rudeness.

Love has no disloyalty.

Love has no lies.

Love has no mistrust.

Love has no violence.

Love has no adultery.

Love has no fornication.

Love has no cheating.

Love has no theft.

Love has no greed.

Love has no abuse.

Love has no tricks.

Love has no selfishness.

Love has no deceit.

Love has no gossip.

Love has no complaints.

Love has no superiority complex.

Love has no riots.

Love has no unnatural affection.

Love has no lust.

Love has no impatience.

Love has no unforgiveness.

Love has no murder.

Love has no disobedience.

Love has no covetousness.

Love has no unfriendliness.

Love has no forcefulness.

Love has no evil.

Love has no false accusations.

Love has no manipulation.

Love has no ill feelings.

Love has no quick temper.

Love has no homelessness.

Love has no bad motives.

Love has no bad intentions.

Love has no molestation.

Love has no degradation.

Love has no malpractice.

Love has no unfairness.

Love has no pretense.

Love has no phoniness.

Love has no bad hygiene.

Love has no gluttony.

Love has no intemperance.

Love has no concerns.

Love has no unhealthiness.

Love has no disbelief about Jesus Christ.

Love has no division in the church.

Love has no retirement in the church.

Love has no doubts about Jesus Christ.

Love has no laziness to not win souls to Jesus Christ.

Love has no secrets to hide Jesus Christ from unbelievers.

Love has no pointing fingers to not judge anyone who Jesus gives His salvation to examine themselves to make their calling sure in Him day after day.

There is a Path

There is a path that good dreams love to take and walk down to come true.

There is a path that time loves to take and walk down to be on time.

There is a path that love will take and walk down to love everybody.

There is a path that hope loves to take and walk down to give hope to everybody.

There is a path that faith loves to take and walk down to not be distinct.

There is a path that freedom loves to take and walk down to always exist.

There is a path that sickness loves to take and walk down to wellness.

There is a path that brokenness loves to take and walk down to wholeness.

There is a path that confession loves to take and walk down to repentance.

There is a path that conviction loves to take and walk down to baptism.

There is a path that true conversion loves to take and walk down to being saved in Jesus Christ.

There is a path that a true Christian loves to take and walk down to be like Jesus Christ.

There is a path that a true Christian loves to take and walk down to win souls to Jesus Christ.

There is a path that a true Christian loves to take and walk down to wearing a long white robe and having stars on one's crown.

There is a path that a true Christian loves to take and walk down to receive eternal life in Jesus Christ when He comes back again on the clouds of glory.

There is Always Room for Improvement

There is always room for improvement on sermons about the Lord.

There is always room for improvement on songs about the Lord.

There is always room for improvement on Sabbath school lessons about the Lord.

There is always room for improvement on poetry about the Lord.

There is always room for improvement on humility unto the Lord.

There is always room for improvement on witnessing about the Lord.

There is always room for improvement on love for the Lord.

There is always room for improvement on faith in the Lord.

There is always room for improvement on obedience unto the Lord.

There is always room for improvement on worshipping the Lord.

There is always room for improvement on serving the Lord.

There is always room for improvement on knowledge about the Lord.

There is always room for improvement on spiritual things about the Lord.

There is always room for improvement on knowing the Lord.

There is always room for improvement on a relationship with the Lord.

There is always room for improvement on trusting the Lord.

There is always room for improvement on depending on the Lord.

There is always room for improvement on living for the Lord.

There is always room for improvement on joy in the Lord.

There is always room for improvement on waiting on the Lord.

There is always room for improvement on working for the Lord.

There is always room for improvement on leaning on the Lord.

There is always room for improvement on keeping our eyes on the Lord.

There is always room for improvement on walking with the Lord.

There is always room for improvement on reverence unto the Lord.

There is always room for improvement on temperance unto the Lord.

There is always room for improvement on holiness unto the Lord.

There is always room for improvement on righteousness unto the Lord.

There is always room for improvement on making the Lord our choice every day that we need the Holy Spirit to help us to improve on loving Jesus and keeping His Commandments.

There is always room for improvement on confessing and repenting of our sins unto the Lord Jesus Christ.

There is always room for improvement on giving the Lord Jesus Christ our whole heart from day to day.

There is always room for improvement on not quenching the Holy Spirit who convicts us of our sins and converts us to repent of our sins and turn to Jesus one day at a time.

There is always room for improvement on letting the Holy Spirit teach us all the truth about the Lord Jesus Christ who is the Son of God and the light of the world and our Lord and Savior who redeemed us back to God with His victory over death and the grave to give us eternal life when He comes back again to take us to heaven with Him and all the angels.

What Can Be More Real?

What can be more real than believing in Jesus Christ?

What can be more real than repenting of our sins and turning to Jesus?

What can be more real than loving Jesus and Keeping His Commandments?

What can be more real than having a relationship with Jesus Christ?

What can be more real than praying to Jesus?

What can be more real than keeping our eyes on Jesus?

What can be more real than working for Jesus?

What can be more real than having the fruit of the Holy Spirit?

What can be more real than giving Jesus all the glory and praise?

What can be more real than humbling ourselves unto Jesus Christ?

What can be more real than worshipping the Lord Jesus Christ?

What can be more real than studying the bible to get to know Jesus?

What can be more real than denying ourselves and picking up our crosses to follow Jesus?

What can be more real than confessing our sins unto Jesus Christ?

What can be more real than Jesus cleansing us of our sins?

What can be more real than going through trials for Jesus' holy name sake?

What can be more real than putting all of our trust in Jesus?

What can be more real than making Jesus our first choice day after day?

What can be more real than returning faithful tithes and offerings unto Jesus Christ?

What can be more real than giving Jesus our time?

What can be more real than giving Jesus our talents.

What can be more real than holding onto Jesus?

What can be more real than going to church to assemble ourselves together to worship the Lord Jesus Christ?

What can be more real than using our spiritual gifts from the Lord to build up the church?

What can be more real than being a witness of Jesus Christ?

What can be more real than giving testimonies of all that Jesus brought us through?

What can be more real than winning souls to Jesus Christ?

What can be more real than not making this world our home, because our home is in heaven for all who have been redeemed?

What can be more real than saved in Jesus Christ?

What can be more real than living right by example before unbelievers who don't know the Lord Jesus Christ?

What can be more real than working out one's own soul's salvation unto the Lord?

What can be more real than knowing what is right unto the Lord and not doing what is right unto the Lord Jesus Christ.

What can be more real than calling on the name of the Lord to cause the demons to flee.

What can be more real than giving up one's life for Jesus' holy name sake.

What can be more real than giving up all that we have for Jesus' holy name sake.

What can be more real than dying and being saved in Jesus who will raise us up in the first resurrection when He comes back again on the clouds of glory?

What can be more real than living for Jesus like it's our last day to live?

What can be more real than laying up our treasures in heaven?

What can be more real than our bodies being the holy temple of God to dwell in us if we eat right and exercise and most of all if we live right unto God by the right that we know even though God winks His eye at our ignorance for what we don't know that is right?

What can be more real than the Lord Jesus Christ answering our prayers on His time that is never too late?

What can be more real than God giving us His mercy and grace when we all deserve to drop dead for sinning against Him even in a thought that God sees when no one else can see our thoughts before we speak one word and before we do anything?

What can be more real than God who cannot lie and will never change on us who can tell a lie and live a lie and can change on God and one another and even want to change His holy word to fit in with what we don't do right and can make excuses and believe that we are fair with God who we can never be more real than?

What can be more real than God who will always do what He says, when you and I can say one thing and do another thing even though we can mean good and well by what we say, especially on the spur of the moment without thinking?

What can be more real than being real with Jesus Christ who can truly help us to be real with ourselves and real with one another?

What can be more real than Jesus who is always very real with you and me every day that we can see and feel Jesus being so very real with us when we read His holy word as well as seeing Jesus being real in every real, true Christian?

What can be more real than Jesus Christ who was a real man who had no sin in His flesh when He lived among sinners who had a hard time accepting Jesus being very real with them in His words that He spoke with no lies.

What can be more real than you and me being like Jesus, even on our bad days that the devil especially loves to use to make us look like hypocrites when our soul is anchored in the Lord who makes sure we can rise up again after we fall, especially unintentionally, that the Lord can use for our good?

Peter didn't intend to deny Jesus three times for the cock to crow, but Peter repented of his sins.

Peter had fallen to rise up again in Jesus and feed Jesus' sheep because the world needed to hear the gospel of Jesus Christ.

What can be more real than Jesus Christ?

What can be more real than Jesus Christ who was tempted in every way by the devil and did not sin against God in the wilderness for forty days and forty nights, even though the devil came at Jesus with the full force of all of his temptations?

What can be more real than Jesus Christ, who was very real with God by saying, "If it be possible let this cup pass from me: nevertheless not as I will, but as thou wilt"?

What can be more real than Jesus Christ, our Lord, who was spit on, slapped in the face, had hair pulled out of his beard, was beaten and nailed on the cross for our sins that He became on the cross and was forsaken by God before He died on the cross?

Nothing and no one can be more real than Jesus Christ, who rose from the grave that Jesus is forevermore real than to give you and me eternal life when He comes back again to take us to heaven if we are saved in Him.

What can be more real than Jesus in anyone's life that can't be more real than Jesus, who is the only life eternal forevermore beyond our life that is like a shadow passing over the landscape and disappearing out of sight as though it never appeared.

Everything in this world and everyone in this world can never be more real than Jesus Christ, who created all existing things seen and unseen that can never be more real than Jesus Christ.

After Jesus had risen from the dead and later appeared before His disciples, they believed Jesus was a ghost.

The doubting Thomas was fully convinced that Jesus was very real when he touched Jesus and ate food with Jesus before Jesus ascended up into heaven in real bodily form.

I am a Man

I am a man and I love being a man.

I love talking like a man.

I love dressing like a man.

I am not rich, but I am glad that God created me to be a man.

I love being the man the mirror shows to me every day.

Women are a blessing to me, but I love being a man.

This world would be so lonely without women in it, but I love being a man who loves to see other men talking like men.

I am a man who loves to see other men dressing like men.

I am a man who loves to see other men looking like men.

I am a man who loves to see other men being with a woman like I love being with a woman called my wife, who I love.

I am a man who loves to act like a man every day.

Most of all, I am a Christian man who wants to be like Jesus Christ, who was the only sinless man to be the right example for me to be a man of God.

Most of all, I am a Christian man who loves to treat my neighbors right every day, including every other man and every woman, boy and girl who are my neighbors.

Most of all, I am a Christian man who loves being a Christian man to be like Jesus Christ who was fully man and God who created a man to be a man and a woman to be a woman from the beginning of time here on earth.

Most of all, I am a Christian man who loves to lay up my treasures in heaven because this world is not my home where many men want to be a woman and many women want to be a man.

Most of all, I am a Christian man who loves being like Jesus Christ in this sinful world where I want to help men, women, boys and girls make it to heaven.

Most of all, I am a Christian man who doesn't want to ever be a carnal-minded man again.

I don't miss being that way because being a Christian man is truly being a real man every day.

Most of all, I am a Christian man who has no desire to sin against God willfully because I truly know today that living in sin is of the devil who hates God and every man, woman, boy and girl.

Whether I was being a Christian man or not being a Christian man, it was in God's will for me to be a man because God doesn't make any mistakes in His likeness.

I am glad that God created me to be a man in His likeness that no animal is created in.

Today I am so blessed by God to be a spiritual-minded man that I don't deserve.

I am so glad that Jesus gave up His life on the cross to save me from my sins as if I was the only sinner man in this world.

I am so glad to be a man who Jesus grew up into from a baby boy.

I am so glad to be a Christian man who is no better than any woman — I just have a different role in life.

I am a man who loves to walk like a man in this world where Jesus once walked without sin in His flesh to set the right example for all men to be a man of God and not of the unnatural effects of life.

The same is for every woman to be a woman of God and not of the unnatural effects of life that were not so from the beginning of God creating a man to be a man and a woman to be a woman given in marriage to each other by God, who created a man and woman naturally from the beginning in the Garden of Eden.

www.ingramcontent.com/pod-product-compliance
Lightning Source LLC
Chambersburg PA
CBHW070854120626
46546CB00001B/6